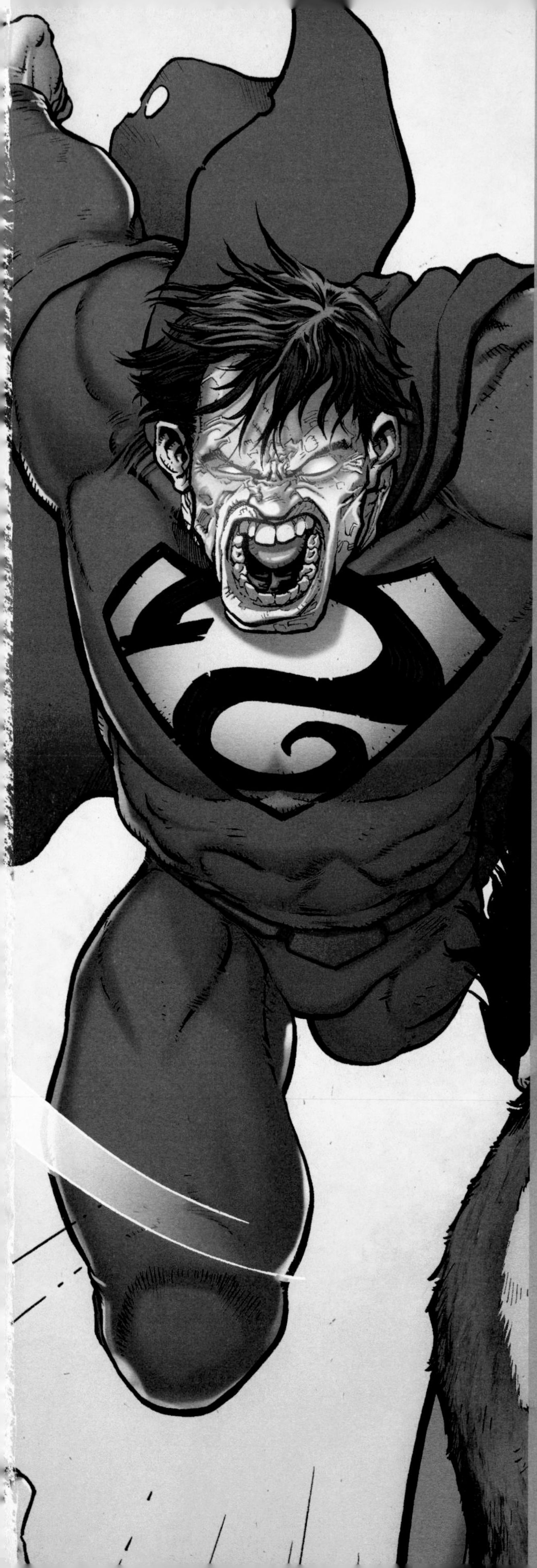

SUPERMAN ACTION COMICS

VOLUME 7
UNDER THE SKIN

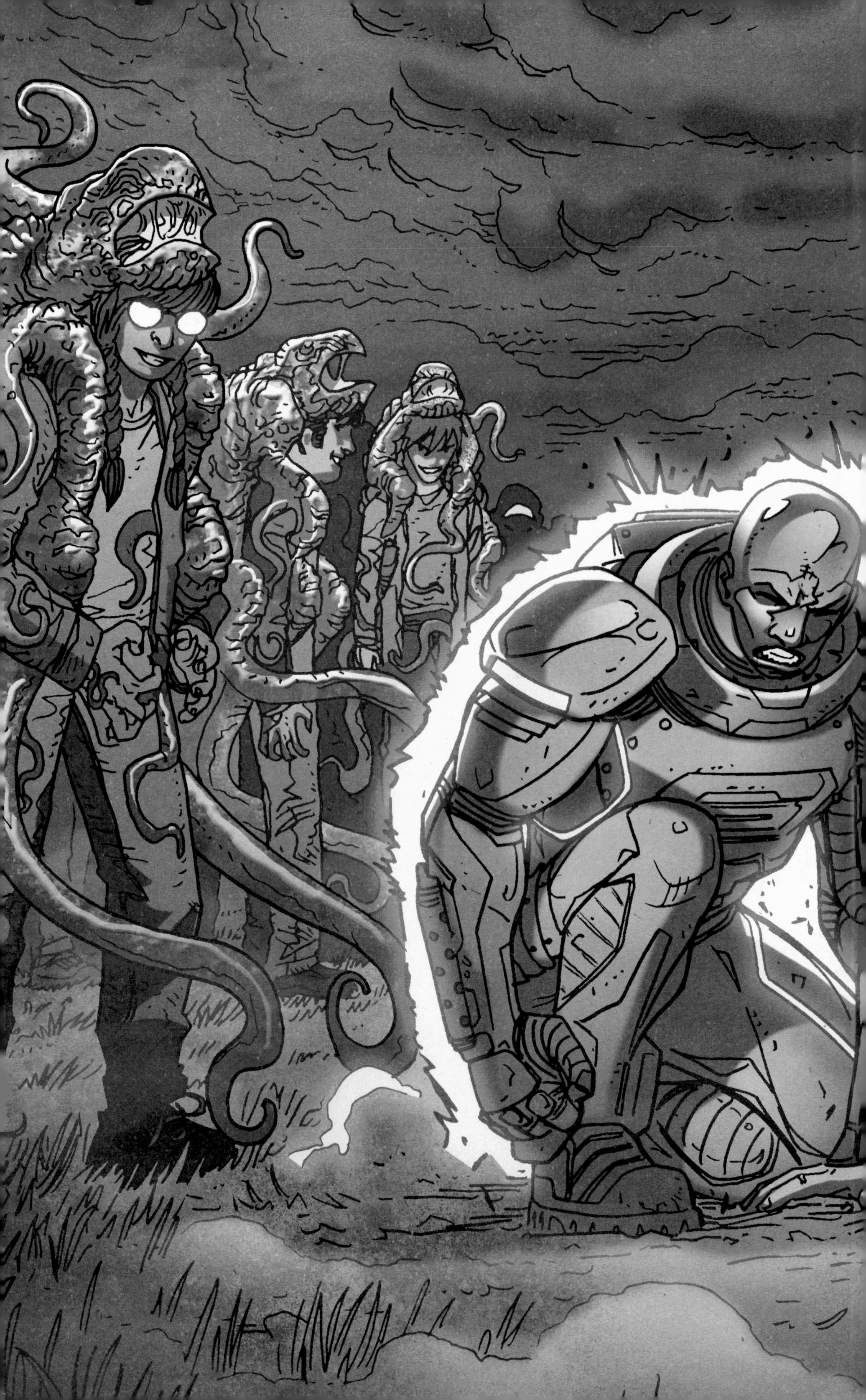

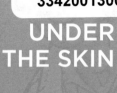
UNDER
THE SKIN

SUPERMAN ACTION COMICS

WRITTEN BY
GREG PAK
SHOLLY FISCH

ART BY
AARON KUDER
SCOTT KOLINS
JAE LEE
PASCAL ALIXE
VICENTE CIFUENTES

COLOR BY
WIL QUINTANA
JUNE CHUNG
PETE PANTAZIS

LETTERS BY
CARLOS M. MANGUAL
DEZI SIENTY
STEVE WANDS

COLLECTION COVER ART BY
AARON KUDER
& WIL QUINTANA

SUPERMAN CREATED BY
JERRY SIEGEL &
JOE SHUSTER
BY SPECIAL ARRANGEMENT
WITH THE JERRY SIEGEL FAMILY

EDDIE BERGANZA Editor – Original Series
JEREMY BENT Assistant Editor – Original Series
JEB WOODARD Group Editor – Collected Editions
LIZ ERICKSON Editor – Collected Edition
DAMIAN RYLAND Publication Design

BOB HARRAS Senior VP – Editor-in-Chief, DC Comics

DIANE NELSON President
DAN DIDIO and JIM LEE Co-Publishers
GEOFF JOHNS Chief Creative Officer
AMIT DESAI Senior VP – Marketing & Global Franchise Management
NAIRI GARDINER Senior VP – Finance
SAM ADES VP – Digital Marketing
BOBBIE CHASE VP –Talent Development
MARK CHIARELLO Senior VP – Art, Design & Collected Editions
JOHN CUNNINGHAM VP – Content Strategy
ANNE DEPIES VP – Strategy Planning & Reporting
DON FALLETTI VP – Manufacturing Operations
LAWRENCE GANEM VP – Editorial Administration & Talent Relations
ALISON GILL Senior VP – Manufacturing & Operations
HANK KANALZ Senior VP – Editorial Strategy & Administration
JAY KOGAN VP – Legal Affairs
DEREK MADDALENA Senior VP – Sales & Business Development
JACK MAHAN VP – Business Affairs
DAN MIRON VP – Sales Planning & Trade Development
NICK NAPOLITANO VP – Manufacturing Administration
CAROL ROEDER VP – Marketing
EDDIE SCANNELL VP - Mass Account & Digital Sales
COURTNEY SIMMONS Senior VP – Publicity & Communications
JIM (SKI) SOKOLOWSKI VP – Comic Book Specialty & Newsstand Sales
SANDY YI Senior VP – Global Franchise Management

SUPERMAN - ACTION COMICS VOLUME 7: UNDER THE SKIN

DC Comics, 4000 Warner Blvd., Burbank, CA 91522
A Warner Bros. Entertainment Company.
Printed by RR Donnelley, Salem, VA, USA. 11/20/15. First Printing.
ISBN: 978-1-4012-5866-5

Pak, Greg.
Superman - Action Comics. Volume 7, Under the skin / Greg Pak, writer ; Aaron Kuder, Lee Weeks, artists.
pages cm. — (The New 52!)
ISBN 978-1-4012-5866-5 (hardback)
1. Graphic novels. I. Kuder, Aaron, illustrator. II. Weeks, Lee, illustrator. III. Title. IV. Title: Under the skin.
PN6728.S9P354 2015
741.5'973—dc23
2015031191

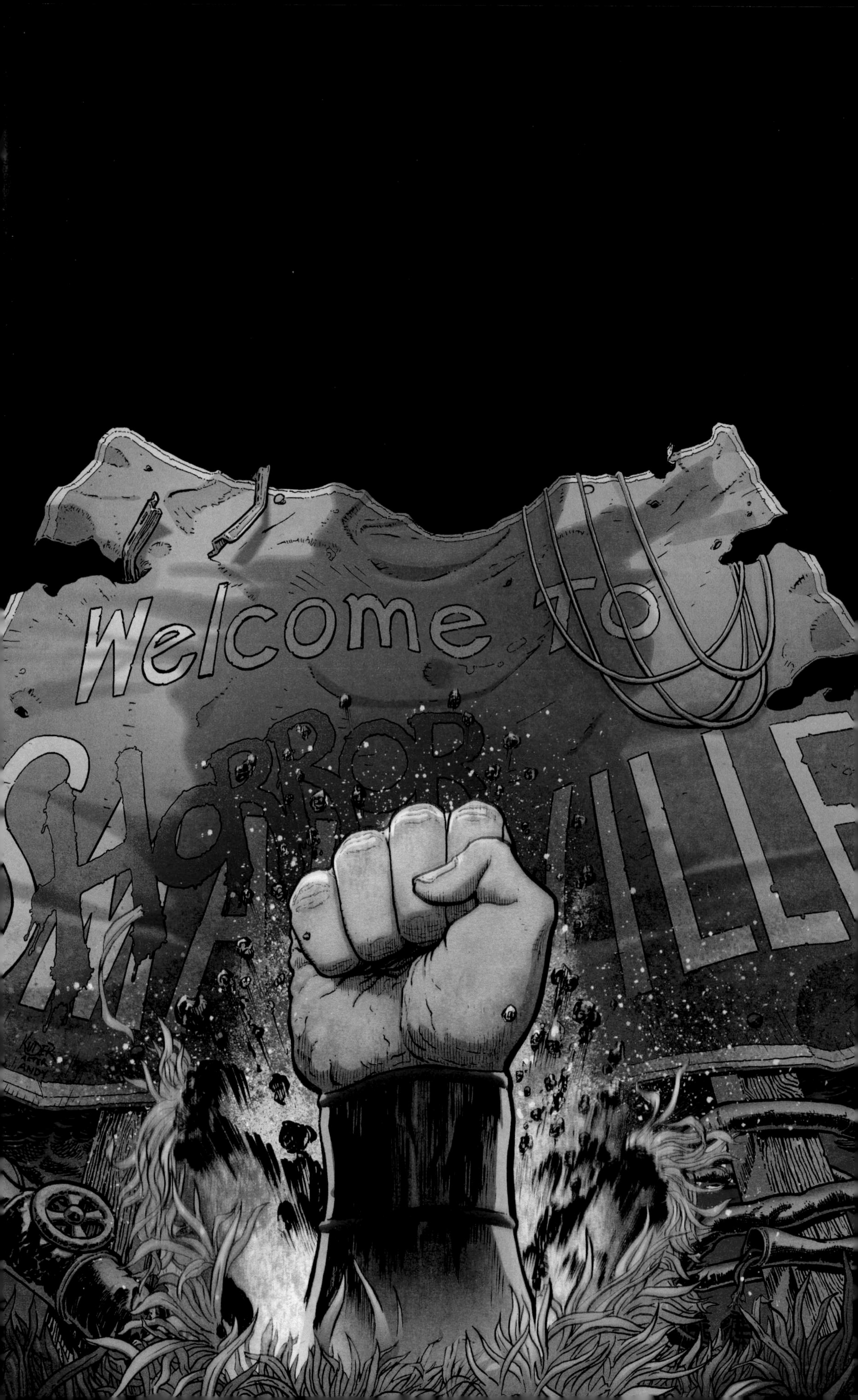
Welcome to
HORROR

HORRORVILLE

GREG PAK writer **AARON KUDER** artist **WIL QUINTANA** colorist **CARLOS M. MANGUAL** letterer cover by **AARON KUDER & WIL QUINTANA**

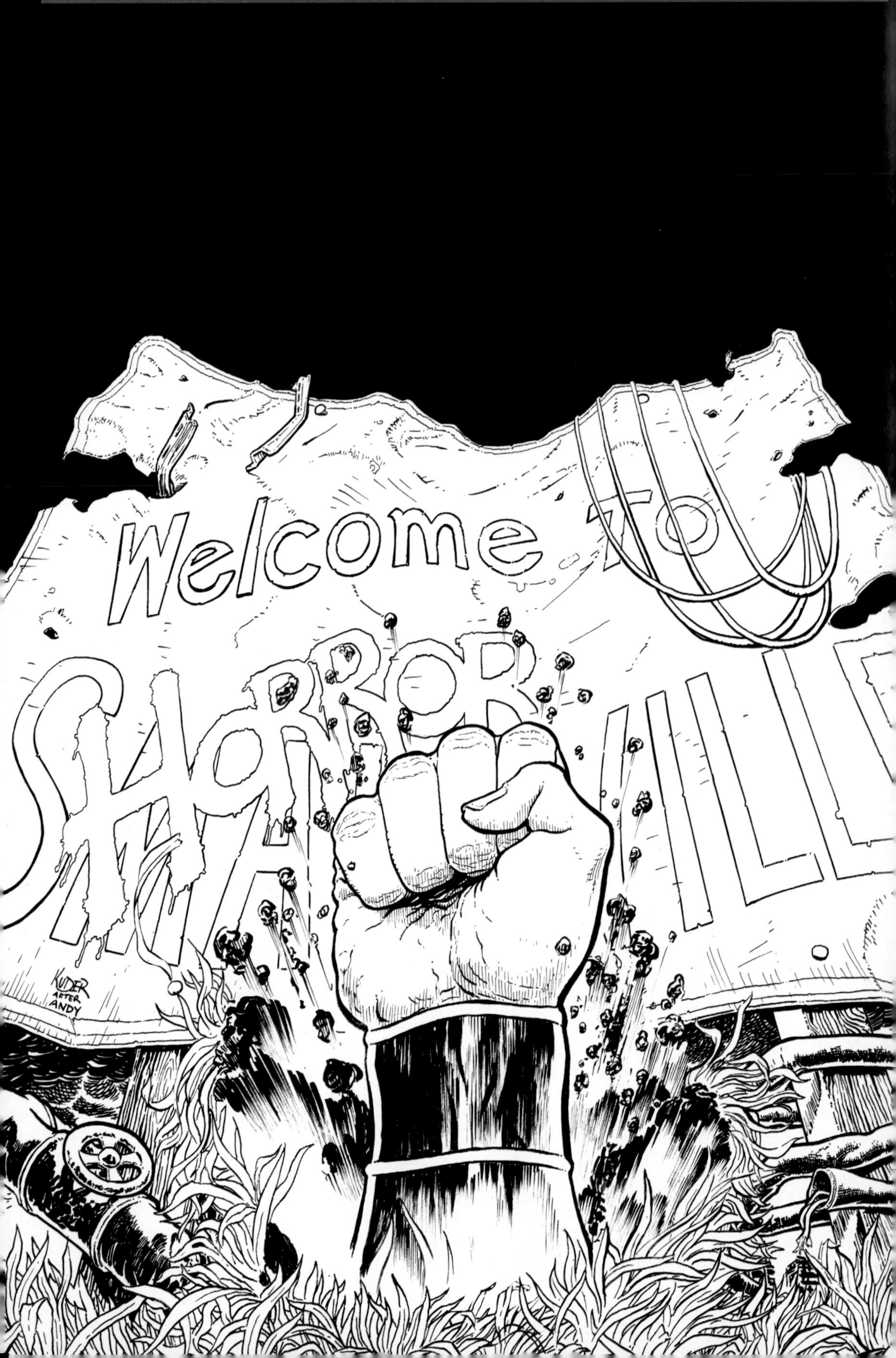
Welcome TO
KUDER AFTER ANDY

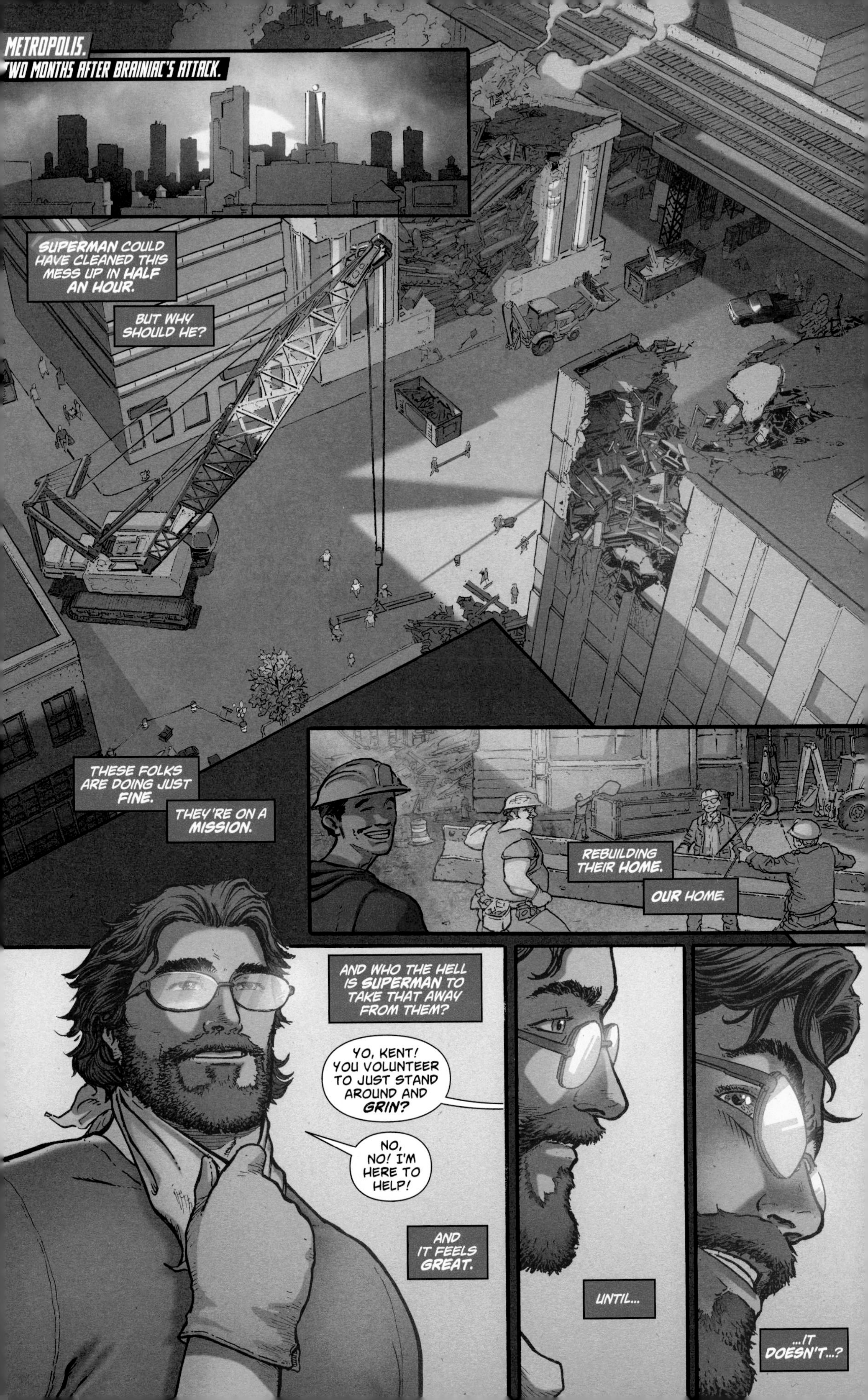

METROPOLIS.
WO MONTHS AFTER BRAINIAC'S ATTACK.
SUPERMAN COULD HAVE CLEANED THIS MESS UP IN HALF AN HOUR.
BUT WHY SHOULD HE?
THESE FOLKS ARE DOING JUST FINE.
THEY'RE ON A MISSION.
REBUILDING THEIR HOME.
OUR HOME.
AND WHO THE HELL IS SUPERMAN TO TAKE THAT AWAY FROM THEM?
YO, KENT! YOU VOLUNTEER TO JUST STAND AROUND AND GRIN?
NO, NO! I'M HERE TO HELP!
AND IT FEELS GREAT.
UNTIL...
...IT DOESN'T...?

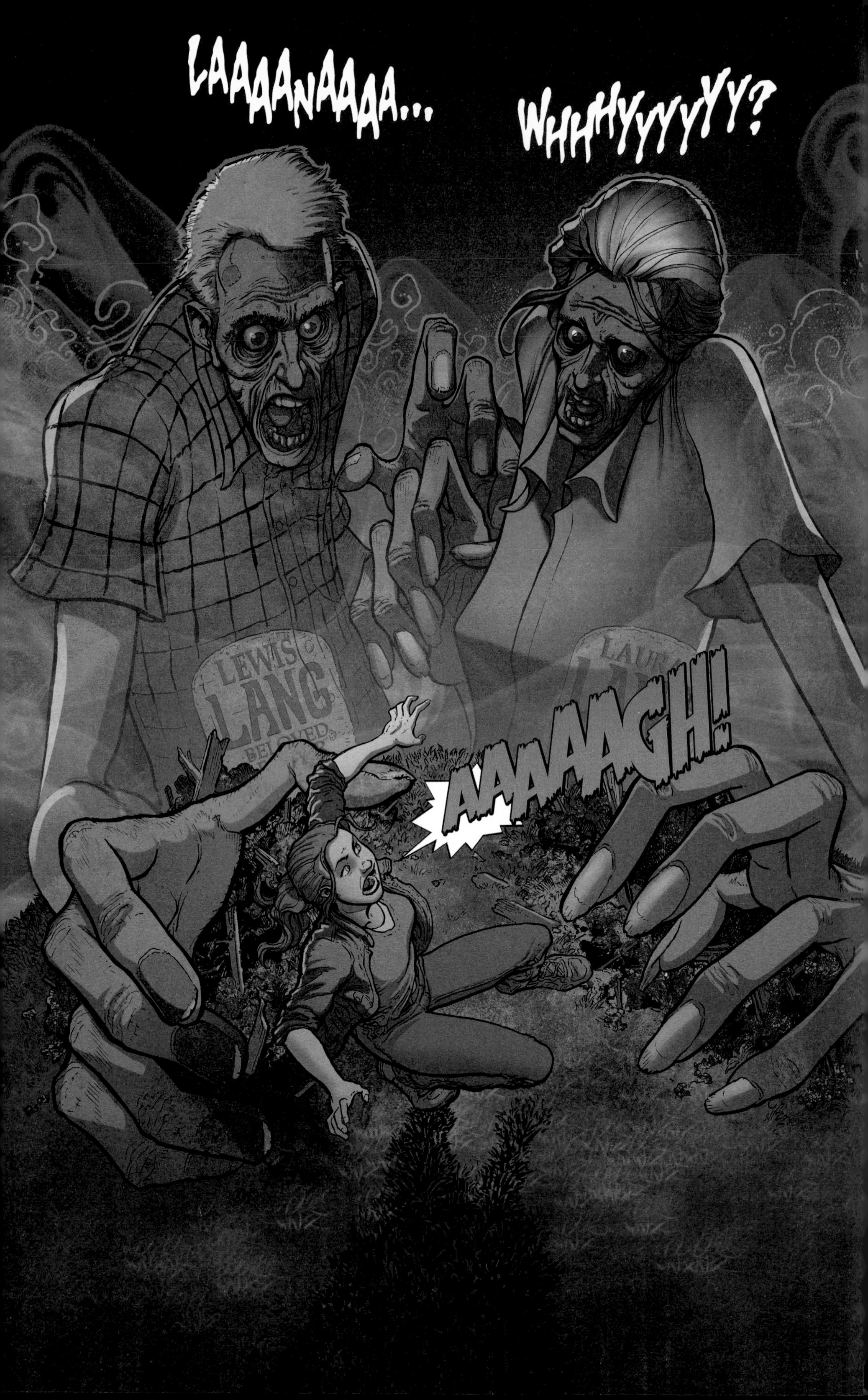
LAAAANAAAA...
WHHHYYYYYY?
LEWIS LANG BELOVED
LAURA
AAAAAGH!

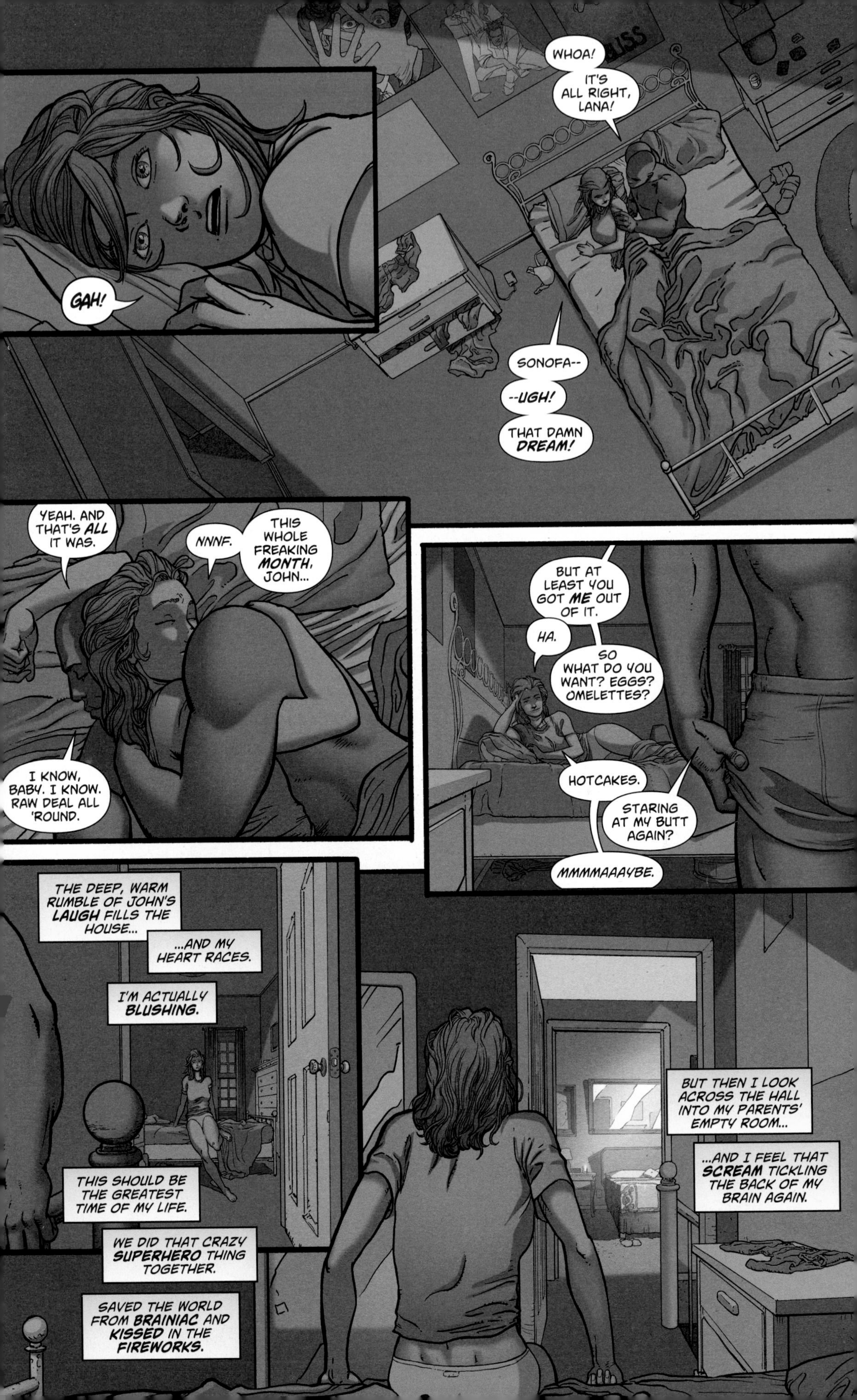
GAH!
WHOA!
IT'S ALL RIGHT, LANA!
SONOFA--
--UGH!
THAT DAMN DREAM!
YEAH. AND THAT'S ALL IT WAS.
NNNF.
THIS WHOLE FREAKING MONTH, JOHN...
I KNOW, BABY. I KNOW. RAW DEAL ALL 'ROUND.
BUT AT LEAST YOU GOT ME OUT OF IT.
HA.
SO WHAT DO YOU WANT? EGGS? OMELETTES?
HOTCAKES.
STARING AT MY BUTT AGAIN?
MMMMAAAYBE.
THE DEEP, WARM RUMBLE OF JOHN'S LAUGH FILLS THE HOUSE...
...AND MY HEART RACES.
I'M ACTUALLY BLUSHING.
THIS SHOULD BE THE GREATEST TIME OF MY LIFE.
WE DID THAT CRAZY SUPERHERO THING TOGETHER.
SAVED THE WORLD FROM BRAINIAC AND KISSED IN THE FIREWORKS.
BUT THEN I LOOK ACROSS THE HALL INTO MY PARENTS' EMPTY ROOM...
...AND I FEEL THAT SCREAM TICKLING THE BACK OF MY BRAIN AGAIN.

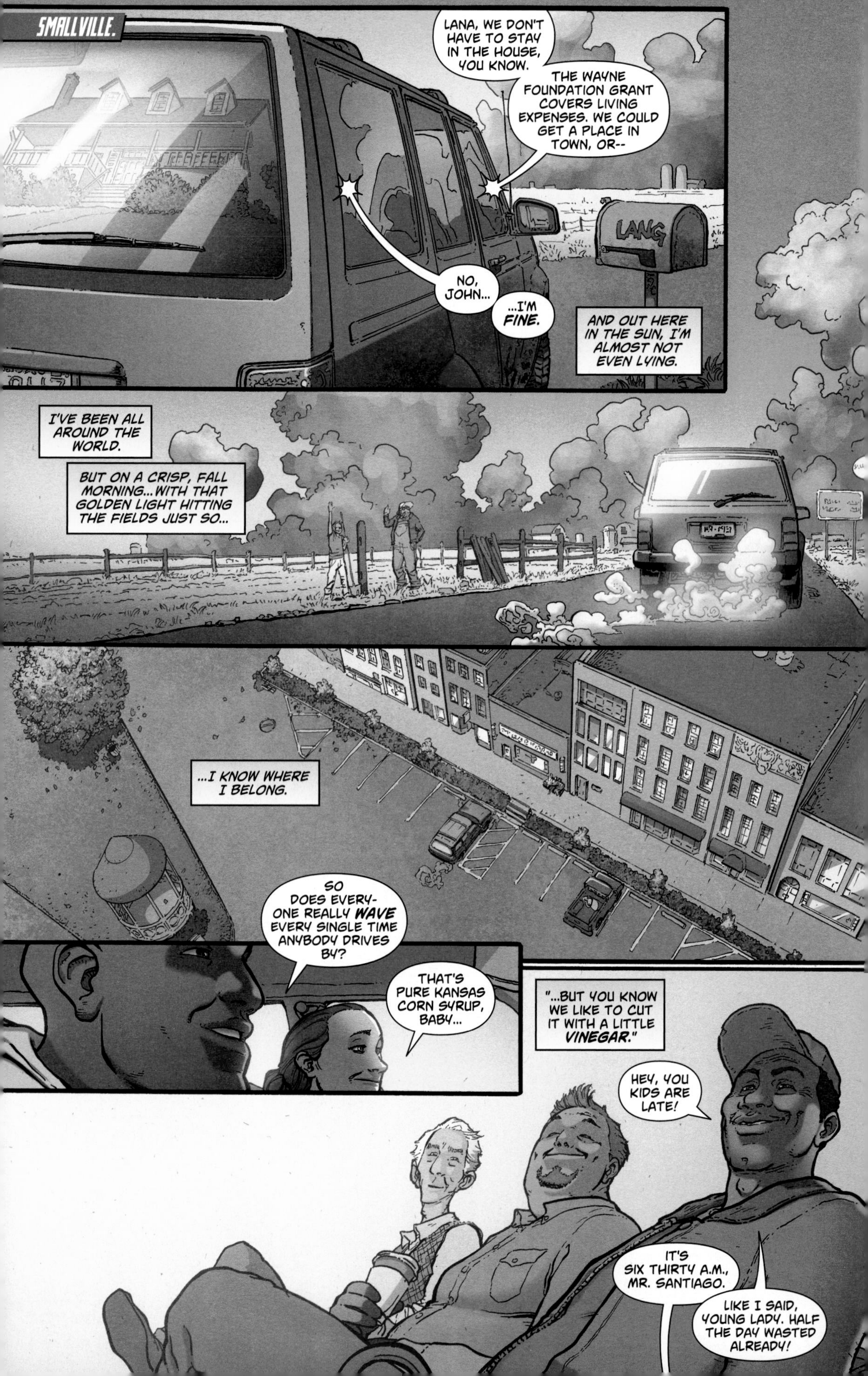
SMALLVILLE.
LANA, WE DON'T HAVE TO STAY IN THE HOUSE, YOU KNOW.
THE WAYNE FOUNDATION GRANT COVERS LIVING EXPENSES. WE COULD GET A PLACE IN TOWN, OR--
LANG
NO, JOHN...
...I'M FINE.
AND OUT HERE IN THE SUN, I'M ALMOST NOT EVEN LYING.
I'VE BEEN ALL AROUND THE WORLD.
BUT ON A CRISP, FALL MORNING...WITH THAT GOLDEN LIGHT HITTING THE FIELDS JUST SO...
...I KNOW WHERE I BELONG.
SO DOES EVERY-ONE REALLY WAVE EVERY SINGLE TIME ANYBODY DRIVES BY?
THAT'S PURE KANSAS CORN SYRUP, BABY...
"...BUT YOU KNOW WE LIKE TO CUT IT WITH A LITTLE VINEGAR."
HEY, YOU KIDS ARE LATE!
IT'S SIX THIRTY A.M., MR. SANTIAGO.
LIKE I SAID, YOUNG LADY. HALF THE DAY WASTED ALREADY!

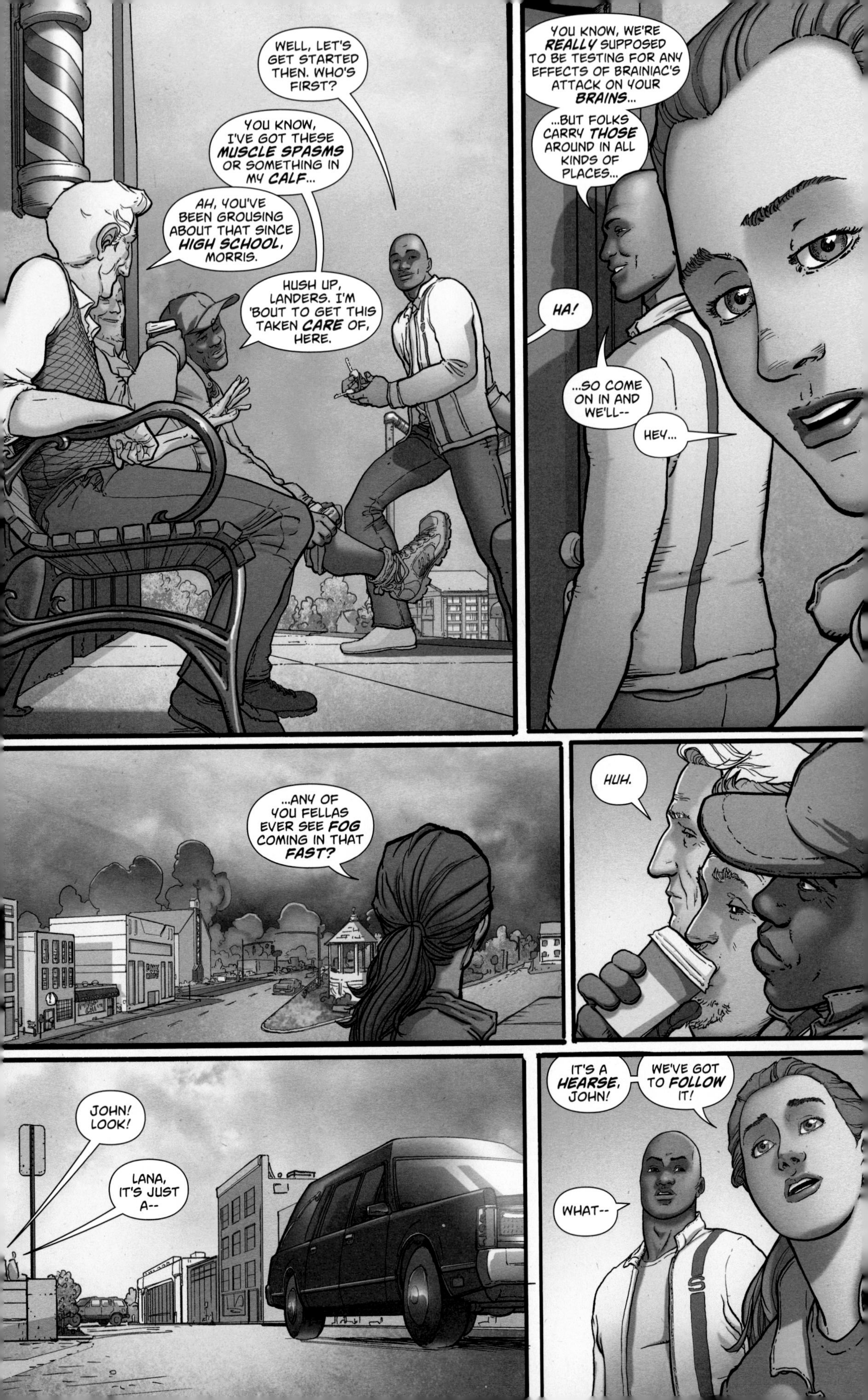
WELL, LET'S GET STARTED THEN. WHO'S FIRST?
YOU KNOW, I'VE GOT THESE MUSCLE SPASMS OR SOMETHING IN MY CALF...
AH, YOU'VE BEEN GROUSING ABOUT THAT SINCE HIGH SCHOOL, MORRIS.
HUSH UP, LANDERS. I'M 'BOUT TO GET THIS TAKEN CARE OF, HERE.
YOU KNOW, WE'RE REALLY SUPPOSED TO BE TESTING FOR ANY EFFECTS OF BRAINIAC'S ATTACK ON YOUR BRAINS...
...BUT FOLKS CARRY THOSE AROUND IN ALL KINDS OF PLACES...
HA!
...SO COME ON IN AND WE'LL--
HEY...
...ANY OF YOU FELLAS EVER SEE FOG COMING IN THAT FAST?
HUH.
JOHN! LOOK!
LANA, IT'S JUST A--
IT'S A HEARSE, JOHN!
WE'VE GOT TO FOLLOW IT!
WHAT--

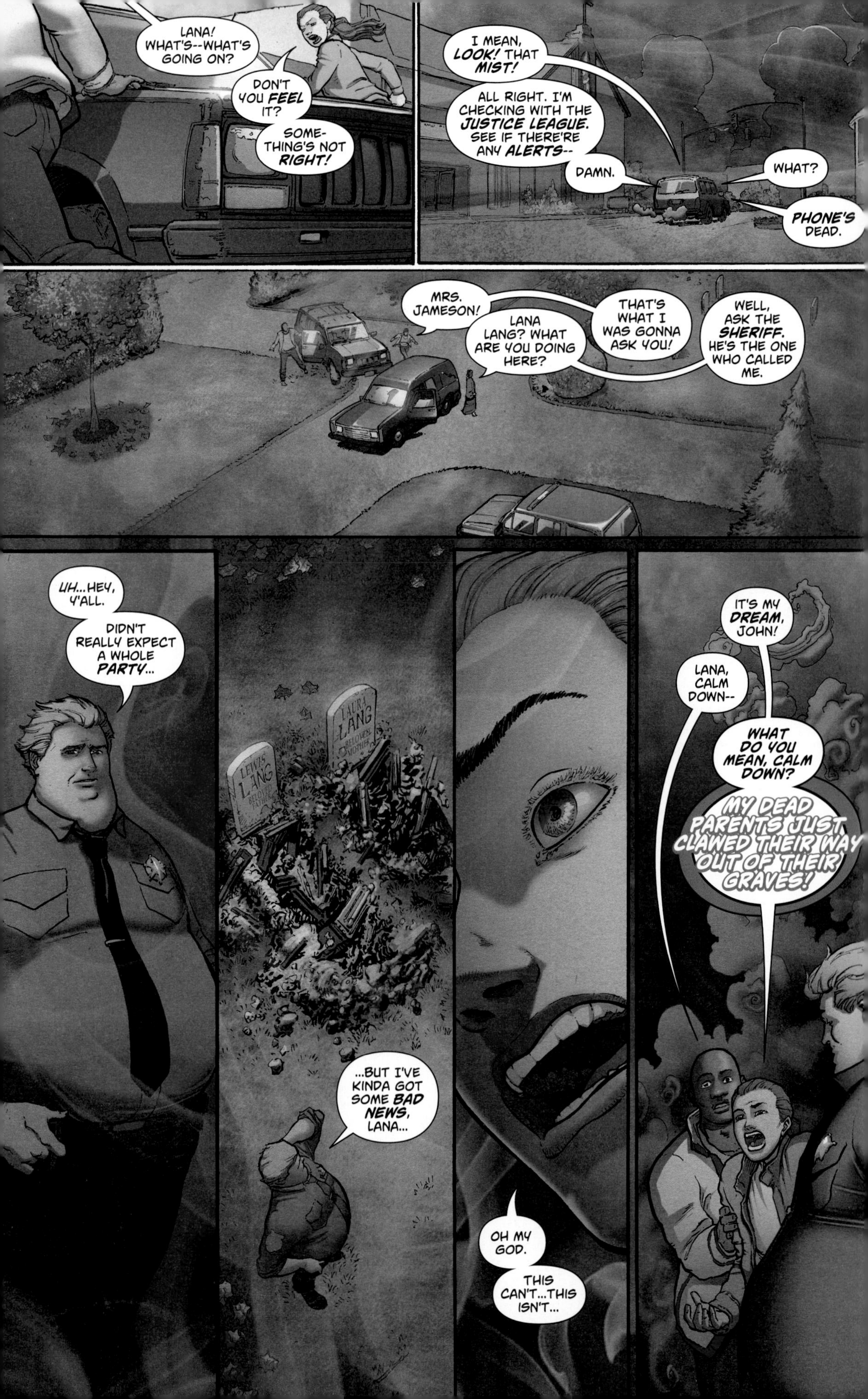
LANA! WHAT'S--WHAT'S GOING ON?
DON'T YOU FEEL IT?
SOME-THING'S NOT RIGHT!
I MEAN, LOOK! THAT MIST!
ALL RIGHT. I'M CHECKING WITH THE JUSTICE LEAGUE. SEE IF THERE'RE ANY ALERTS--
DAMN.
WHAT?
PHONE'S DEAD.
MRS. JAMESON!
LANA LANG? WHAT ARE YOU DOING HERE?
THAT'S WHAT I WAS GONNA ASK YOU!
WELL, ASK THE SHERIFF. HE'S THE ONE WHO CALLED ME.
UH...HEY, Y'ALL.
DIDN'T REALLY EXPECT A WHOLE PARTY...
LAURA LANG BELOVED MOTHER
LEWIS LANG BELOVED FATHER
...BUT I'VE KINDA GOT SOME BAD NEWS, LANA...
OH MY GOD.
THIS CAN'T...THIS ISN'T...
IT'S MY DREAM, JOHN!
LANA, CALM DOWN--
WHAT DO YOU MEAN, CALM DOWN?
MY DEAD PARENTS JUST CLAWED THEIR WAY OUT OF THEIR GRAVES!

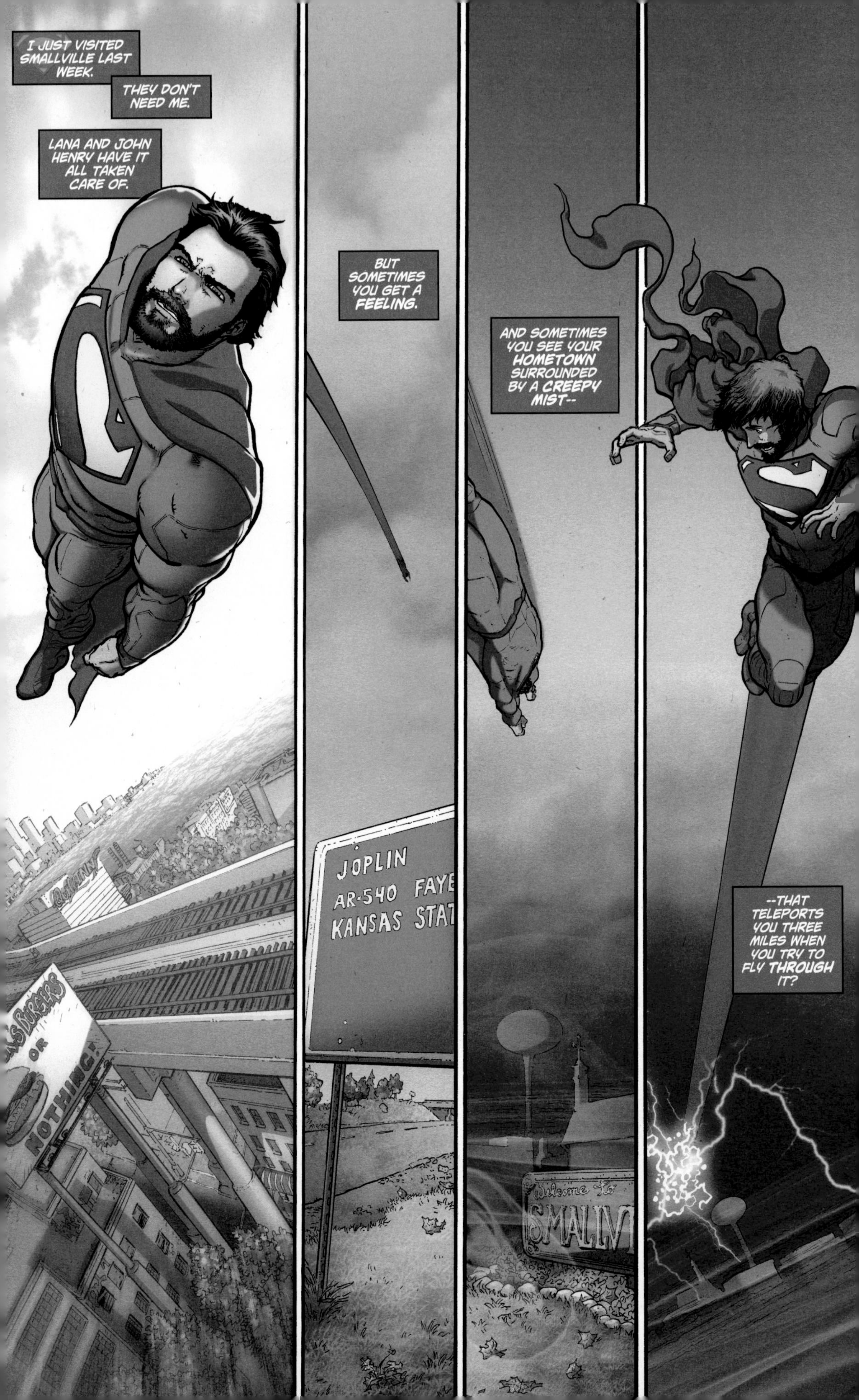
I JUST VISITED SMALLVILLE LAST WEEK.
THEY DON'T NEED ME.
LANA AND JOHN HENRY HAVE IT ALL TAKEN CARE OF.
BURGERS OR NOTHING!
BUT SOMETIMES YOU GET A FEELING.
JOPLIN
AR-540 FAYE
KANSAS STAT
AND SOMETIMES YOU SEE YOUR HOMETOWN SURROUNDED BY A CREEPY MIST--
SMALLVI
--THAT TELEPORTS YOU THREE MILES WHEN YOU TRY TO FLY THROUGH IT?

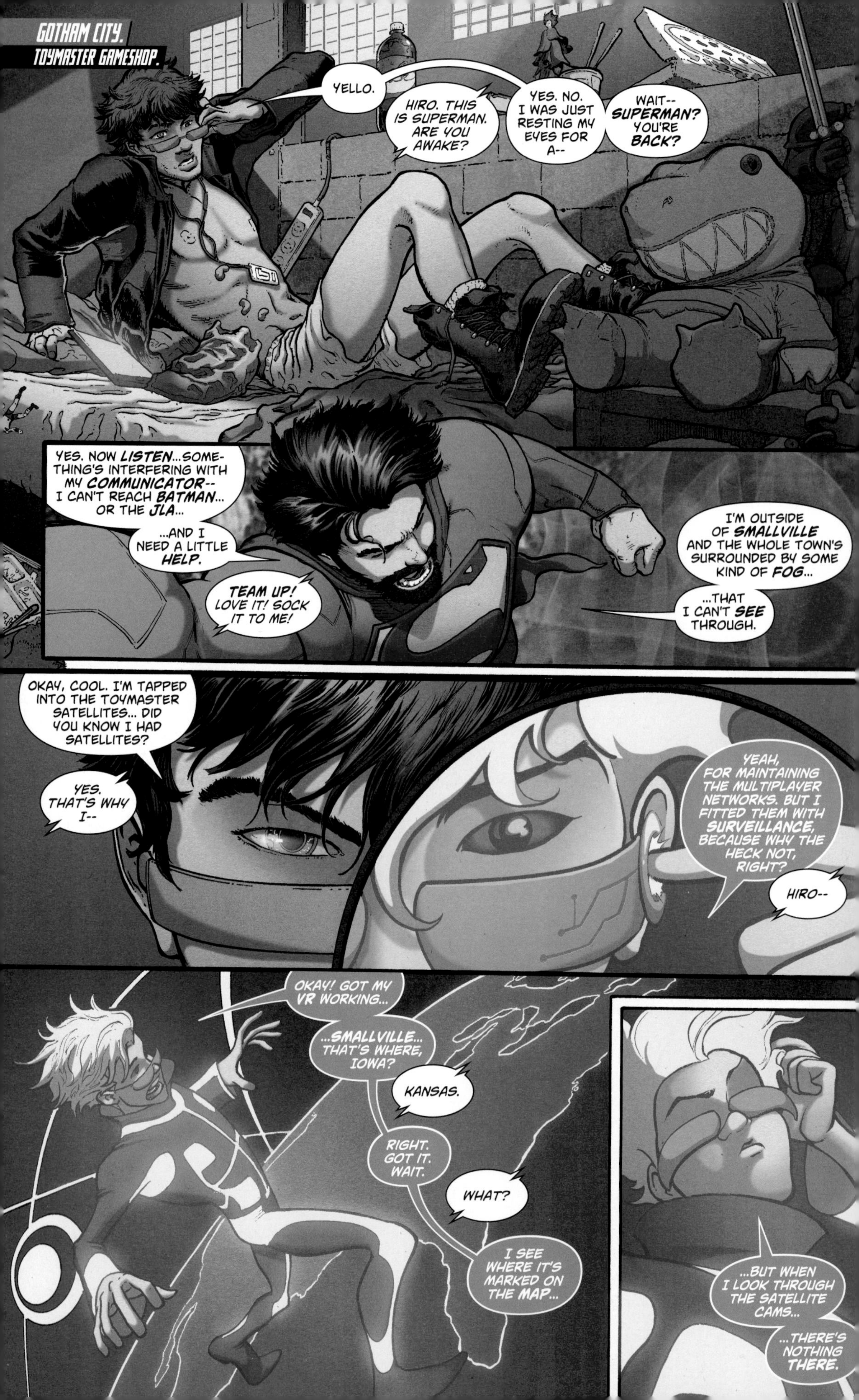
GOTHAM CITY.
TOYMASTER GAMESHOP.
YELLO.
HIRO. THIS IS SUPERMAN. ARE YOU AWAKE?
YES. NO. I WAS JUST RESTING MY EYES FOR A--
WAIT-- SUPERMAN? YOU'RE BACK?
YES. NOW LISTEN...SOMETHING'S INTERFERING WITH MY COMMUNICATOR-- I CAN'T REACH BATMAN... OR THE JLA...
...AND I NEED A LITTLE HELP.
TEAM UP! LOVE IT! SOCK IT TO ME!
I'M OUTSIDE OF SMALLVILLE AND THE WHOLE TOWN'S SURROUNDED BY SOME KIND OF FOG...
...THAT I CAN'T SEE THROUGH.
OKAY, COOL. I'M TAPPED INTO THE TOYMASTER SATELLITES... DID YOU KNOW I HAD SATELLITES?
YES. THAT'S WHY I--
YEAH, FOR MAINTAINING THE MULTIPLAYER NETWORKS. BUT I FITTED THEM WITH SURVEILLANCE, BECAUSE WHY THE HECK NOT, RIGHT?
HIRO--
OKAY! GOT MY VR WORKING...
...SMALLVILLE... THAT'S WHERE, IOWA?
KANSAS.
RIGHT. GOT IT. WAIT.
WHAT?
I SEE WHERE IT'S MARKED ON THE MAP...
...BUT WHEN I LOOK THROUGH THE SATELLITE CAMS...
...THERE'S NOTHING THERE.

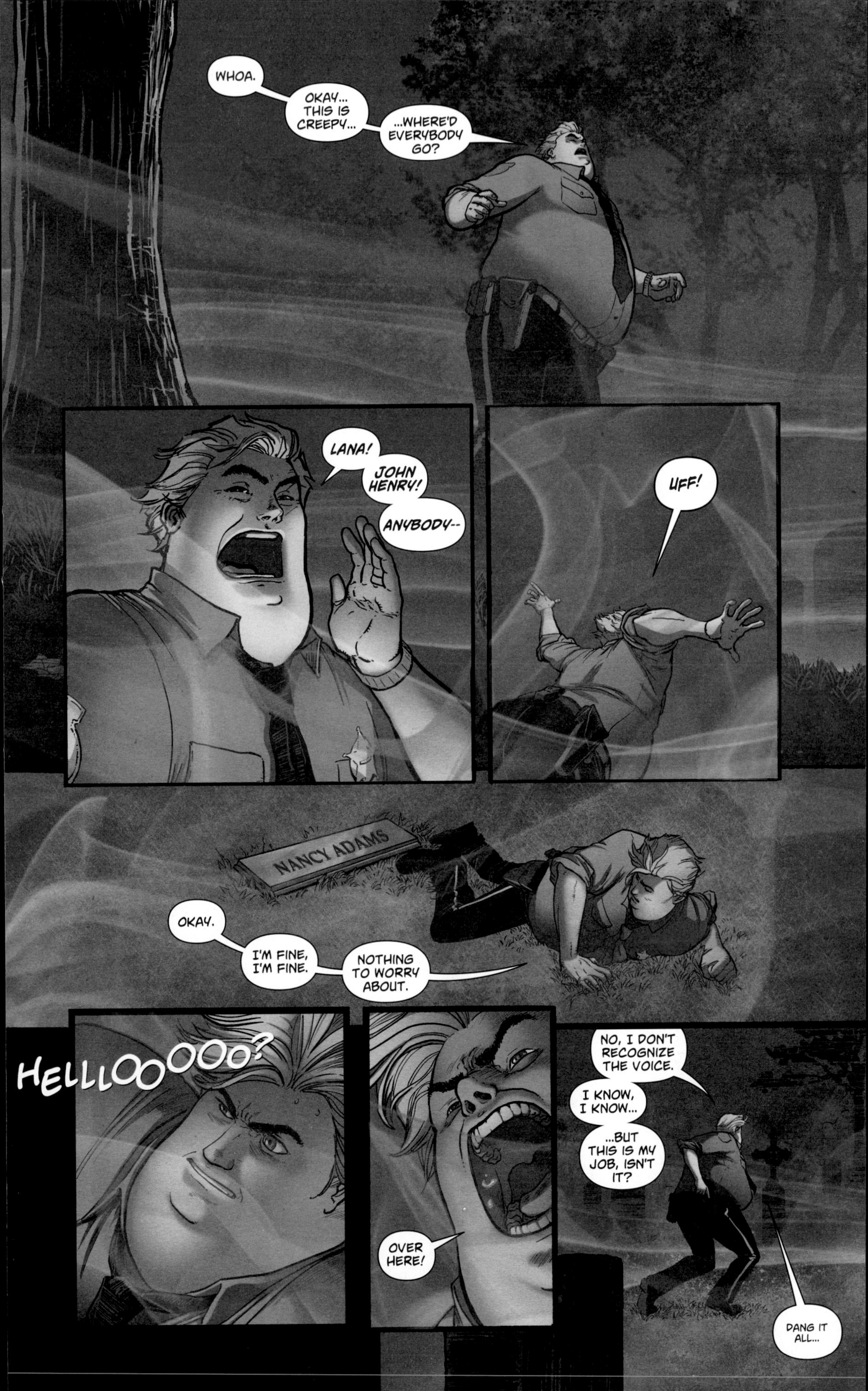
WHOA.
OKAY... THIS IS CREEPY...
...WHERE'D EVERYBODY GO?
LANA!
JOHN HENRY!
ANYBODY--
UFF!
NANCY ADAMS
OKAY.
I'M FINE, I'M FINE.
NOTHING TO WORRY ABOUT.
HELLLOOOOO?
OVER HERE!
NO, I DON'T RECOGNIZE THE VOICE.
I KNOW, I KNOW...
...BUT THIS IS MY JOB, ISN'T IT?
DANG IT ALL...

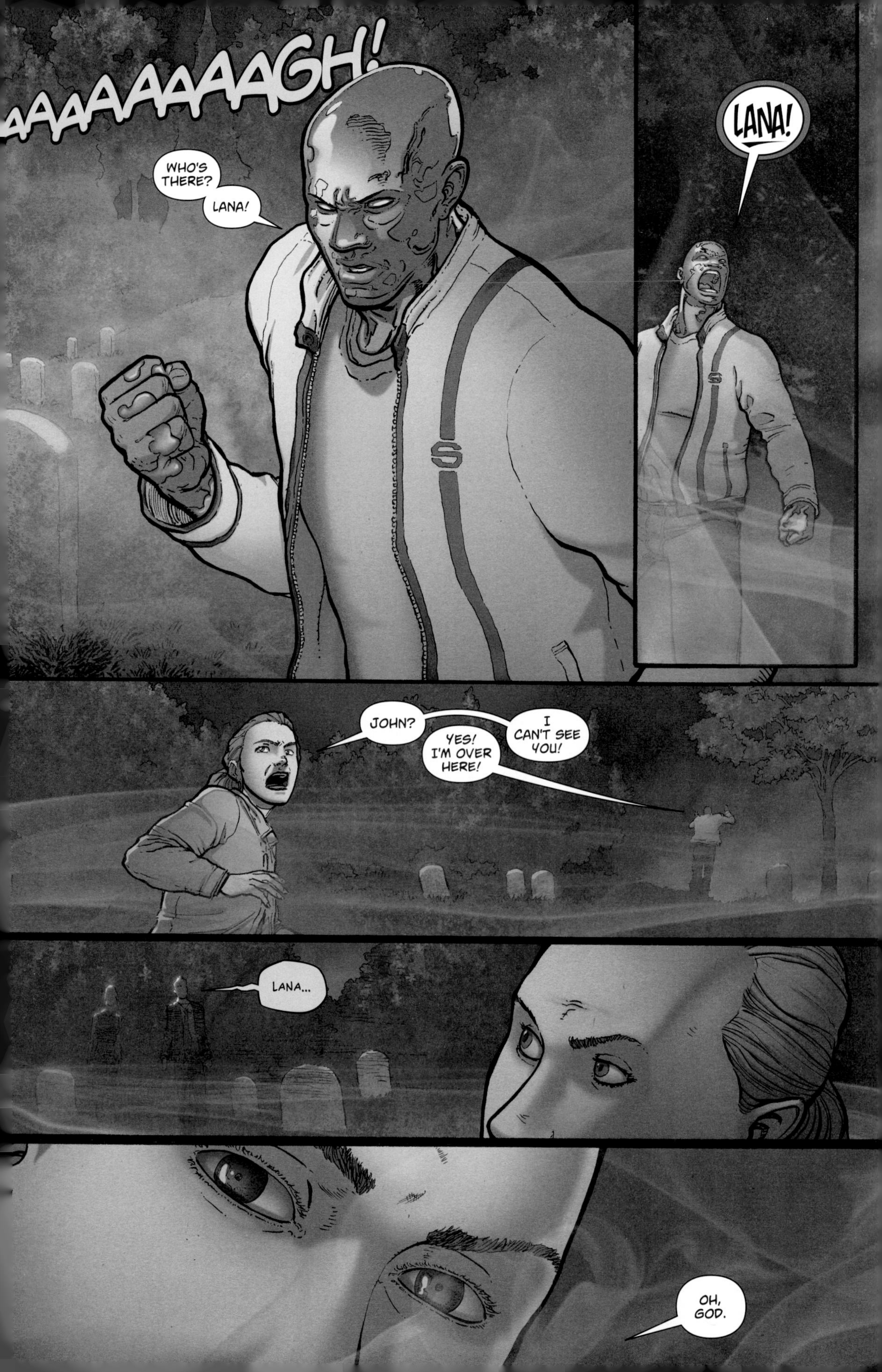
AAAAAAAAAAGH!
WHO'S THERE?
LANA!
LANA!
JOHN?
I CAN'T SEE YOU!
YES! I'M OVER HERE!
LANA...
OH, GOD.

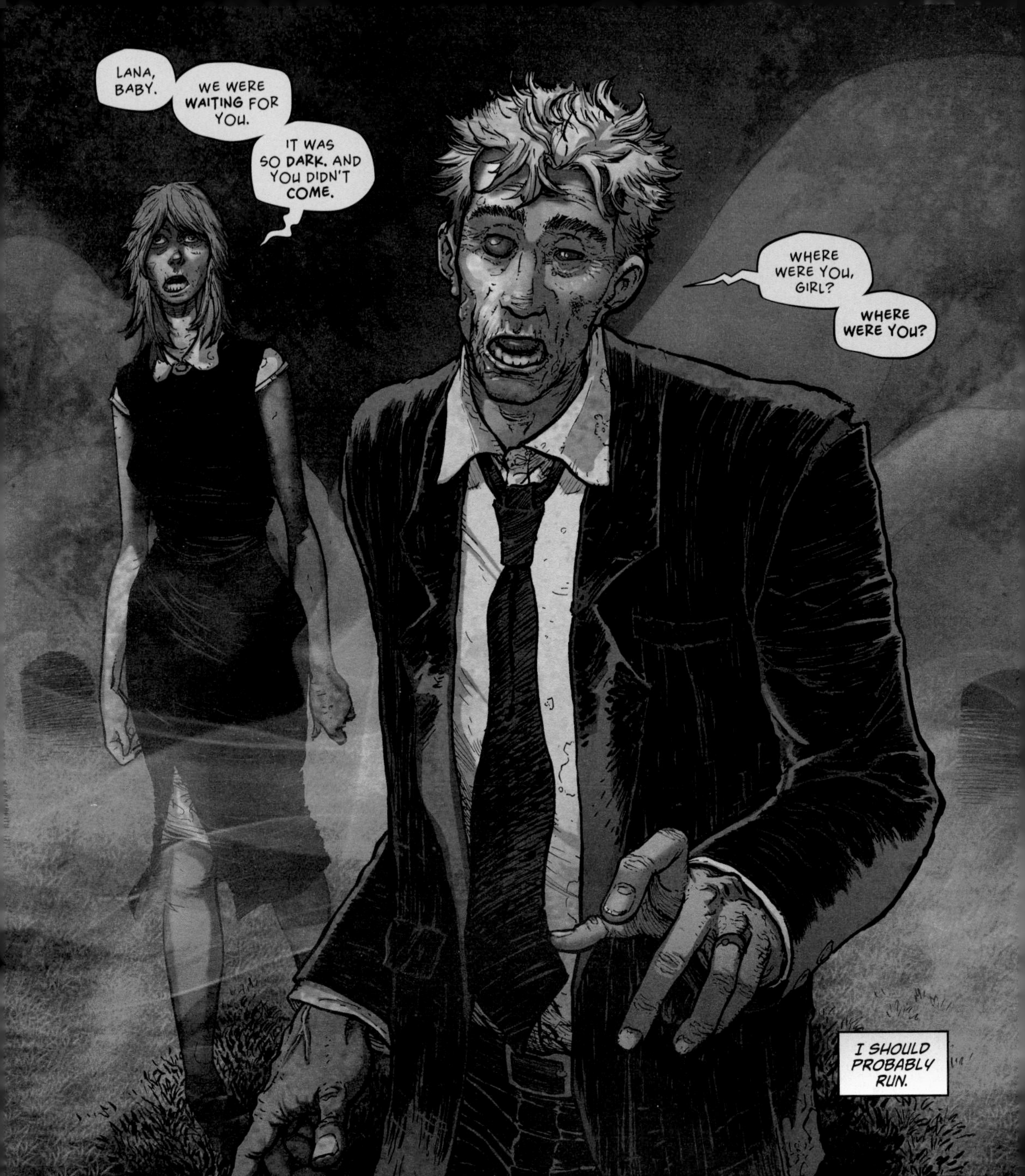
LANA, BABY.
WE WERE WAITING FOR YOU.
IT WAS SO DARK. AND YOU DIDN'T COME.
WHERE WERE YOU, GIRL?
WHERE WERE YOU?
I SHOULD PROBABLY RUN.

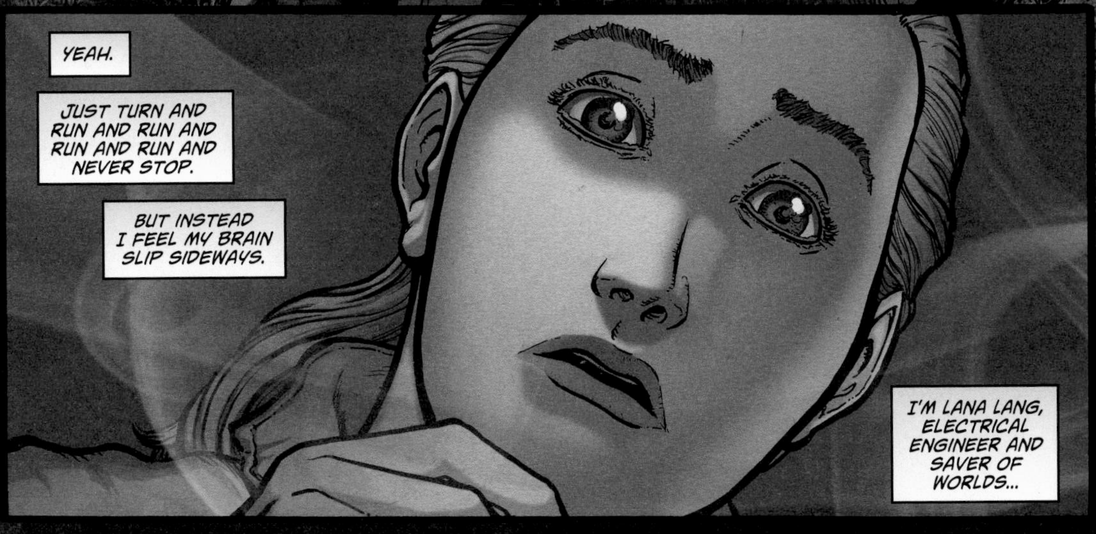
YEAH.
JUST TURN AND RUN AND RUN AND RUN AND RUN AND NEVER STOP.
BUT INSTEAD I FEEL MY BRAIN SLIP SIDEWAYS.
I'M LANA LANG, ELECTRICAL ENGINEER AND SAVER OF WORLDS...

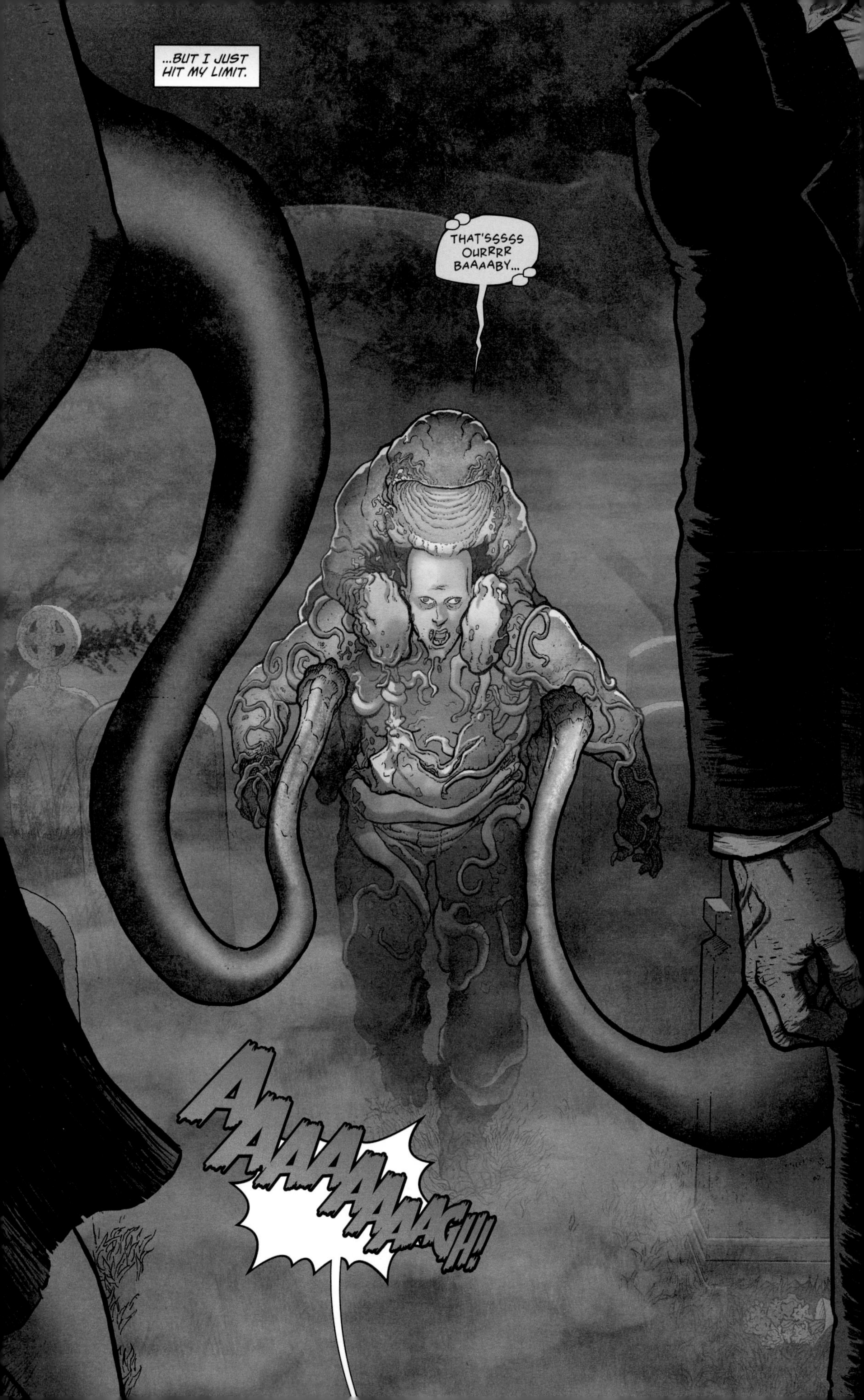
...BUT I JUST HIT MY LIMIT.
THAT'SSSSS OURRRR BAAAABY...
AAAAAAAAAGH!!

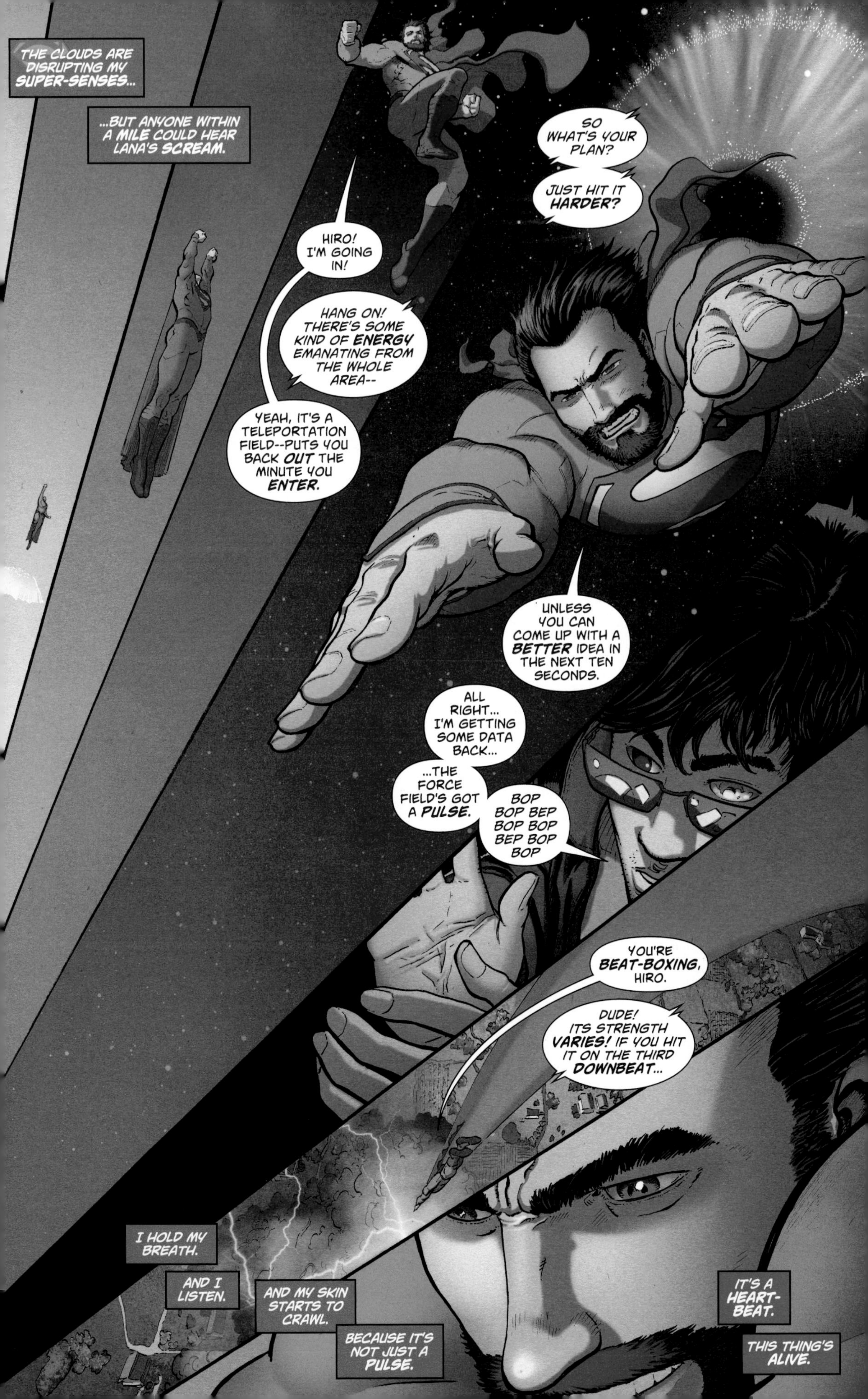
THE CLOUDS ARE DISRUPTING MY SUPER-SENSES...
...BUT ANYONE WITHIN A MILE COULD HEAR LANA'S SCREAM.
HIRO! I'M GOING IN!
SO WHAT'S YOUR PLAN?
JUST HIT IT HARDER?
HANG ON! THERE'S SOME KIND OF ENERGY EMANATING FROM THE WHOLE AREA--
YEAH, IT'S A TELEPORTATION FIELD--PUTS YOU BACK OUT THE MINUTE YOU ENTER.
UNLESS YOU CAN COME UP WITH A BETTER IDEA IN THE NEXT TEN SECONDS.
ALL RIGHT... I'M GETTING SOME DATA BACK...
...THE FORCE FIELD'S GOT A PULSE.
BOP BOP BEP BOP BOP BEP BOP BOP
YOU'RE BEAT-BOXING, HIRO.
DUDE! ITS STRENGTH VARIES! IF YOU HIT IT ON THE THIRD DOWNBEAT...
I HOLD MY BREATH.
AND I LISTEN.
AND MY SKIN STARTS TO CRAWL.
BECAUSE IT'S NOT JUST A PULSE.
IT'S A HEART-BEAT.
THIS THING'S ALIVE.

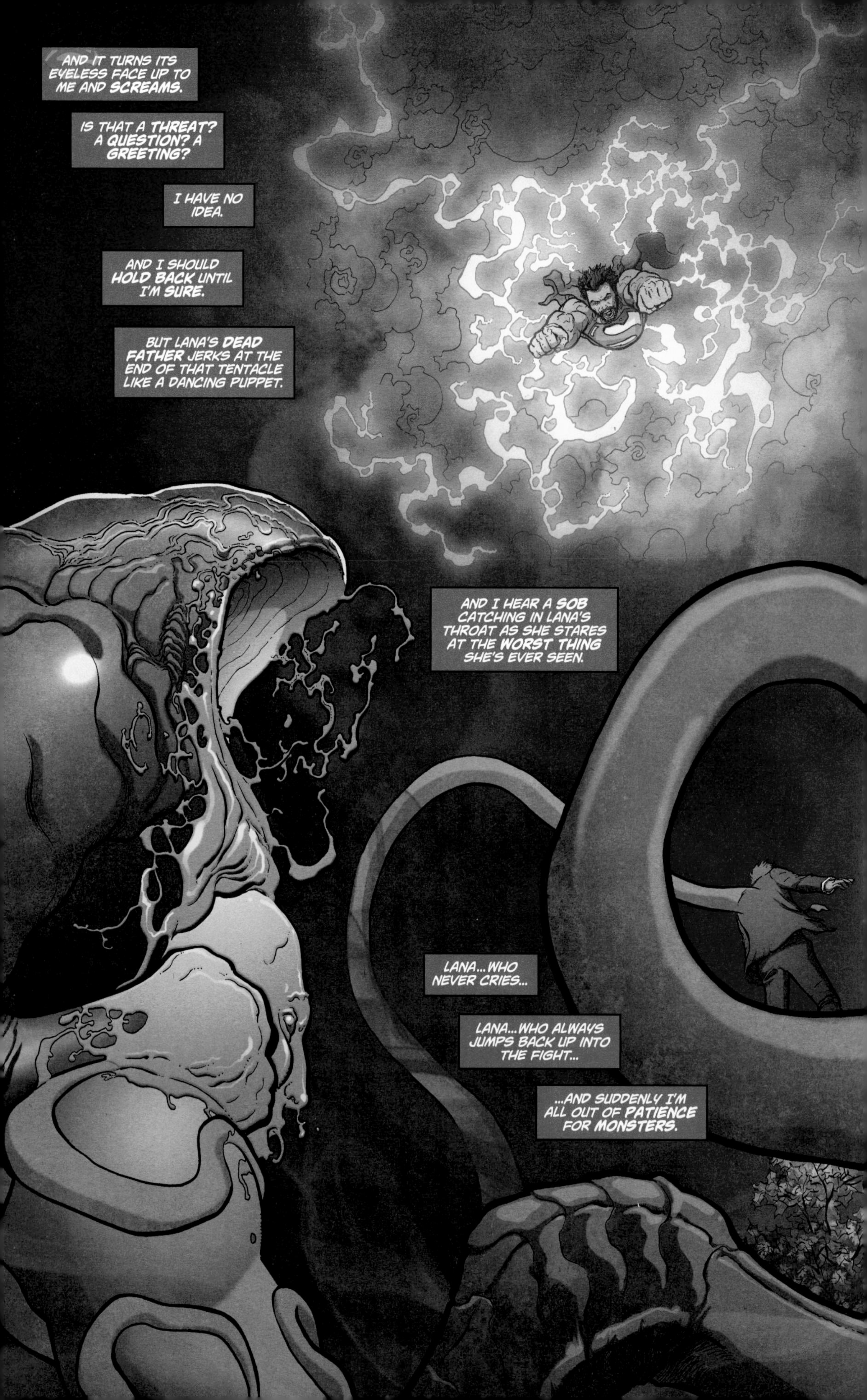
AND IT TURNS ITS EYELESS FACE UP TO ME AND SCREAMS.
IS THAT A THREAT? A QUESTION? A GREETING?
I HAVE NO IDEA.
AND I SHOULD HOLD BACK UNTIL I'M SURE.
BUT LANA'S DEAD FATHER JERKS AT THE END OF THAT TENTACLE LIKE A DANCING PUPPET.
AND I HEAR A SOB CATCHING IN LANA'S THROAT AS SHE STARES AT THE WORST THING SHE'S EVER SEEN.
LANA... WHO NEVER CRIES...
LANA... WHO ALWAYS JUMPS BACK UP INTO THE FIGHT...
...AND SUDDENLY I'M ALL OUT OF PATIENCE FOR MONSTERS.

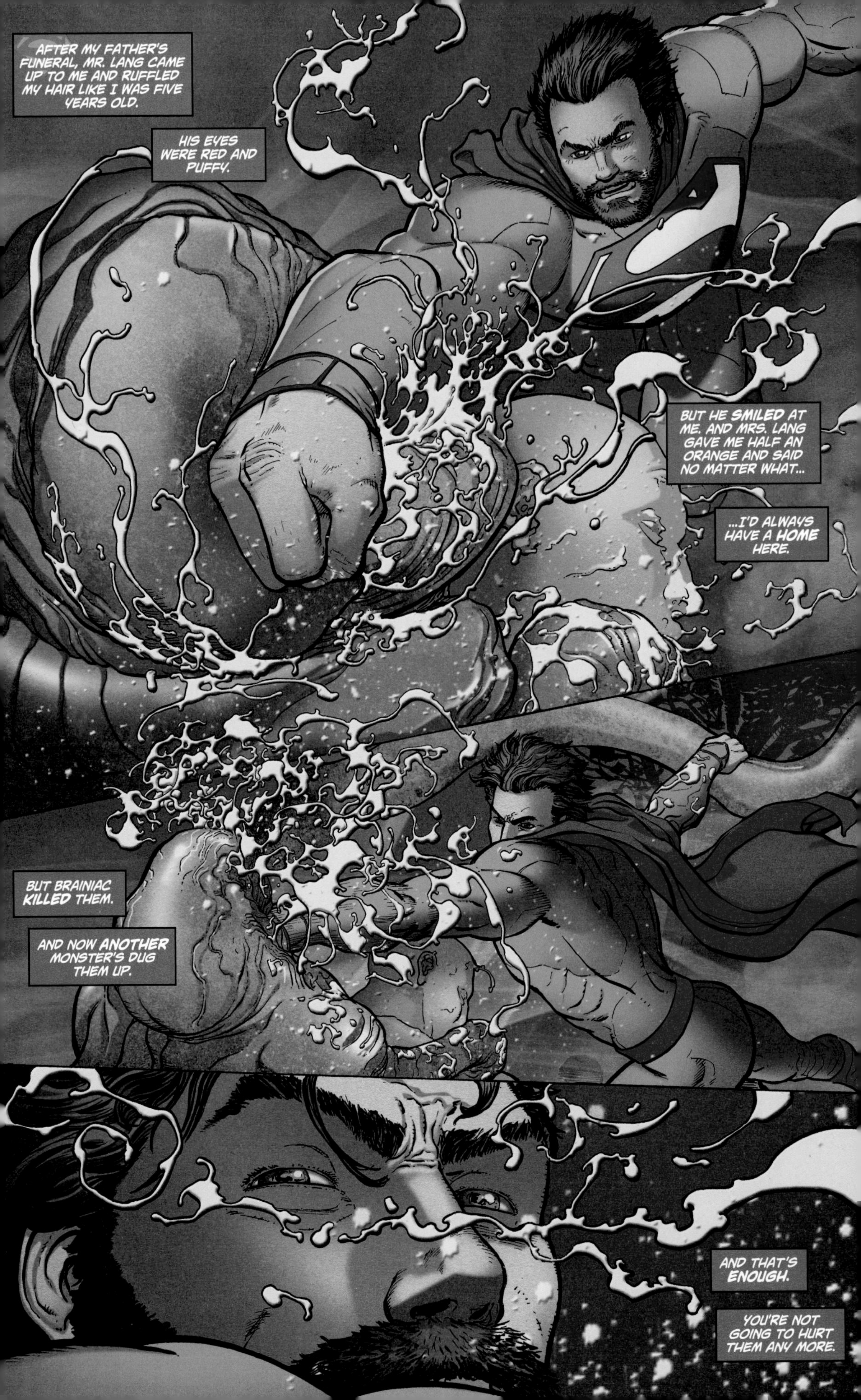
AFTER MY FATHER'S FUNERAL, MR. LANG CAME UP TO ME AND RUFFLED MY HAIR LIKE I WAS FIVE YEARS OLD.
HIS EYES WERE RED AND PUFFY.
BUT HE SMILED AT ME. AND MRS. LANG GAVE ME HALF AN ORANGE AND SAID NO MATTER WHAT...
...I'D ALWAYS HAVE A HOME HERE.
BUT BRAINIAC KILLED THEM.
AND NOW ANOTHER MONSTER'S DUG THEM UP.
AND THAT'S ENOUGH.
YOU'RE NOT GOING TO HURT THEM ANY MORE.

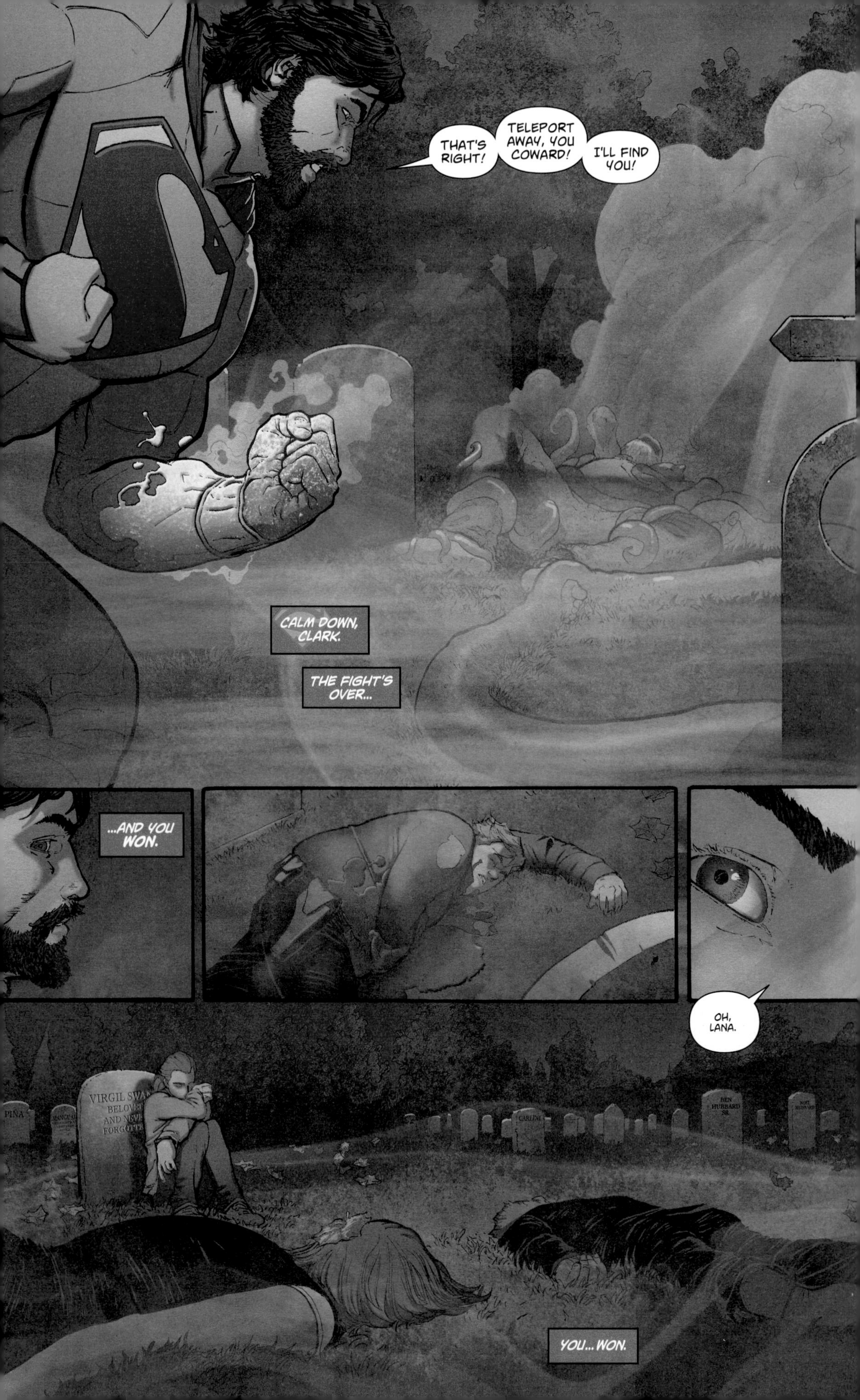
THAT'S RIGHT!
TELEPORT AWAY, YOU COWARD!
I'LL FIND YOU!
CALM DOWN, CLARK.
THE FIGHT'S OVER...
...AND YOU WON.
OH, LANA.
PINA
CARLINI
BEN HUBBARD
YOU...WON.

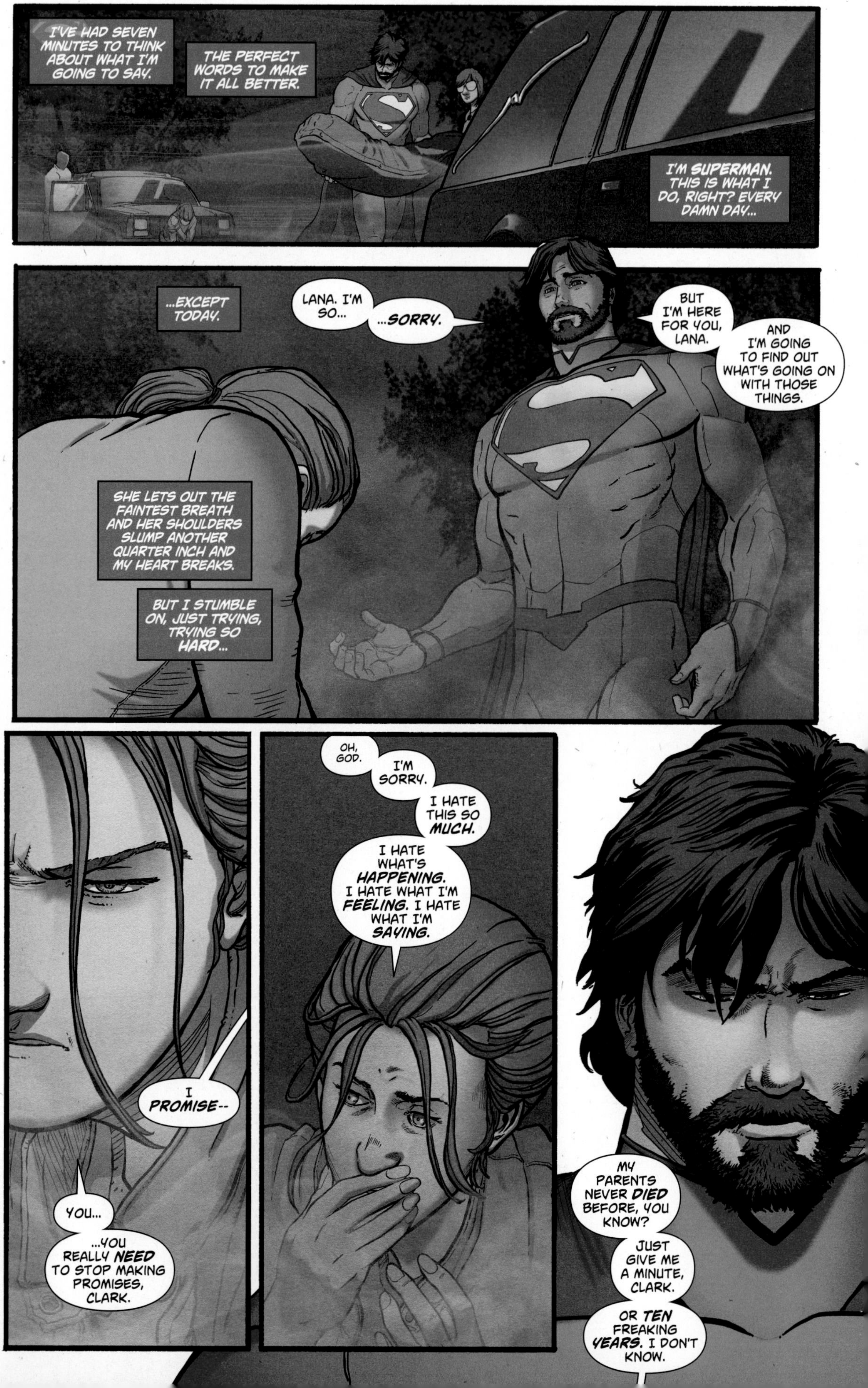
I'VE HAD SEVEN MINUTES TO THINK ABOUT WHAT I'M GOING TO SAY.
THE PERFECT WORDS TO MAKE IT ALL BETTER.
I'M SUPERMAN. THIS IS WHAT I DO, RIGHT? EVERY DAMN DAY...
...EXCEPT TODAY.
LANA. I'M SO...
...SORRY.
BUT I'M HERE FOR YOU, LANA.
AND I'M GOING TO FIND OUT WHAT'S GOING ON WITH THOSE THINGS.
SHE LETS OUT THE FAINTEST BREATH AND HER SHOULDERS SLUMP ANOTHER QUARTER INCH AND MY HEART BREAKS.
BUT I STUMBLE ON, JUST TRYING, TRYING SO HARD...
I PROMISE--
YOU...
...YOU REALLY NEED TO STOP MAKING PROMISES, CLARK.
OH, GOD.
I'M SORRY.
I HATE THIS SO MUCH.
I HATE WHAT'S HAPPENING. I HATE WHAT I'M FEELING. I HATE WHAT I'M SAYING.
MY PARENTS NEVER DIED BEFORE, YOU KNOW?
JUST GIVE ME A MINUTE, CLARK.
OR TEN FREAKING YEARS. I DON'T KNOW.

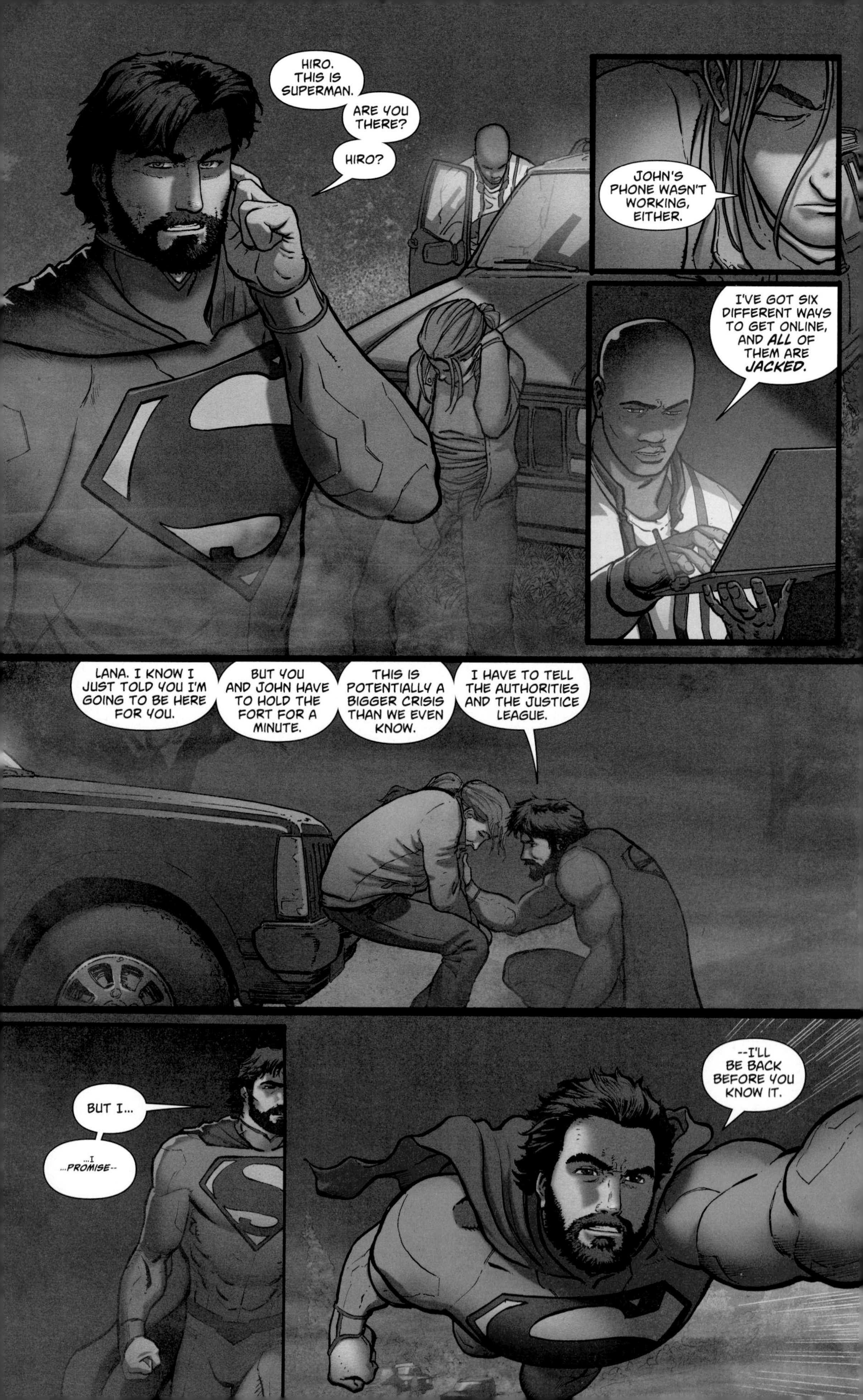
HIRO. THIS IS SUPERMAN.
ARE YOU THERE?
HIRO?
JOHN'S PHONE WASN'T WORKING, EITHER.
I'VE GOT SIX DIFFERENT WAYS TO GET ONLINE, AND ALL OF THEM ARE JACKED.
LANA. I KNOW I JUST TOLD YOU I'M GOING TO BE HERE FOR YOU.
BUT YOU AND JOHN HAVE TO HOLD THE FORT FOR A MINUTE.
THIS IS POTENTIALLY A BIGGER CRISIS THAN WE EVEN KNOW.
I HAVE TO TELL THE AUTHORITIES AND THE JUSTICE LEAGUE.
BUT I...
...I ...PROMISE--
--I'LL BE BACK BEFORE YOU KNOW IT.

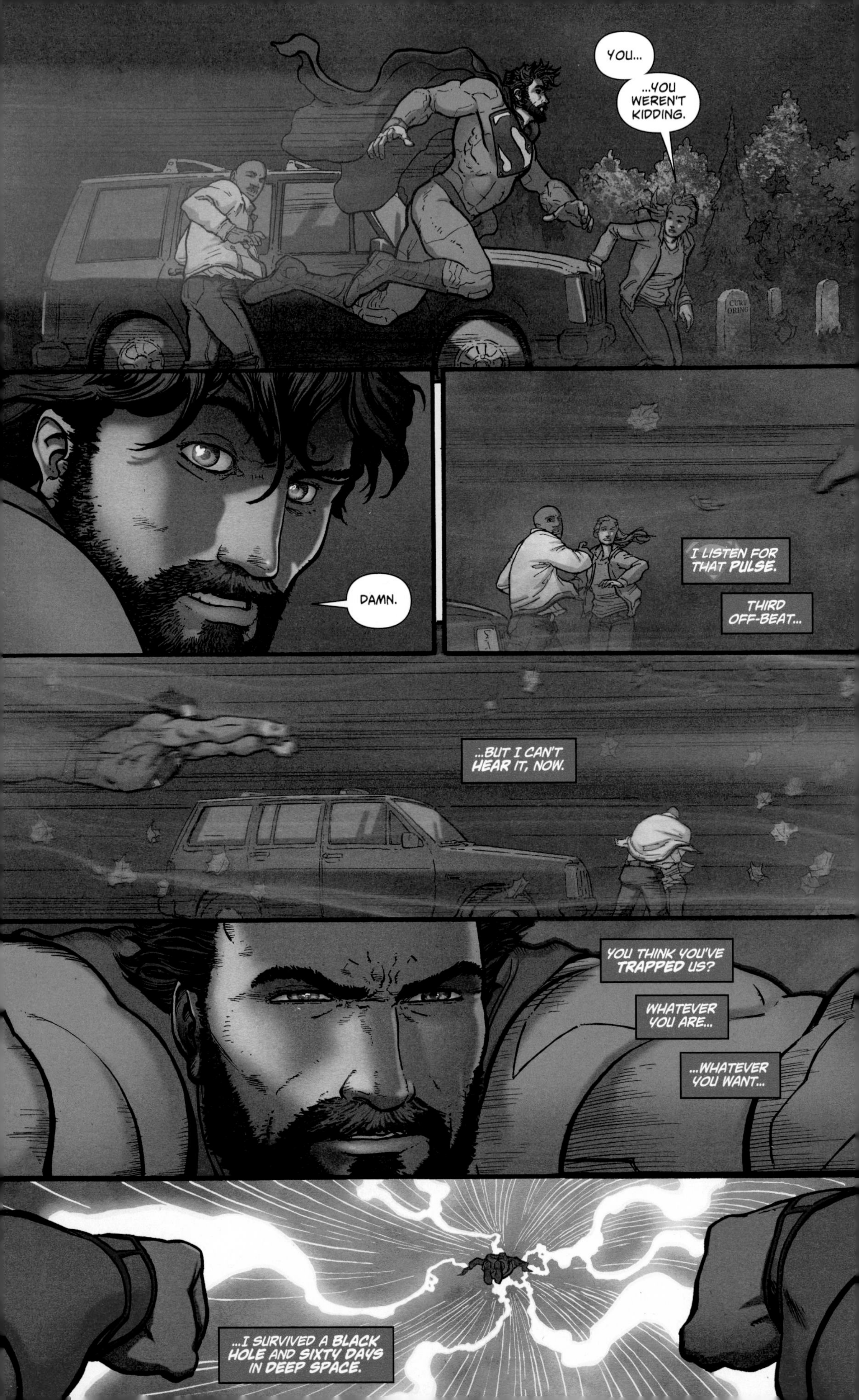
YOU...
...YOU WEREN'T KIDDING.
CURT ORING
DAMN.
I LISTEN FOR THAT PULSE.
THIRD OFF-BEAT...
...BUT I CAN'T HEAR IT, NOW.
YOU THINK YOU'VE TRAPPED US?
WHATEVER YOU ARE...
...WHATEVER YOU WANT...
...I SURVIVED A BLACK HOLE AND SIXTY DAYS IN DEEP SPACE.

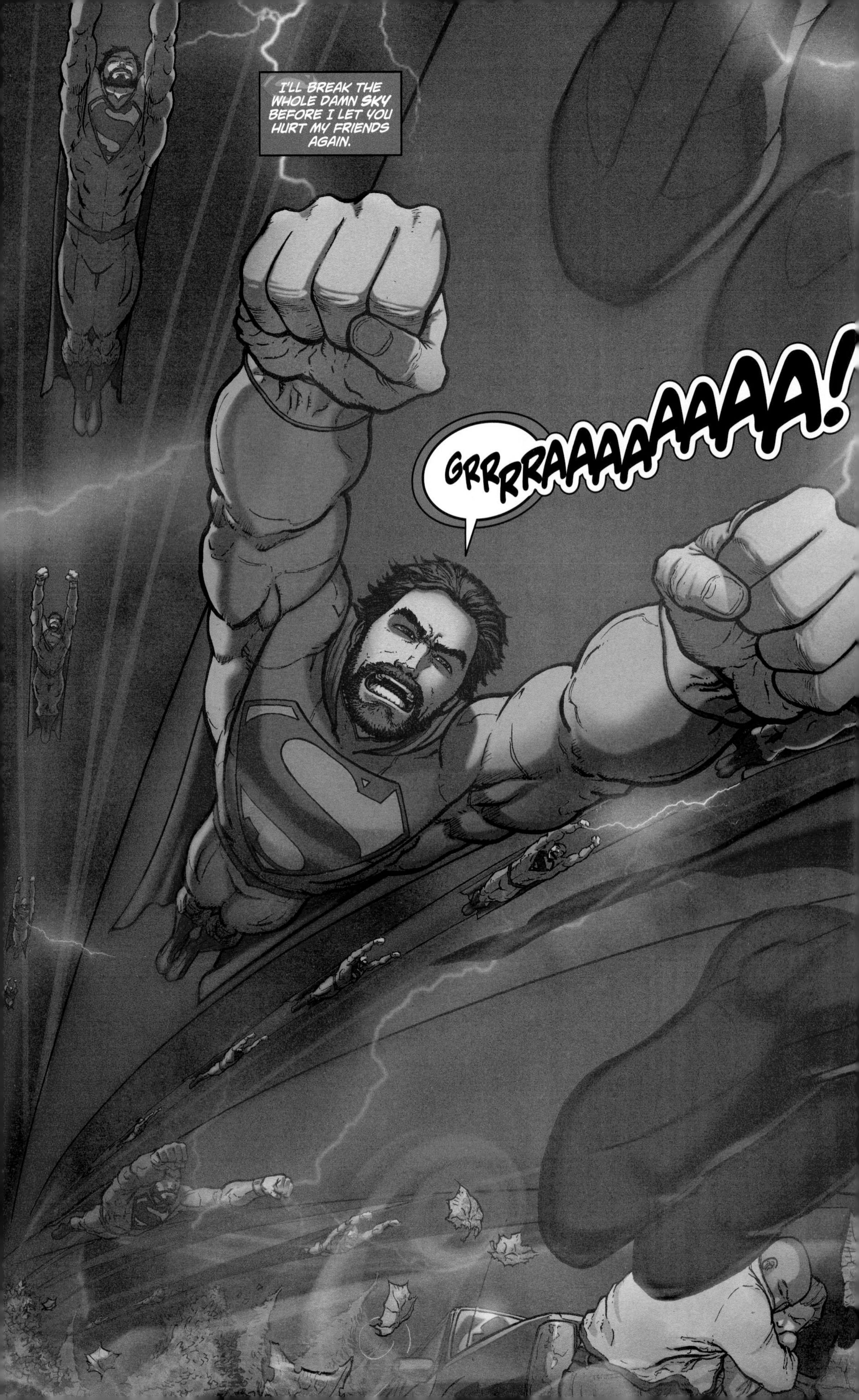
I'LL BREAK THE WHOLE DAMN SKY BEFORE I LET YOU HURT MY FRIENDS AGAIN.
GRRRRAAAAAAAAA!

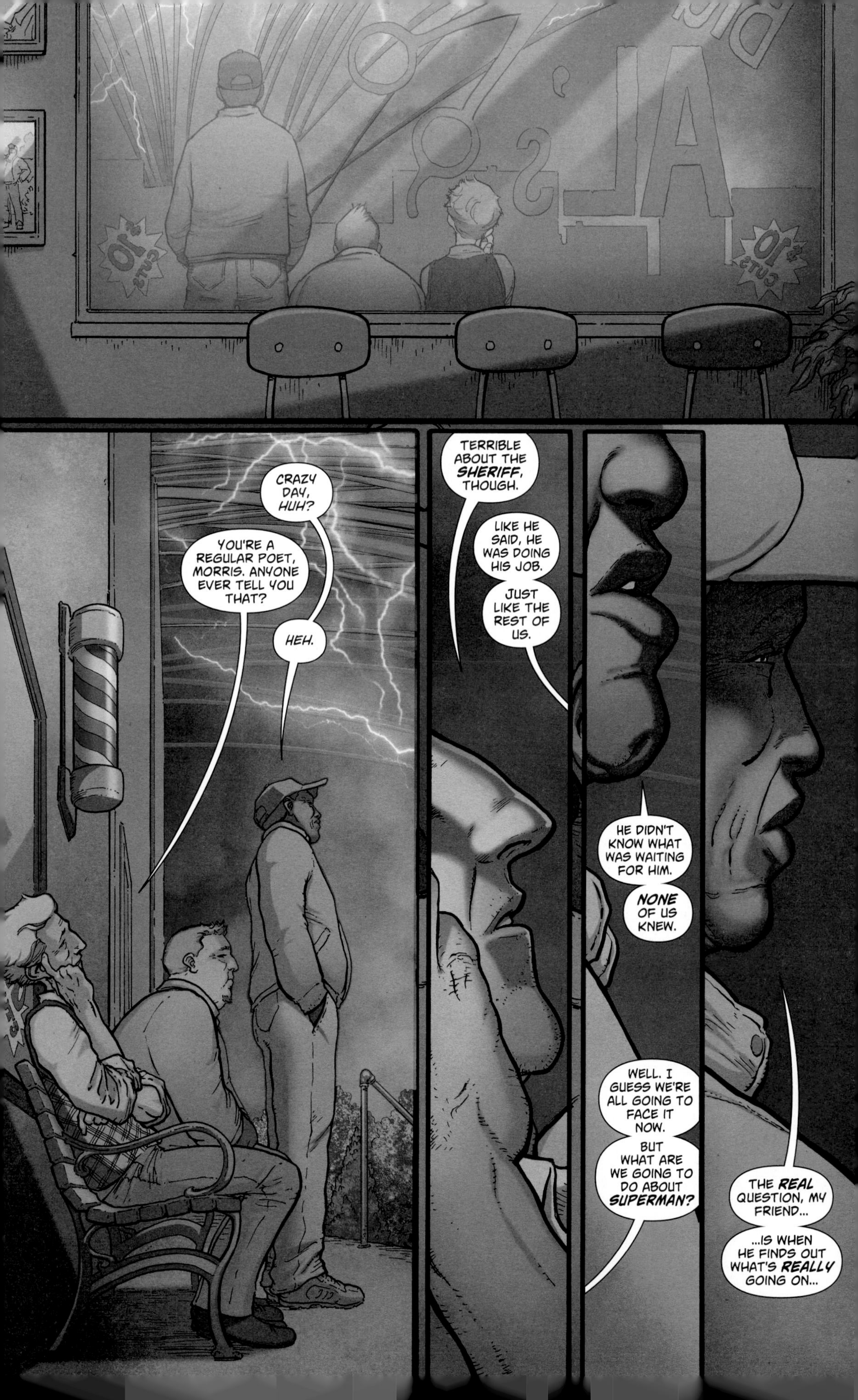
$10 CUTS
$10 CUTS
CRAZY DAY, HUH?
YOU'RE A REGULAR POET, MORRIS. ANYONE EVER TELL YOU THAT?
HEH.
TERRIBLE ABOUT THE SHERIFF, THOUGH.
LIKE HE SAID, HE WAS DOING HIS JOB.
JUST LIKE THE REST OF US.
HE DIDN'T KNOW WHAT WAS WAITING FOR HIM.
NONE OF US KNEW.
WELL. I GUESS WE'RE ALL GOING TO FACE IT NOW.
BUT WHAT ARE WE GOING TO DO ABOUT SUPERMAN?
THE REAL QUESTION, MY FRIEND...
...IS WHEN HE FINDS OUT WHAT'S REALLY GOING ON...

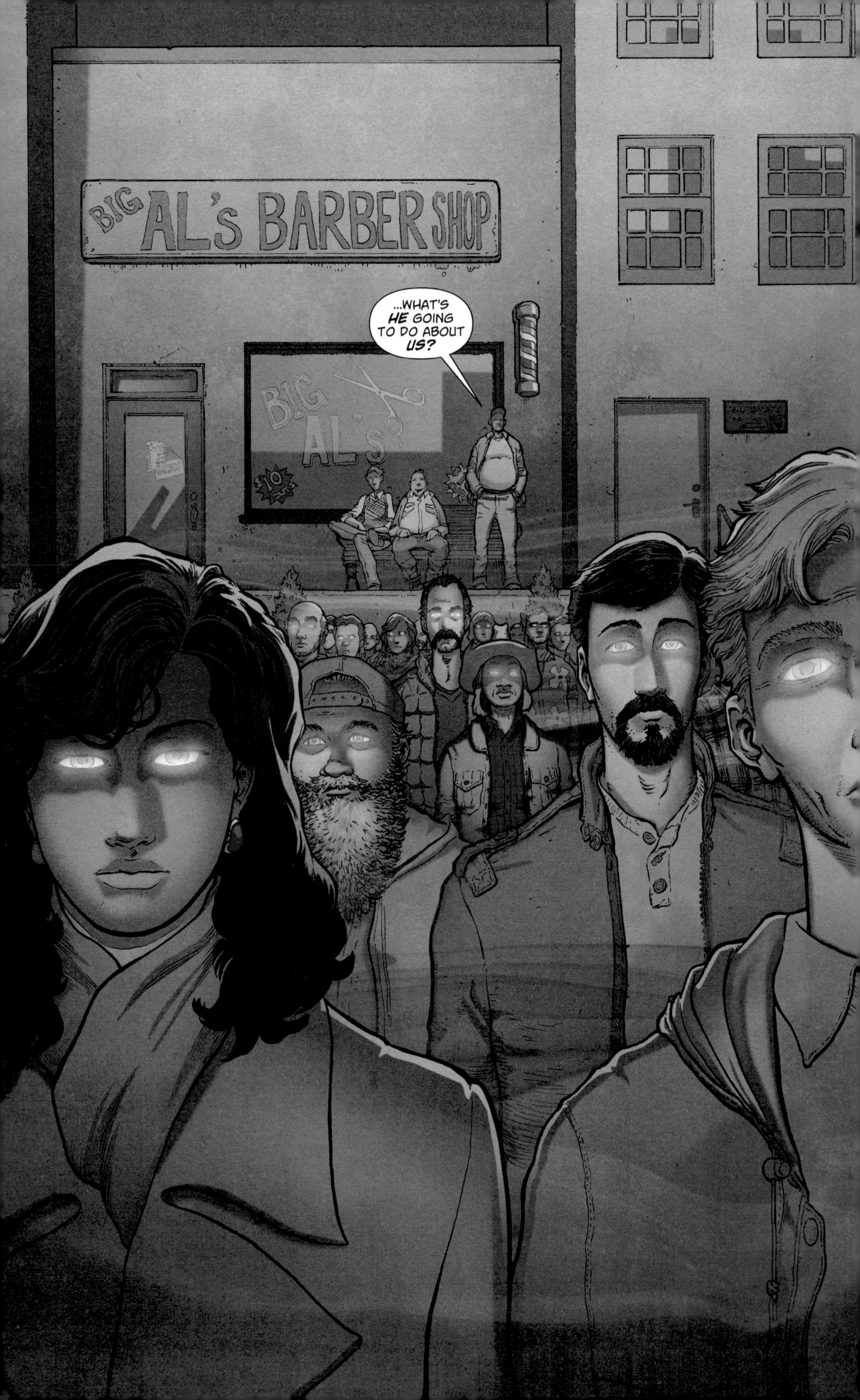
BIG AL's BARBER SHOP
BIG AL'S
...WHAT'S HE GOING TO DO ABOUT US?

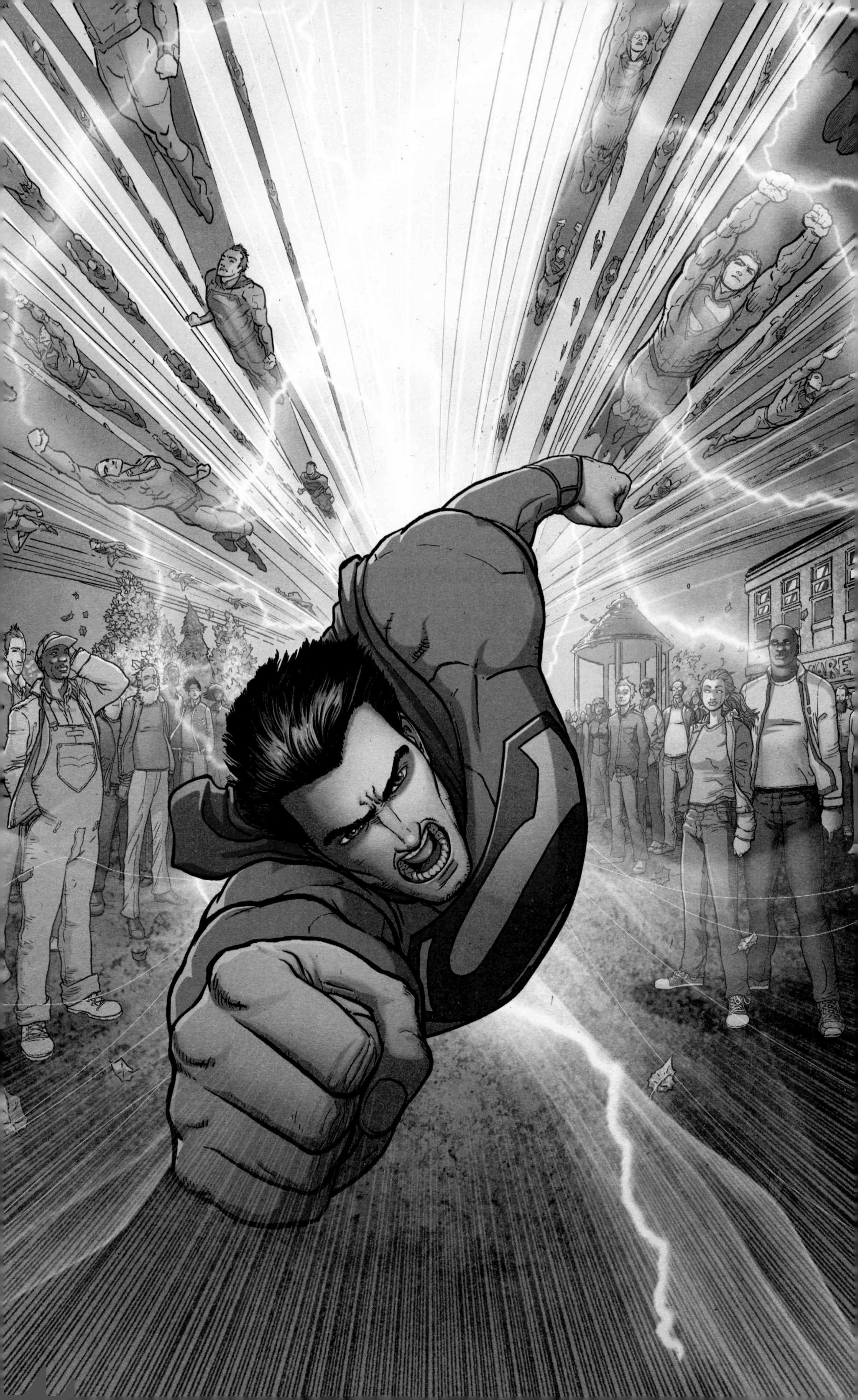

SMALLVILLAINS
GREG PAK writer AARON KUDER artist WIL QUINTANA colorist DC LETTERING letterer cover by AARON KUDER & WIL QUINTANA

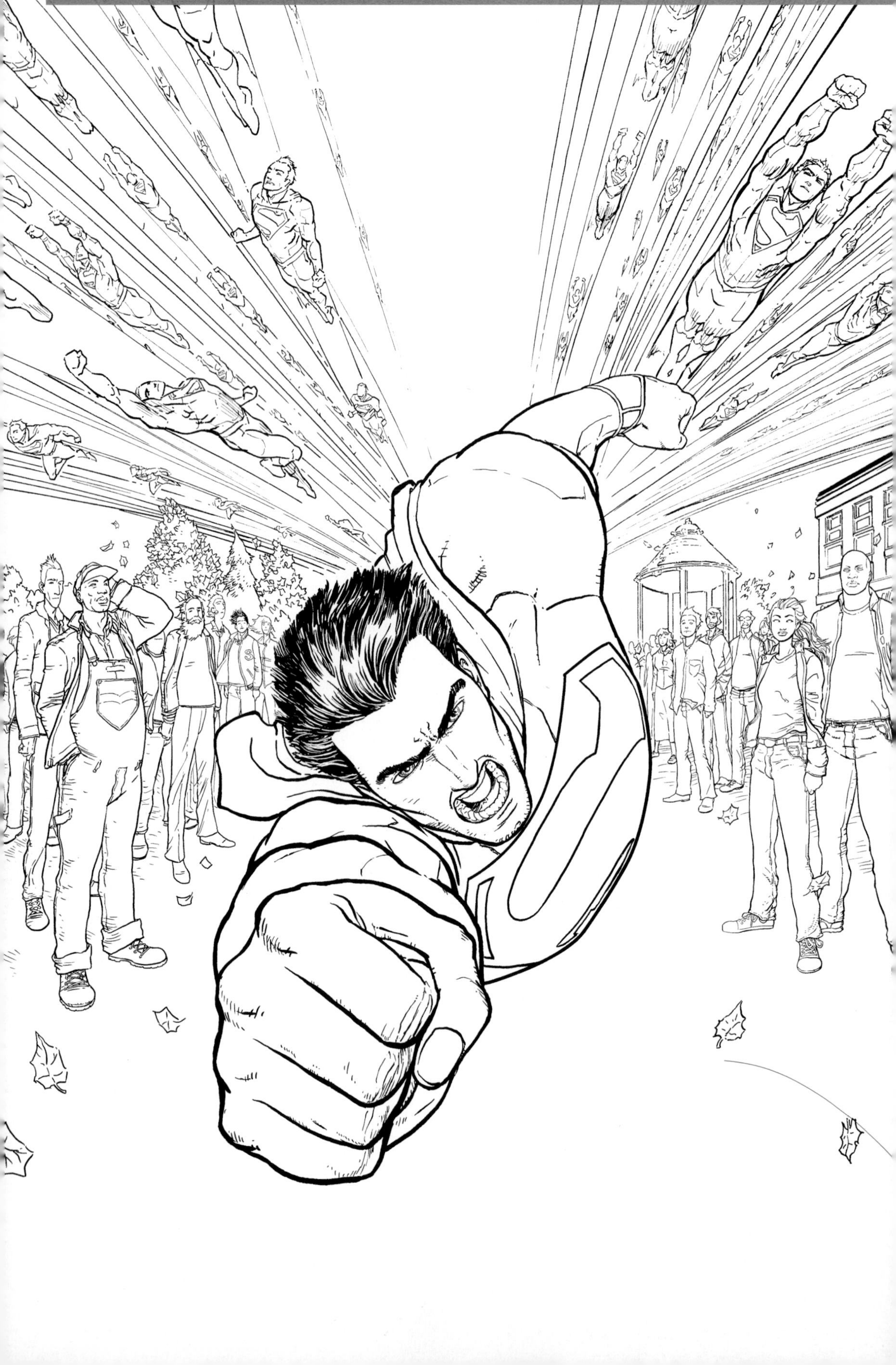

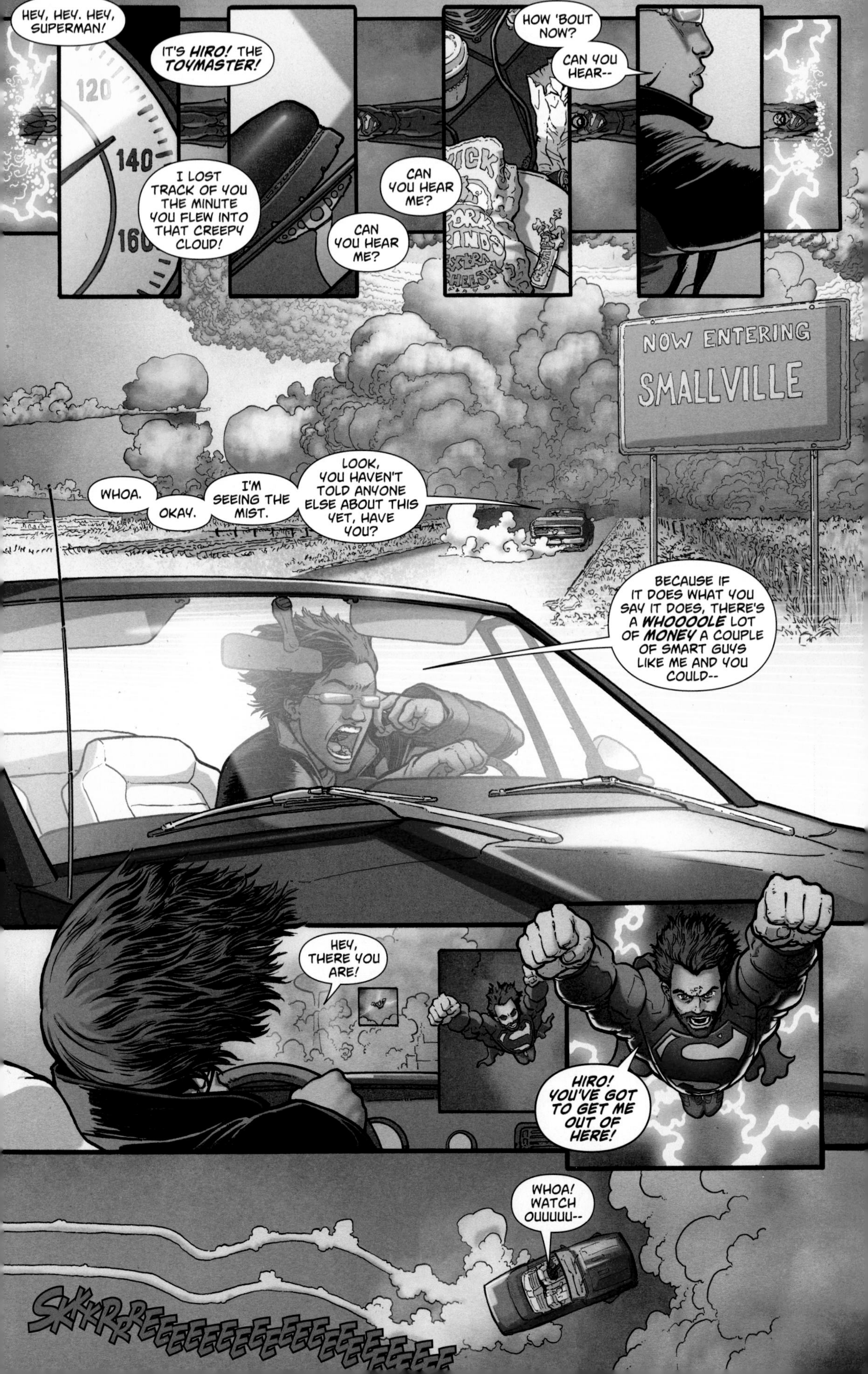
HEY, HEY. HEY, SUPERMAN!
IT'S HIRO! THE TOYMASTER!
I LOST TRACK OF YOU THE MINUTE YOU FLEW INTO THAT CREEPY CLOUD!
CAN YOU HEAR ME?
CAN YOU HEAR ME?
HOW 'BOUT NOW?
CAN YOU HEAR--
NOW ENTERING
SMALLVILLE
WHOA.
OKAY.
I'M SEEING THE MIST.
LOOK, YOU HAVEN'T TOLD ANYONE ELSE ABOUT THIS YET, HAVE YOU?
BECAUSE IF IT DOES WHAT YOU SAY IT DOES, THERE'S A WHOOOOLE LOT OF MONEY A COUPLE OF SMART GUYS LIKE ME AND YOU COULD--
HEY, THERE YOU ARE!
HIRO! YOU'VE GOT TO GET ME OUT OF HERE!
WHOA! WATCH OUUUUU--
SKKRRREEEEEEEEEEEEEEEEEEEEE

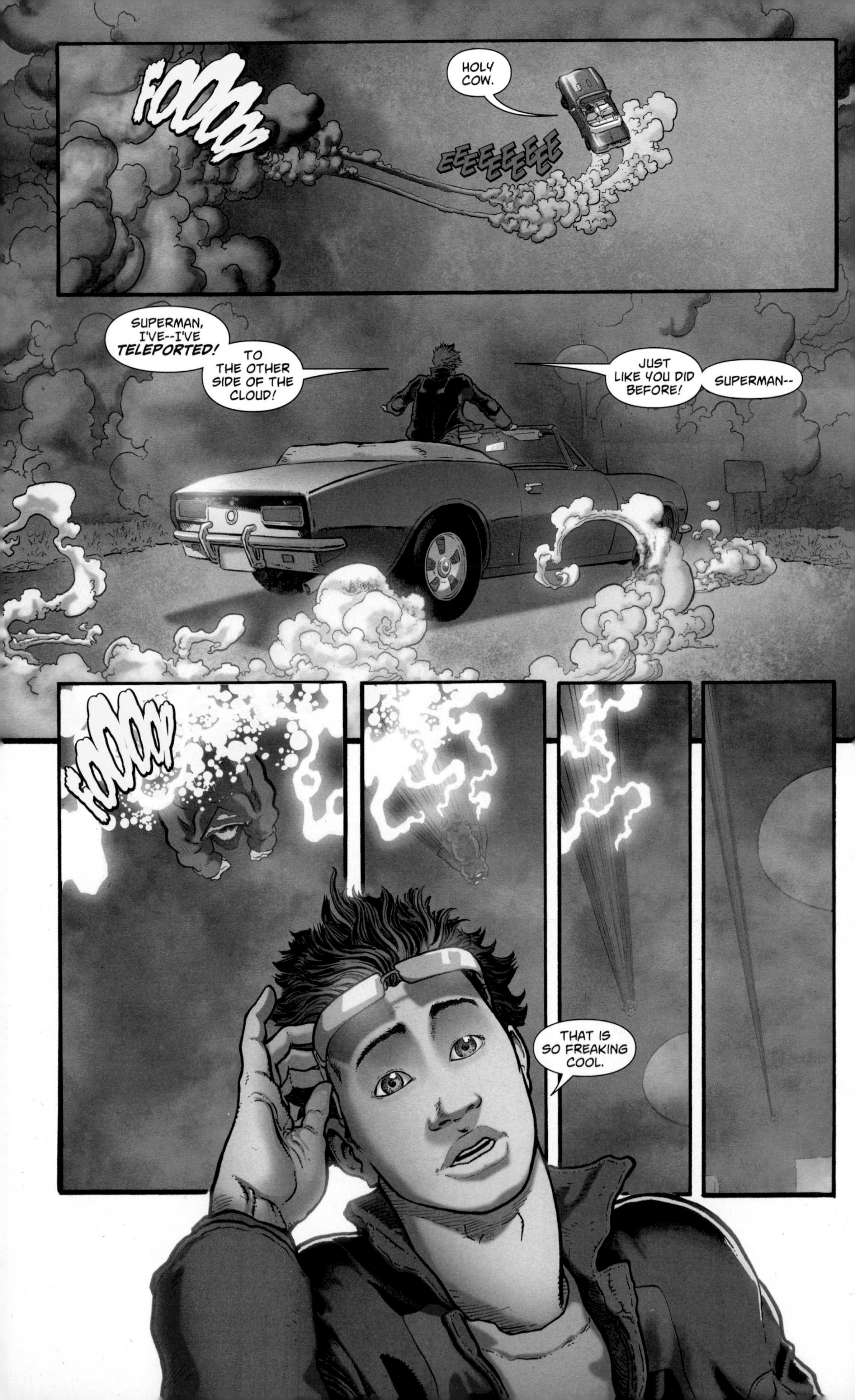
FOOOOP
HOLY COW.
EEEEEEEEE
SUPERMAN, I'VE--I'VE TELEPORTED!
TO THE OTHER SIDE OF THE CLOUD!
JUST LIKE YOU DID BEFORE!
SUPERMAN--
FOOOOP
THAT IS SO FREAKING COOL.

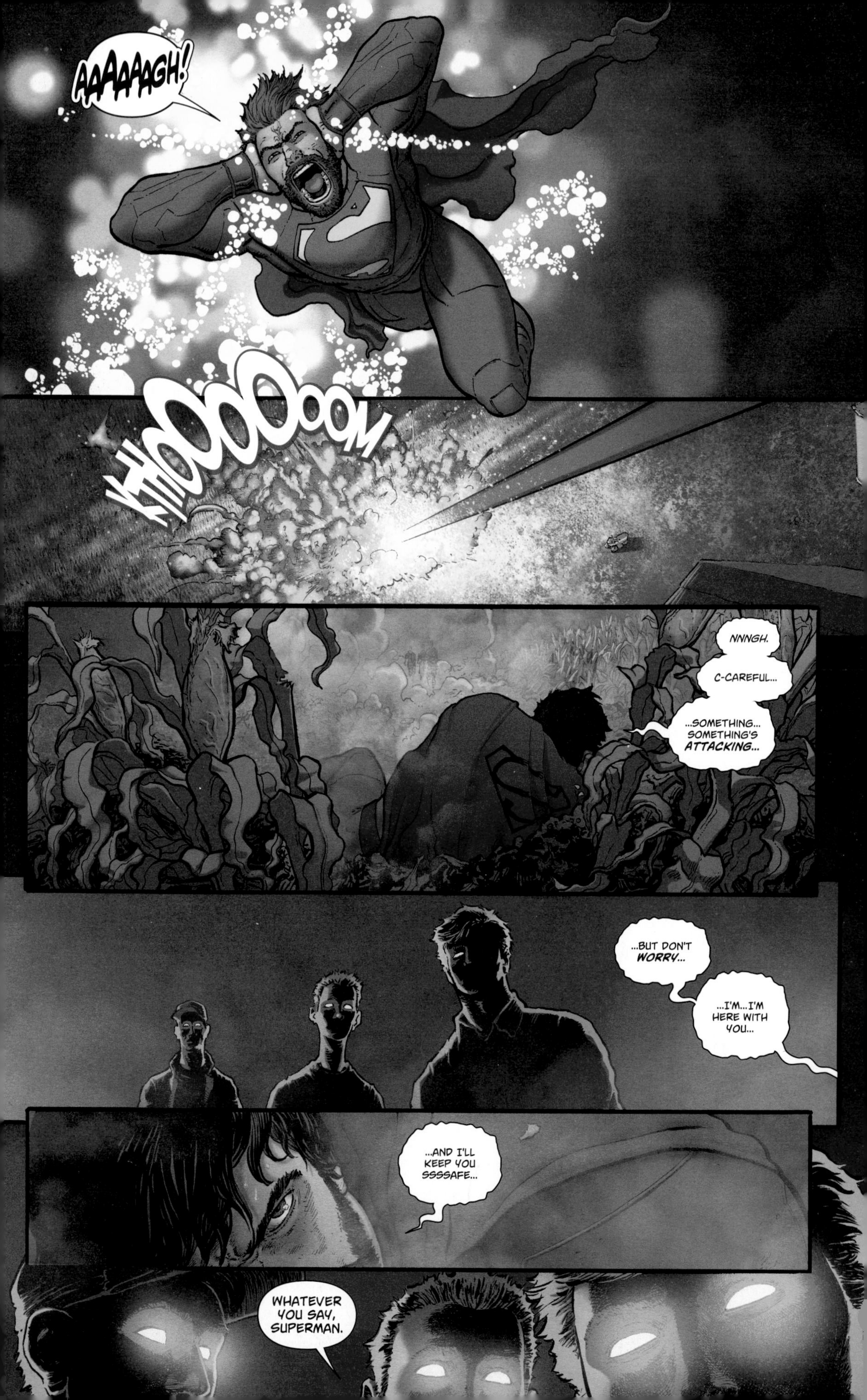
AAAAAAGH!
KHOOOOOOM
NNNGH.
C-CAREFUL...
...SOMETHING... SOMETHING'S ATTACKING...
...BUT DON'T WORRY...
...I'M...I'M HERE WITH YOU...
...AND I'LL KEEP YOU SSSSAFE...
WHATEVER YOU SAY, SUPERMAN.

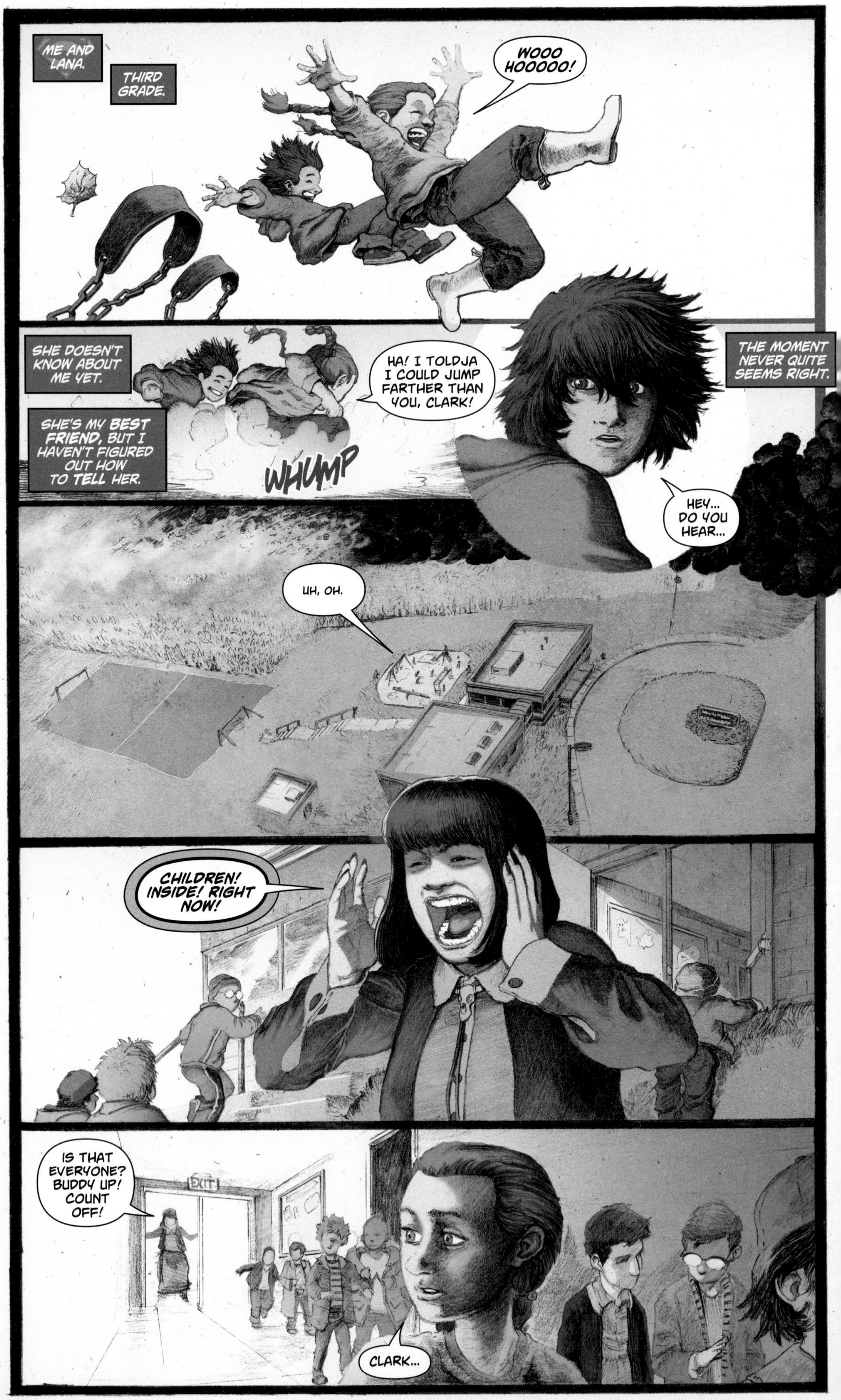

ME AND LANA.
THIRD GRADE.
WOOO HOOOOO!
SHE DOESN'T KNOW ABOUT ME YET.
SHE'S MY BEST FRIEND, BUT I HAVEN'T FIGURED OUT HOW TO TELL HER.
HA! I TOLDJA I COULD JUMP FARTHER THAN YOU, CLARK!
WHUMP
THE MOMENT NEVER QUITE SEEMS RIGHT.
HEY... DO YOU HEAR...
UH, OH.
CHILDREN! INSIDE! RIGHT NOW!
IS THAT EVERYONE? BUDDY UP! COUNT OFF!
EXIT
CLARK...

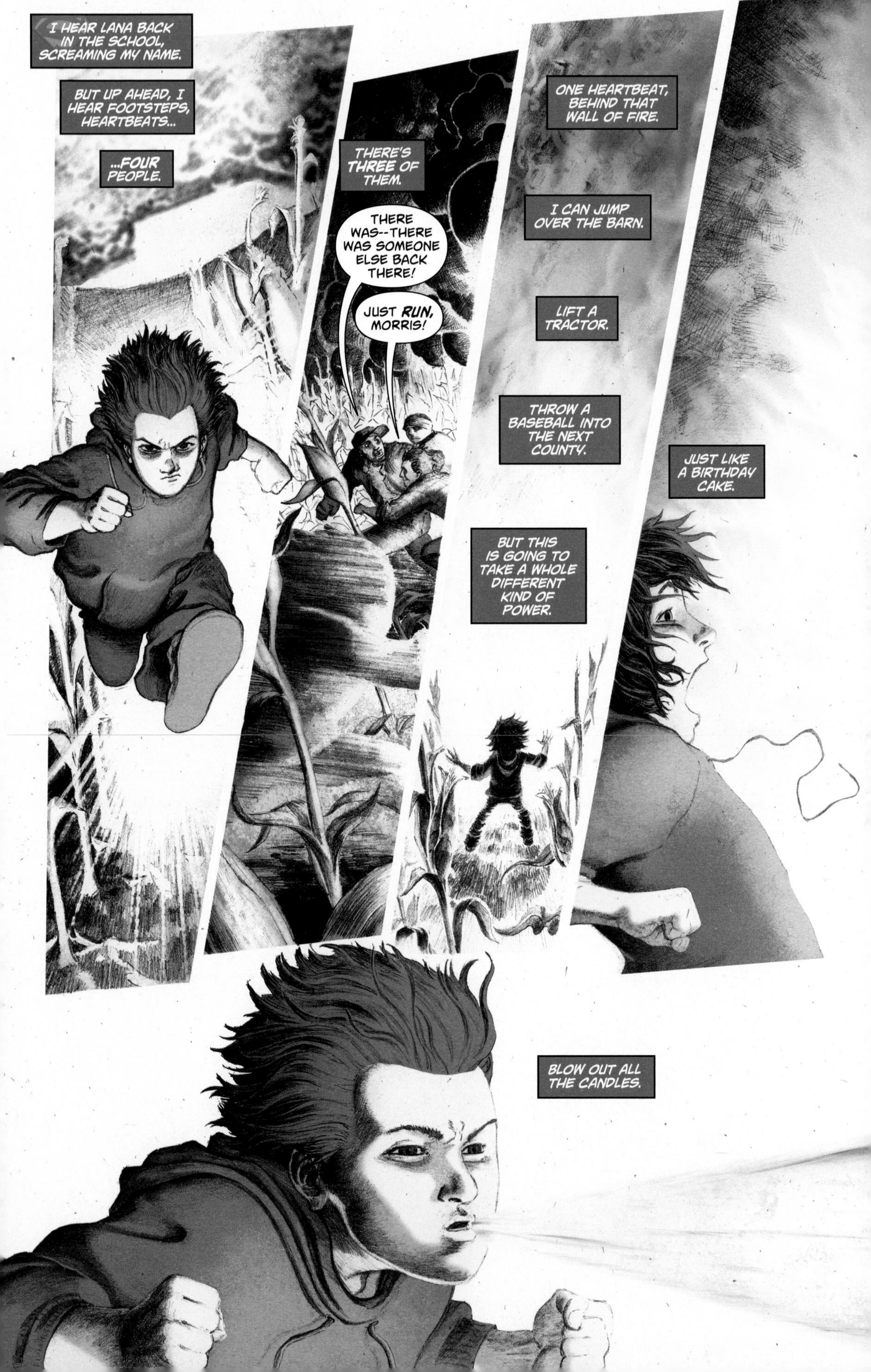
I HEAR LANA BACK IN THE SCHOOL, SCREAMING MY NAME.
BUT UP AHEAD, I HEAR FOOTSTEPS, HEARTBEATS...
...FOUR PEOPLE.
THERE'S THREE OF THEM.
THERE WAS--THERE WAS SOMEONE ELSE BACK THERE!
JUST RUN, MORRIS!
ONE HEARTBEAT, BEHIND THAT WALL OF FIRE.
I CAN JUMP OVER THE BARN.
LIFT A TRACTOR.
THROW A BASEBALL INTO THE NEXT COUNTY.
BUT THIS IS GOING TO TAKE A WHOLE DIFFERENT KIND OF POWER.
JUST LIKE A BIRTHDAY CAKE.
BLOW OUT ALL THE CANDLES.

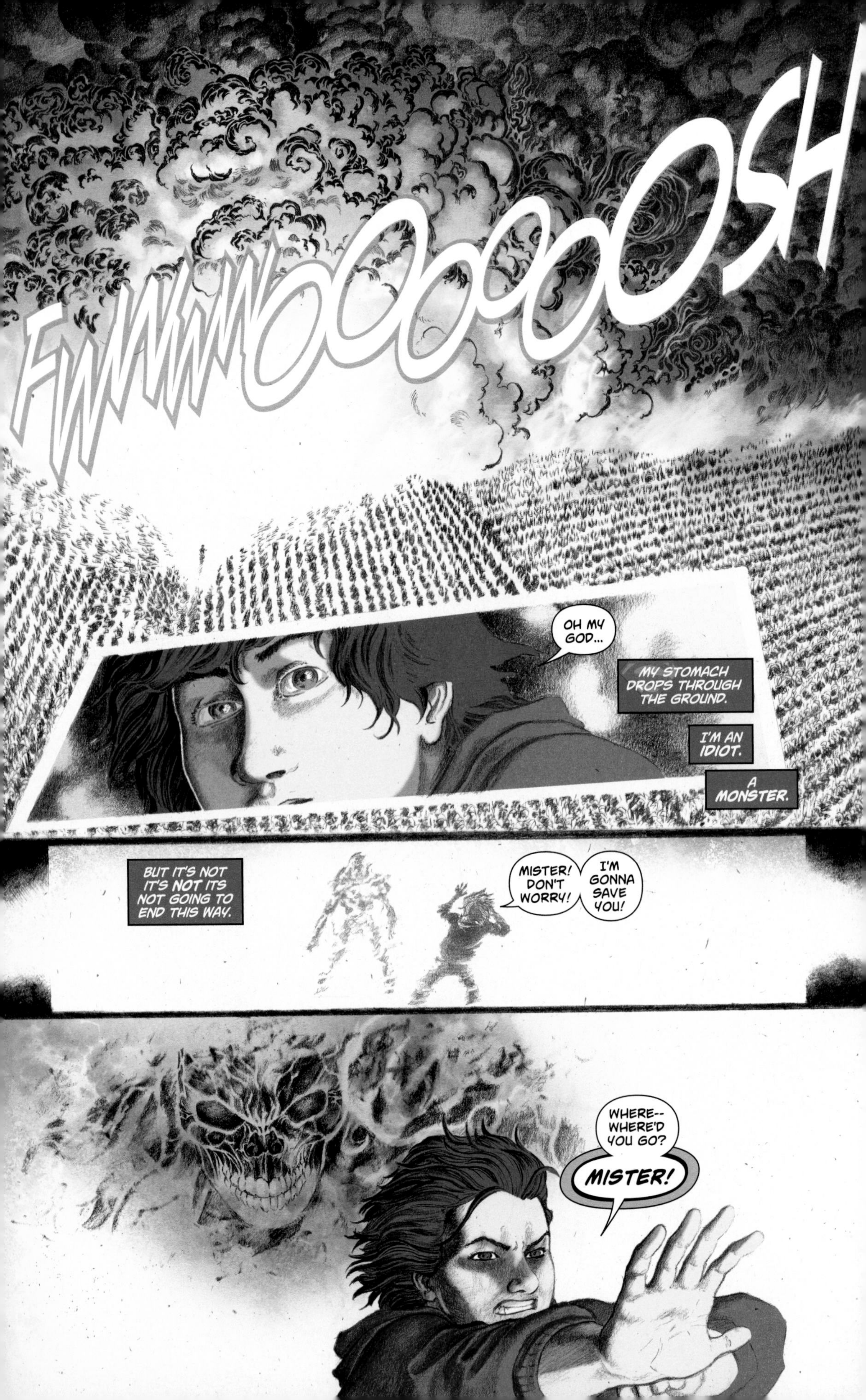
FWMMMOOOOOOSH
OH MY GOD...
MY STOMACH DROPS THROUGH THE GROUND.
I'M AN IDIOT.
A MONSTER.
BUT IT'S NOT IT'S NOT ITS NOT GOING TO END THIS WAY.
MISTER! DON'T WORRY!
I'M GONNA SAVE YOU!
WHERE-- WHERE'D YOU GO?
MISTER!

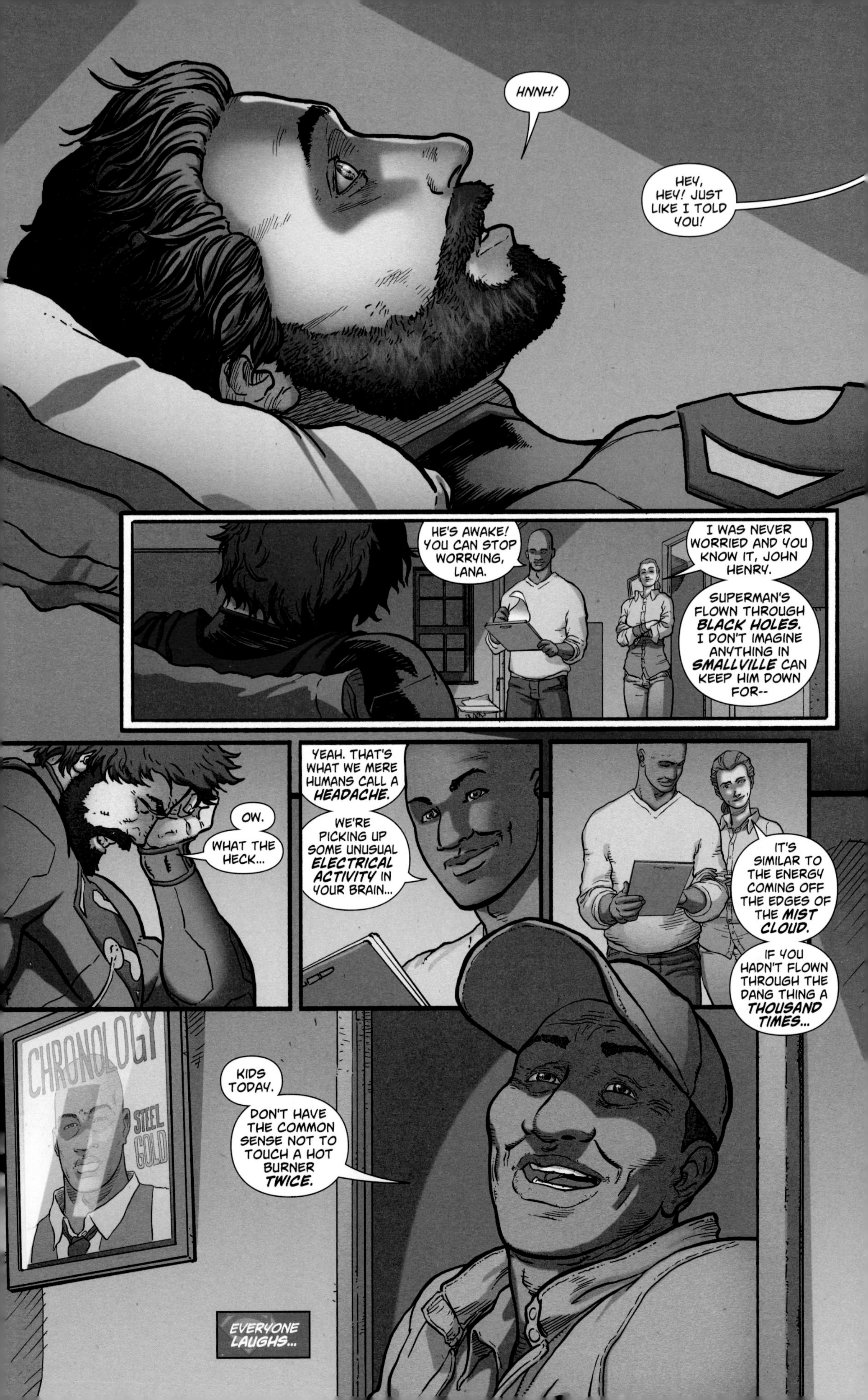
HNNH!
HEY, HEY! JUST LIKE I TOLD YOU!
HE'S AWAKE! YOU CAN STOP WORRYING, LANA.
I WAS NEVER WORRIED AND YOU KNOW IT, JOHN HENRY.
SUPERMAN'S FLOWN THROUGH BLACK HOLES. I DON'T IMAGINE ANYTHING IN SMALLVILLE CAN KEEP HIM DOWN FOR--
OW.
WHAT THE HECK...
YEAH. THAT'S WHAT WE MERE HUMANS CALL A HEADACHE.
WE'RE PICKING UP SOME UNUSUAL ELECTRICAL ACTIVITY IN YOUR BRAIN...
IT'S SIMILAR TO THE ENERGY COMING OFF THE EDGES OF THE MIST CLOUD.
IF YOU HADN'T FLOWN THROUGH THE DANG THING A THOUSAND TIMES...
CHRONOLOGY
STEEL
GOLD
KIDS TODAY.
DON'T HAVE THE COMMON SENSE NOT TO TOUCH A HOT BURNER TWICE.
EVERYONE LAUGHS...

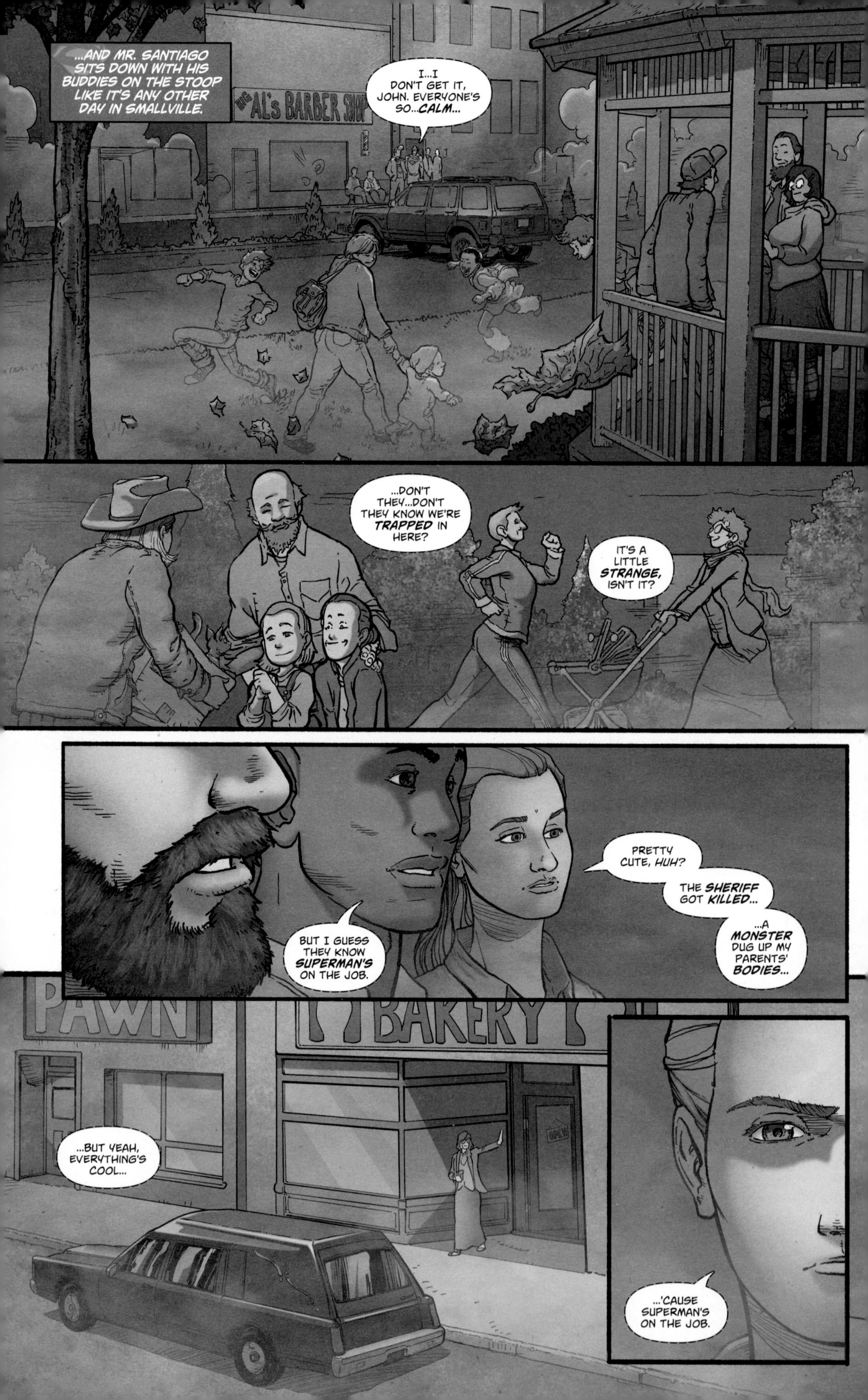

...AND MR. SANTIAGO SITS DOWN WITH HIS BUDDIES ON THE STOOP LIKE IT'S ANY OTHER DAY IN SMALLVILLE.
BIG AL's BARBER SHOP
I...I DON'T GET IT, JOHN. EVERYONE'S SO...CALM...
...DON'T THEY...DON'T THEY KNOW WE'RE TRAPPED IN HERE?
IT'S A LITTLE STRANGE, ISN'T IT?
PRETTY CUTE, HUH?
THE SHERIFF GOT KILLED...
...A MONSTER DUG UP MY PARENTS' BODIES...
BUT I GUESS THEY KNOW SUPERMAN'S ON THE JOB.
PAWN
BAKERY
...BUT YEAH, EVERYTHING'S COOL...
...'CAUSE SUPERMAN'S ON THE JOB.

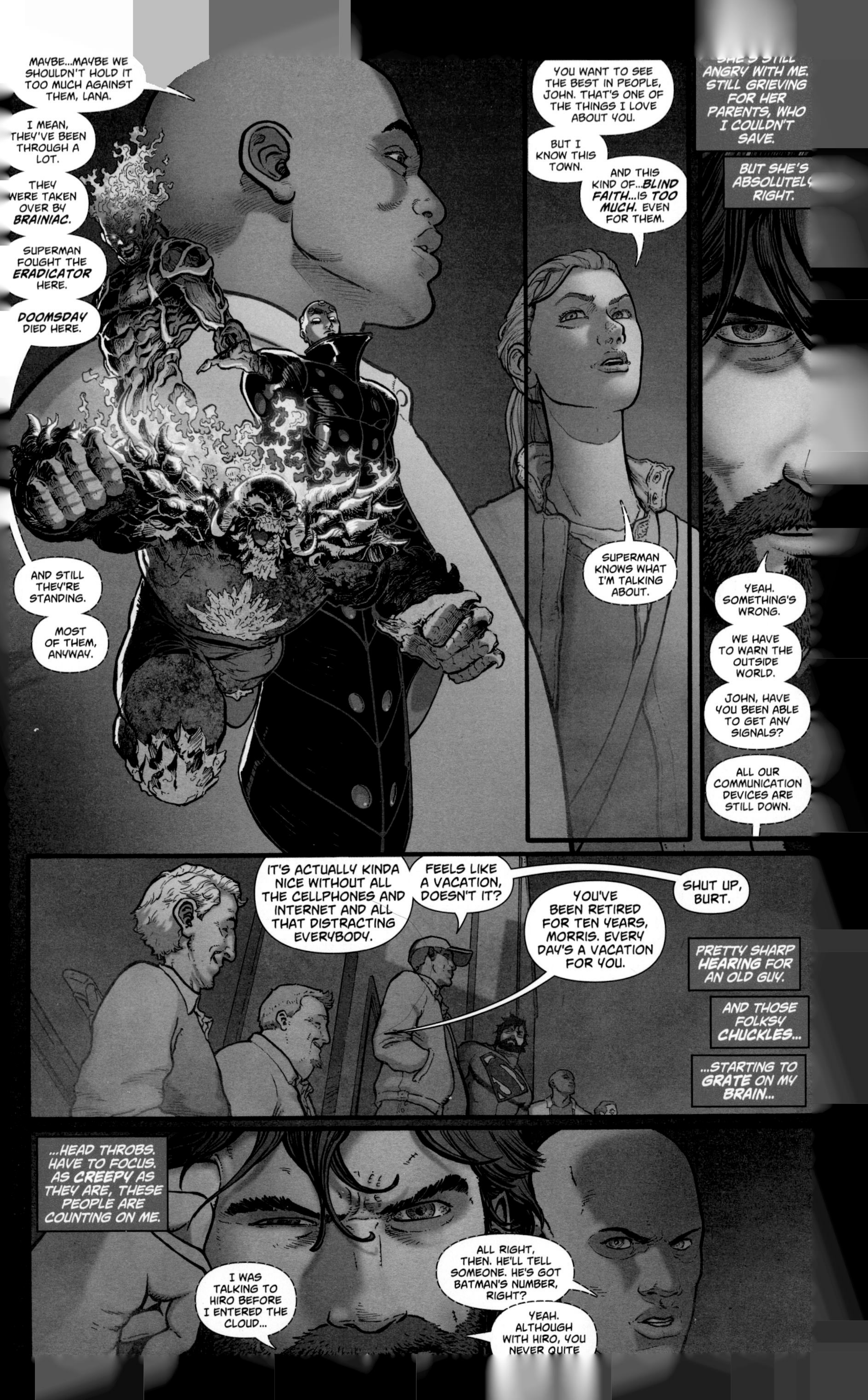

MAYBE...MAYBE WE SHOULDN'T HOLD IT TOO MUCH AGAINST THEM, LANA.
I MEAN, THEY'VE BEEN THROUGH A LOT.
THEY WERE TAKEN OVER BY BRAINIAC.
SUPERMAN FOUGHT THE ERADICATOR HERE.
DOOMSDAY DIED HERE.
AND STILL THEY'RE STANDING.
MOST OF THEM, ANYWAY.
YOU WANT TO SEE THE BEST IN PEOPLE, JOHN. THAT'S ONE OF THE THINGS I LOVE ABOUT YOU.
BUT I KNOW THIS TOWN.
AND THIS KIND OF...BLIND FAITH...IS TOO MUCH. EVEN FOR THEM.
SUPERMAN KNOWS WHAT I'M TALKING ABOUT.
ANGRY WITH ME. STILL GRIEVING FOR HER PARENTS, WHO I COULDN'T SAVE.
BUT SHE'S ABSOLUTEL RIGHT.
YEAH. SOMETHING'S WRONG.
WE HAVE TO WARN THE OUTSIDE WORLD.
JOHN, HAVE YOU BEEN ABLE TO GET ANY SIGNALS?
ALL OUR COMMUNICATION DEVICES ARE STILL DOWN.
IT'S ACTUALLY KINDA NICE WITHOUT ALL THE CELLPHONES AND INTERNET AND ALL THAT DISTRACTING EVERYBODY.
FEELS LIKE A VACATION, DOESN'T IT?
SHUT UP, BURT.
YOU'VE BEEN RETIRED FOR TEN YEARS, MORRIS. EVERY DAY'S A VACATION FOR YOU.
PRETTY SHARP HEARING FOR AN OLD GUY.
AND THOSE FOLKSY CHUCKLES...
...STARTING TO GRATE ON MY BRAIN...
...HEAD THROBS. HAVE TO FOCUS. AS CREEPY AS THEY ARE, THESE PEOPLE ARE COUNTING ON ME.
I WAS TALKING TO HIRO BEFORE I ENTERED THE CLOUD...
ALL RIGHT, THEN. HE'LL TELL SOMEONE. HE'S GOT BATMAN'S NUMBER, RIGHT?
YEAH. ALTHOUGH WITH HIRO, YOU NEVER QUITE

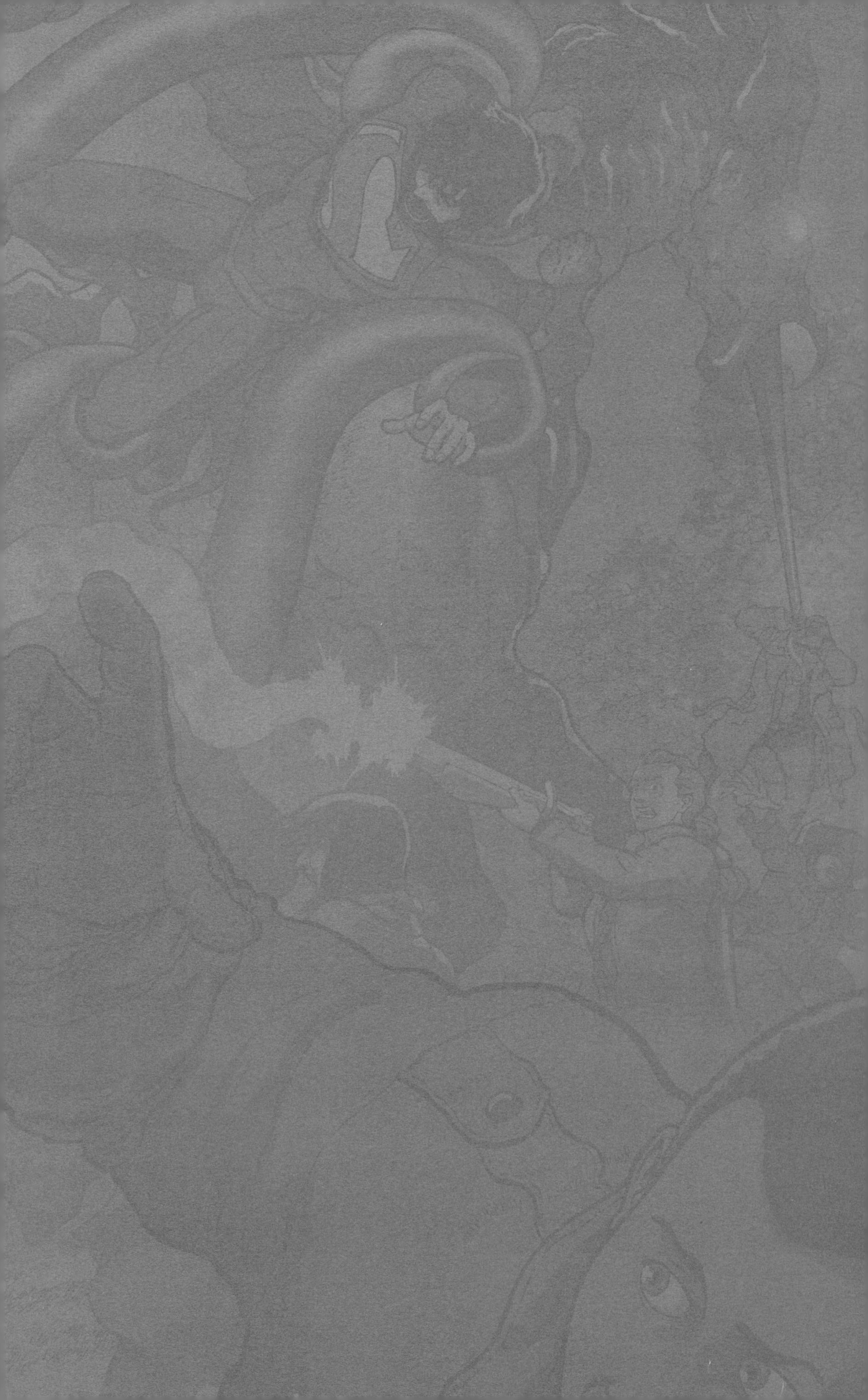

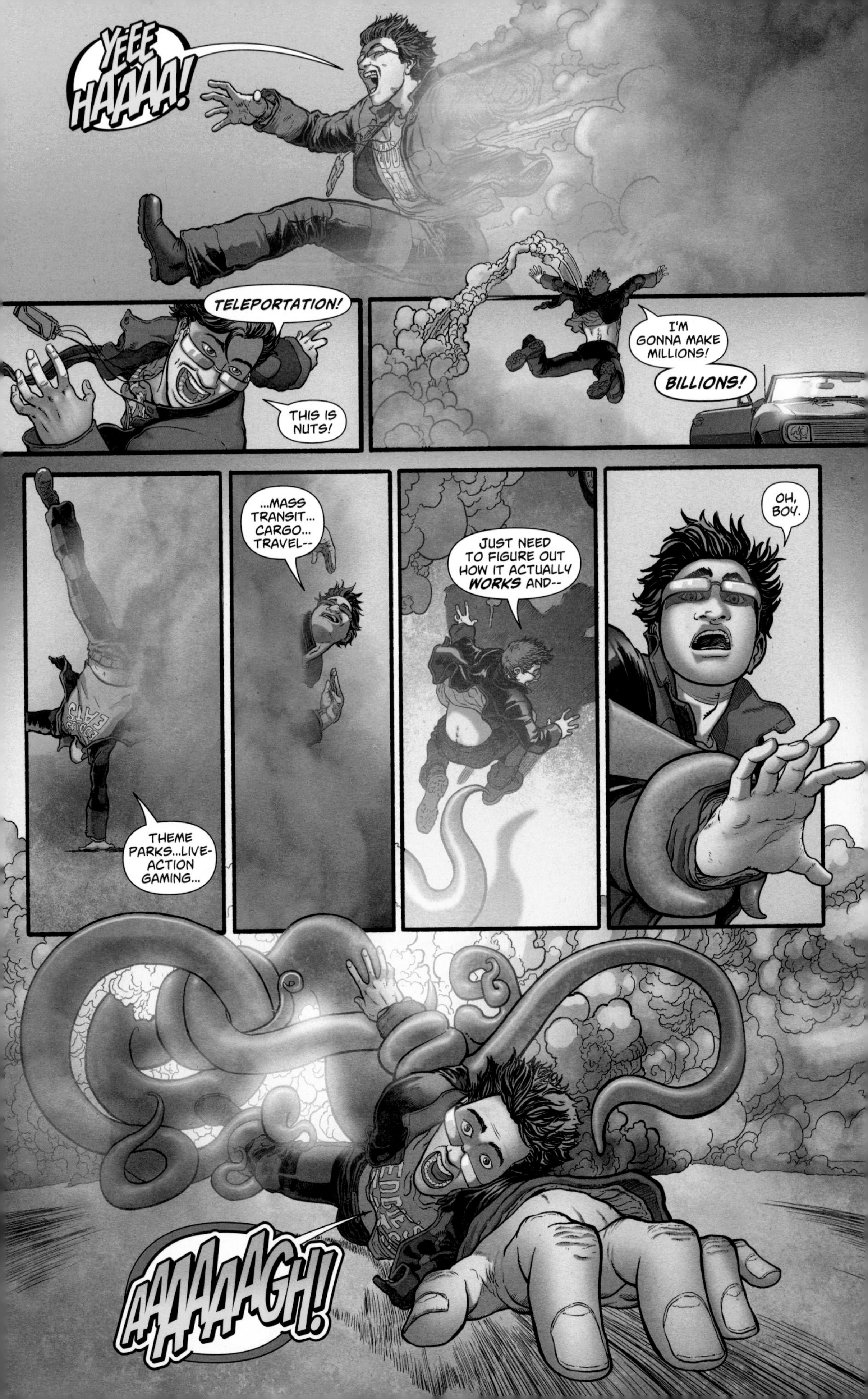
YEEE HAAAA!
TELEPORTATION!
THIS IS NUTS!
I'M GONNA MAKE MILLIONS!
BILLIONS!
THEME PARKS...LIVE-ACTION GAMING...
...MASS TRANSIT... CARGO... TRAVEL--
JUST NEED TO FIGURE OUT HOW IT ACTUALLY WORKS AND--
OH, BOY.
AAAAAAGH!

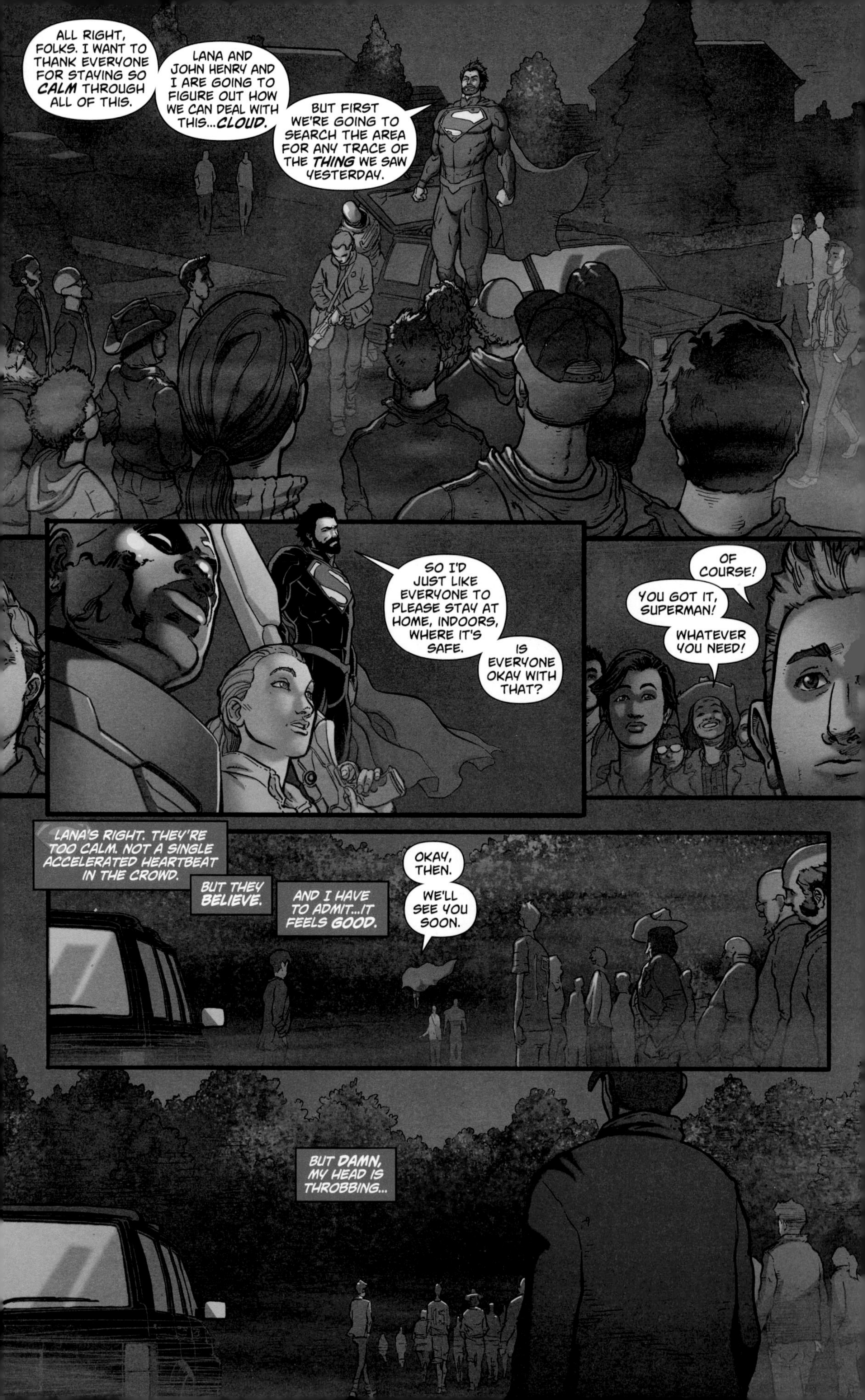
ALL RIGHT, FOLKS. I WANT TO THANK EVERYONE FOR STAYING SO CALM THROUGH ALL OF THIS.
LANA AND JOHN HENRY AND I ARE GOING TO FIGURE OUT HOW WE CAN DEAL WITH THIS...CLOUD.
BUT FIRST WE'RE GOING TO SEARCH THE AREA FOR ANY TRACE OF THE THING WE SAW YESTERDAY.
SO I'D JUST LIKE EVERYONE TO PLEASE STAY AT HOME, INDOORS, WHERE IT'S SAFE.
IS EVERYONE OKAY WITH THAT?
OF COURSE!
YOU GOT IT, SUPERMAN!
WHATEVER YOU NEED!
LANA'S RIGHT. THEY'RE TOO CALM. NOT A SINGLE ACCELERATED HEARTBEAT IN THE CROWD.
BUT THEY BELIEVE.
AND I HAVE TO ADMIT...IT FEELS GOOD.
OKAY, THEN.
WE'LL SEE YOU SOON.
BUT DAMN, MY HEAD IS THROBBING...

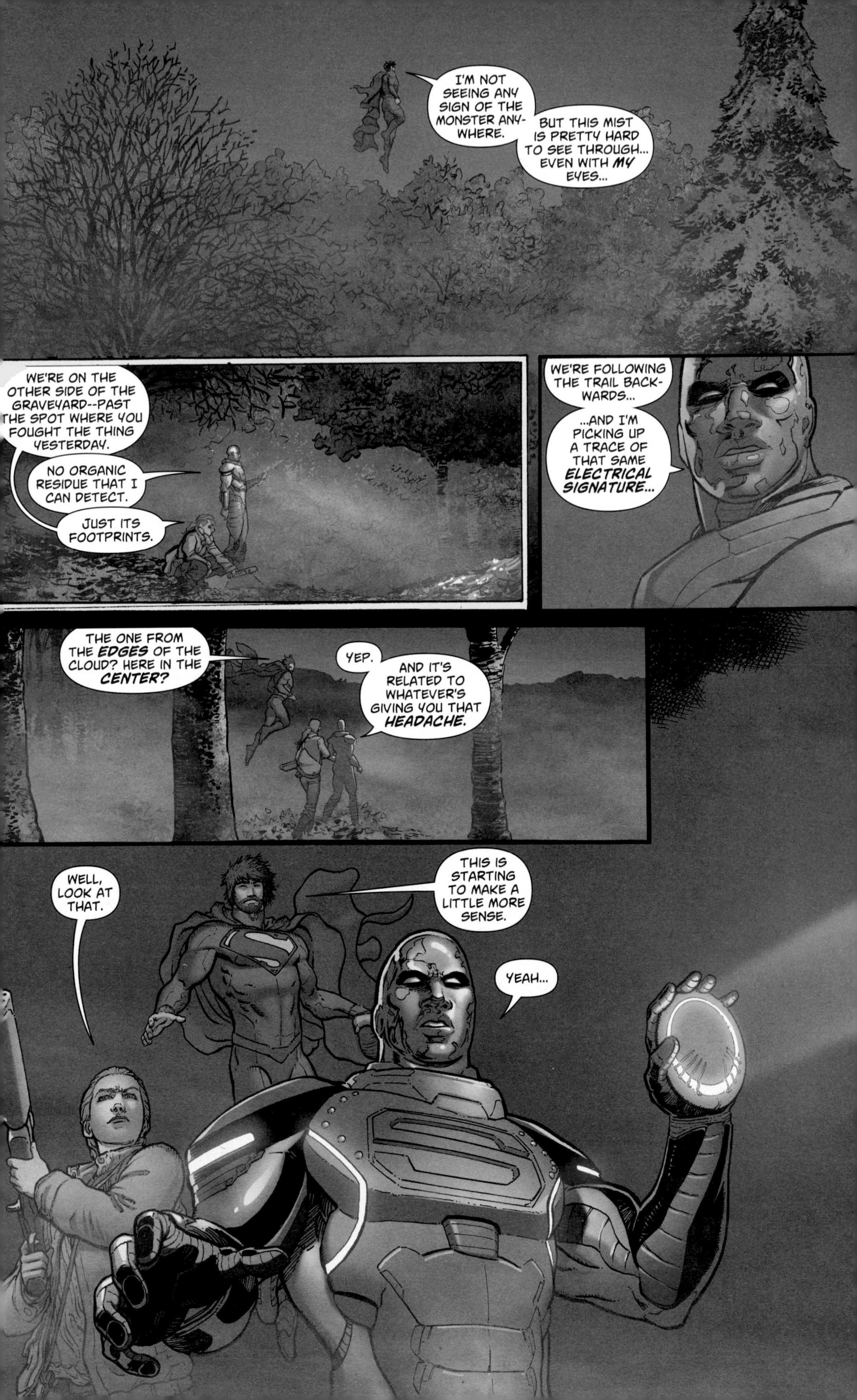

I'M NOT SEEING ANY SIGN OF THE MONSTER ANY-WHERE.
BUT THIS MIST IS PRETTY HARD TO SEE THROUGH... EVEN WITH *MY* EYES...
WE'RE ON THE OTHER SIDE OF THE GRAVEYARD--PAST THE SPOT WHERE YOU FOUGHT THE THING YESTERDAY.
NO ORGANIC RESIDUE THAT I CAN DETECT.
JUST ITS FOOTPRINTS.
WE'RE FOLLOWING THE TRAIL BACK-WARDS...
...AND I'M PICKING UP A TRACE OF THAT SAME **ELECTRICAL SIGNATURE...**
THE ONE FROM THE **EDGES** OF THE CLOUD? HERE IN THE **CENTER?**
YEP.
AND IT'S RELATED TO WHATEVER'S GIVING YOU THAT **HEADACHE.**
WELL, LOOK AT THAT.
THIS IS STARTING TO MAKE A LITTLE MORE SENSE.
YEAH...

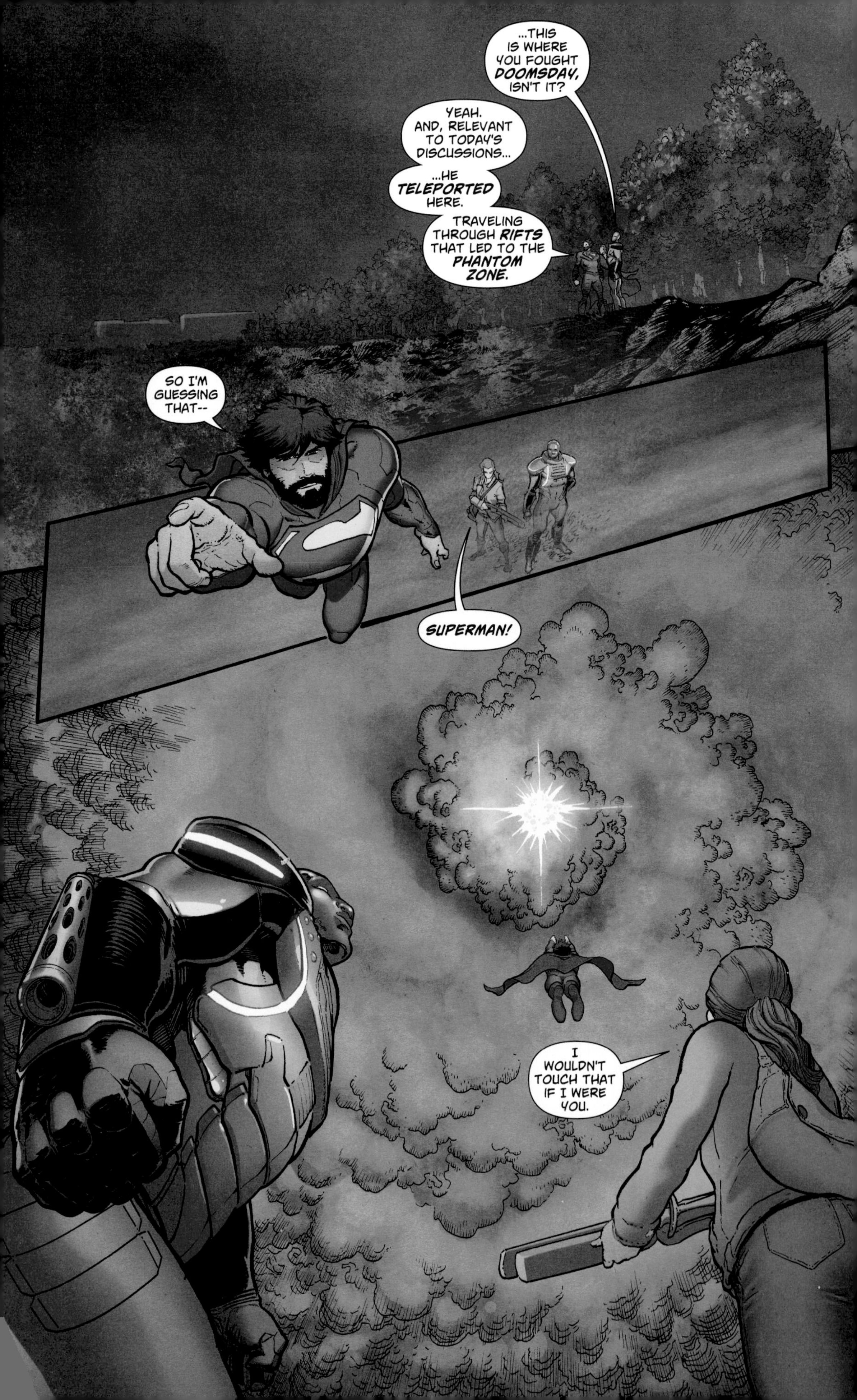
...THIS IS WHERE YOU FOUGHT DOOMSDAY, ISN'T IT?
YEAH. AND, RELEVANT TO TODAY'S DISCUSSIONS...
...HE TELEPORTED HERE.
TRAVELING THROUGH RIFTS THAT LED TO THE PHANTOM ZONE.
SO I'M GUESSING THAT--
SUPERMAN!
I WOULDN'T TOUCH THAT IF I WERE YOU.

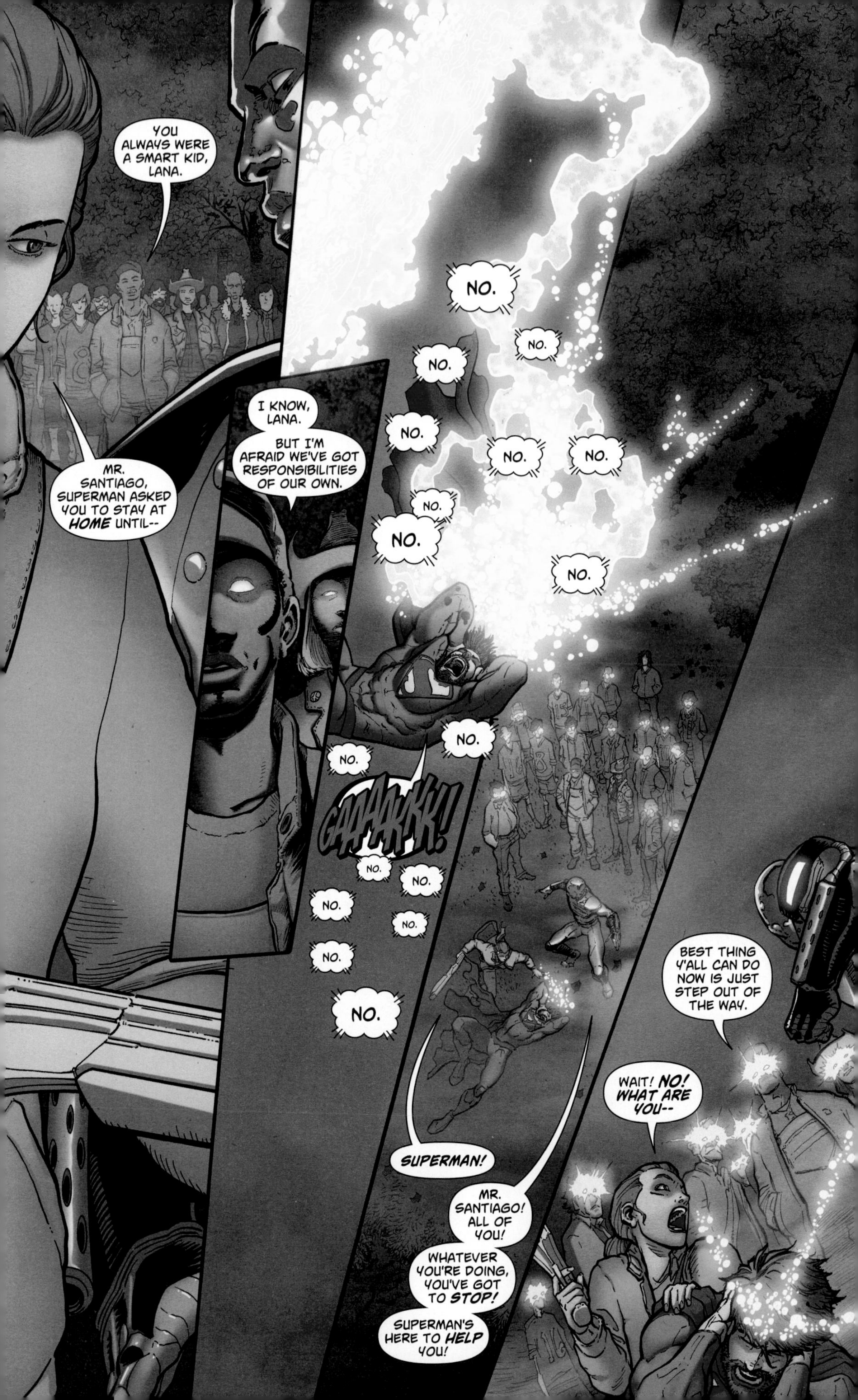
YOU ALWAYS WERE A SMART KID, LANA.
MR. SANTIAGO, SUPERMAN ASKED YOU TO STAY AT HOME UNTIL--
I KNOW, LANA.
BUT I'M AFRAID WE'VE GOT RESPONSIBILITIES OF OUR OWN.
NO.
NO.
NO.
NO.
NO.
NO.
NO.
NO.
NO.
NO.
NO.
NO.
GAAAARKK!
NO.
NO.
NO.
NO.
NO.
NO.
SUPERMAN!
MR. SANTIAGO! ALL OF YOU!
WHATEVER YOU'RE DOING, YOU'VE GOT TO STOP!
SUPERMAN'S HERE TO HELP YOU!
BEST THING Y'ALL CAN DO NOW IS JUST STEP OUT OF THE WAY.
WAIT! NO! WHAT ARE YOU--

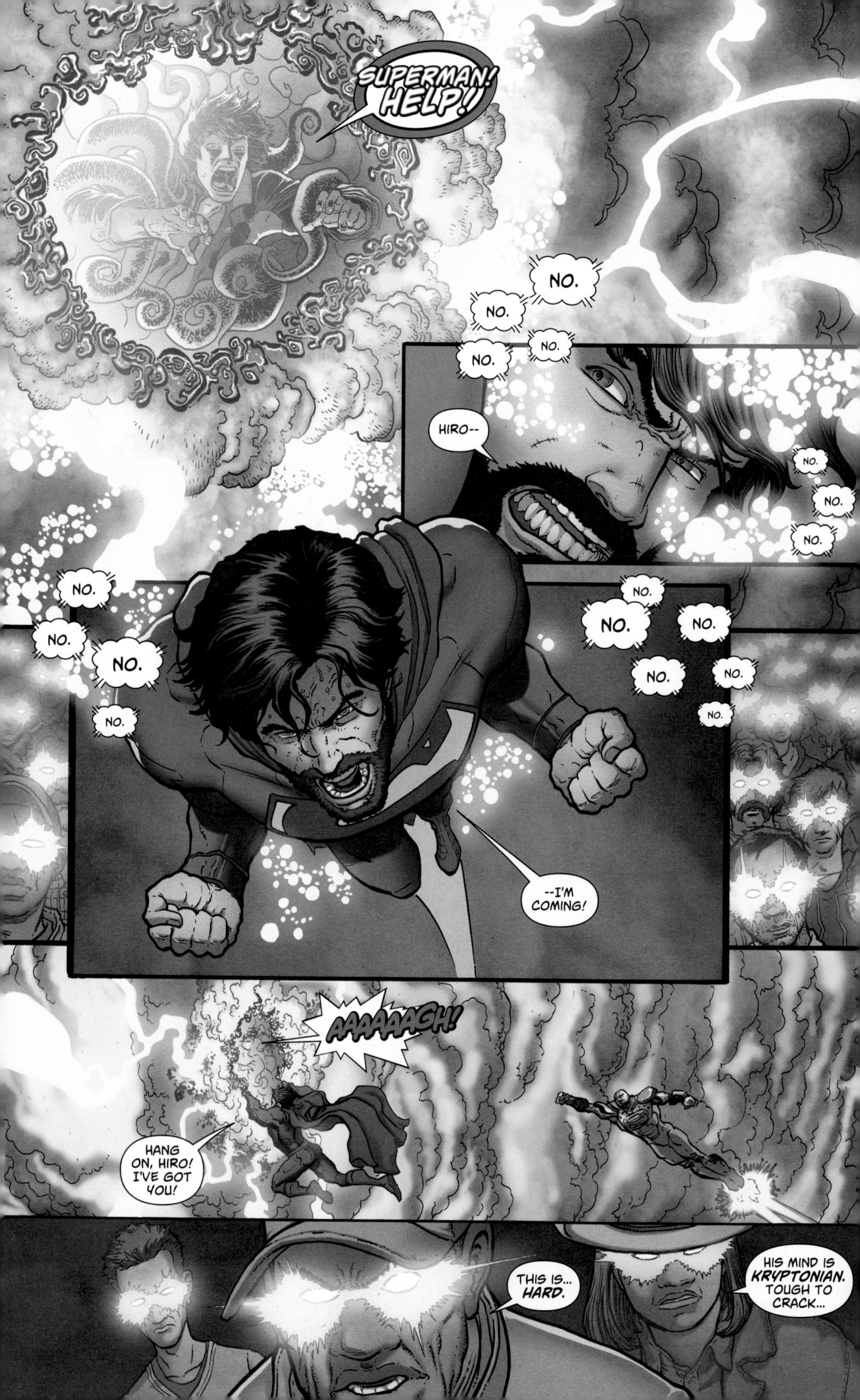
SUPERMAN! HELP!
NO.
NO.
NO.
NO.
HIRO--
NO.
NO.
NO.
NO.
NO.
NO.
NO.
NO.
NO.
NO.
NO.
NO.
NO.
--I'M COMING!
AAAAAAGH!
HANG ON, HIRO! I'VE GOT YOU!
THIS IS... HARD.
HIS MIND IS KRYPTONIAN. TOUGH TO CRACK...

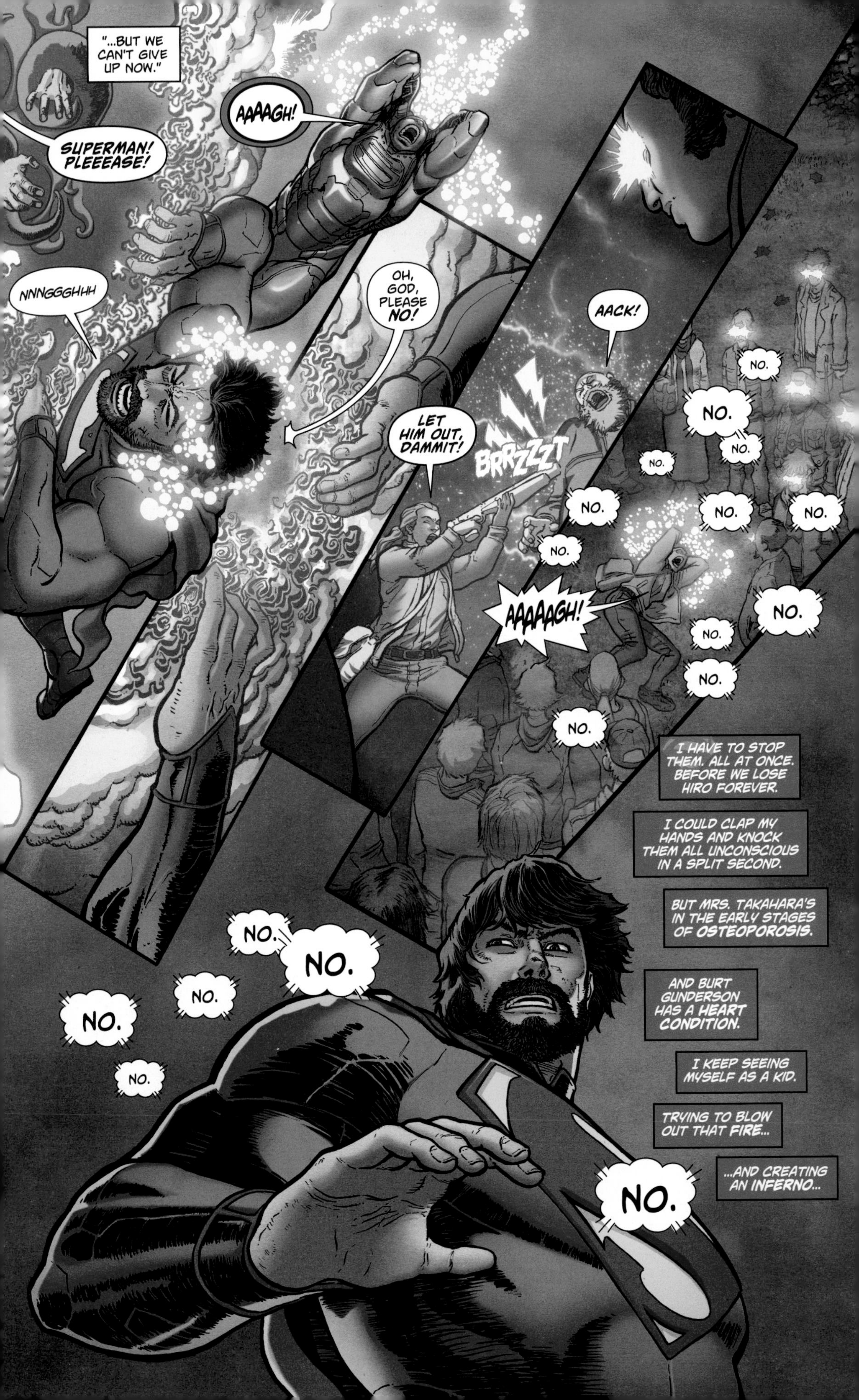
"...BUT WE CAN'T GIVE UP NOW."
AAAAGH!
SUPERMAN! PLEEEASE!
NNNGGGHHH
OH, GOD, PLEASE NO!
LET HIM OUT, DAMMIT!
AACK!
BRRZZZT
AAAAAGH!
NO.
NO.
NO.
NO.
NO.
NO.
NO.
NO.
NO.
NO.
NO.
NO.
I HAVE TO STOP THEM. ALL AT ONCE. BEFORE WE LOSE HIRO FOREVER.
I COULD CLAP MY HANDS AND KNOCK THEM ALL UNCONSCIOUS IN A SPLIT SECOND.
BUT MRS. TAKAHARA'S IN THE EARLY STAGES OF OSTEOPOROSIS.
AND BURT GUNDERSON HAS A HEART CONDITION.
I KEEP SEEING MYSELF AS A KID.
TRYING TO BLOW OUT THAT FIRE...
...AND CREATING AN INFERNO...
NO.
NO.
NO.
NO.
NO.
NO.

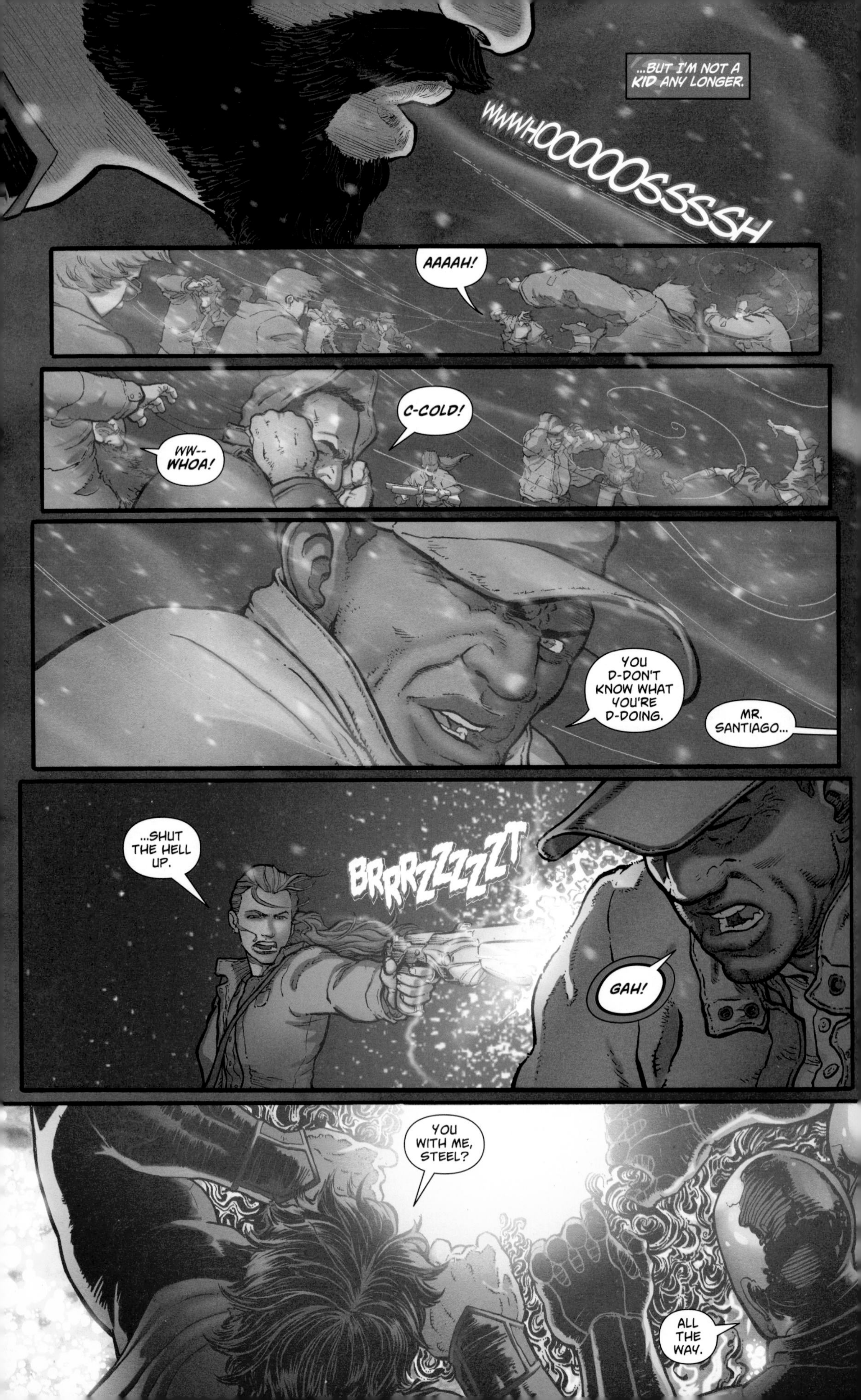
...BUT I'M NOT A KID ANY LONGER.
WWWHOOOOOSSSSSH
AAAAH!
WW-- WHOA!
C-COLD!
YOU D-DON'T KNOW WHAT YOU'RE D-DOING.
MR. SANTIAGO...
...SHUT THE HELL UP.
BRRRZZZZZZT
GAH!
YOU WITH ME, STEEL?
ALL THE WAY.

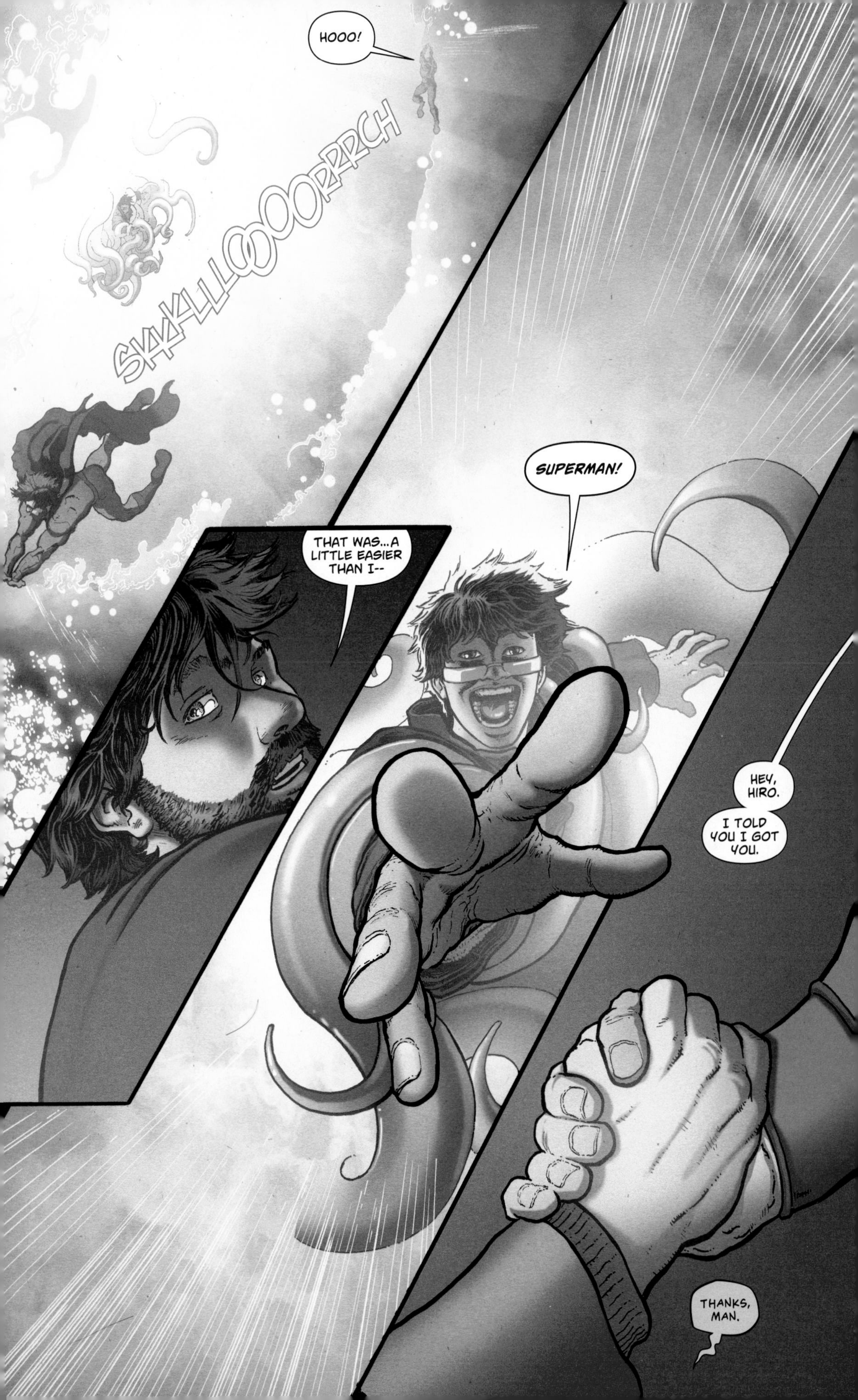
HOOO!
SKKKLLLOOOORRRRCH
THAT WAS...A LITTLE EASIER THAN I--
SUPERMAN!
HEY, HIRO.
I TOLD YOU I GOT YOU.
THANKS, MAN.

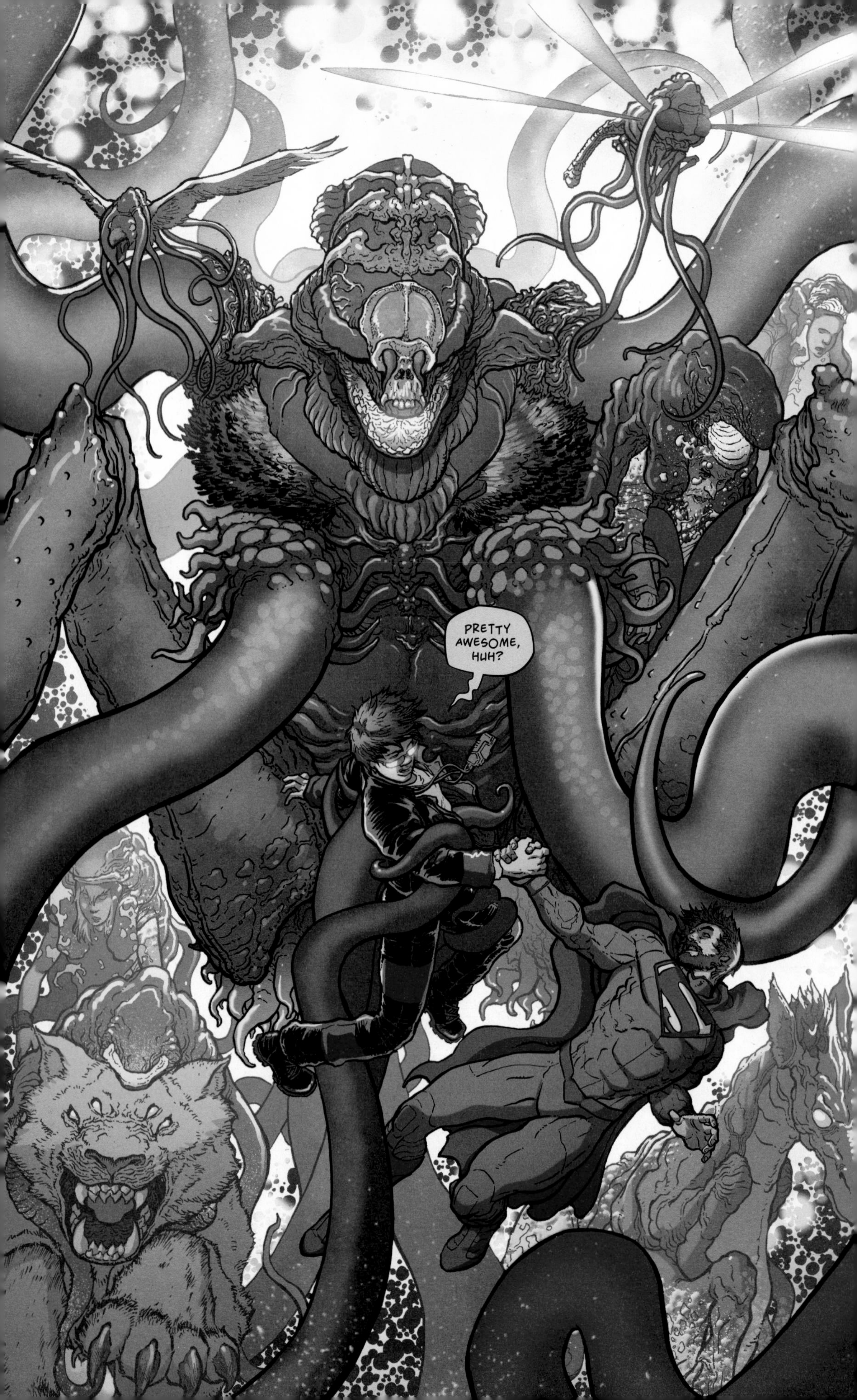
PRETTY AWESOME, HUH?

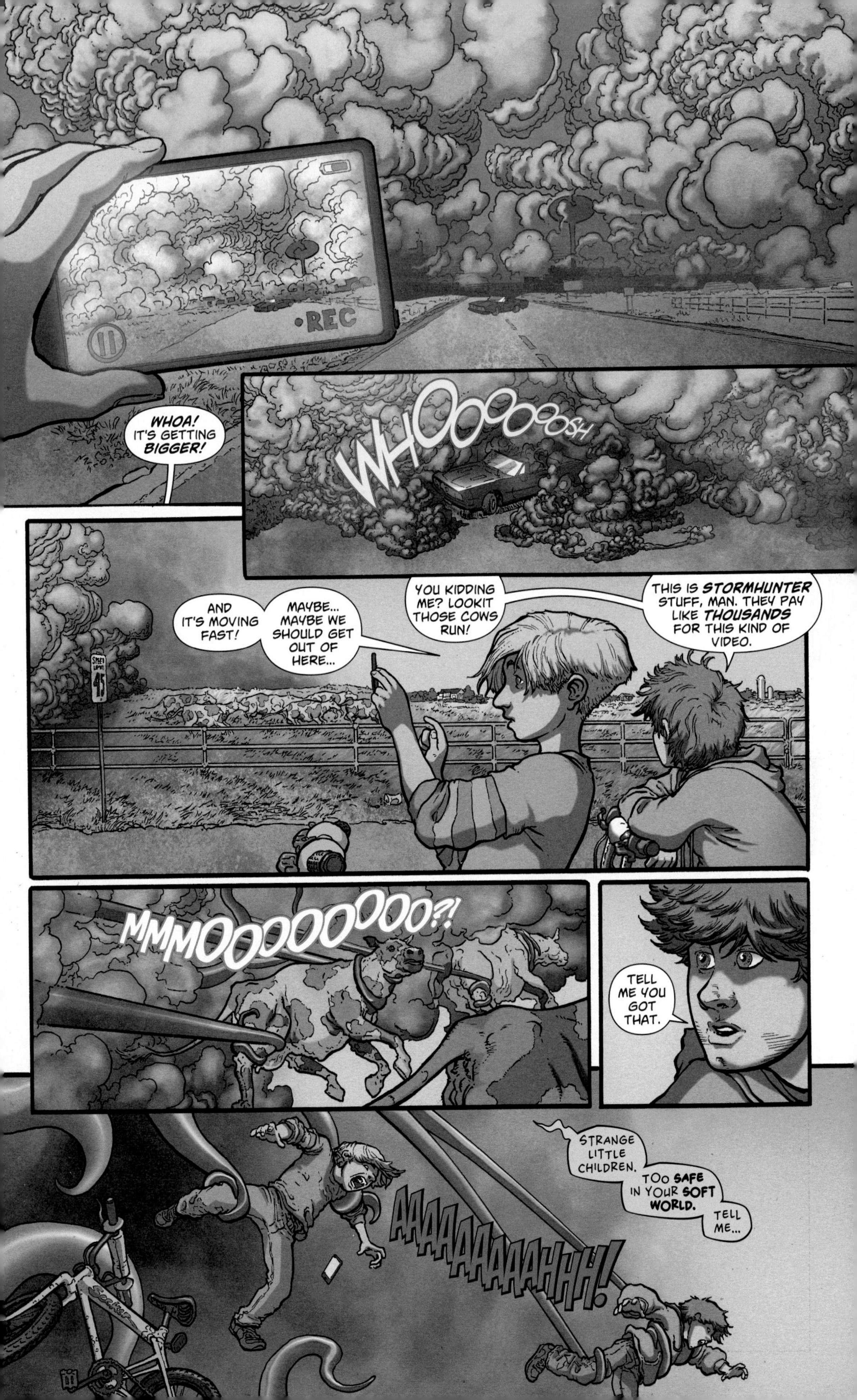

•REC
WHOA! IT'S GETTING BIGGER!
WHOOOOOOOSH
AND IT'S MOVING FAST!
MAYBE... MAYBE WE SHOULD GET OUT OF HERE...
YOU KIDDING ME? LOOKIT THOSE COWS RUN!
THIS IS STORMHUNTER STUFF, MAN. THEY PAY LIKE THOUSANDS FOR THIS KIND OF VIDEO.
SPEED LIMIT 45
MMMOOOOOOOOOO?!
TELL ME YOU GOT THAT.
STRANGE LITTLE CHILDREN.
TOO SAFE IN YOUR SOFT WORLD.
TELL ME...
AAAAAAAAAAAHHH!
Seeker

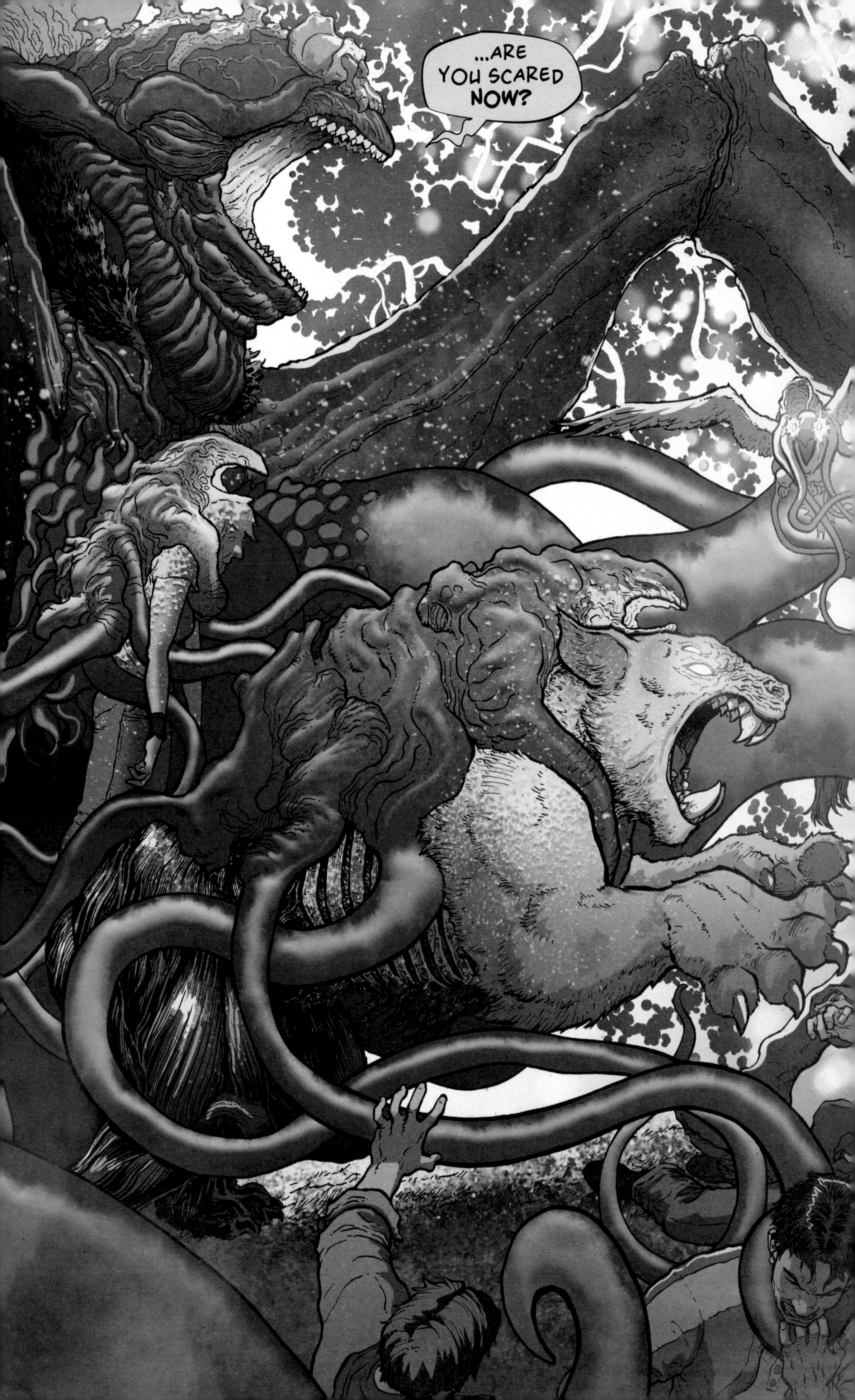
...ARE YOU SCARED NOW?

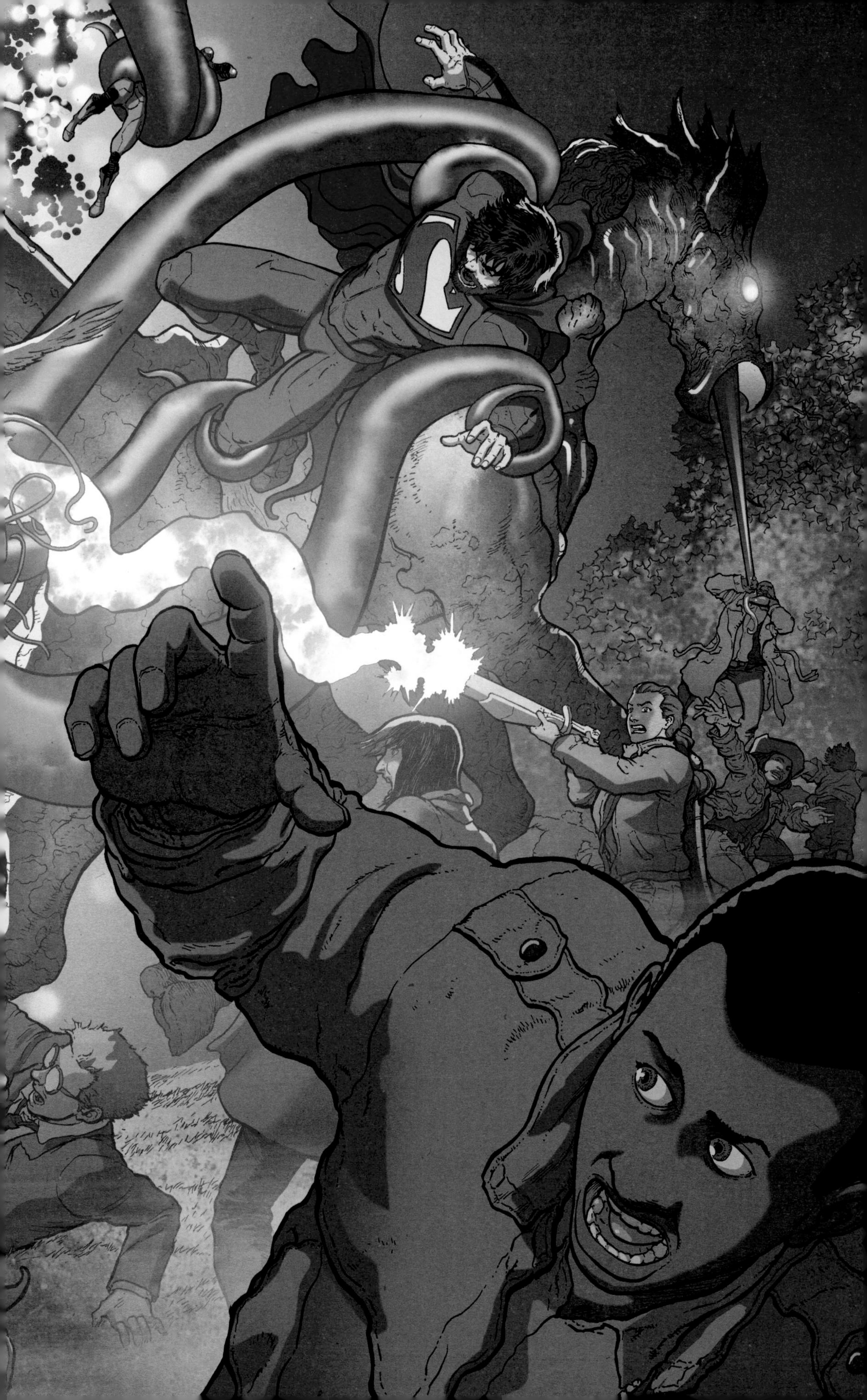

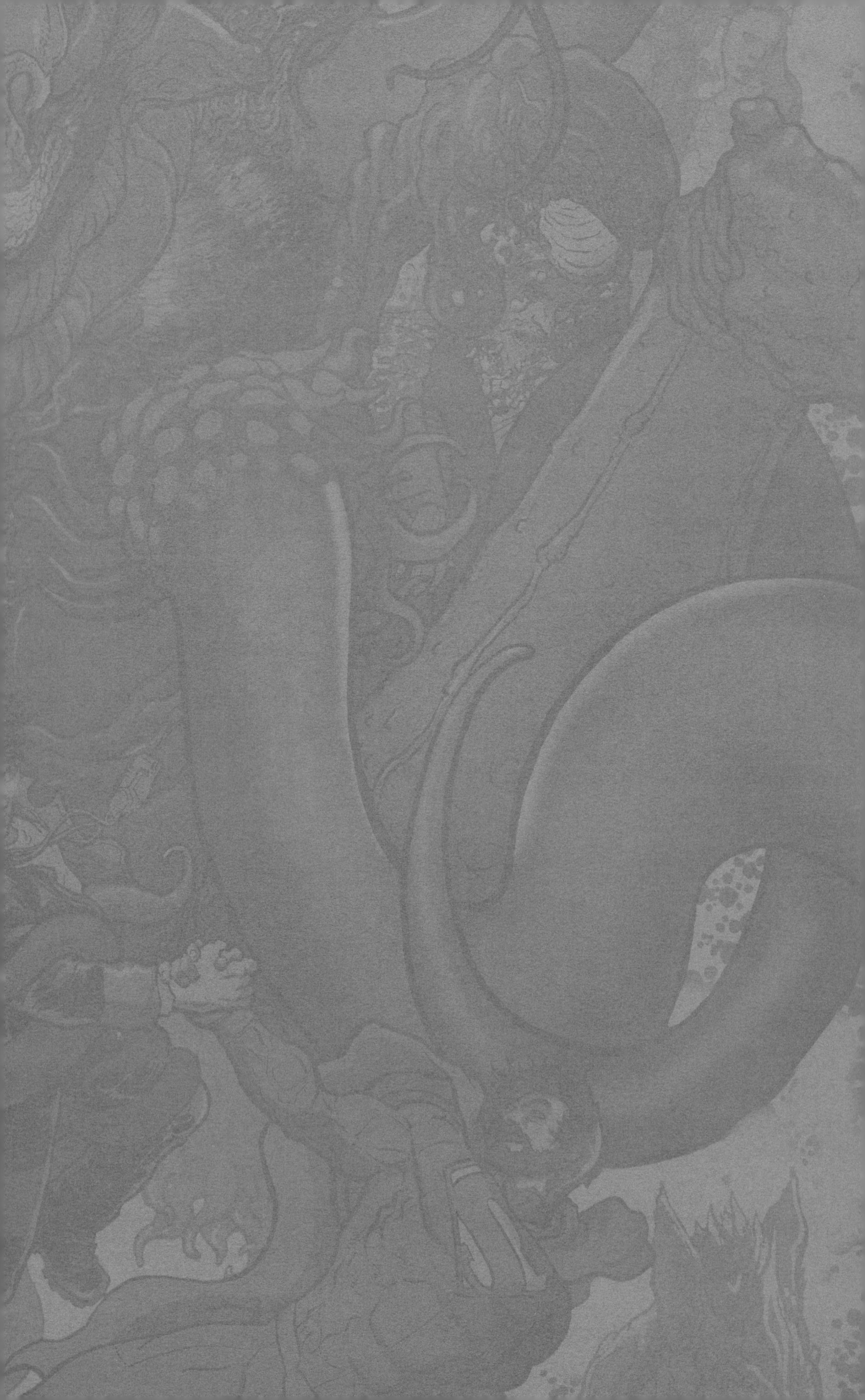

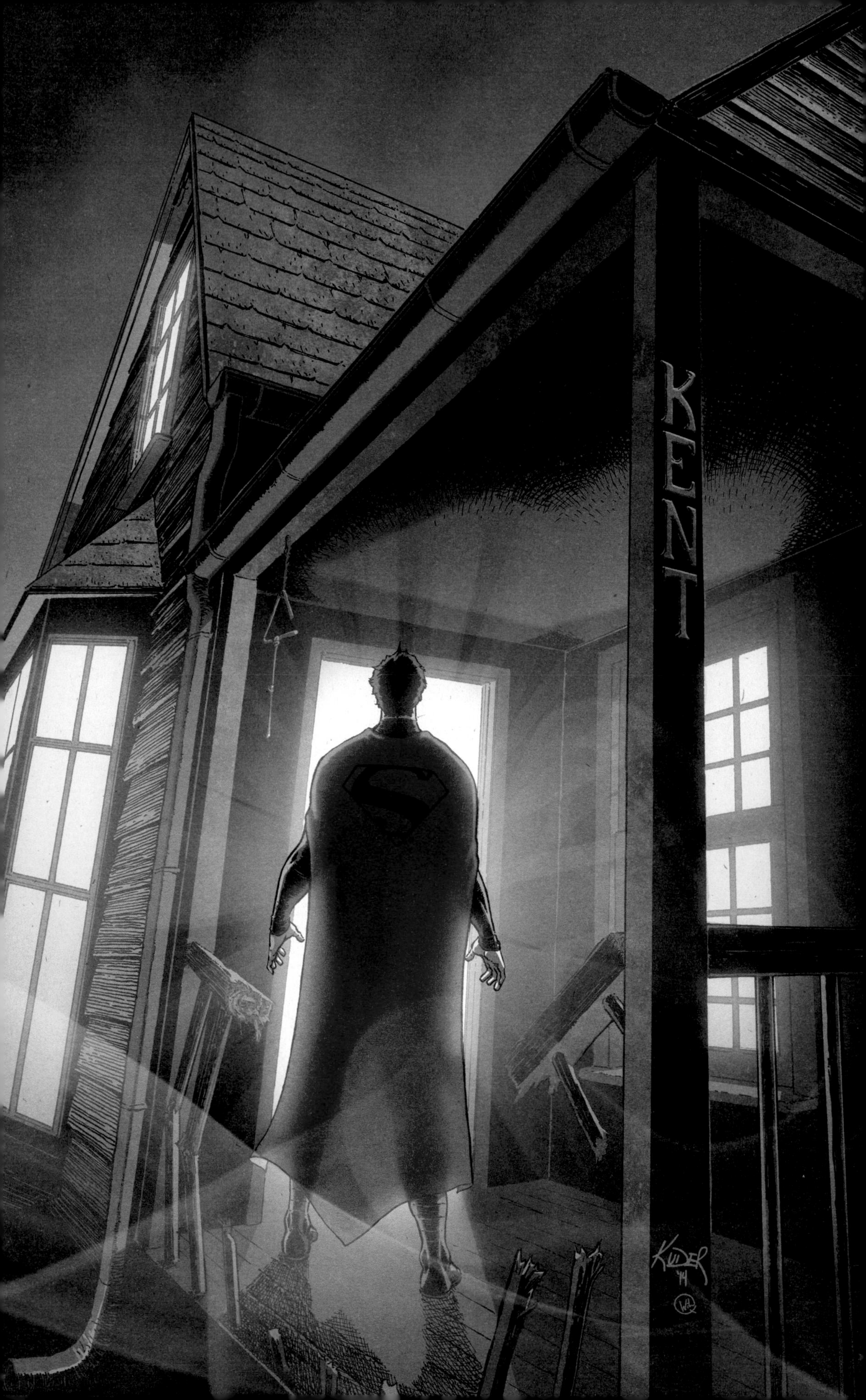
KENT

HOME IS WHERE THE HELL IS

GREG PAK writer **AARON KUDER JAE LEE (flashback sequence)** artists **WIL QUINTANA JUNE CHUNG (flashback sequence)** colorists **DEZI SIENTY** letterer

cover by **AARON KUDER & WIL QUINTANA**

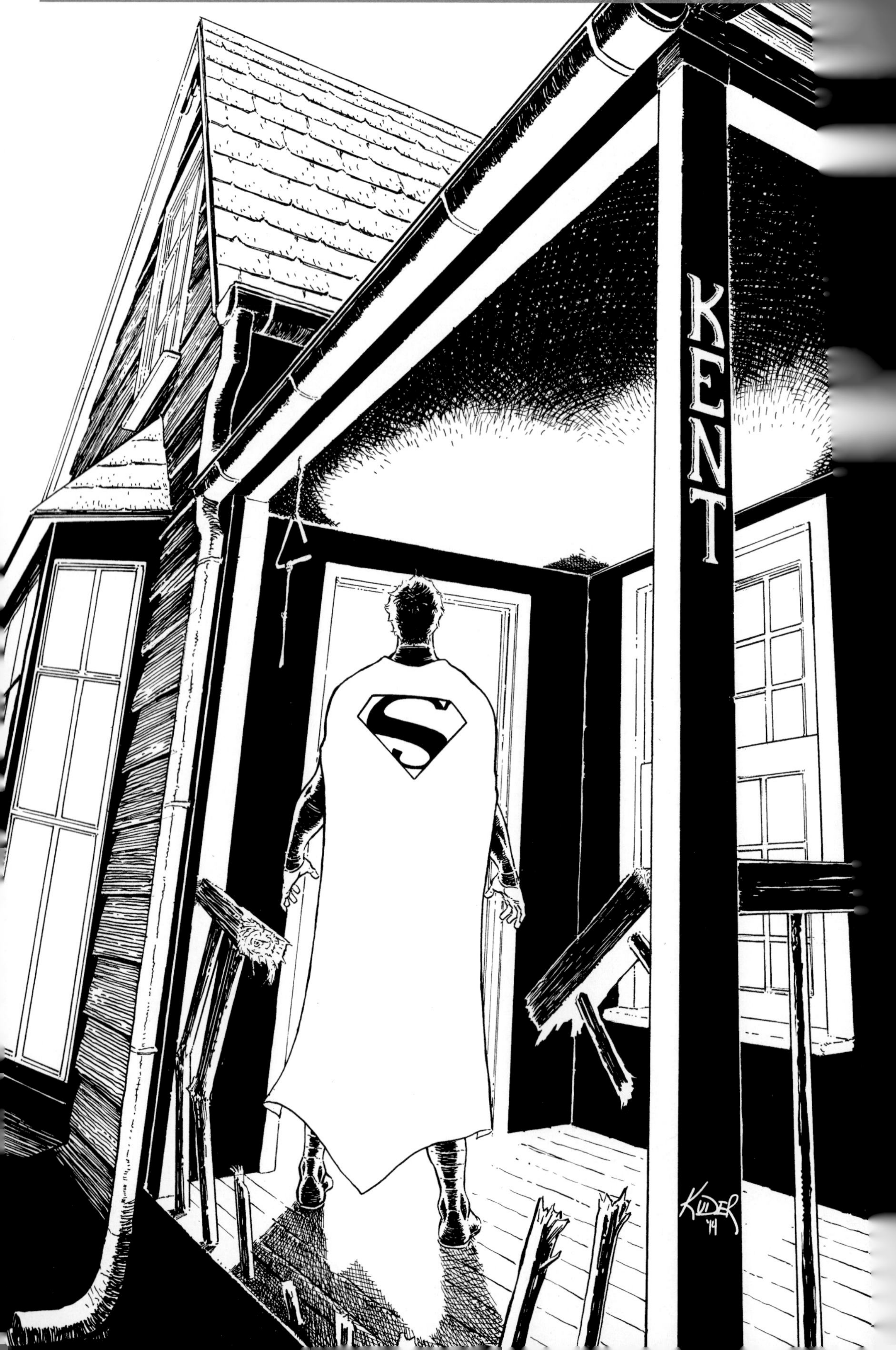
KENT
KUDER '14

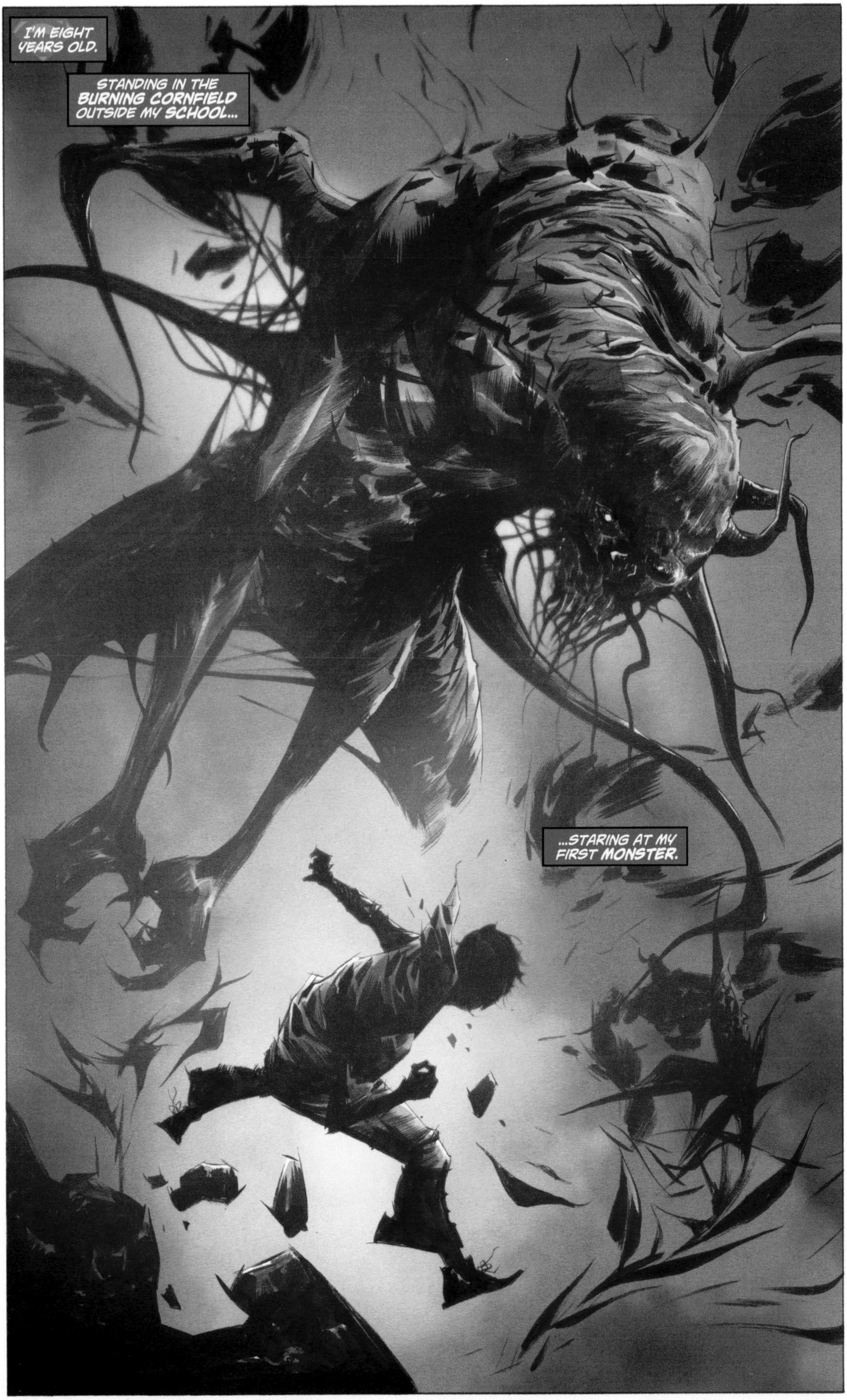
I'M EIGHT YEARS OLD.
STANDING IN THE BURNING CORNFIELD OUTSIDE MY SCHOOL...
...STARING AT MY FIRST MONSTER.

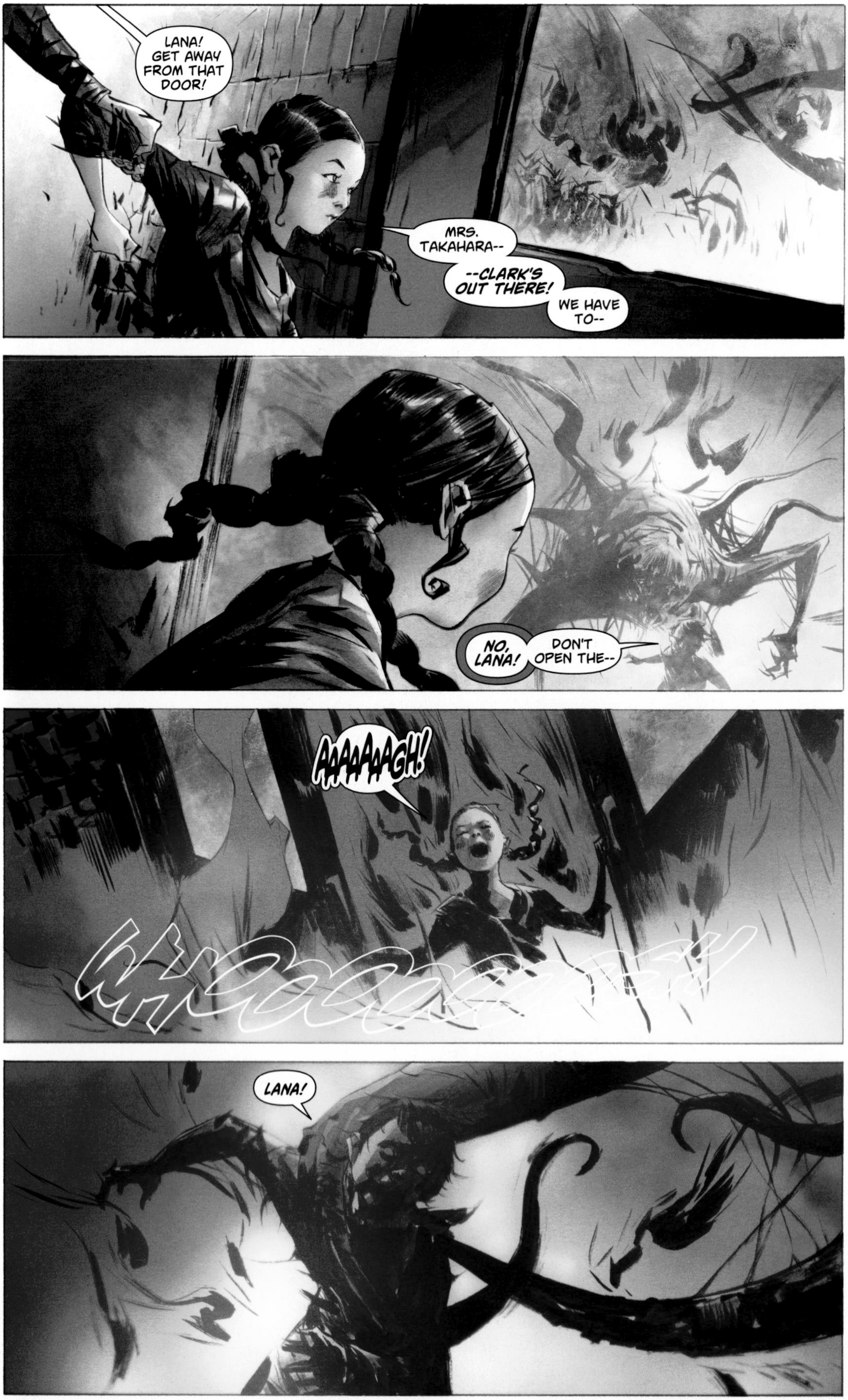
LANA! GET AWAY FROM THAT DOOR!
MRS. TAKAHARA--
--CLARK'S OUT THERE!
WE HAVE TO--
NO, LANA!
DON'T OPEN THE--
AAAAAAAGH!
LANA!

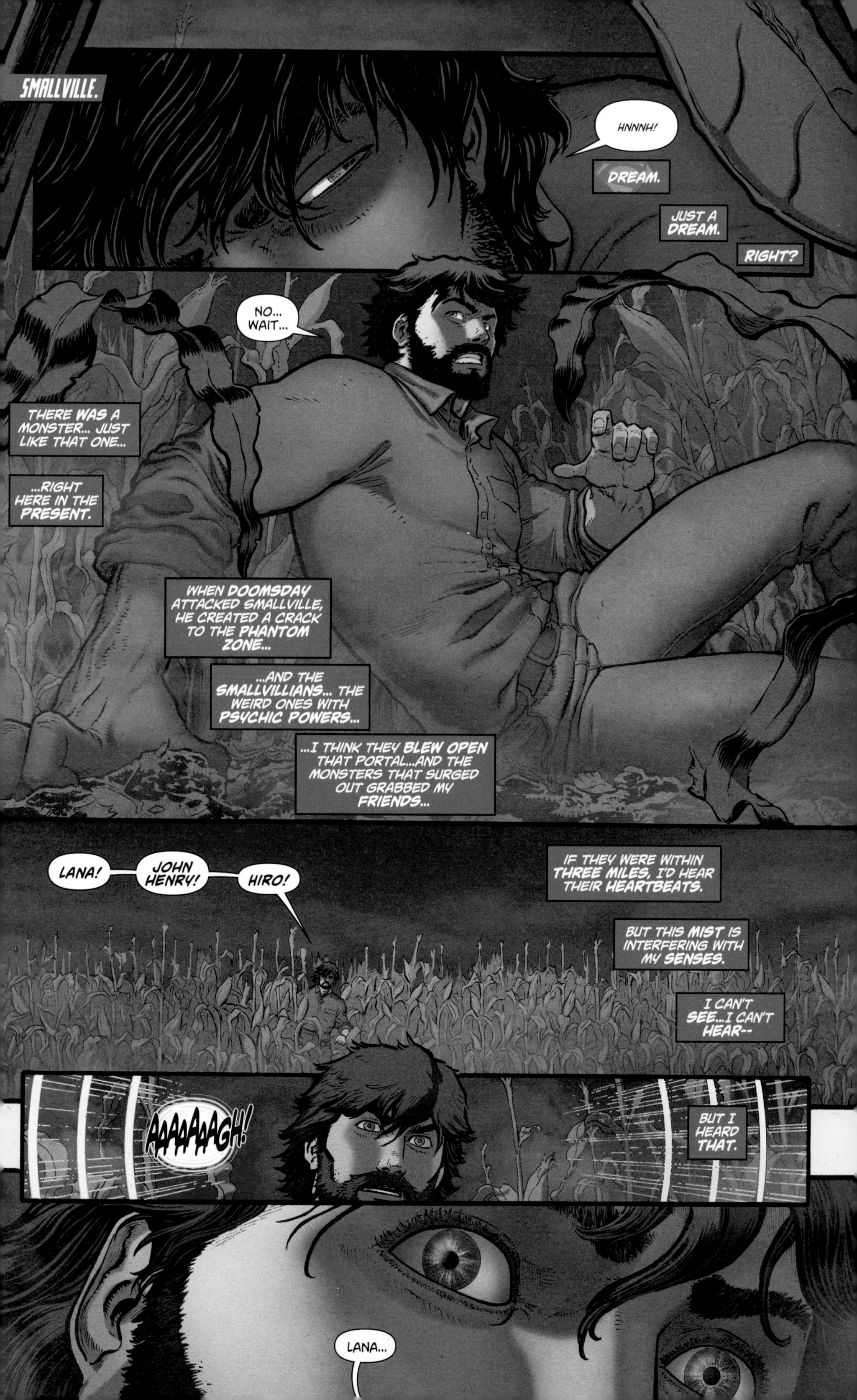

SMALLVILLE.
HNNNH!
DREAM.
JUST A DREAM.
RIGHT?
NO... WAIT...
THERE WAS A MONSTER... JUST LIKE THAT ONE...
...RIGHT HERE IN THE PRESENT.
WHEN DOOMSDAY ATTACKED SMALLVILLE, HE CREATED A CRACK TO THE PHANTOM ZONE...
...AND THE SMALLVILLIANS... THE WEIRD ONES WITH PSYCHIC POWERS...
...I THINK THEY BLEW OPEN THAT PORTAL...AND THE MONSTERS THAT SURGED OUT GRABBED MY FRIENDS...
LANA!
JOHN HENRY!
HIRO!
IF THEY WERE WITHIN THREE MILES, I'D HEAR THEIR HEARTBEATS.
BUT THIS MIST IS INTERFERING WITH MY SENSES.
I CAN'T SEE...I CAN'T HEAR--
AAAAAAAGH!
BUT I HEARD THAT.
LANA...

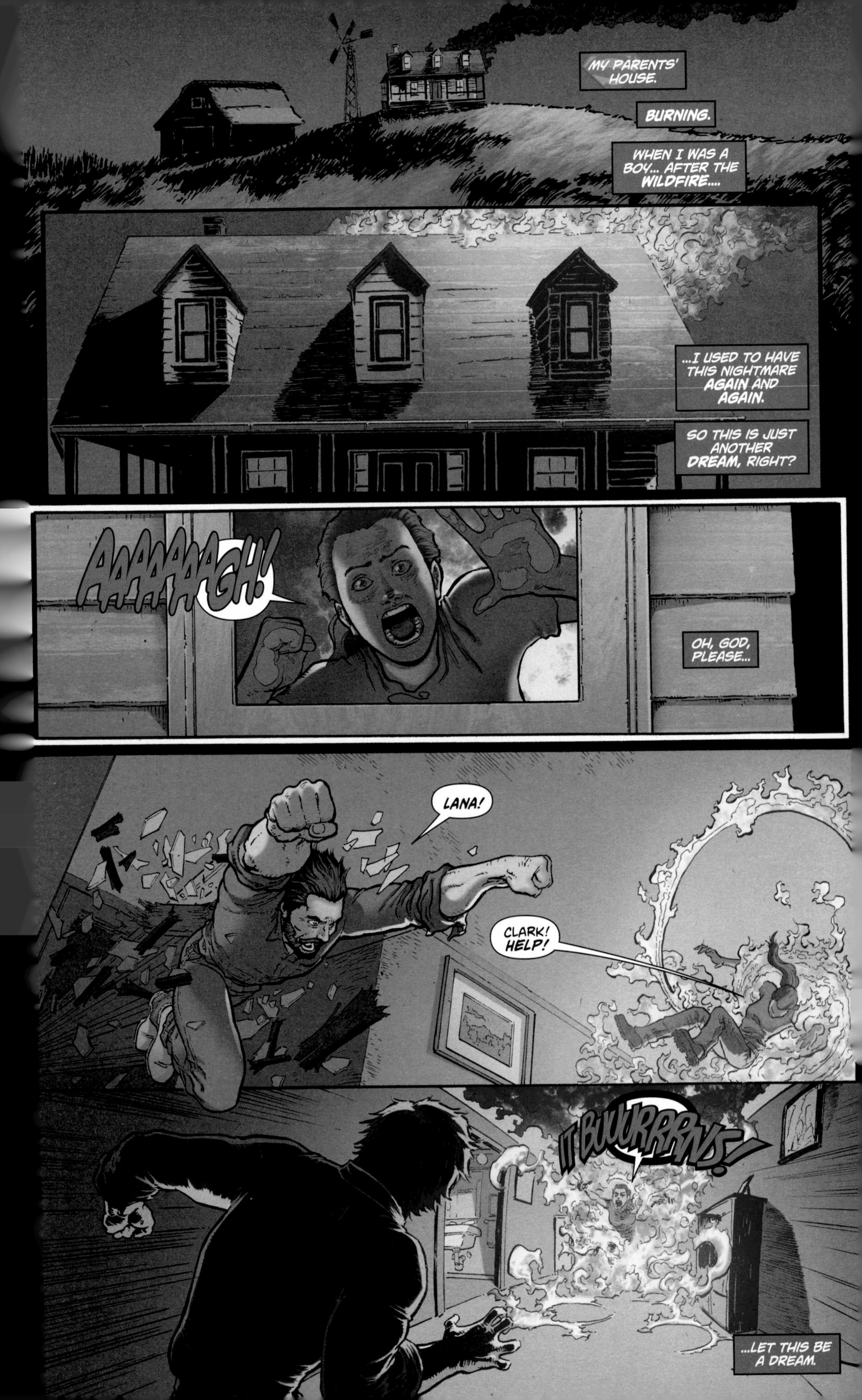
MY PARENTS' HOUSE.
BURNING.
WHEN I WAS A BOY... AFTER THE WILDFIRE....
...I USED TO HAVE THIS NIGHTMARE AGAIN AND AGAIN.
SO THIS IS JUST ANOTHER DREAM, RIGHT?
AAAAAAAGH!
OH, GOD, PLEASE...
LANA!
CLARK! HELP!
IT BUUURRRNS!
...LET THIS BE A DREAM.

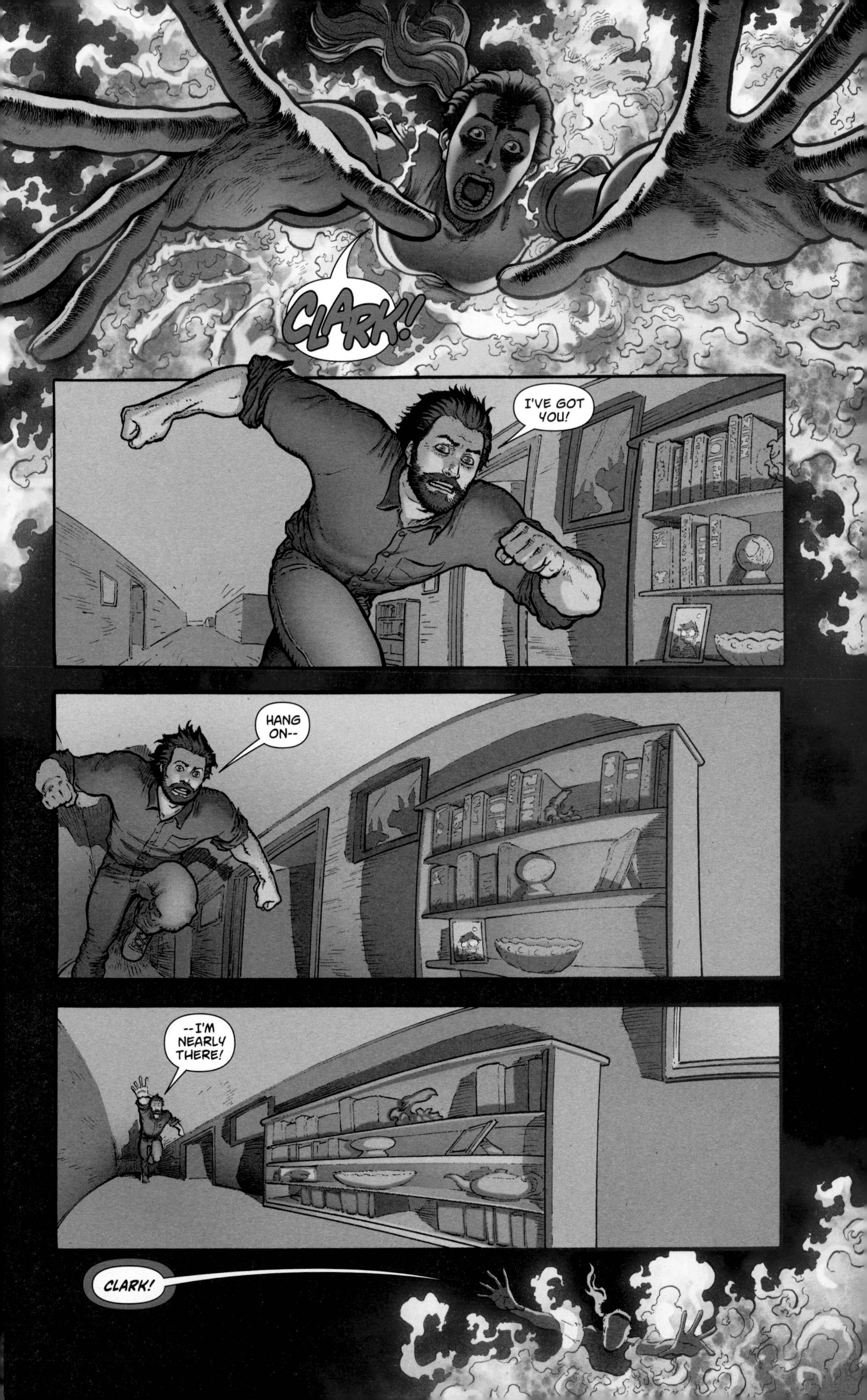
CLARK!
I'VE GOT YOU!
HANG ON--
--I'M NEARLY THERE!
CLARK!

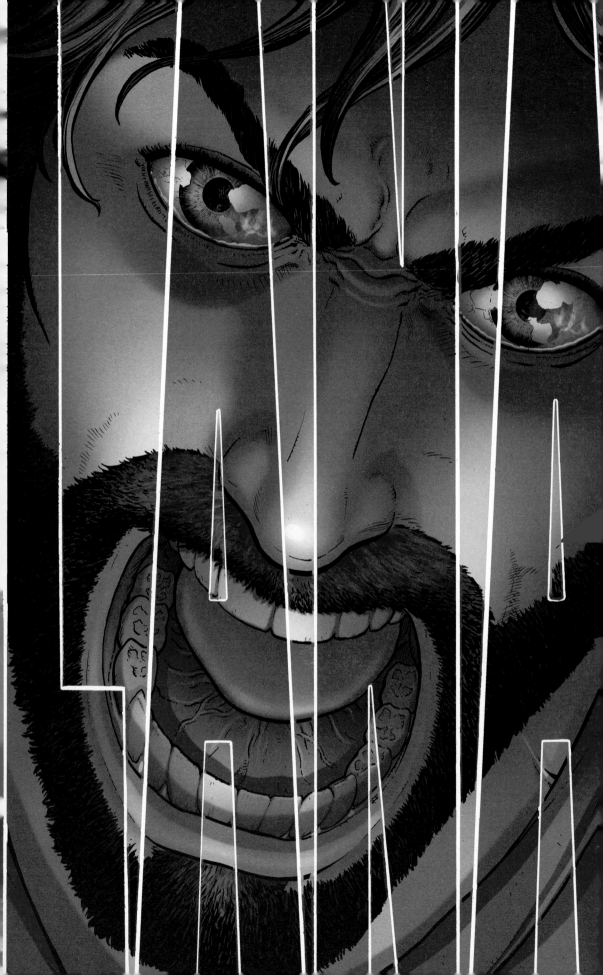

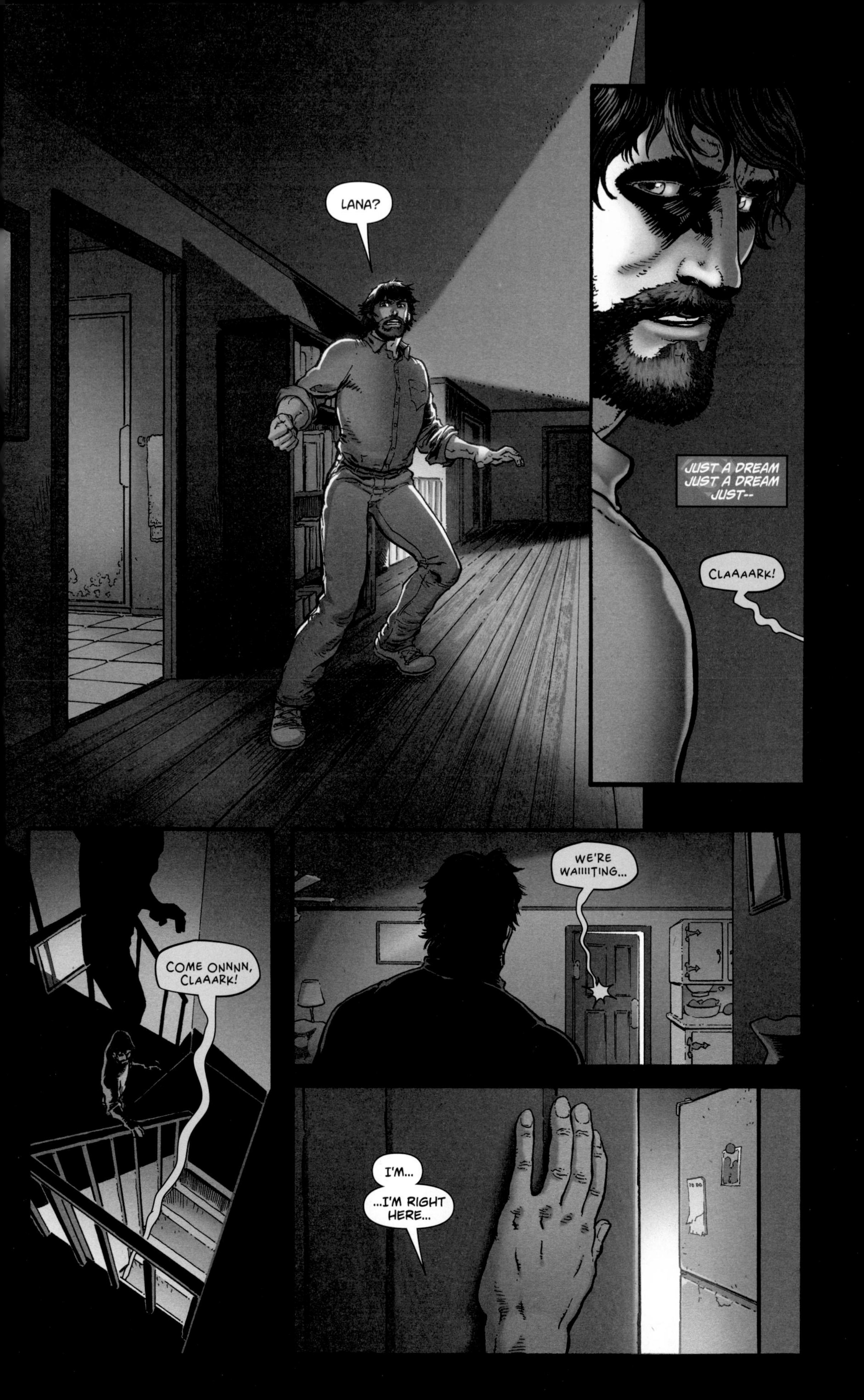
LANA?
JUST A DREAM
JUST A DREAM
JUST--
CLAAAARK!
WE'RE WAIIIITING...
COME ONNNN, CLAAARK!
I'M...
...I'M RIGHT HERE...

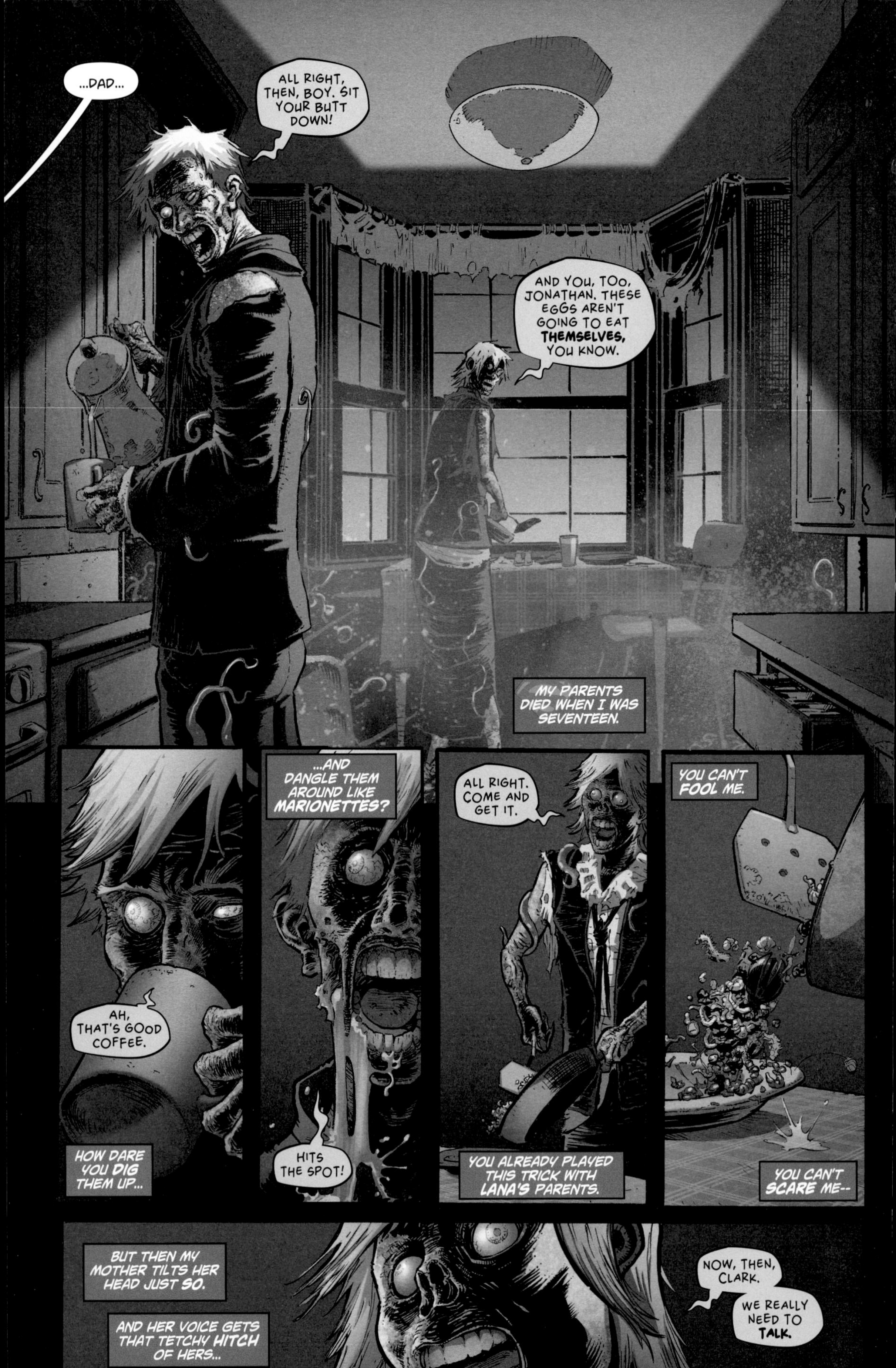
...DAD...
ALL RIGHT, THEN, BOY. SIT YOUR BUTT DOWN!
AND YOU, TOO, JONATHAN. THESE EGGS AREN'T GOING TO EAT THEMSELVES, YOU KNOW.
MY PARENTS DIED WHEN I WAS SEVENTEEN.
AH, THAT'S GOOD COFFEE.
HOW DARE YOU DIG THEM UP...
...AND DANGLE THEM AROUND LIKE MARIONETTES?
HITS THE SPOT!
ALL RIGHT. COME AND GET IT.
YOU ALREADY PLAYED THIS TRICK WITH LANA'S PARENTS.
YOU CAN'T FOOL ME.
YOU CAN'T SCARE ME--
BUT THEN MY MOTHER TILTS HER HEAD JUST SO.
AND HER VOICE GETS THAT TETCHY HITCH OF HERS...
NOW, THEN, CLARK.
WE REALLY NEED TO TALK.

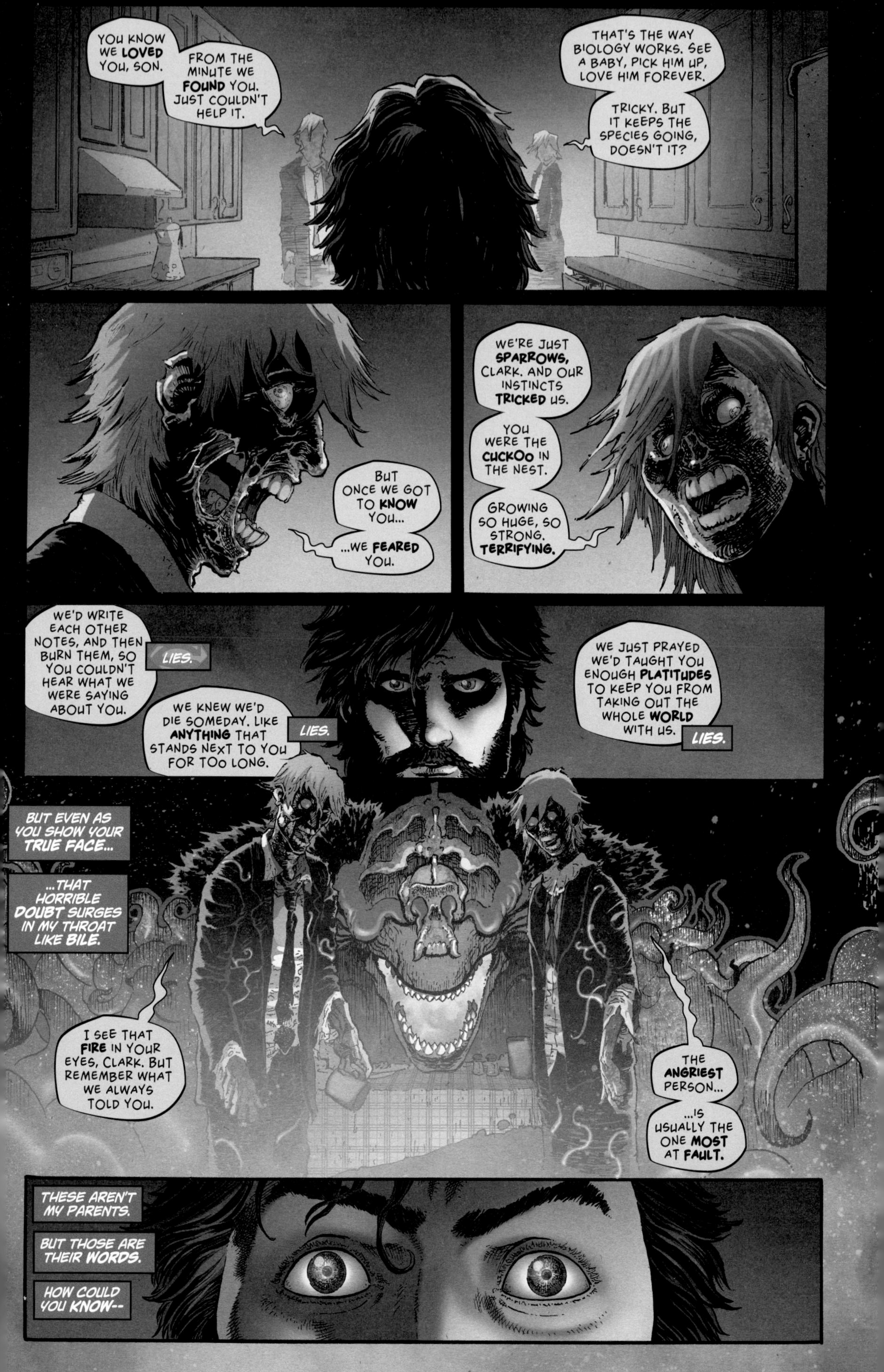

YOU KNOW WE LOVED YOU, SON.
FROM THE MINUTE WE FOUND YOU. JUST COULDN'T HELP IT.
THAT'S THE WAY BIOLOGY WORKS. SEE A BABY, PICK HIM UP, LOVE HIM FOREVER.
TRICKY. BUT IT KEEPS THE SPECIES GOING, DOESN'T IT?
BUT ONCE WE GOT TO KNOW YOU...
...WE FEARED YOU.
WE'RE JUST SPARROWS, CLARK. AND OUR INSTINCTS TRICKED US.
YOU WERE THE CUCKOO IN THE NEST.
GROWING SO HUGE, SO STRONG. TERRIFYING.
WE'D WRITE EACH OTHER NOTES, AND THEN BURN THEM, SO YOU COULDN'T HEAR WHAT WE WERE SAYING ABOUT YOU.
LIES.
WE KNEW WE'D DIE SOMEDAY. LIKE ANYTHING THAT STANDS NEXT TO YOU FOR TOO LONG.
LIES.
WE JUST PRAYED WE'D TAUGHT YOU ENOUGH PLATITUDES TO KEEP YOU FROM TAKING OUT THE WHOLE WORLD WITH US.
LIES.
BUT EVEN AS YOU SHOW YOUR TRUE FACE...
...THAT HORRIBLE DOUBT SURGES IN MY THROAT LIKE BILE.
I SEE THAT FIRE IN YOUR EYES, CLARK. BUT REMEMBER WHAT WE ALWAYS TOLD YOU.
THE ANGRIEST PERSON...
...IS USUALLY THE ONE MOST AT FAULT.
THESE AREN'T MY PARENTS.
BUT THOSE ARE THEIR WORDS.
HOW COULD YOU KNOW--

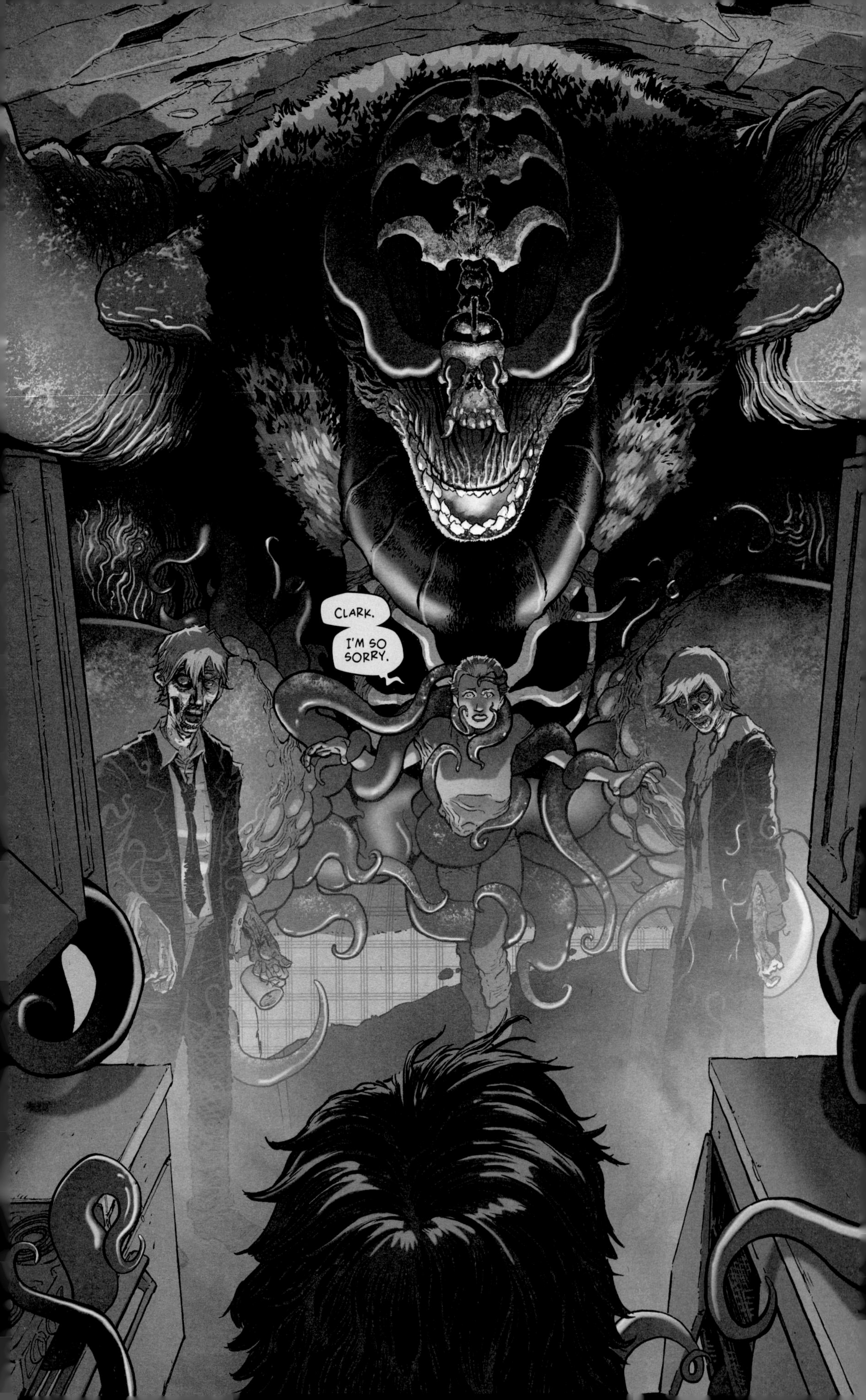
CLARK.
I'M SO SORRY.

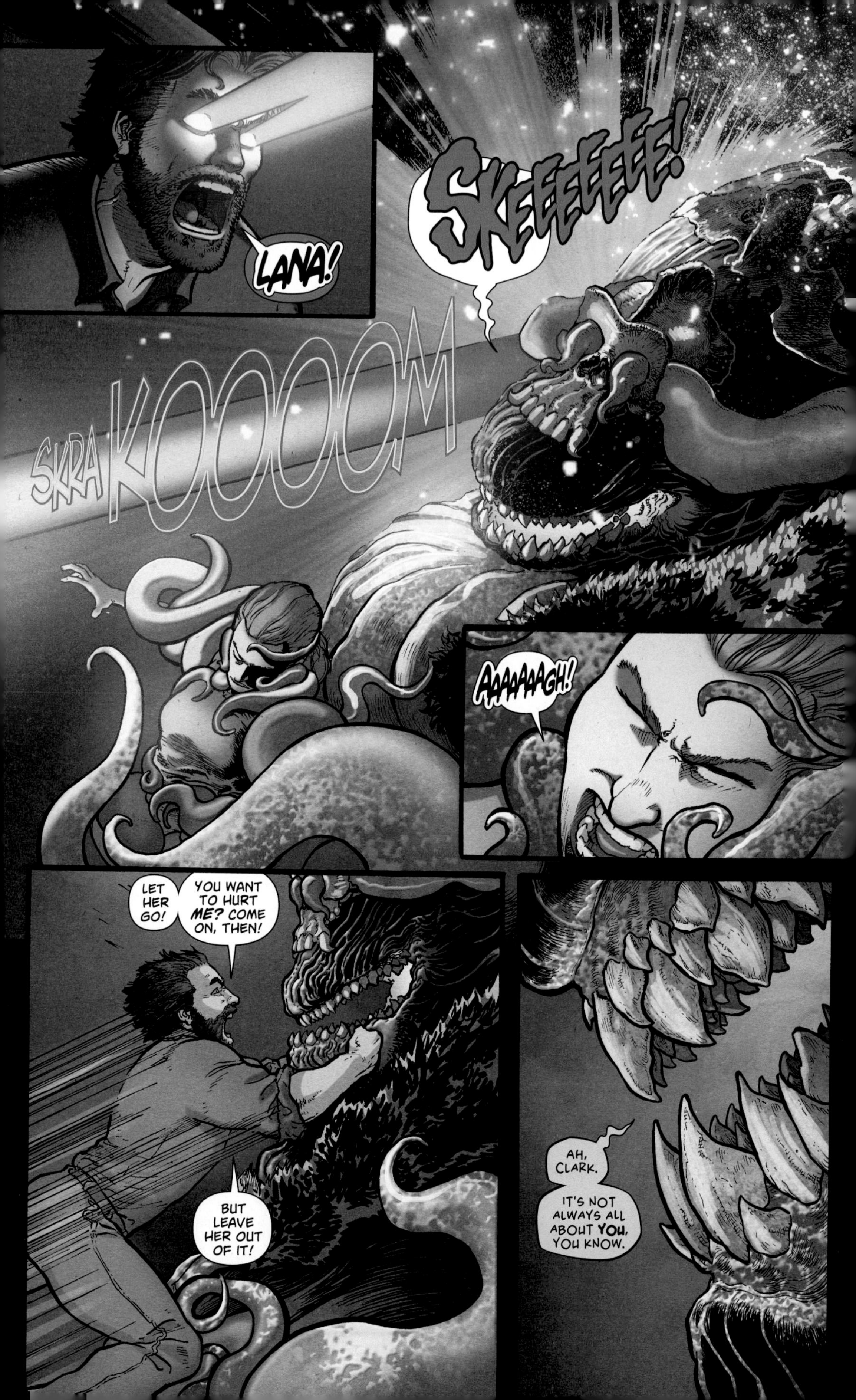
LANA!
SKEEEEEEE!
SKRAKOOOOOM
AAAAAAAGH!
LET HER GO!
YOU WANT TO HURT ME? COME ON, THEN!
BUT LEAVE HER OUT OF IT!
AH, CLARK.
IT'S NOT ALWAYS ALL ABOUT YOU, YOU KNOW.

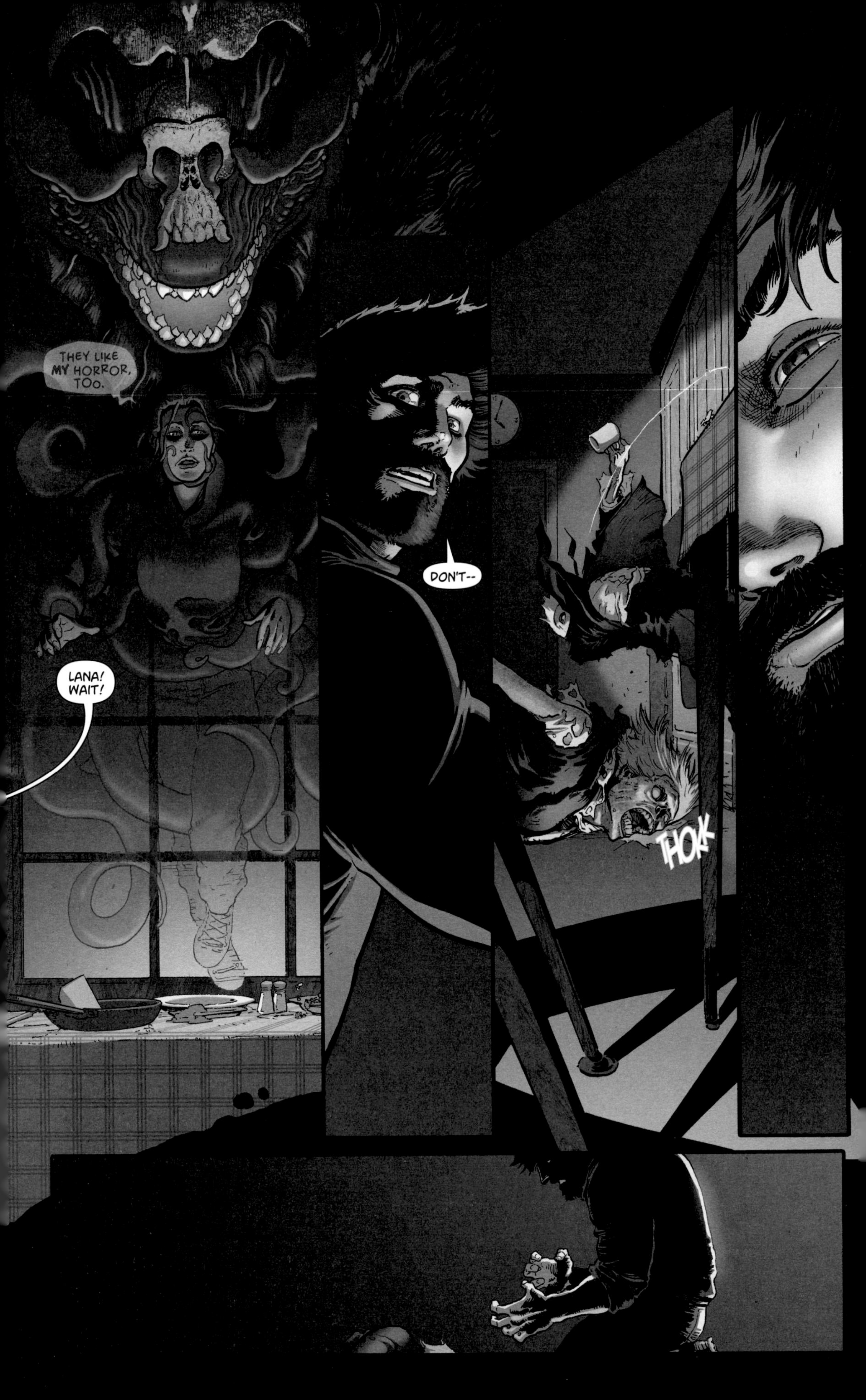
THEY LIKE MY HORROR, TOO.
LANA! WAIT!
DON'T--
THOK

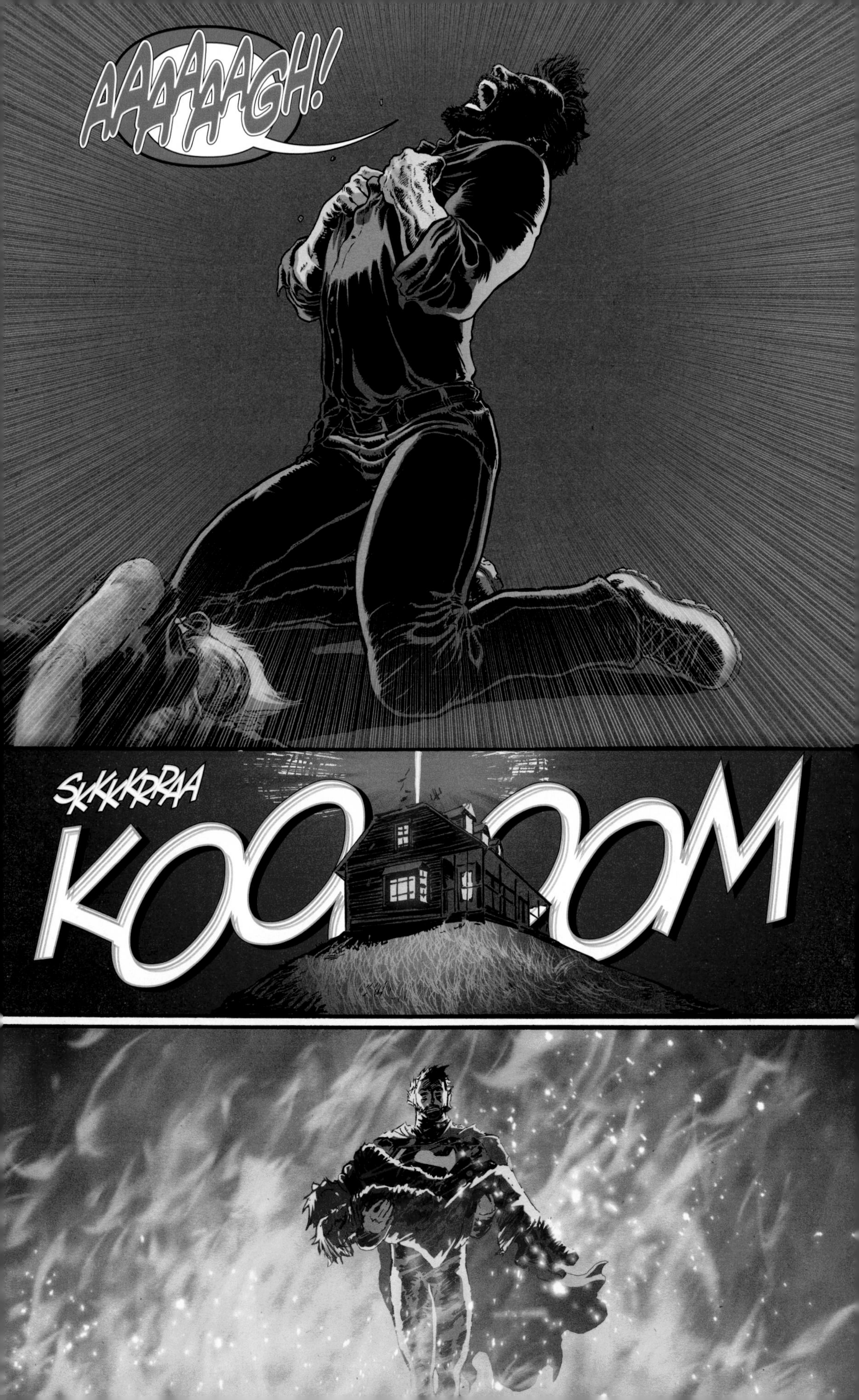
AAAAAAGH!
SKKKKRRAA
KOOOOOM

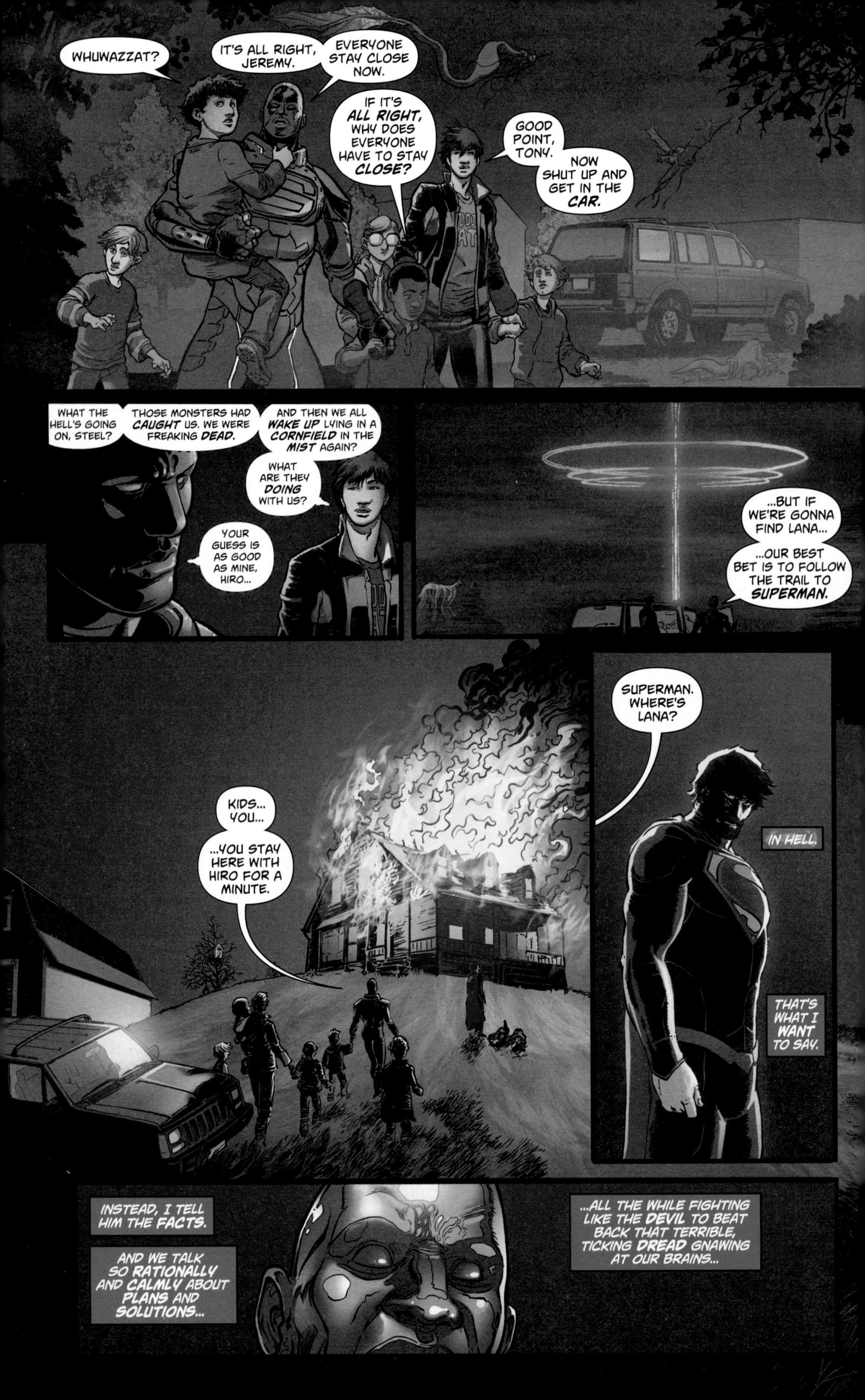
WHUWAZZAT?
IT'S ALL RIGHT, JEREMY.
EVERYONE STAY CLOSE NOW.
IF IT'S ALL RIGHT, WHY DOES EVERYONE HAVE TO STAY CLOSE?
GOOD POINT, TONY.
NOW SHUT UP AND GET IN THE CAR.
WHAT THE HELL'S GOING ON, STEEL?
THOSE MONSTERS HAD CAUGHT US. WE WERE FREAKING DEAD.
AND THEN WE ALL WAKE UP LYING IN A CORNFIELD IN THE MIST AGAIN?
WHAT ARE THEY DOING WITH US?
YOUR GUESS IS AS GOOD AS MINE, HIRO...
...BUT IF WE'RE GONNA FIND LANA...
...OUR BEST BET IS TO FOLLOW THE TRAIL TO SUPERMAN.
KIDS... YOU...
...YOU STAY HERE WITH HIRO FOR A MINUTE.
SUPERMAN. WHERE'S LANA?
IN HELL.
THAT'S WHAT I WANT TO SAY.
INSTEAD, I TELL HIM THE FACTS.
AND WE TALK SO RATIONALLY AND CALMLY ABOUT PLANS AND SOLUTIONS...
...ALL THE WHILE FIGHTING LIKE THE DEVIL TO BEAT BACK THAT TERRIBLE, TICKING DREAD GNAWING AT OUR BRAINS...

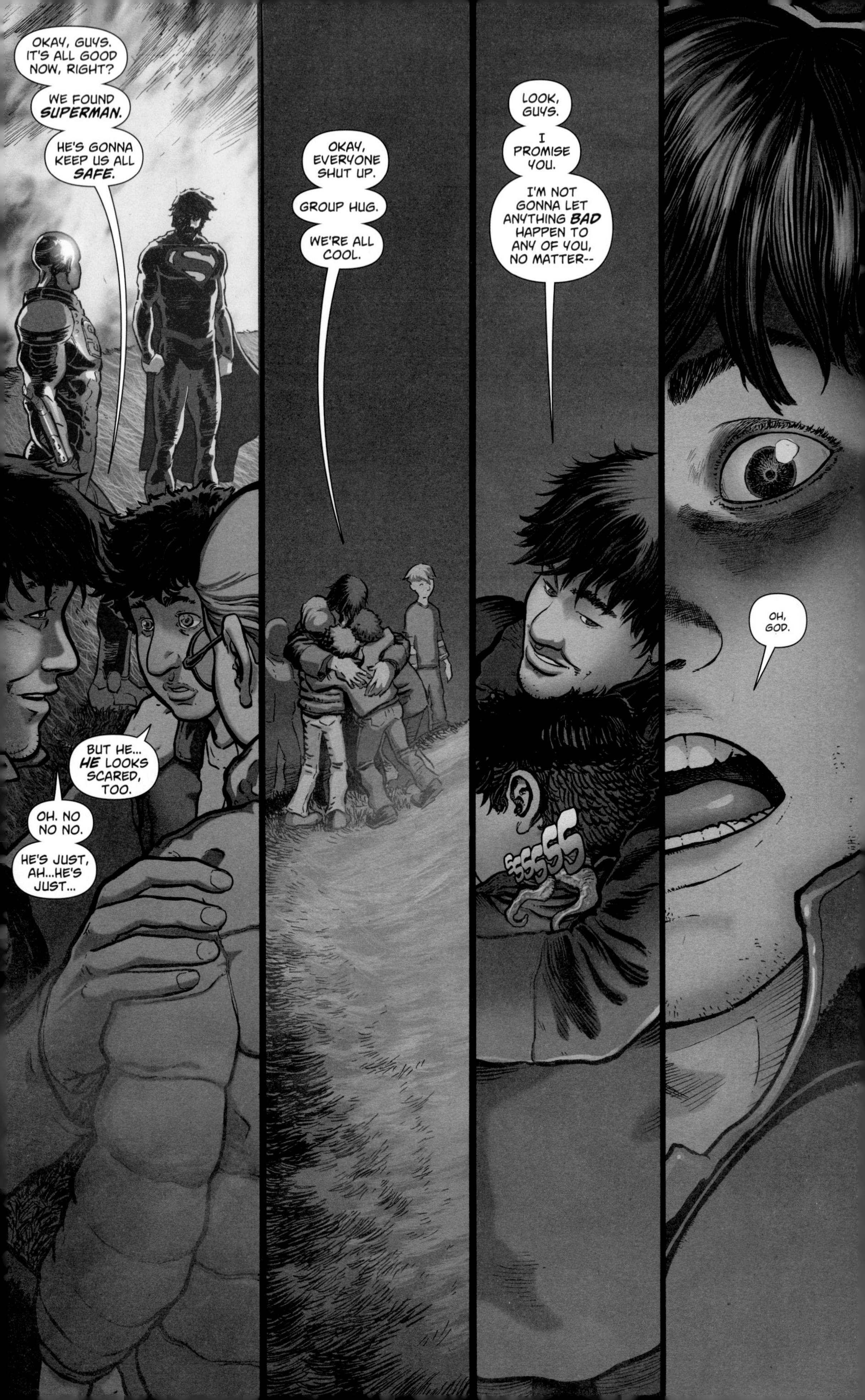
OKAY, GUYS. IT'S ALL GOOD NOW, RIGHT?
WE FOUND SUPERMAN.
HE'S GONNA KEEP US ALL SAFE.
BUT HE... HE LOOKS SCARED, TOO.
OH. NO NO NO.
HE'S JUST, AH...HE'S JUST...
OKAY, EVERYONE SHUT UP.
GROUP HUG.
WE'RE ALL COOL.
LOOK, GUYS.
I PROMISE YOU.
I'M NOT GONNA LET ANYTHING BAD HAPPEN TO ANY OF YOU, NO MATTER--
SSSSSS
OH, GOD.

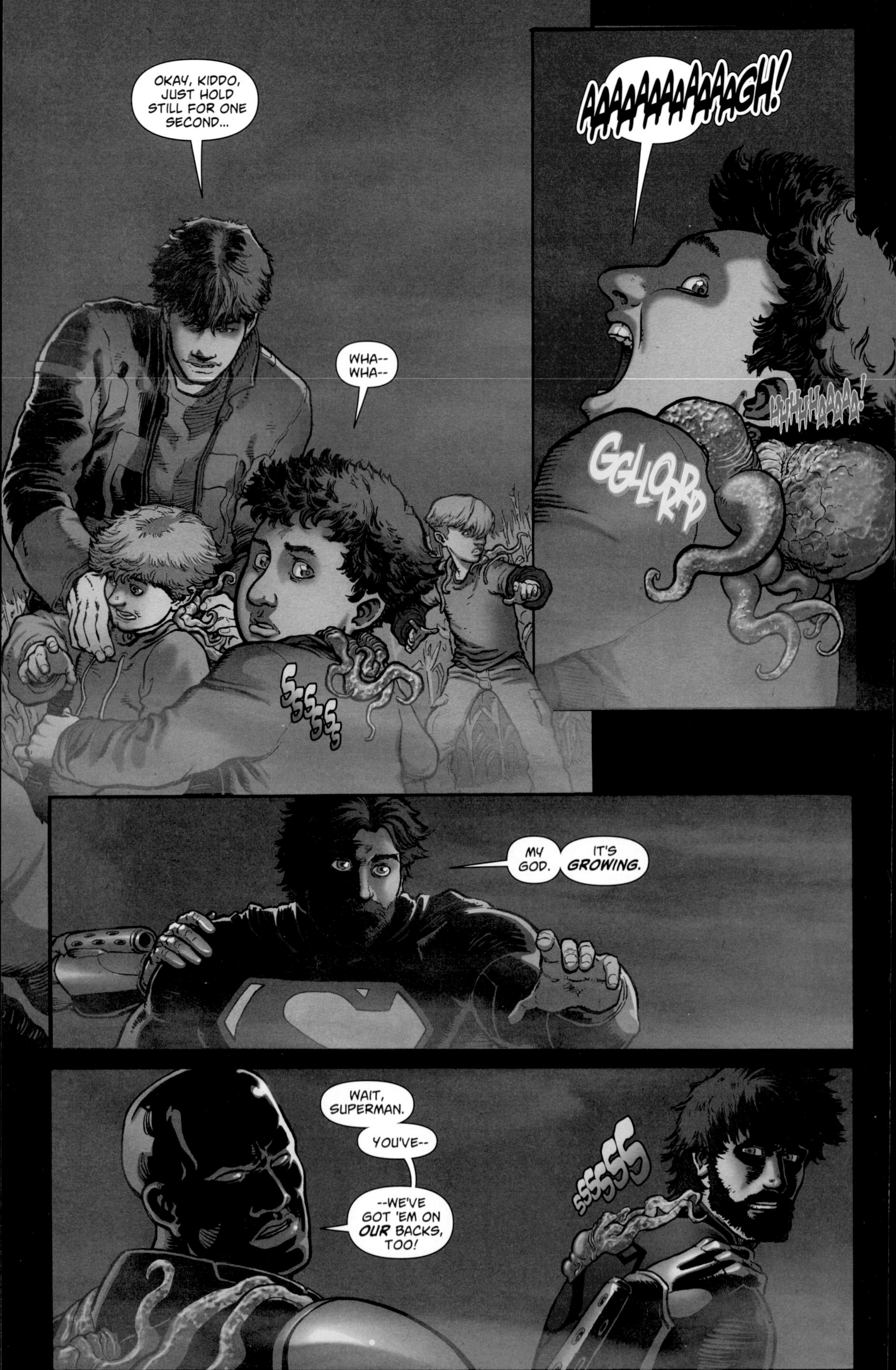
OKAY, KIDDO, JUST HOLD STILL FOR ONE SECOND...
WHA-- WHA--
SSSSS
AAAAAAAAAAAGH!
GGLLORRP
HHHHHAAAAA!
MY GOD.
IT'S GROWING.
WAIT, SUPERMAN.
YOU'VE--
--WE'VE GOT 'EM ON OUR BACKS, TOO!
SSSSS

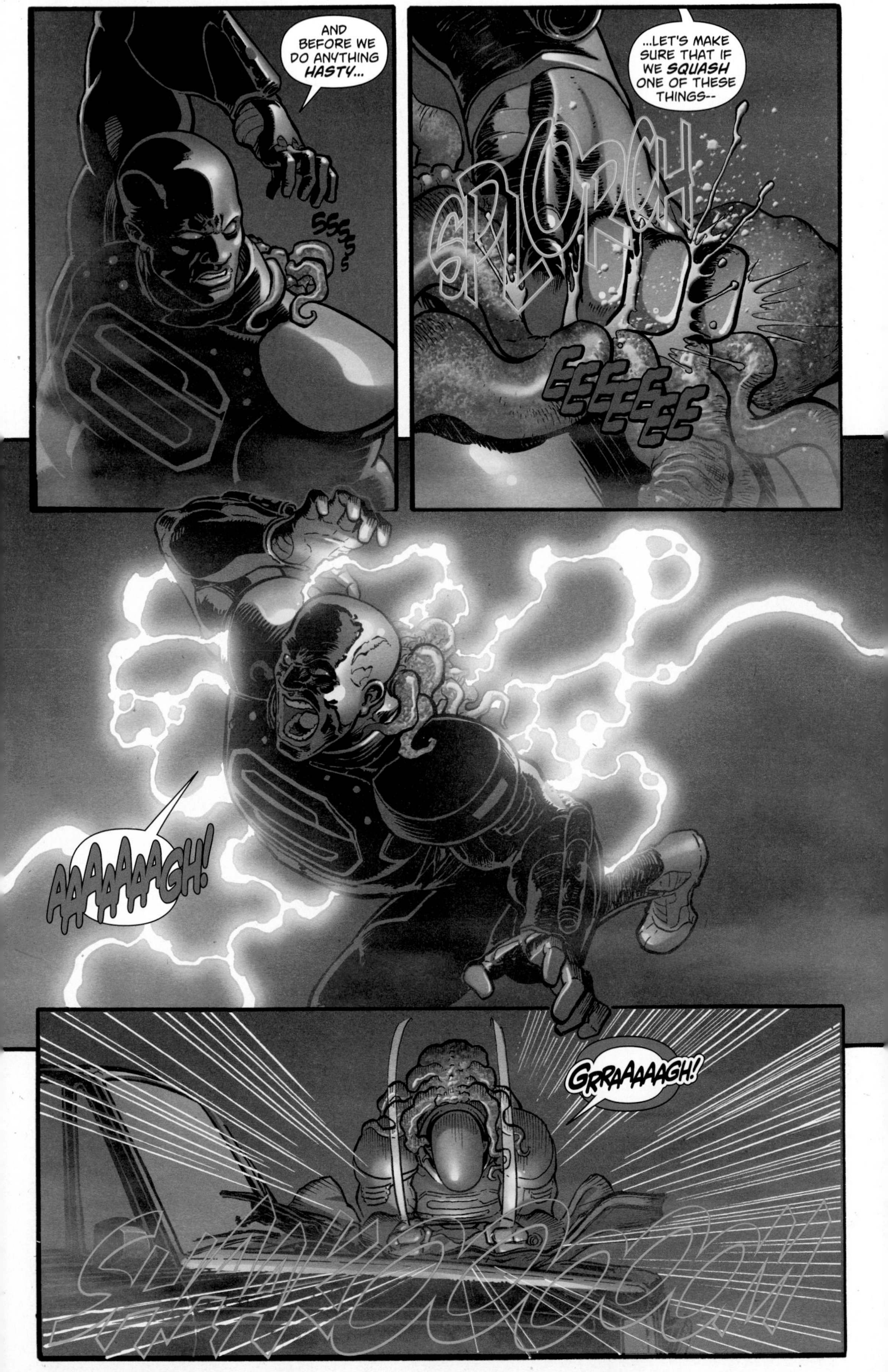
AND BEFORE WE DO ANYTHING HASTY...
...LET'S MAKE SURE THAT IF WE SQUASH ONE OF THESE THINGS--
SPLORCH
EEEEEEEEE
AAAAAAAGH!
GRRAAAAAGH!

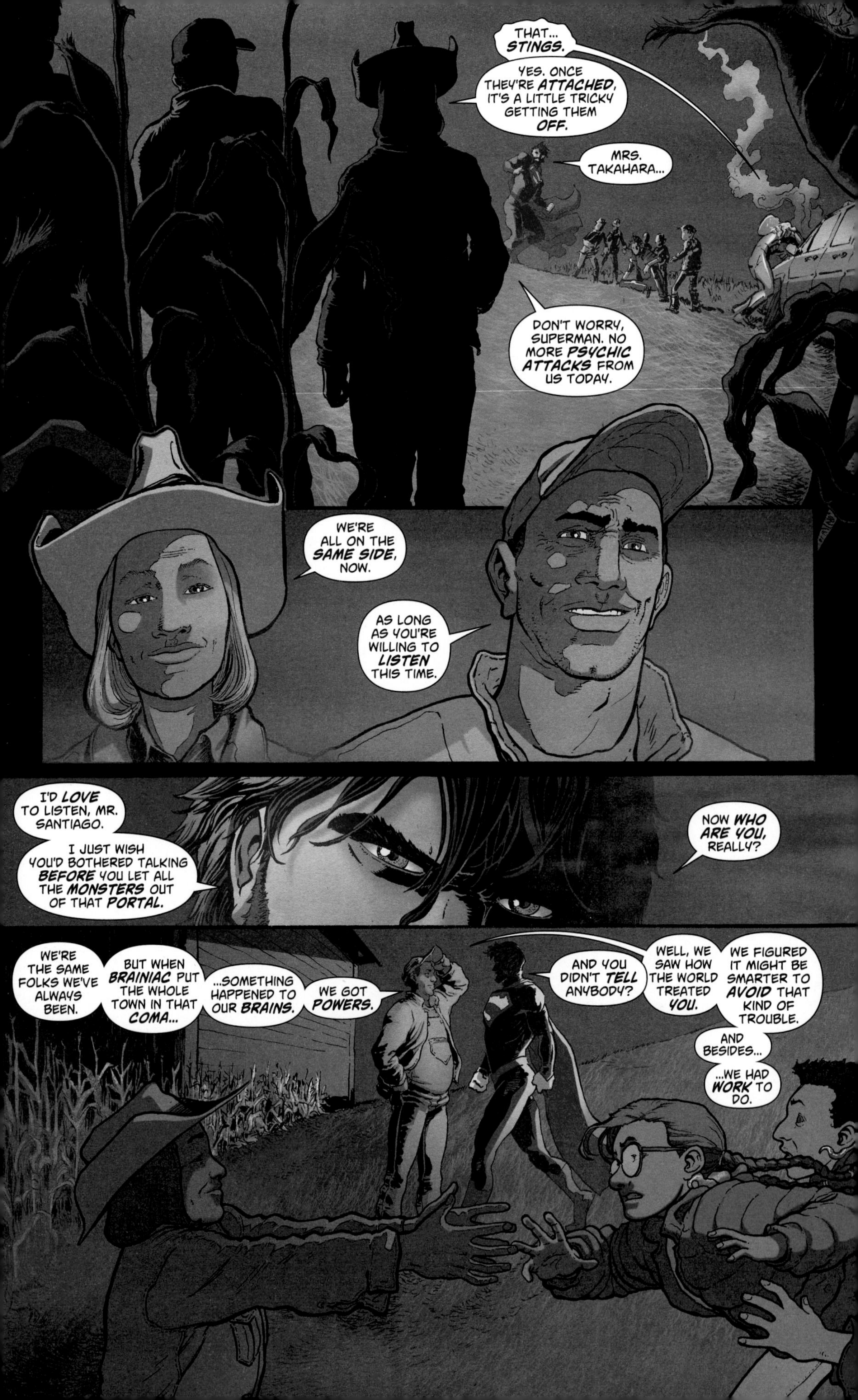
THAT... STINGS.
YES. ONCE THEY'RE ATTACHED, IT'S A LITTLE TRICKY GETTING THEM OFF.
MRS. TAKAHARA...
DON'T WORRY, SUPERMAN. NO MORE PSYCHIC ATTACKS FROM US TODAY.
WE'RE ALL ON THE SAME SIDE, NOW.
AS LONG AS YOU'RE WILLING TO LISTEN THIS TIME.
I'D LOVE TO LISTEN, MR. SANTIAGO.
I JUST WISH YOU'D BOTHERED TALKING BEFORE YOU LET ALL THE MONSTERS OUT OF THAT PORTAL.
NOW WHO ARE YOU, REALLY?
WE'RE THE SAME FOLKS WE'VE ALWAYS BEEN.
BUT WHEN BRAINIAC PUT THE WHOLE TOWN IN THAT COMA...
...SOMETHING HAPPENED TO OUR BRAINS.
WE GOT POWERS.
AND YOU DIDN'T TELL ANYBODY?
WELL, WE SAW HOW THE WORLD TREATED YOU.
WE FIGURED IT MIGHT BE SMARTER TO AVOID THAT KIND OF TROUBLE.
AND BESIDES...
...WE HAD WORK TO DO.

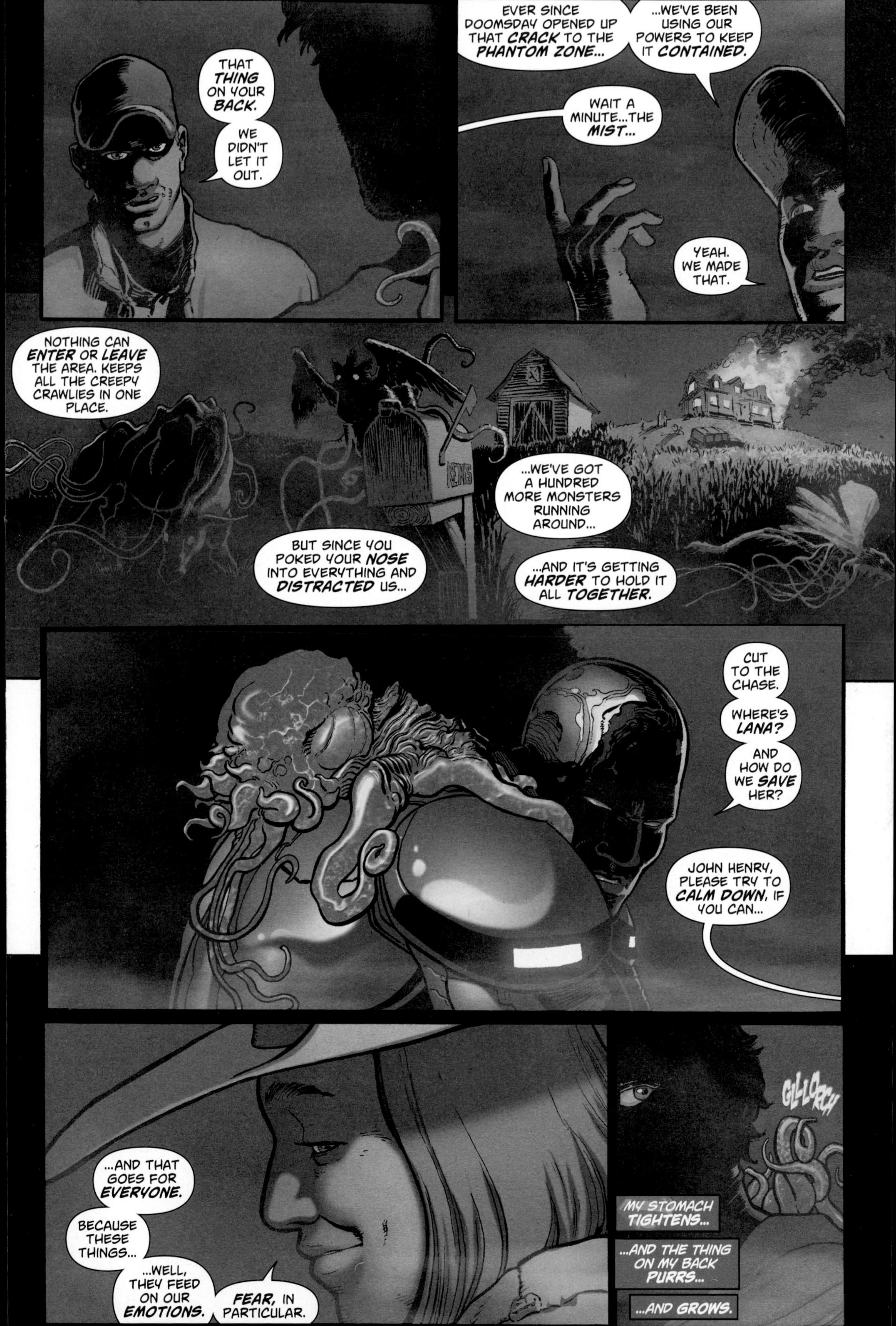
THAT THING ON YOUR BACK.
WE DIDN'T LET IT OUT.
EVER SINCE DOOMSDAY OPENED UP THAT CRACK TO THE PHANTOM ZONE...
...WE'VE BEEN USING OUR POWERS TO KEEP IT CONTAINED.
WAIT A MINUTE...THE MIST...
YEAH. WE MADE THAT.
NOTHING CAN ENTER OR LEAVE THE AREA. KEEPS ALL THE CREEPY CRAWLIES IN ONE PLACE.
BUT SINCE YOU POKED YOUR NOSE INTO EVERYTHING AND DISTRACTED US...
...WE'VE GOT A HUNDRED MORE MONSTERS RUNNING AROUND...
...AND IT'S GETTING HARDER TO HOLD IT ALL TOGETHER.
CUT TO THE CHASE.
WHERE'S LANA?
AND HOW DO WE SAVE HER?
JOHN HENRY, PLEASE TRY TO CALM DOWN, IF YOU CAN...
...AND THAT GOES FOR EVERYONE.
BECAUSE THESE THINGS...
...WELL, THEY FEED ON OUR EMOTIONS.
FEAR, IN PARTICULAR.
GLLLORCH
MY STOMACH TIGHTENS...
...AND THE THING ON MY BACK PURRS...
...AND GROWS.

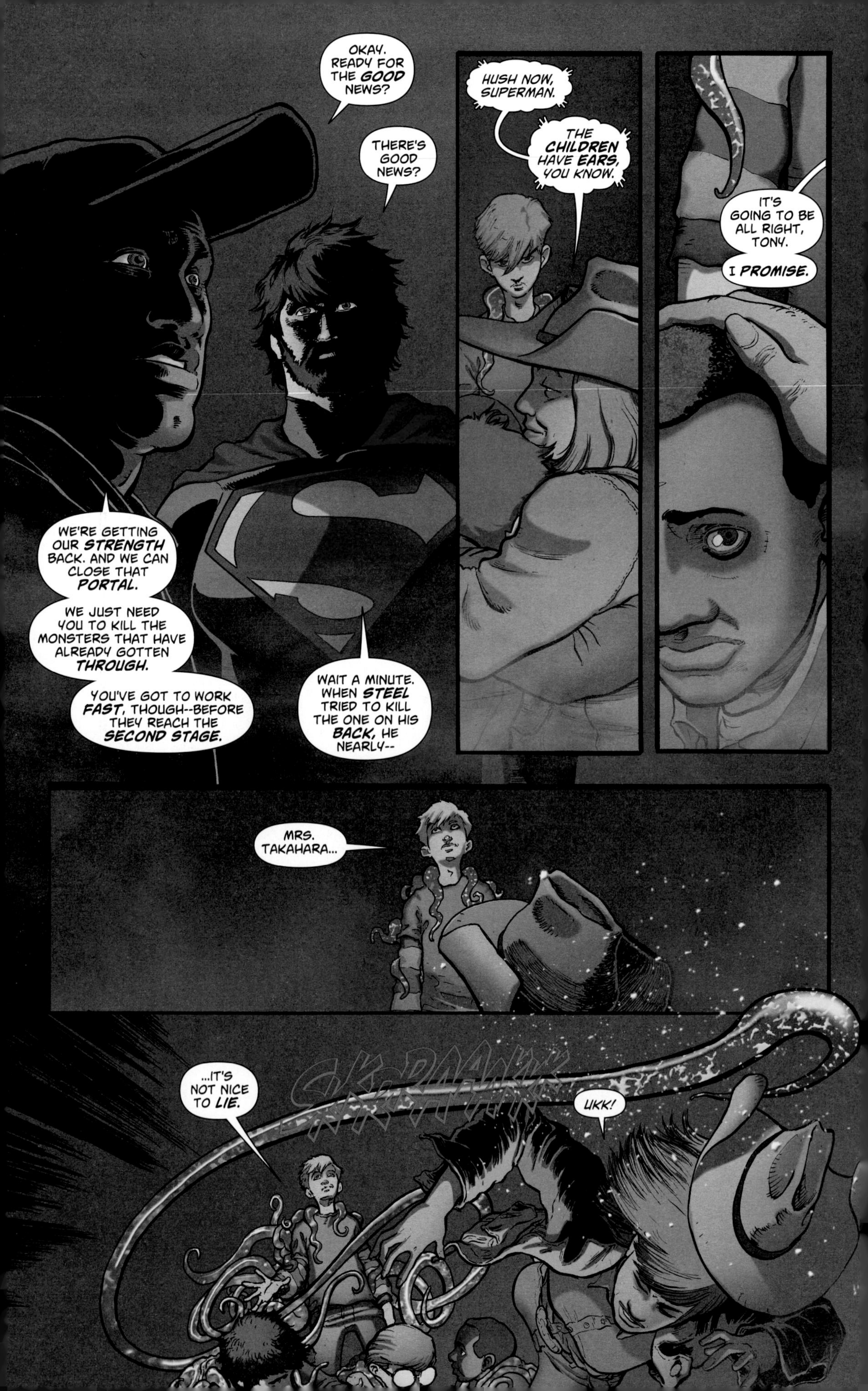
OKAY. READY FOR THE GOOD NEWS?
THERE'S GOOD NEWS?
WE'RE GETTING OUR STRENGTH BACK. AND WE CAN CLOSE THAT PORTAL.
WE JUST NEED YOU TO KILL THE MONSTERS THAT HAVE ALREADY GOTTEN THROUGH.
YOU'VE GOT TO WORK FAST, THOUGH--BEFORE THEY REACH THE SECOND STAGE.
WAIT A MINUTE. WHEN STEEL TRIED TO KILL THE ONE ON HIS BACK, HE NEARLY--
HUSH NOW, SUPERMAN.
THE CHILDREN HAVE EARS, YOU KNOW.
IT'S GOING TO BE ALL RIGHT, TONY.
I PROMISE.
MRS. TAKAHARA...
...IT'S NOT NICE TO LIE.
UKK!

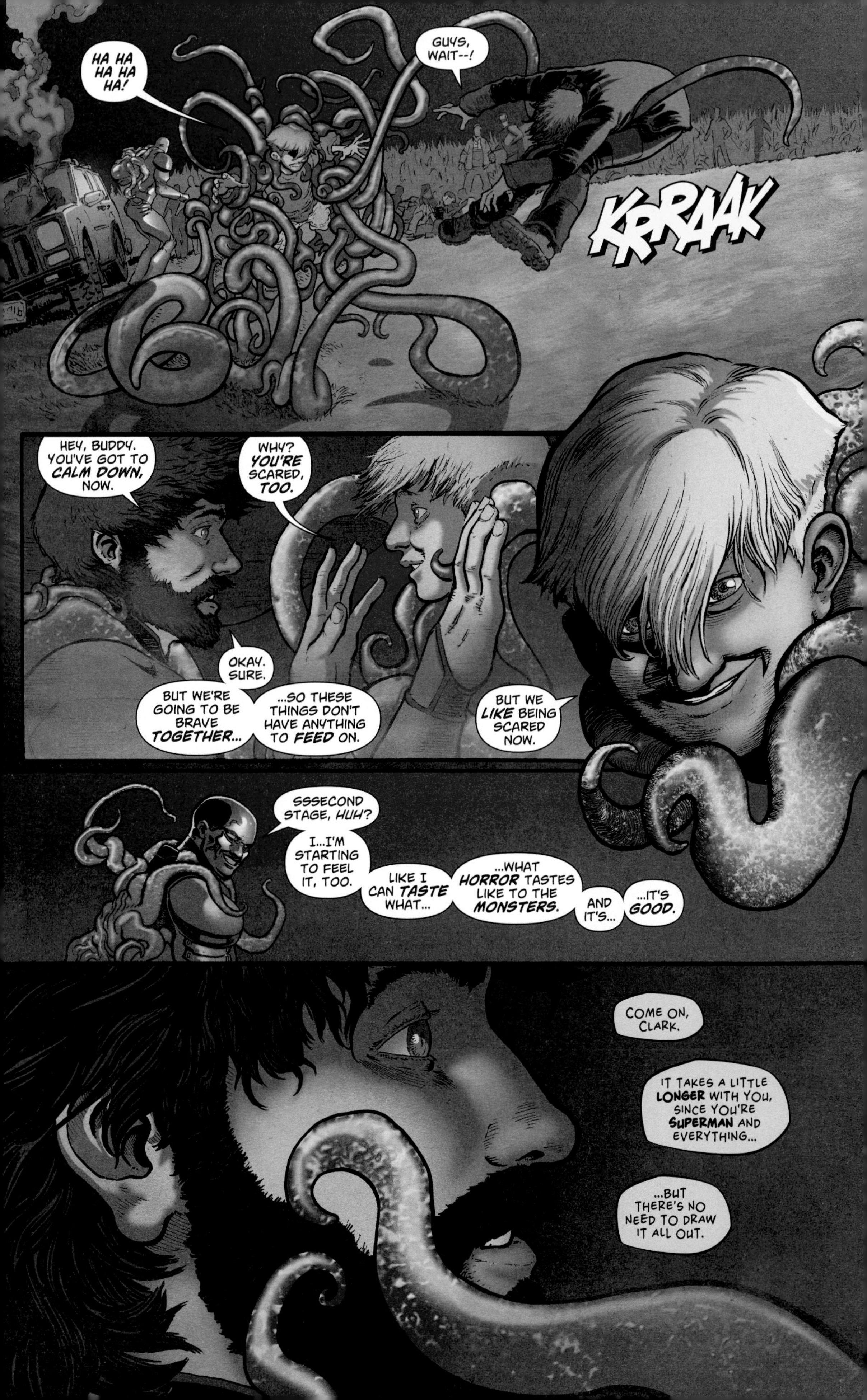
HA HA HA HA HA!
GUYS, WAIT--!
KRRAAK
HEY, BUDDY. YOU'VE GOT TO CALM DOWN, NOW.
WHY? YOU'RE SCARED, TOO.
OKAY. SURE.
BUT WE'RE GOING TO BE BRAVE TOGETHER...
...SO THESE THINGS DON'T HAVE ANYTHING TO FEED ON.
BUT WE LIKE BEING SCARED NOW.
SSSECOND STAGE, HUH?
I...I'M STARTING TO FEEL IT, TOO.
LIKE I CAN TASTE WHAT...
...WHAT HORROR TASTES LIKE TO THE MONSTERS.
AND IT'S...
...IT'S GOOD.
COME ON, CLARK.
IT TAKES A LITTLE LONGER WITH YOU, SINCE YOU'RE SUPERMAN AND EVERYTHING...
...BUT THERE'S NO NEED TO DRAW IT ALL OUT.

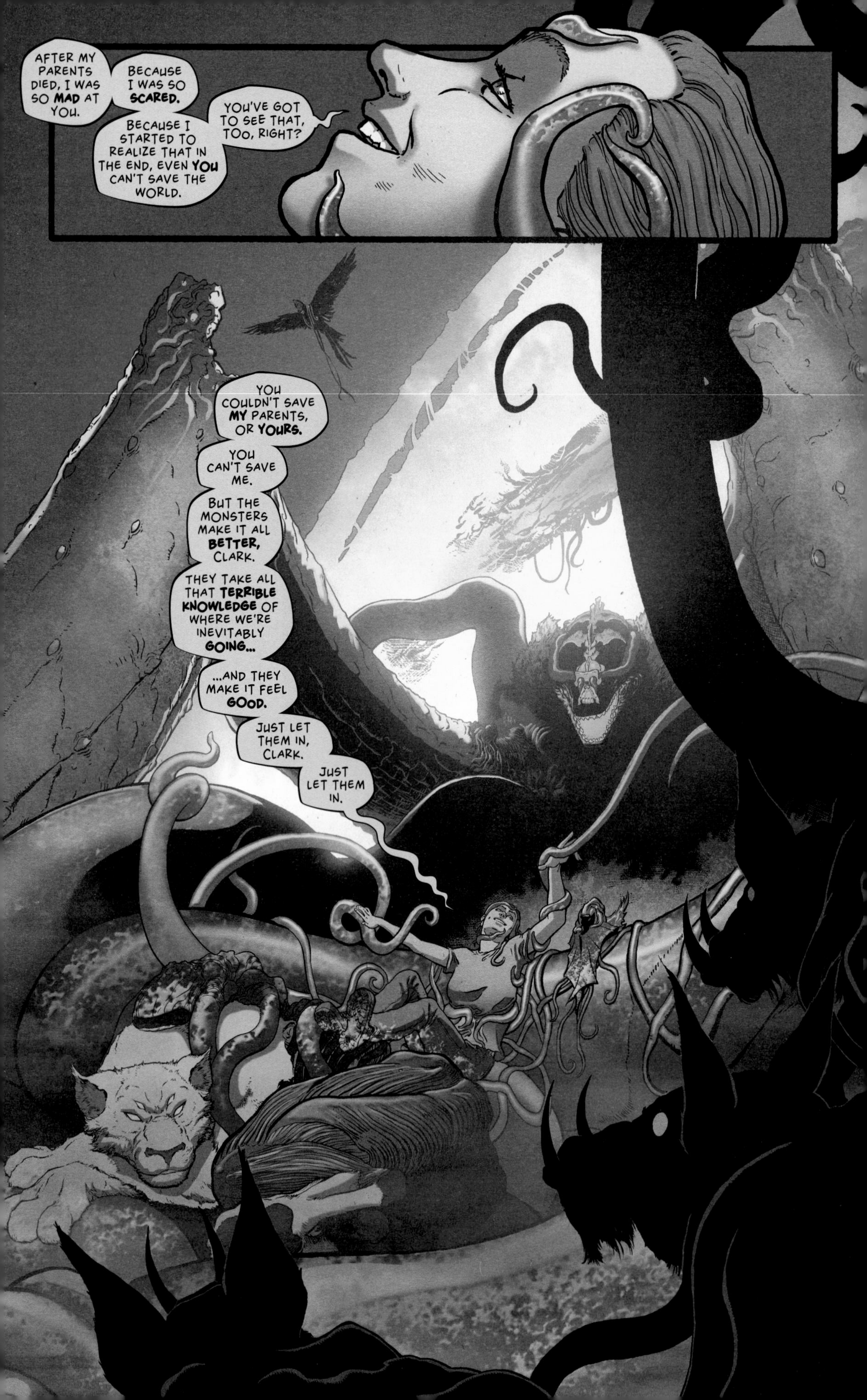
AFTER MY PARENTS DIED, I WAS SO MAD AT YOU.
BECAUSE I WAS SO SCARED.
BECAUSE I STARTED TO REALIZE THAT IN THE END, EVEN YOU CAN'T SAVE THE WORLD.
YOU'VE GOT TO SEE THAT, TOO, RIGHT?
YOU COULDN'T SAVE MY PARENTS, OR YOURS.
YOU CAN'T SAVE ME.
BUT THE MONSTERS MAKE IT ALL BETTER, CLARK.
THEY TAKE ALL THAT TERRIBLE KNOWLEDGE OF WHERE WE'RE INEVITABLY GOING...
...AND THEY MAKE IT FEEL GOOD.
JUST LET THEM IN, CLARK.
JUST LET THEM IN.

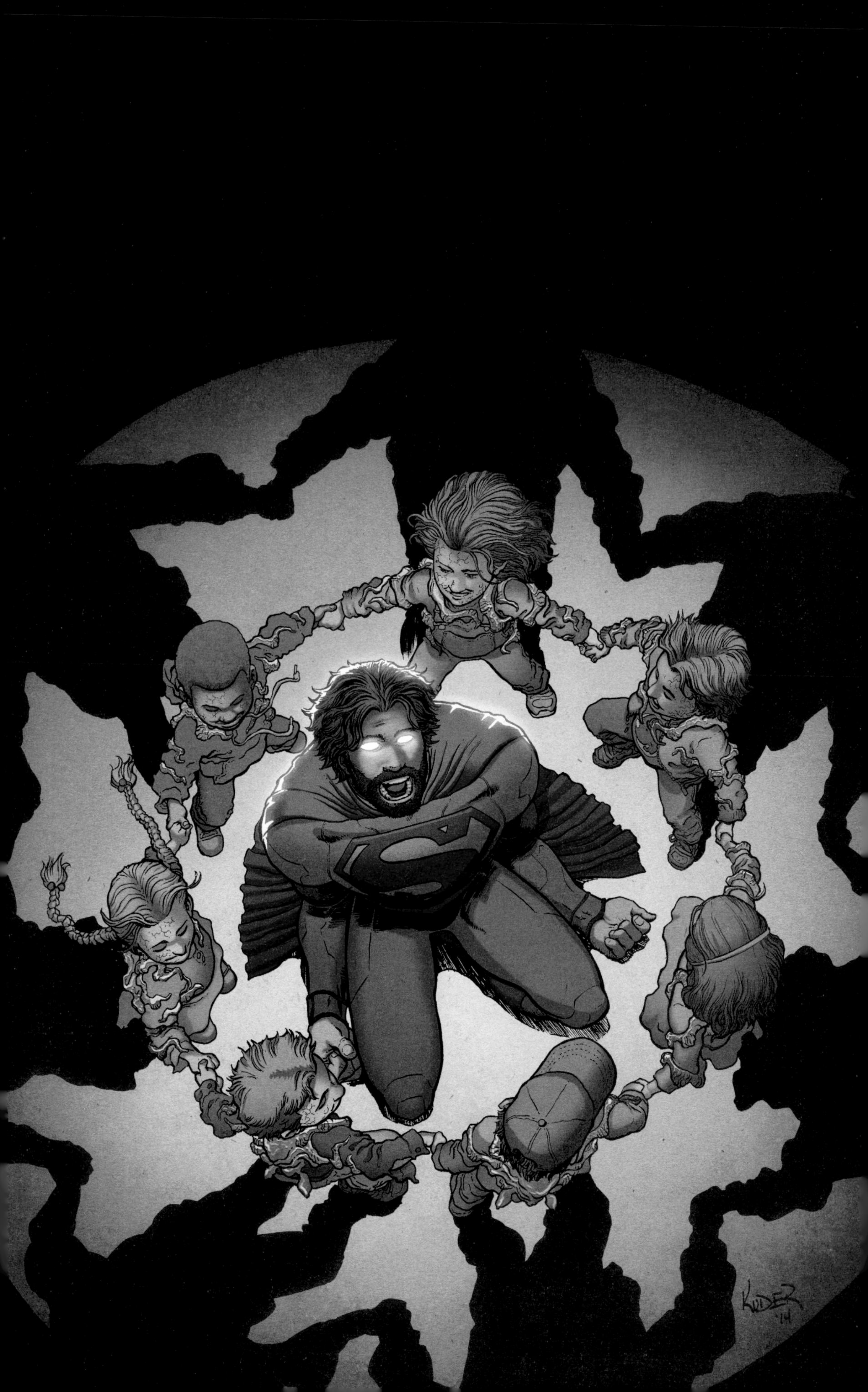

UNDER THE SKIN

GREG PAK writer **SCOTT KOLINS AARON KUDER** artists **WIL QUINTANA** colorist **STEVE WANDS** letterer cover by **AARON KUDER & WIL QUINTANA**

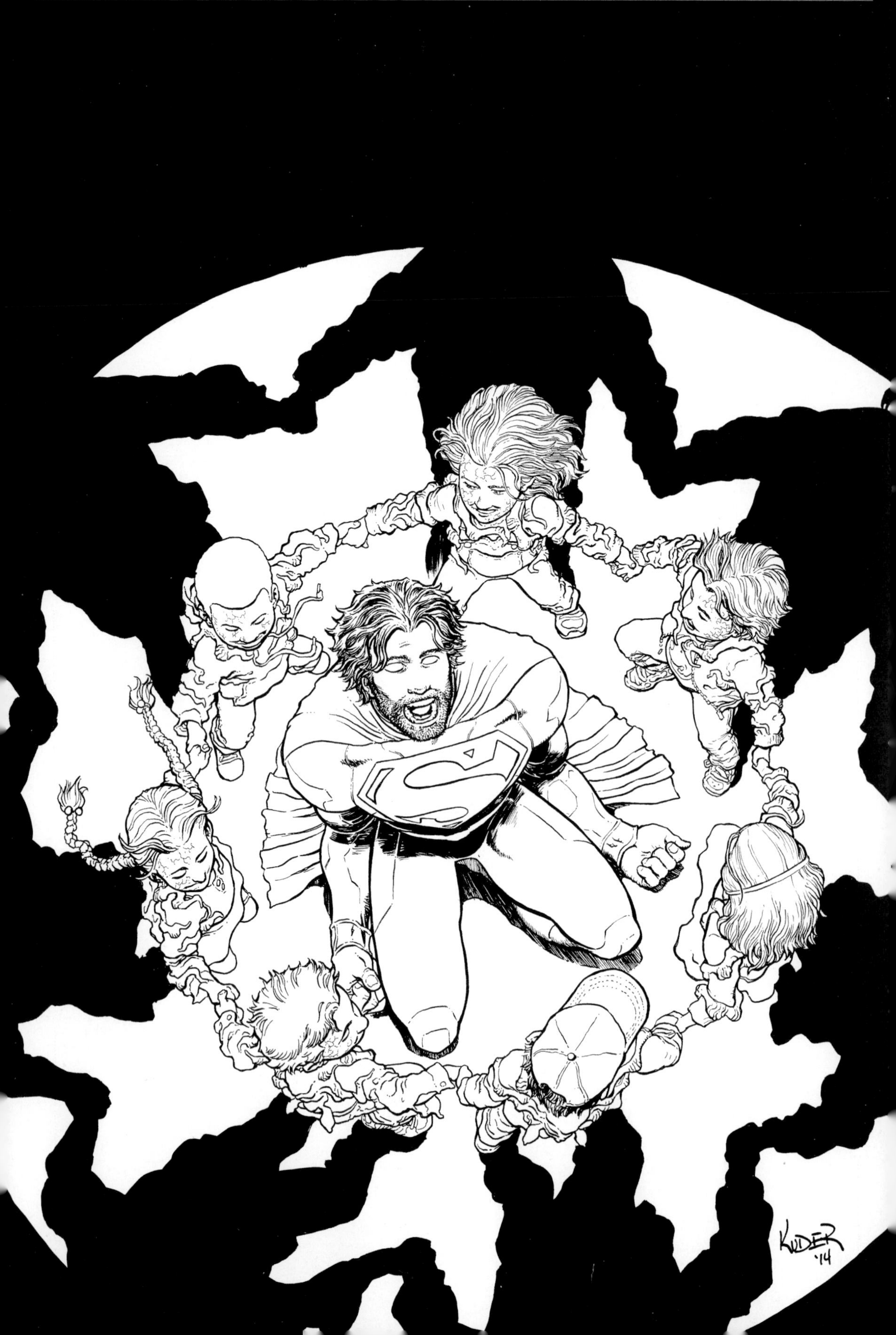
KUDER '14

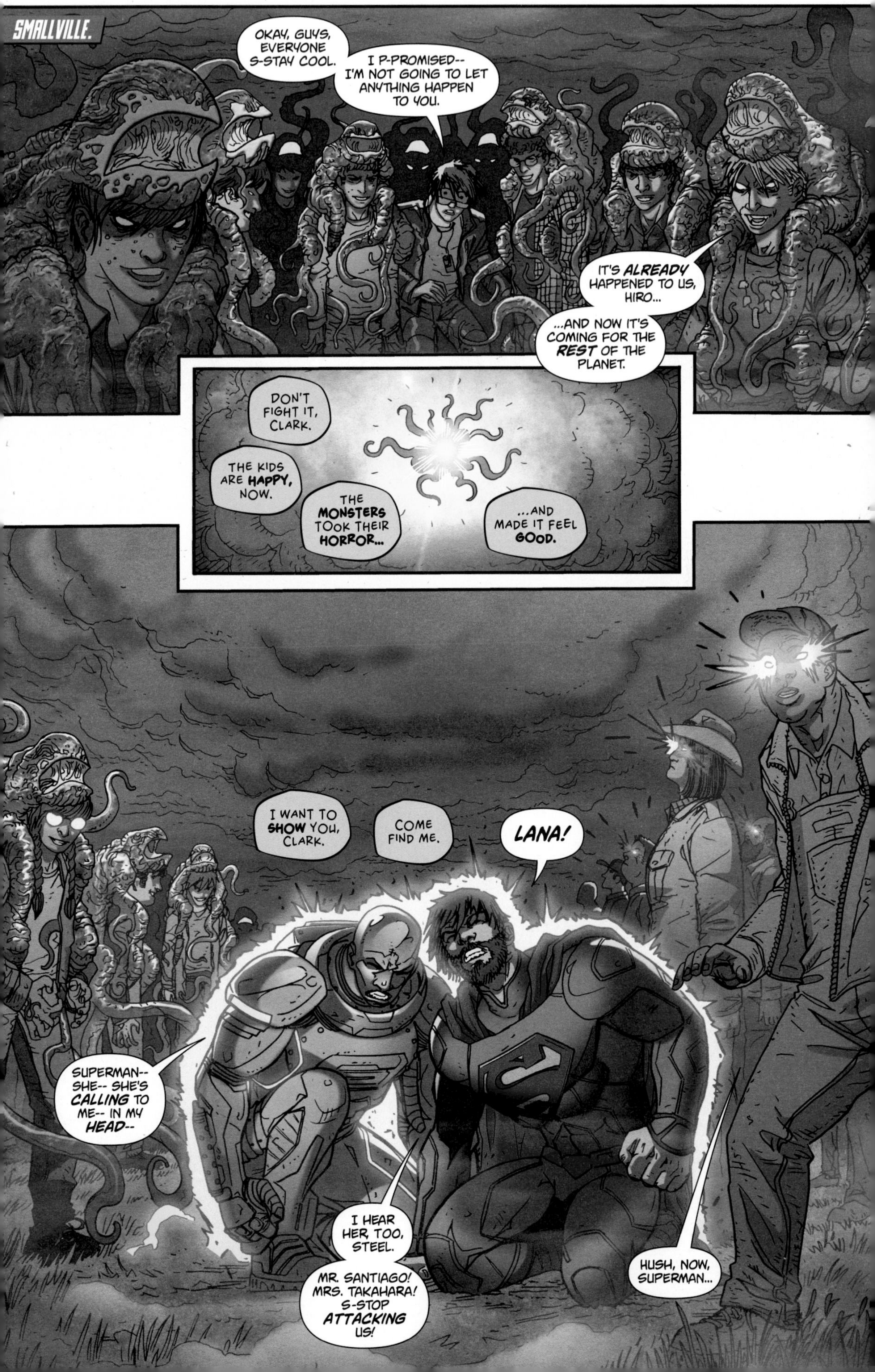
SMALLVILLE.
OKAY, GUYS, EVERYONE S-STAY COOL.
I P-PROMISED-- I'M NOT GOING TO LET ANYTHING HAPPEN TO YOU.
IT'S ALREADY HAPPENED TO US, HIRO...
...AND NOW IT'S COMING FOR THE REST OF THE PLANET.
DON'T FIGHT IT, CLARK.
THE KIDS ARE HAPPY, NOW.
THE MONSTERS TOOK THEIR HORROR...
...AND MADE IT FEEL GOOD.
I WANT TO SHOW YOU, CLARK.
COME FIND ME.
LANA!
SUPERMAN-- SHE-- SHE'S CALLING TO ME-- IN MY HEAD--
I HEAR HER, TOO, STEEL.
MR. SANTIAGO! MRS. TAKAHARA! S-STOP ATTACKING US!
HUSH, NOW, SUPERMAN...

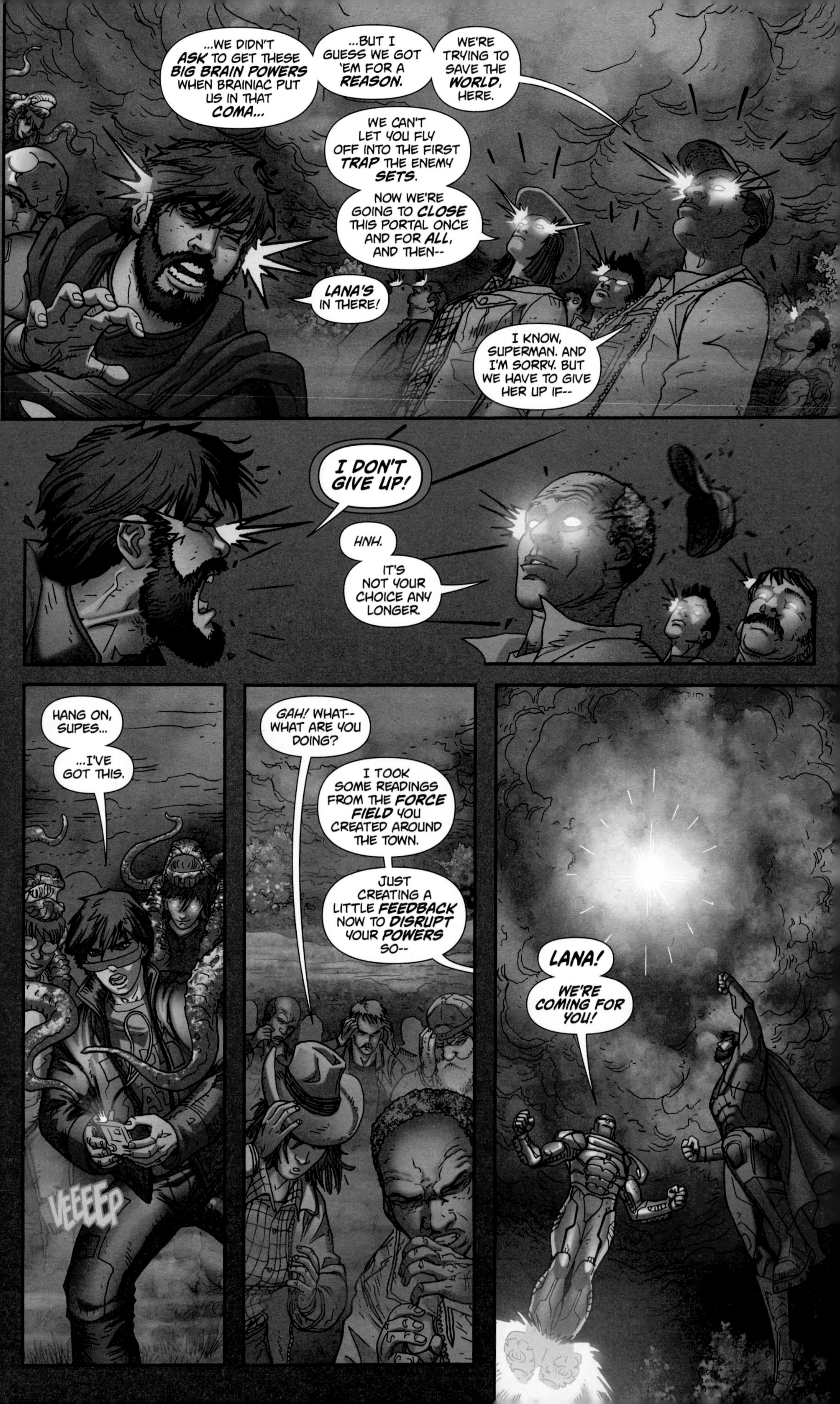
...WE DIDN'T ASK TO GET THESE BIG BRAIN POWERS WHEN BRAINIAC PUT US IN THAT COMA...
...BUT I GUESS WE GOT 'EM FOR A REASON.
WE'RE TRYING TO SAVE THE WORLD, HERE.
WE CAN'T LET YOU FLY OFF INTO THE FIRST TRAP THE ENEMY SETS.
NOW WE'RE GOING TO CLOSE THIS PORTAL ONCE AND FOR ALL, AND THEN--
LANA'S IN THERE!
I KNOW, SUPERMAN. AND I'M SORRY. BUT WE HAVE TO GIVE HER UP IF--
I DON'T GIVE UP!
HNH.
IT'S NOT YOUR CHOICE ANY LONGER.
HANG ON, SUPES...
...I'VE GOT THIS.
VEEEEP
GAH! WHAT-- WHAT ARE YOU DOING?
I TOOK SOME READINGS FROM THE FORCE FIELD YOU CREATED AROUND THE TOWN.
JUST CREATING A LITTLE FEEDBACK NOW TO DISRUPT YOUR POWERS SO--
LANA!
WE'RE COMING FOR YOU!

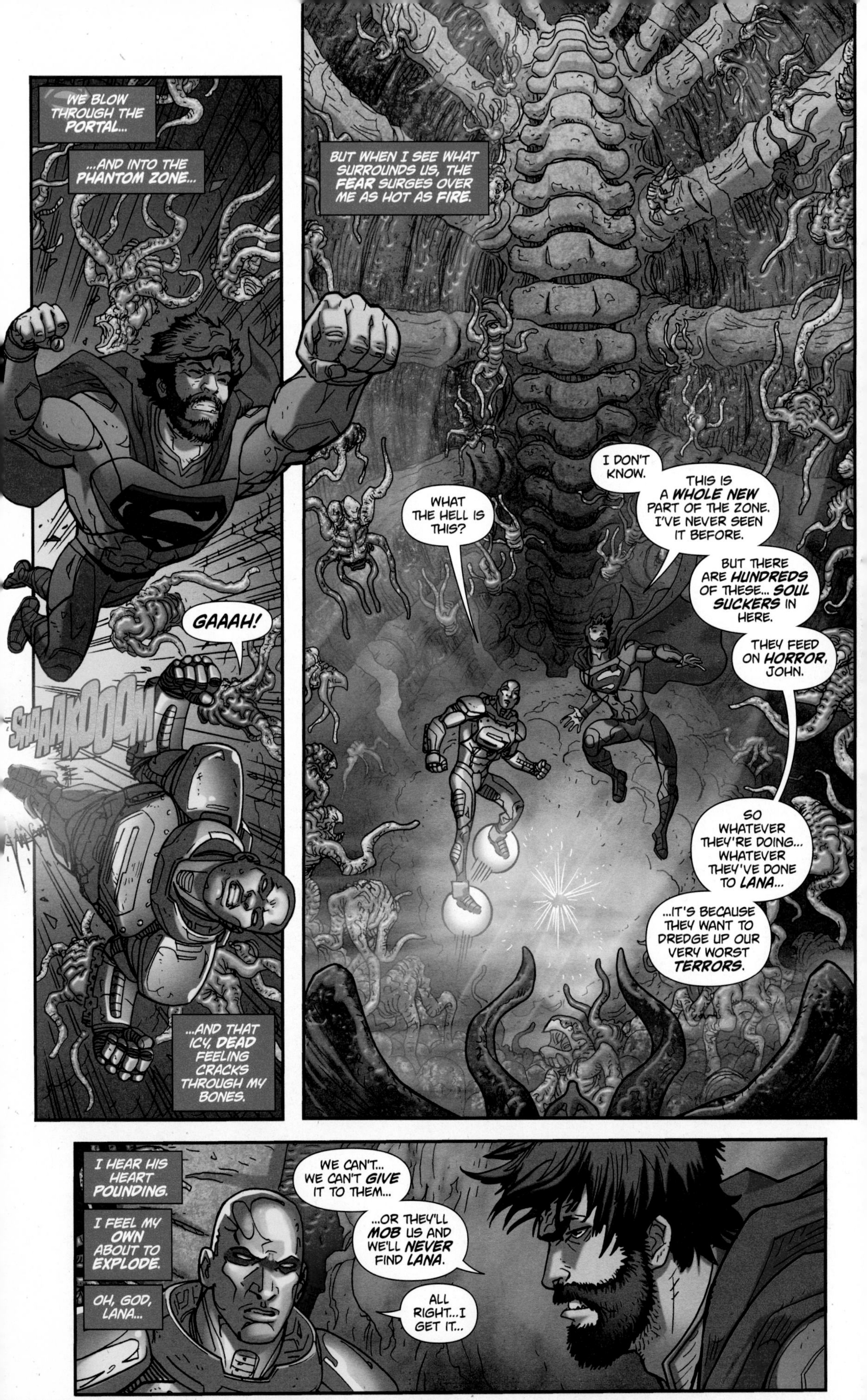
WE BLOW THROUGH THE PORTAL...
...AND INTO THE PHANTOM ZONE...
GAAAH!
SHAAAKOOOM
...AND THAT ICY, DEAD FEELING CRACKS THROUGH MY BONES.
BUT WHEN I SEE WHAT SURROUNDS US, THE FEAR SURGES OVER ME AS HOT AS FIRE.
WHAT THE HELL IS THIS?
I DON'T KNOW.
THIS IS A WHOLE NEW PART OF THE ZONE. I'VE NEVER SEEN IT BEFORE.
BUT THERE ARE HUNDREDS OF THESE... SOUL SUCKERS IN HERE.
THEY FEED ON HORROR, JOHN.
SO WHATEVER THEY'RE DOING... WHATEVER THEY'VE DONE TO LANA...
...IT'S BECAUSE THEY WANT TO DREDGE UP OUR VERY WORST TERRORS.
I HEAR HIS HEART POUNDING.
I FEEL MY OWN ABOUT TO EXPLODE.
OH, GOD, LANA...
WE CAN'T... WE CAN'T GIVE IT TO THEM...
...OR THEY'LL MOB US AND WE'LL NEVER FIND LANA.
ALL RIGHT...I GET IT...

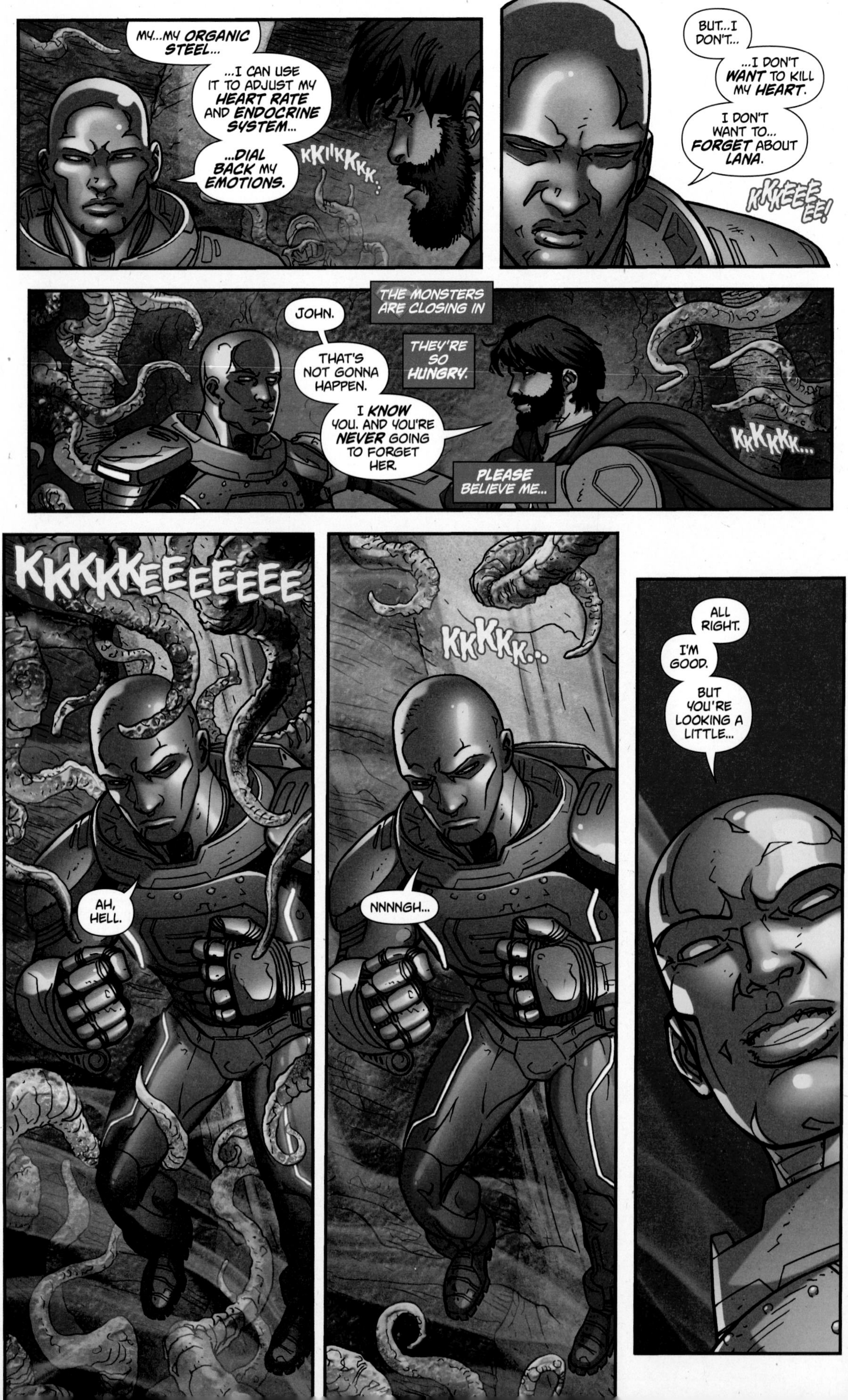
MY...MY ORGANIC STEEL...
...I CAN USE IT TO ADJUST MY HEART RATE AND ENDOCRINE SYSTEM...
...DIAL BACK MY EMOTIONS.
KKIIKKKK...
BUT...I DON'T...
...I DON'T WANT TO KILL MY HEART.
I DON'T WANT TO... FORGET ABOUT LANA.
KKKEEEEE!
THE MONSTERS ARE CLOSING IN
JOHN.
THAT'S NOT GONNA HAPPEN.
THEY'RE SO HUNGRY.
I KNOW YOU. AND YOU'RE NEVER GOING TO FORGET HER.
PLEASE BELIEVE ME...
KKKKKK...
KKKKKEEEEEEE
AH, HELL.
KKKKK..
NNNNGH...
ALL RIGHT.
I'M GOOD.
BUT YOU'RE LOOKING A LITTLE...

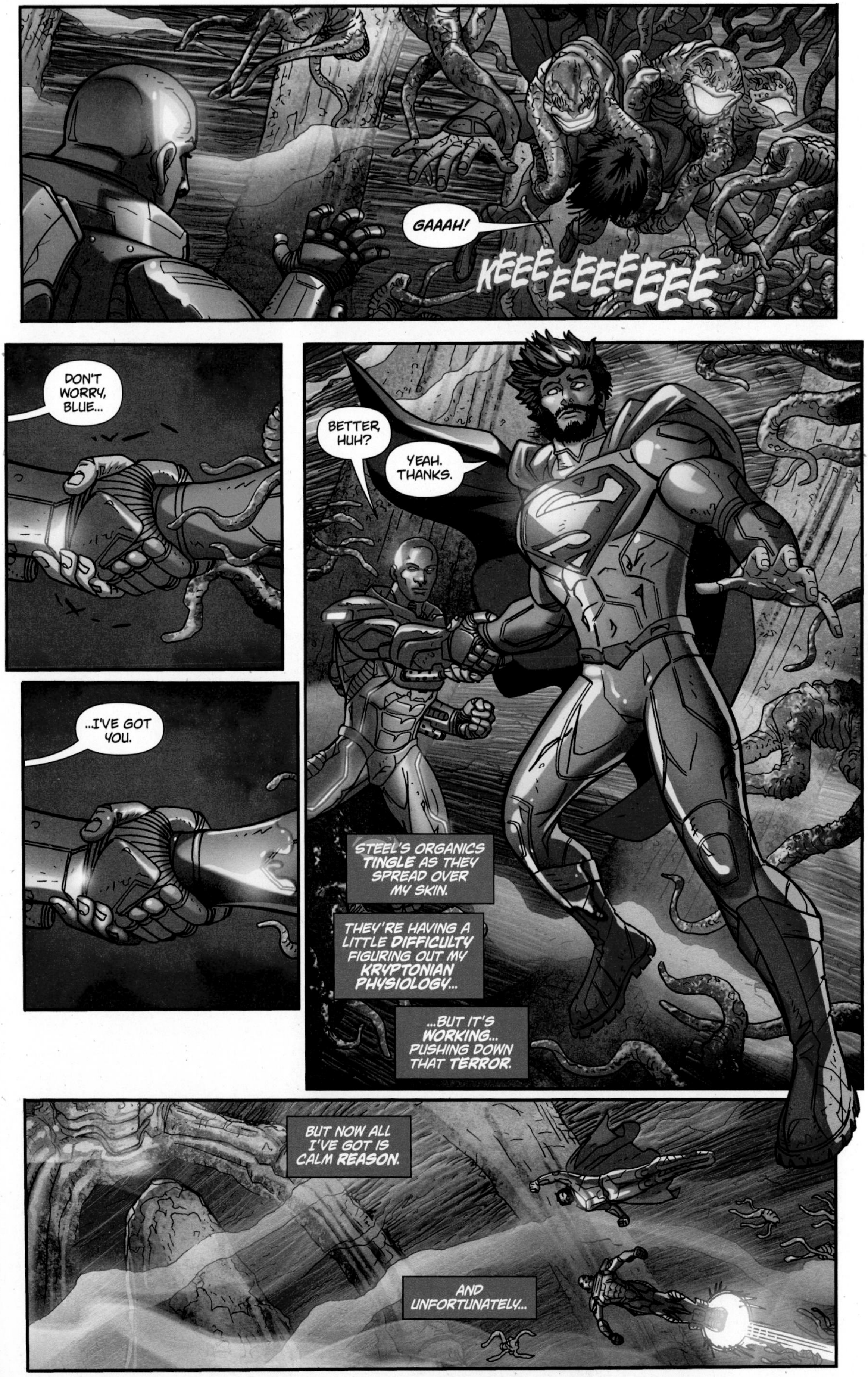
GAAAH!
KEEEEEEEEEEE
DON'T WORRY, BLUE...
...I'VE GOT YOU.
BETTER, HUH?
YEAH. THANKS.
STEEL'S ORGANICS TINGLE AS THEY SPREAD OVER MY SKIN.
THEY'RE HAVING A LITTLE DIFFICULTY FIGURING OUT MY KRYPTONIAN PHYSIOLOGY...
...BUT IT'S WORKING... PUSHING DOWN THAT TERROR.
BUT NOW ALL I'VE GOT IS CALM REASON.
AND UNFORTUNATELY...

...THAT MEANS I DON'T HAVE ANY WAY TO AVOID UNDERSTANDING HOW BAD OUR ODDS LOOK.

AH. THIS MUST BE THE THIRD STAGE OF THE PROCESS.

WHEN THE HOST BODIES GET USED UP.

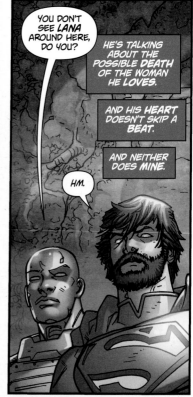

YOU DON'T SEE LANA AROUND HERE, DO YOU?

HE'S TALKING ABOUT THE POSSIBLE DEATH OF THE WOMAN HE LOVES.

AND HIS HEART DOESN'T SKIP A BEAT.

AND NEITHER DOES MINE.

HM.

NO.

NOT THAT I CAN TELL.

WELL, THAT'S GOOD.

YES.

CLARK... SO NICE TO SEE YOU.

THERE... SHE'S IN MY HEAD AGAIN.

SHE'S TALKING TO ME, TOO, GIVING ME DIRECTIONS...

OH, NO.

LANA!

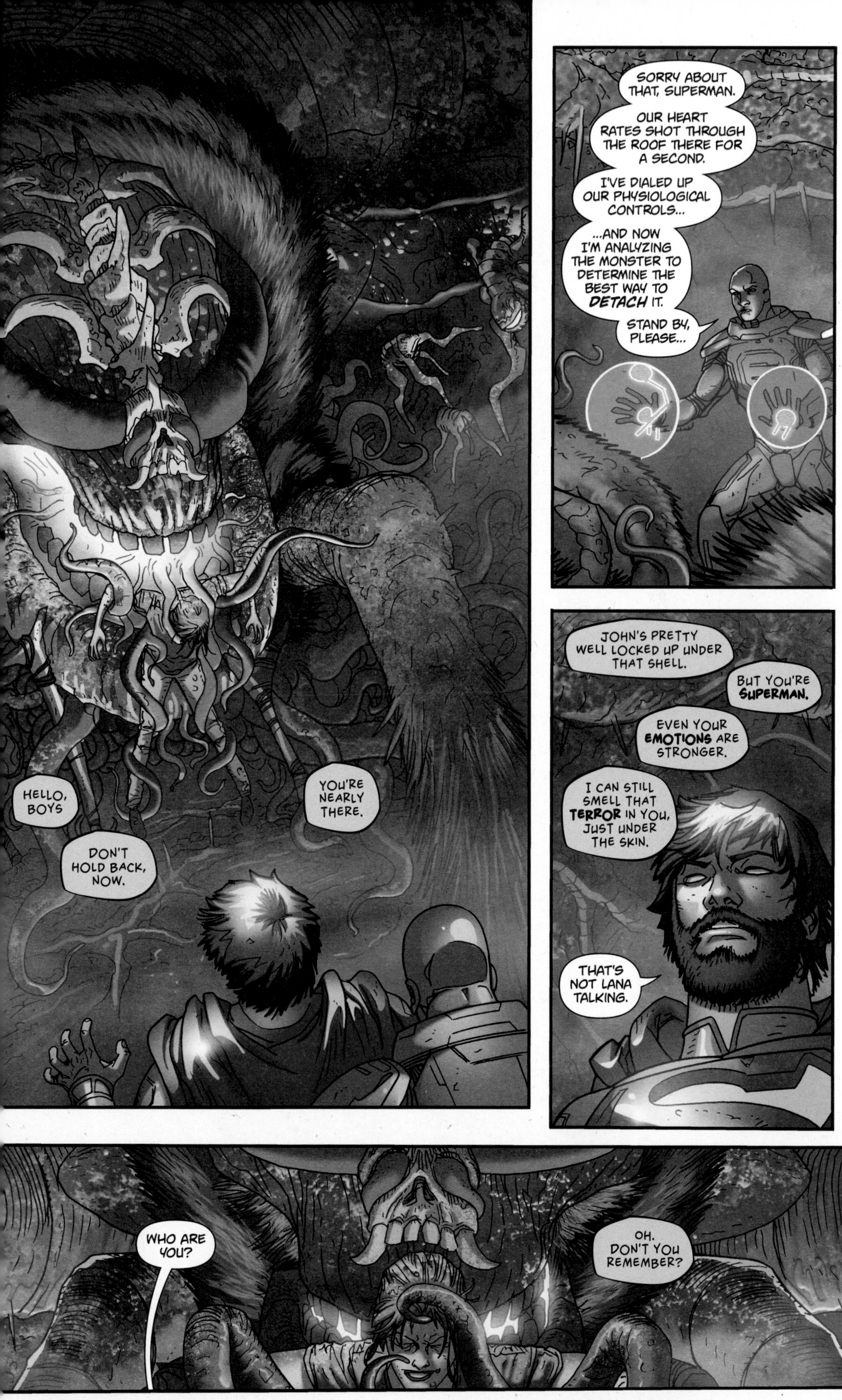
HELLO, BOYS
YOU'RE NEARLY THERE.
DON'T HOLD BACK, NOW.
SORRY ABOUT THAT, SUPERMAN.
OUR HEART RATES SHOT THROUGH THE ROOF THERE FOR A SECOND.
I'VE DIALED UP OUR PHYSIOLOGICAL CONTROLS...
...AND NOW I'M ANALYZING THE MONSTER TO DETERMINE THE BEST WAY TO DETACH IT.
STAND BY, PLEASE...
JOHN'S PRETTY WELL LOCKED UP UNDER THAT SHELL.
BUT YOU'RE SUPERMAN.
EVEN YOUR EMOTIONS ARE STRONGER.
I CAN STILL SMELL THAT TERROR IN YOU, JUST UNDER THE SKIN.
THAT'S NOT LANA TALKING.
WHO ARE YOU?
OH. DON'T YOU REMEMBER?

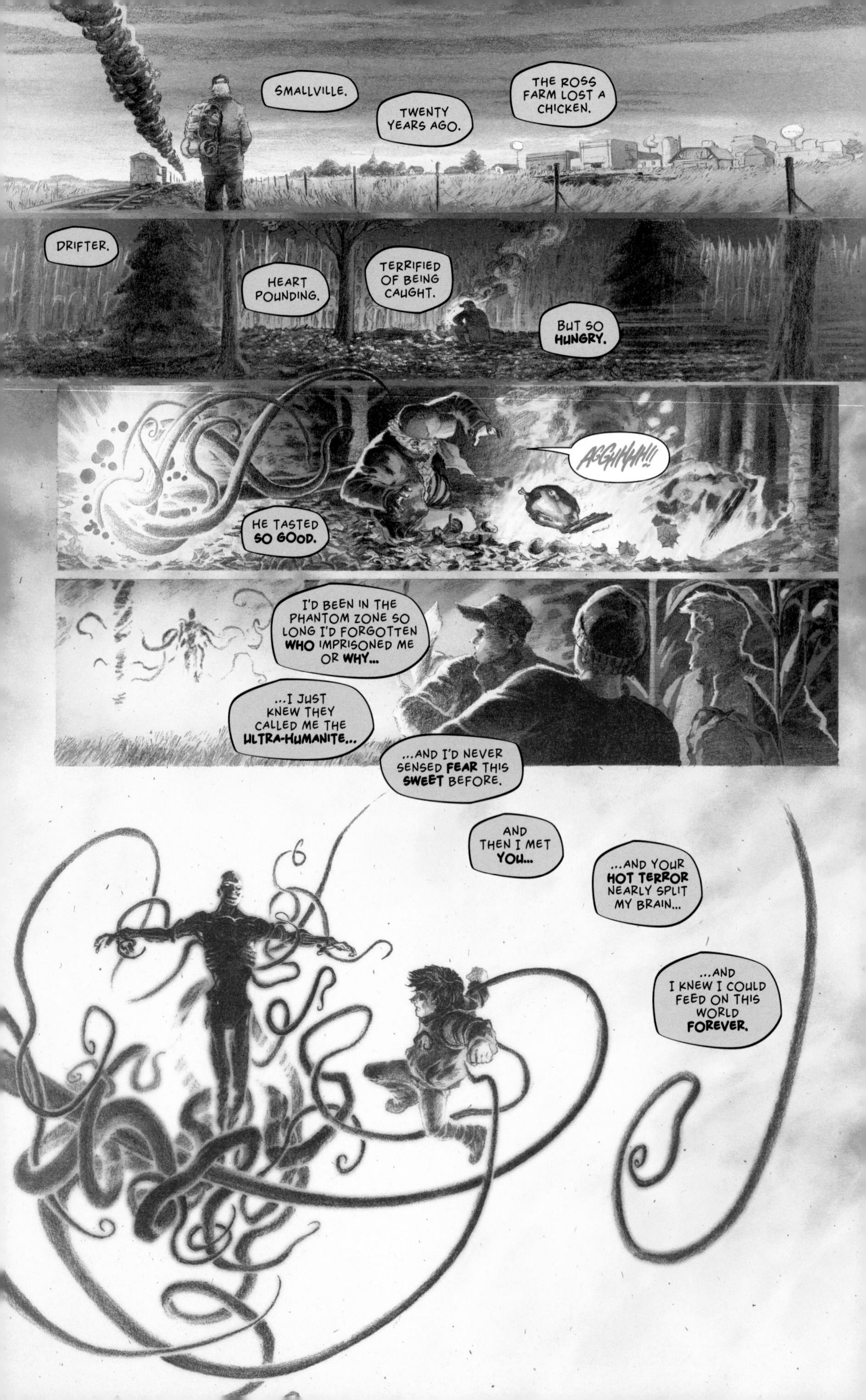
SMALLVILLE.
TWENTY YEARS AGO.
THE ROSS FARM LOST A CHICKEN.
DRIFTER.
HEART POUNDING.
TERRIFIED OF BEING CAUGHT.
BUT SO HUNGRY.
AGGHHH!!
HE TASTED SO GOOD.
I'D BEEN IN THE PHANTOM ZONE SO LONG I'D FORGOTTEN WHO IMPRISONED ME OR WHY...
...I JUST KNEW THEY CALLED ME THE ULTRA-HUMANITE...
...AND I'D NEVER SENSED FEAR THIS SWEET BEFORE.
AND THEN I MET YOU...
...AND YOUR HOT TERROR NEARLY SPLIT MY BRAIN...
...AND I KNEW I COULD FEED ON THIS WORLD FOREVER.

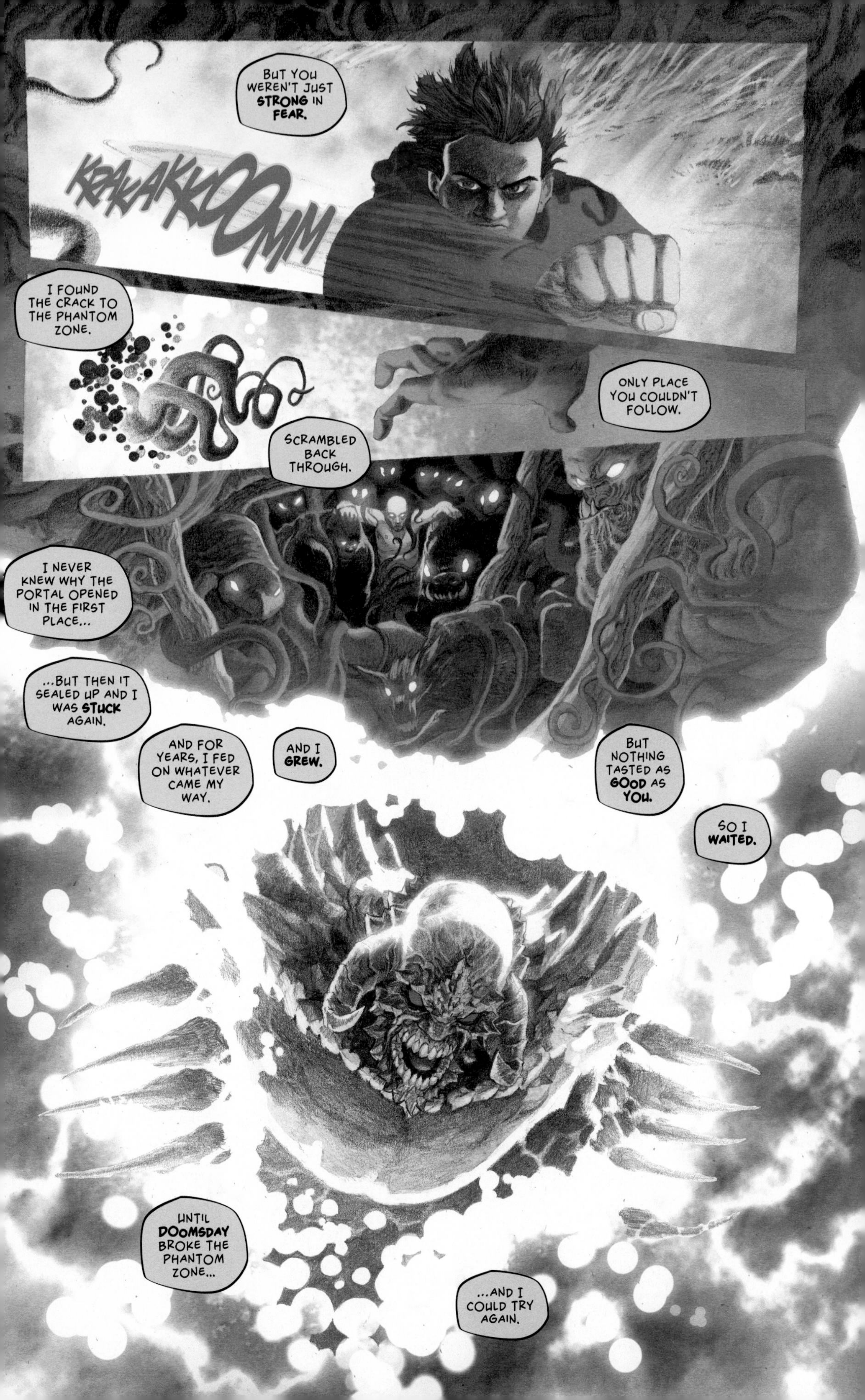
BUT YOU WEREN'T JUST STRONG IN FEAR.
KRAKAKKOOMM
I FOUND THE CRACK TO THE PHANTOM ZONE.
ONLY PLACE YOU COULDN'T FOLLOW.
SCRAMBLED BACK THROUGH.
I NEVER KNEW WHY THE PORTAL OPENED IN THE FIRST PLACE...
...BUT THEN IT SEALED UP AND I WAS STUCK AGAIN.
AND FOR YEARS, I FED ON WHATEVER CAME MY WAY.
AND I GREW.
BUT NOTHING TASTED AS GOOD AS YOU.
SO I WAITED.
UNTIL DOOMSDAY BROKE THE PHANTOM ZONE...
...AND I COULD TRY AGAIN.

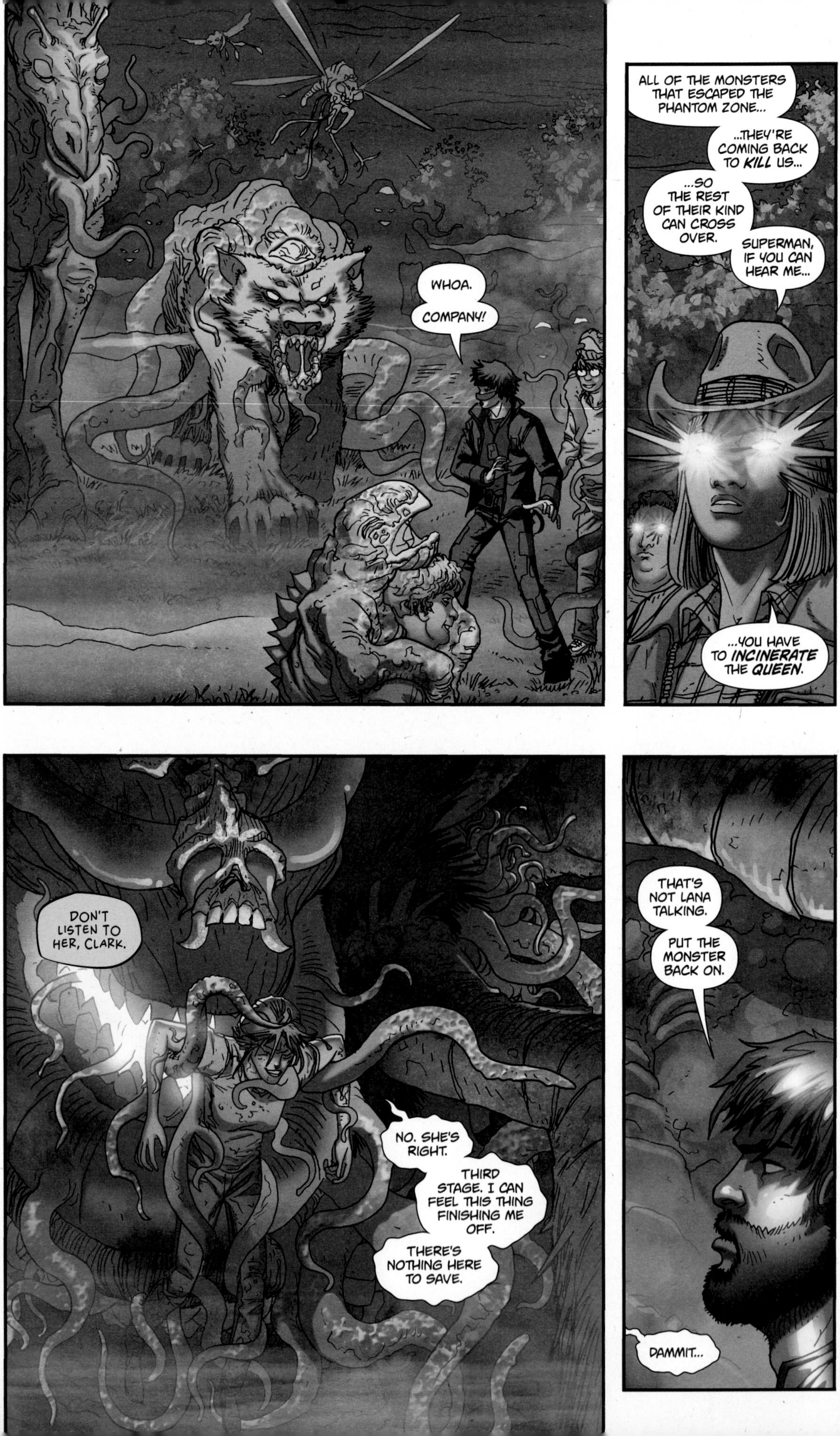
WHOA.
COMPANY!
ALL OF THE MONSTERS THAT ESCAPED THE PHANTOM ZONE...
...THEY'RE COMING BACK TO *KILL* US...
...SO THE REST OF THEIR KIND CAN CROSS OVER.
SUPERMAN, IF YOU CAN HEAR ME...
...YOU HAVE TO ***INCINERATE*** THE ***QUEEN***.
DON'T LISTEN TO HER, CLARK.
NO. SHE'S RIGHT.
THIRD STAGE. I CAN FEEL THIS THING FINISHING ME OFF.
THERE'S NOTHING HERE TO SAVE.
THAT'S NOT LANA TALKING.
PUT THE MONSTER BACK ON.
DAMMIT...

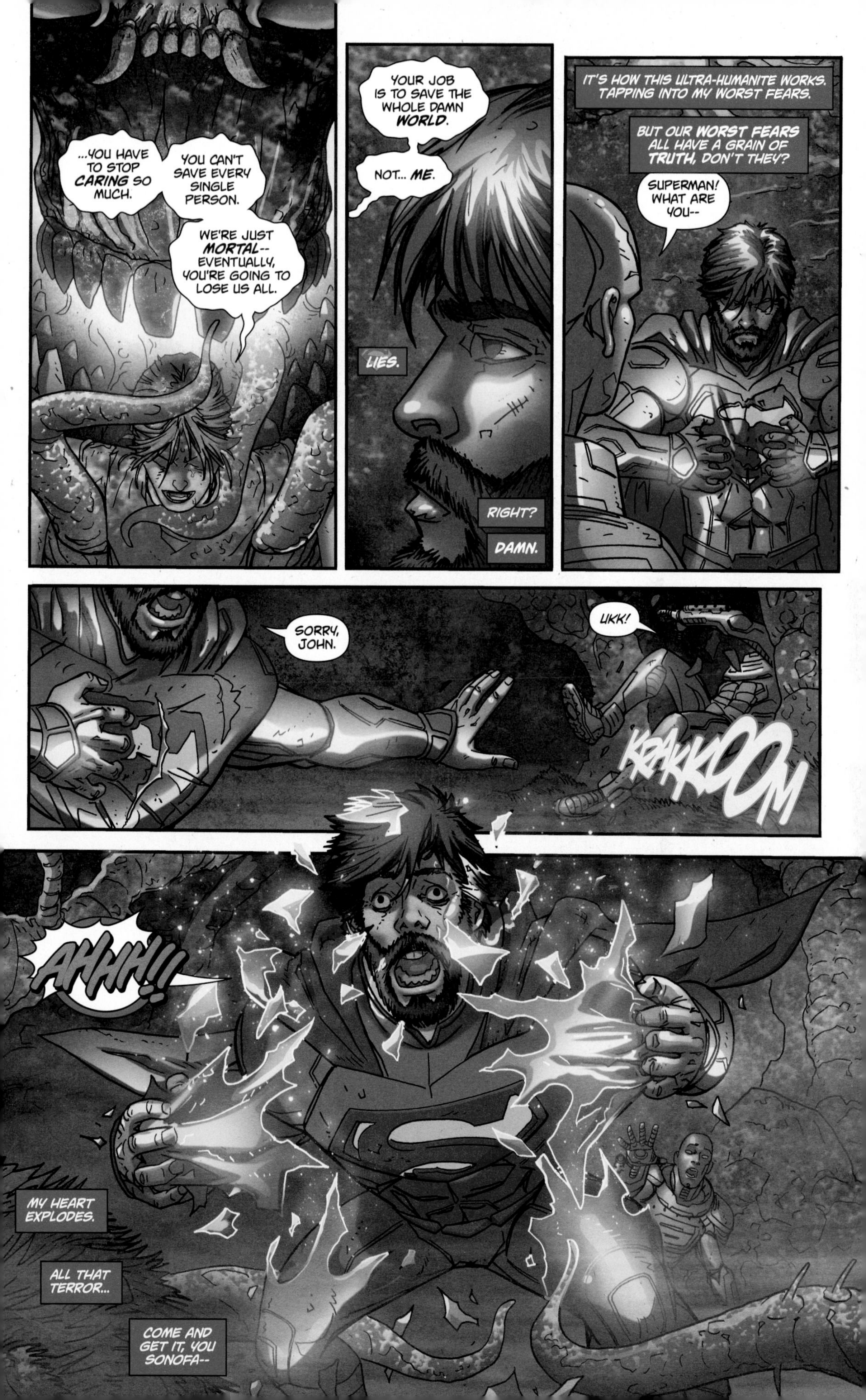
...YOU HAVE TO STOP CARING SO MUCH.
YOU CAN'T SAVE EVERY SINGLE PERSON.
WE'RE JUST MORTAL-- EVENTUALLY, YOU'RE GOING TO LOSE US ALL.
YOUR JOB IS TO SAVE THE WHOLE DAMN WORLD.
NOT... ME.
LIES.
RIGHT?
DAMN.
IT'S HOW THIS ULTRA-HUMANITE WORKS. TAPPING INTO MY WORST FEARS.
BUT OUR WORST FEARS ALL HAVE A GRAIN OF TRUTH, DON'T THEY?
SUPERMAN! WHAT ARE YOU--
SORRY, JOHN.
UKK!
KRAKKOOM
AHHH!!!
MY HEART EXPLODES.
ALL THAT TERROR...
COME AND GET IT, YOU SONOFA--

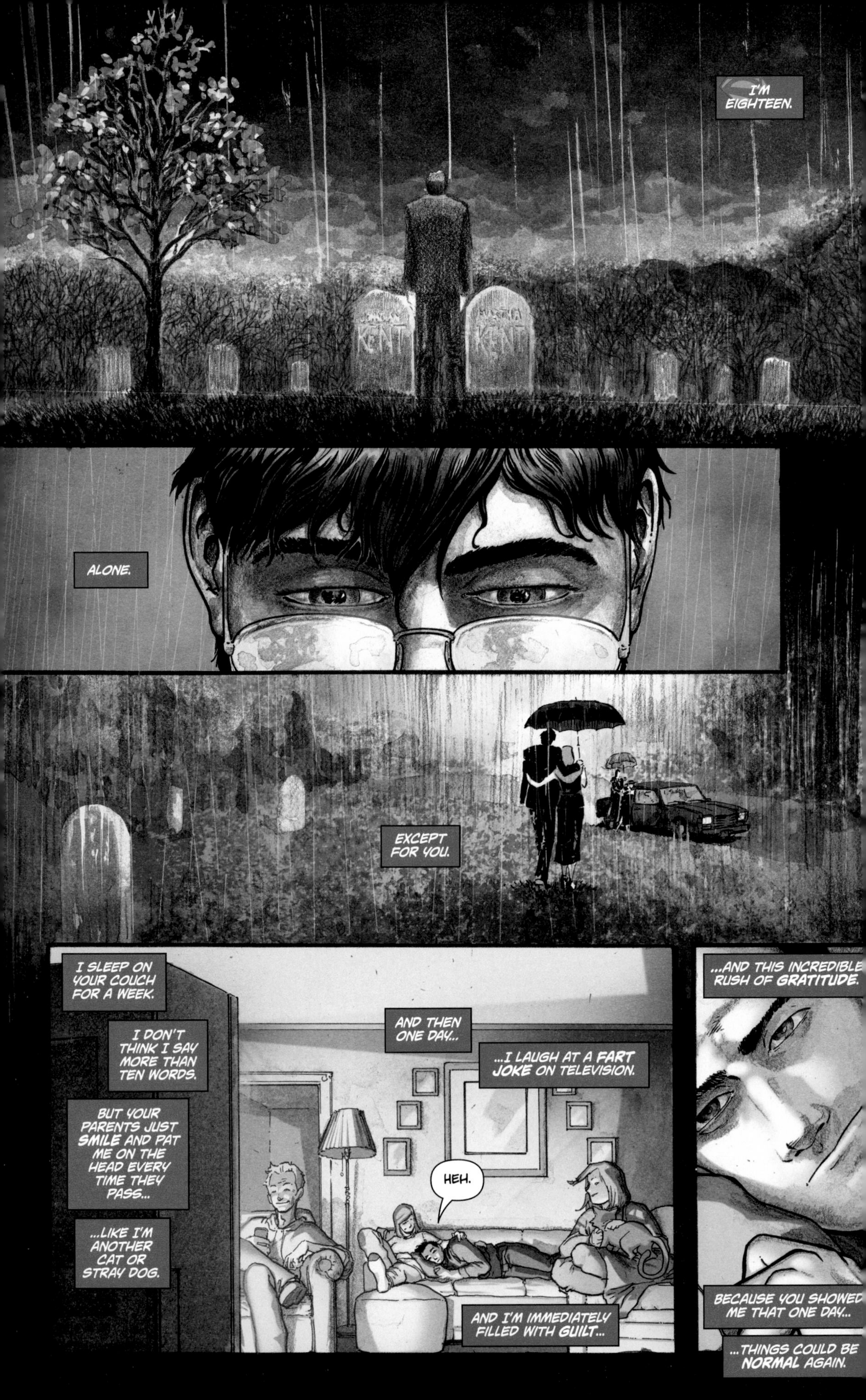
I'M EIGHTEEN.
ALONE.
EXCEPT FOR YOU.
I SLEEP ON YOUR COUCH FOR A WEEK.
I DON'T THINK I SAY MORE THAN TEN WORDS.
BUT YOUR PARENTS JUST SMILE AND PAT ME ON THE HEAD EVERY TIME THEY PASS...
...LIKE I'M ANOTHER CAT OR STRAY DOG.
AND THEN ONE DAY...
...I LAUGH AT A FART JOKE ON TELEVISION.
HEH.
AND I'M IMMEDIATELY FILLED WITH GUILT...
...AND THIS INCREDIBLE RUSH OF GRATITUDE.
BECAUSE YOU SHOWED ME THAT ONE DAY...
...THINGS COULD BE NORMAL AGAIN.

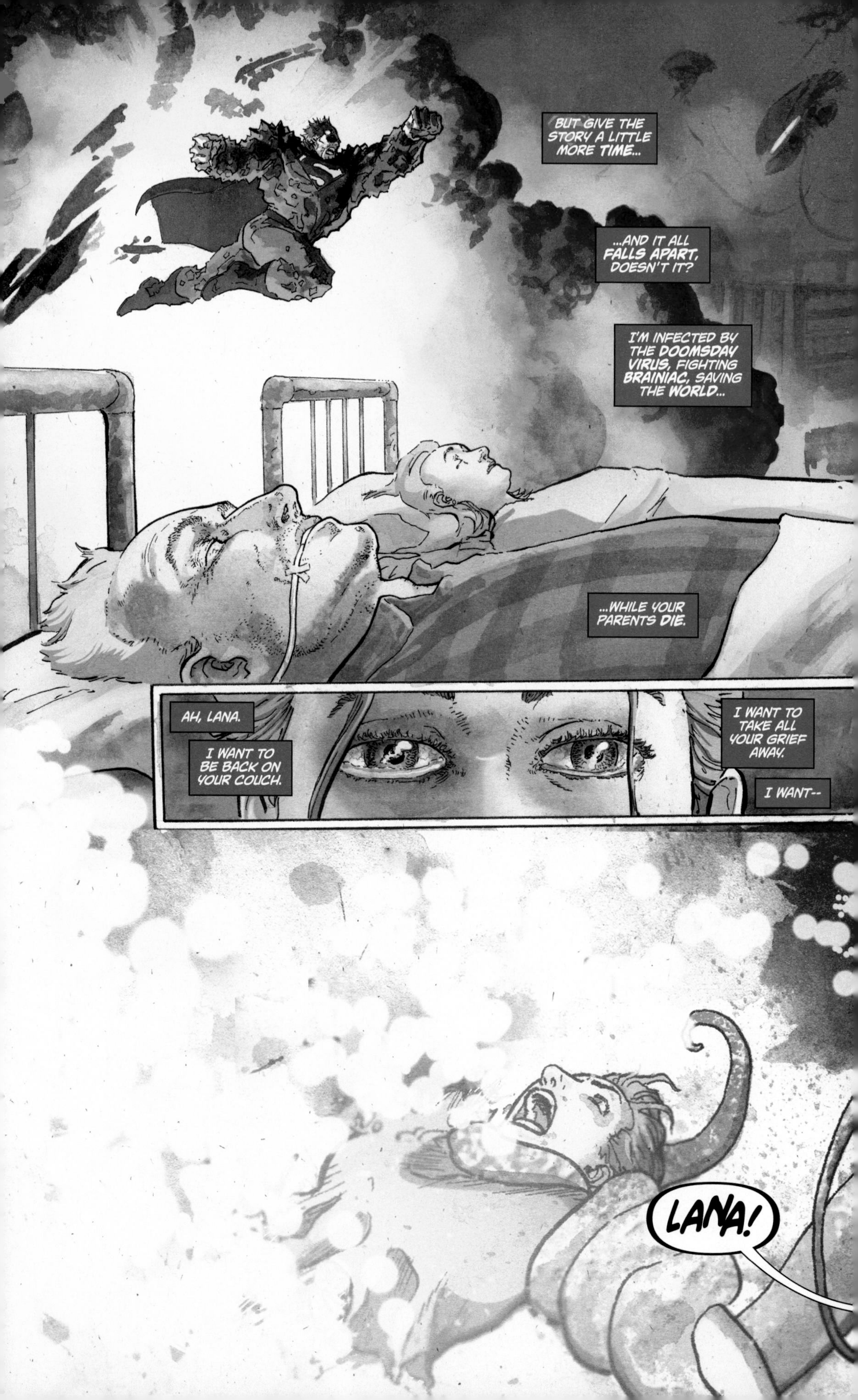
BUT GIVE THE STORY A LITTLE MORE TIME...
...AND IT ALL FALLS APART, DOESN'T IT?
I'M INFECTED BY THE DOOMSDAY VIRUS, FIGHTING BRAINIAC, SAVING THE WORLD...
...WHILE YOUR PARENTS DIE.
AH, LANA.
I WANT TO BE BACK ON YOUR COUCH.
I WANT TO TAKE ALL YOUR GRIEF AWAY.
I WANT--
LANA!

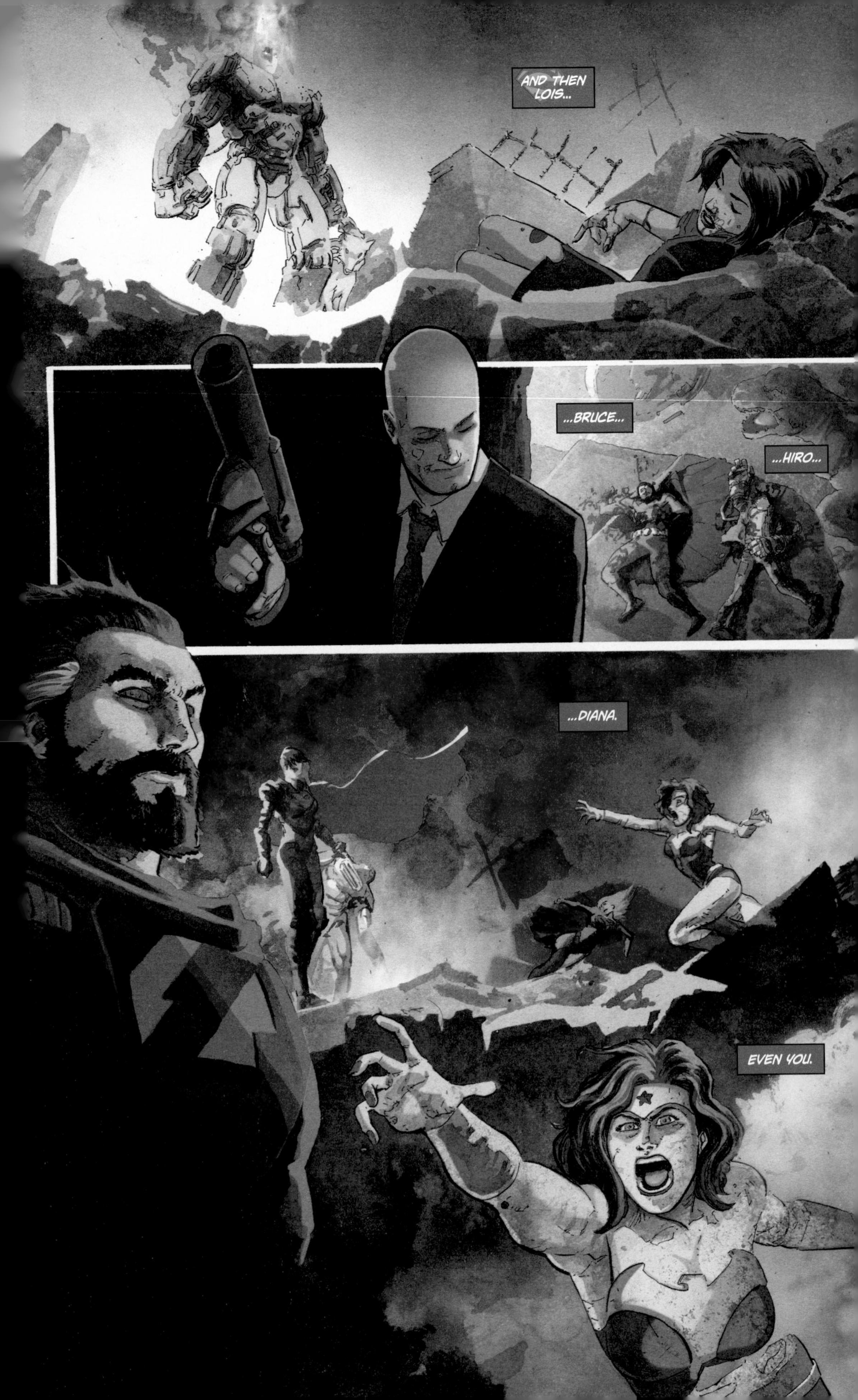
AND THEN LOIS...
...BRUCE...
...HIRO...
...DIANA.
EVEN YOU.

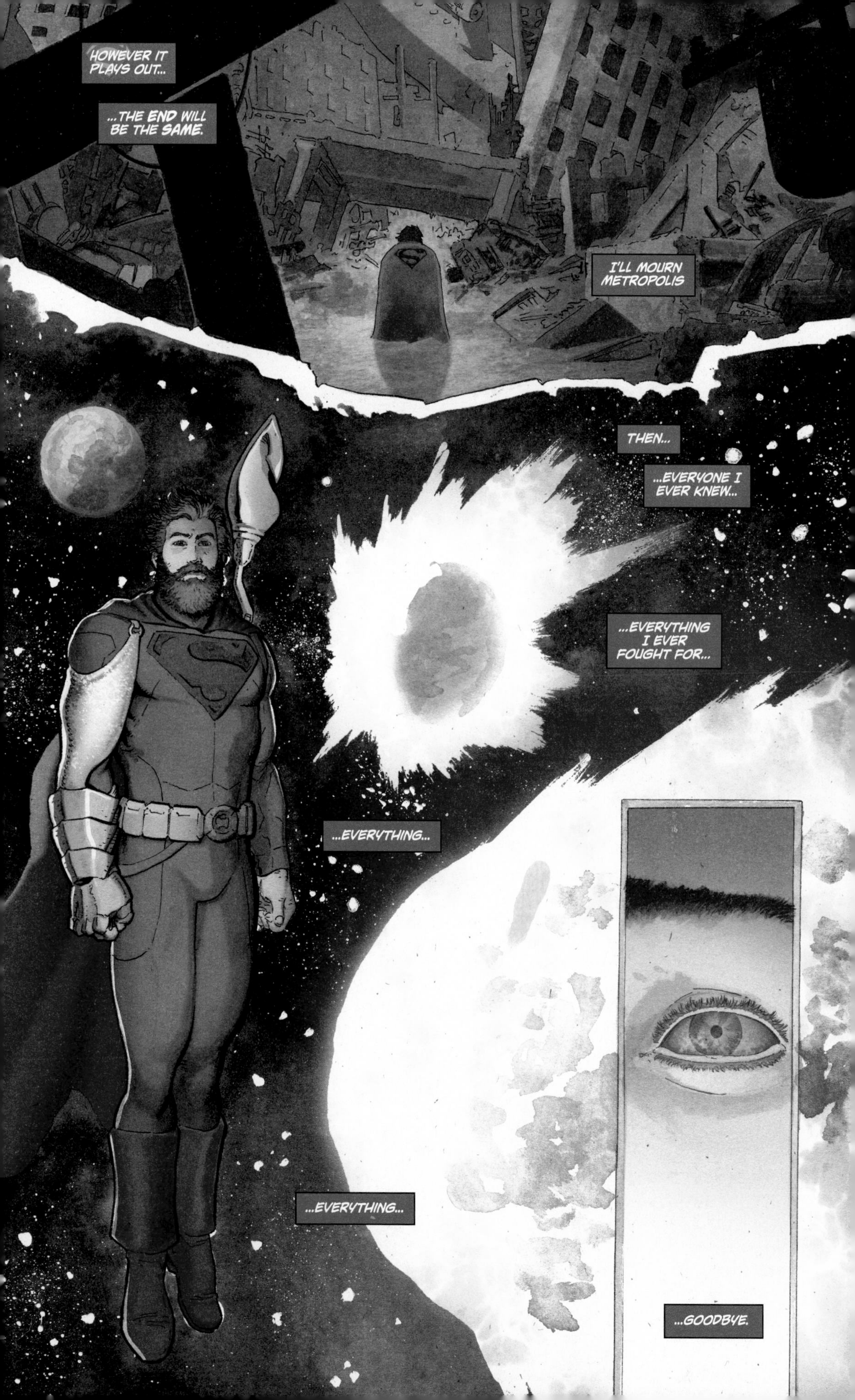
HOWEVER IT PLAYS OUT...
...THE END WILL BE THE SAME.
I'LL MOURN METROPOLIS
THEN...
...EVERYONE I EVER KNEW...
...EVERYTHING I EVER FOUGHT FOR...
...EVERYTHING...
...EVERYTHING...
...GOODBYE.

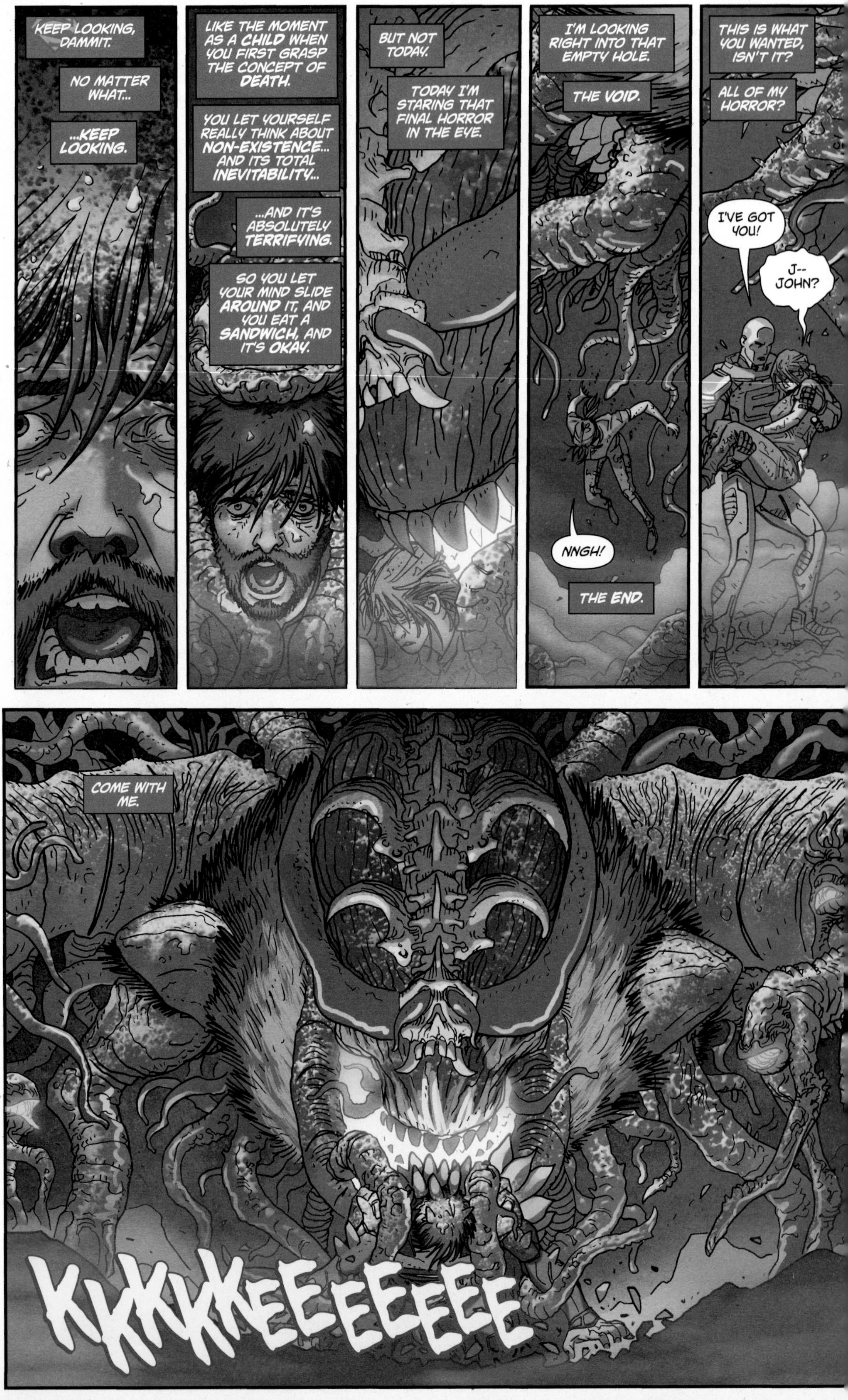
KEEP LOOKING, DAMMIT.
NO MATTER WHAT...
...KEEP LOOKING.
LIKE THE MOMENT AS A CHILD WHEN YOU FIRST GRASP THE CONCEPT OF DEATH.
YOU LET YOURSELF REALLY THINK ABOUT NON-EXISTENCE... AND ITS TOTAL INEVITABILITY...
...AND IT'S ABSOLUTELY TERRIFYING.
SO YOU LET YOUR MIND SLIDE AROUND IT, AND YOU EAT A SANDWICH, AND IT'S OKAY.
BUT NOT TODAY.
TODAY I'M STARING THAT FINAL HORROR IN THE EYE.
I'M LOOKING RIGHT INTO THAT EMPTY HOLE.
THE VOID.
NNGH!
THE END.
THIS IS WHAT YOU WANTED, ISN'T IT?
ALL OF MY HORROR?
I'VE GOT YOU!
J-- JOHN?
COME WITH ME.
KKKKKEEEEEEEE

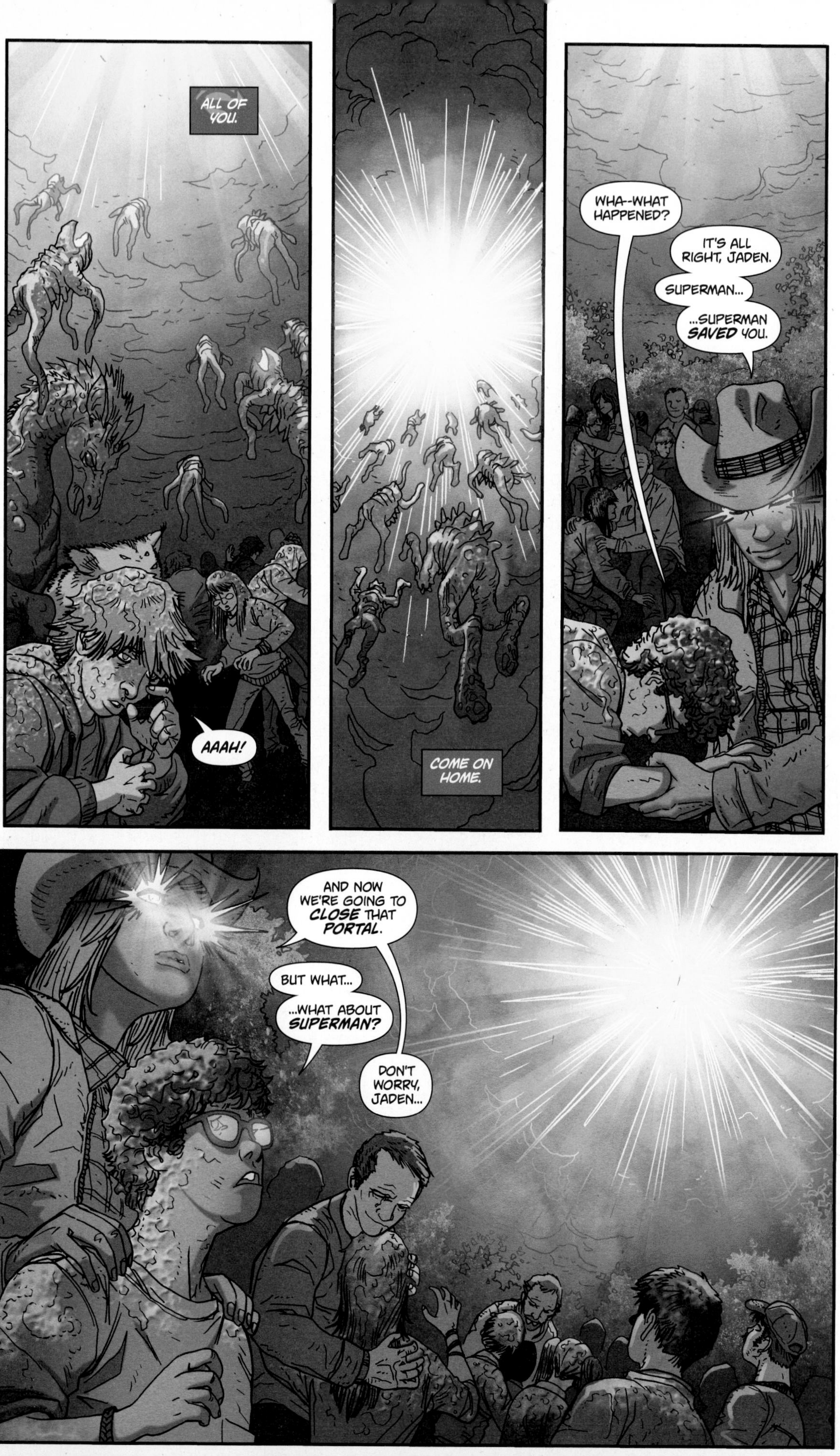
ALL OF YOU.
AAAH!
COME ON HOME.
WHA--WHAT HAPPENED?
IT'S ALL RIGHT, JADEN.
SUPERMAN...
...SUPERMAN SAVED YOU.
AND NOW WE'RE GOING TO CLOSE THAT PORTAL.
BUT WHAT...
...WHAT ABOUT SUPERMAN?
DON'T WORRY, JADEN...

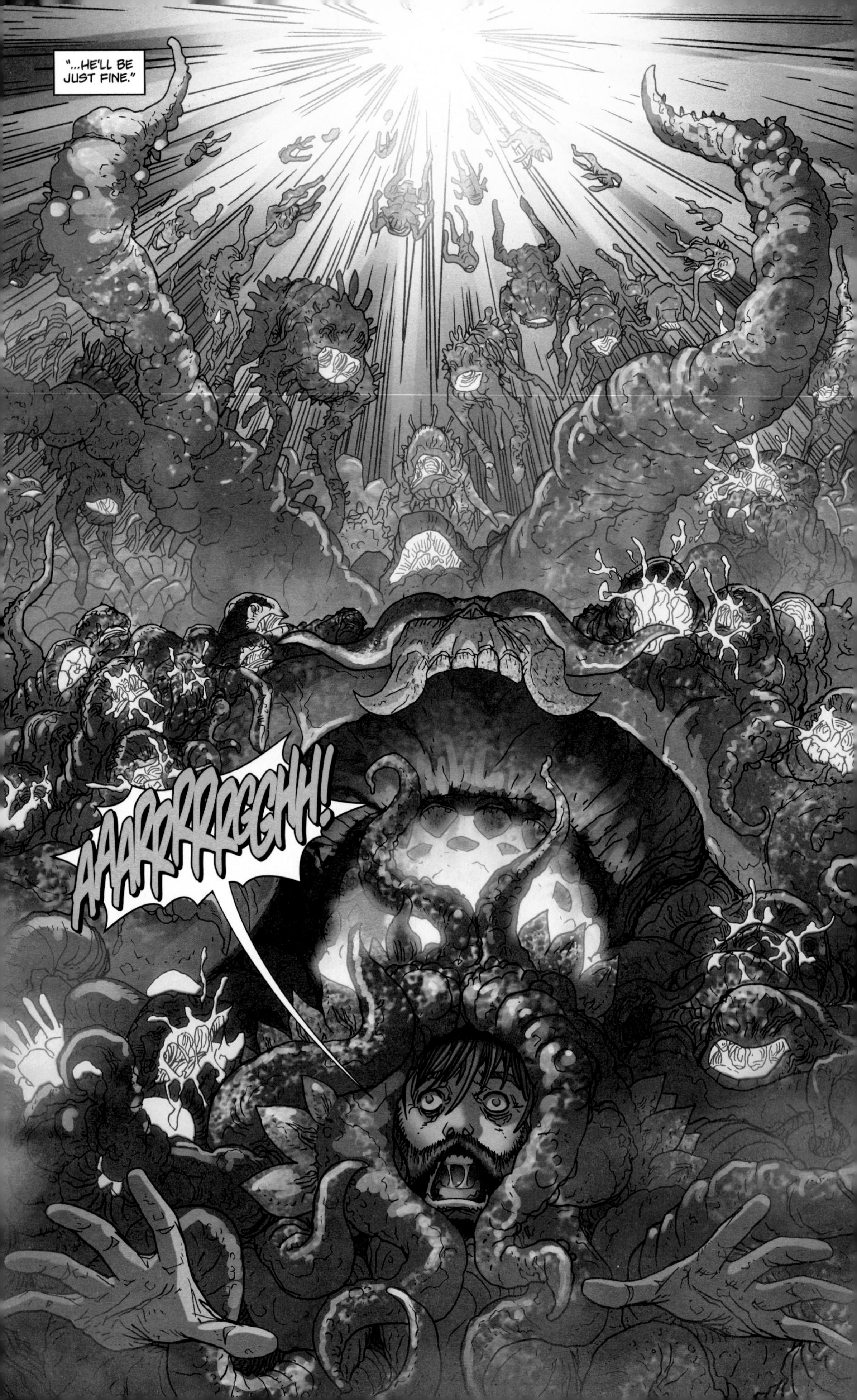
"...HE'LL BE JUST FINE."
AAARRRRRGHH!

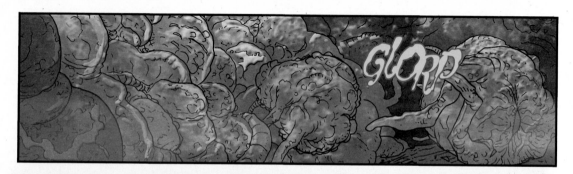

GLORP

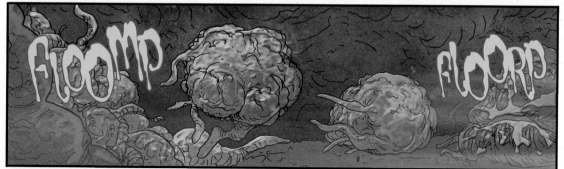

FLOOMP

FLOORD

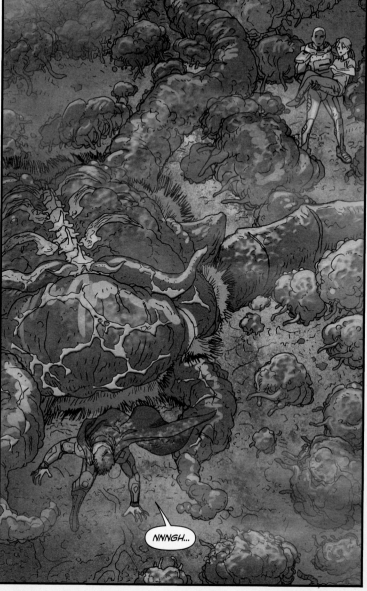

NNNGH...

SUPERMAN...

THEY'RE... FINALLY... *FULL*.

WE'D BETTER GET OUT OF HERE BEFORE THEY WAKE UP.

...ARE YOU...

I'M *FINE*.

LIES.

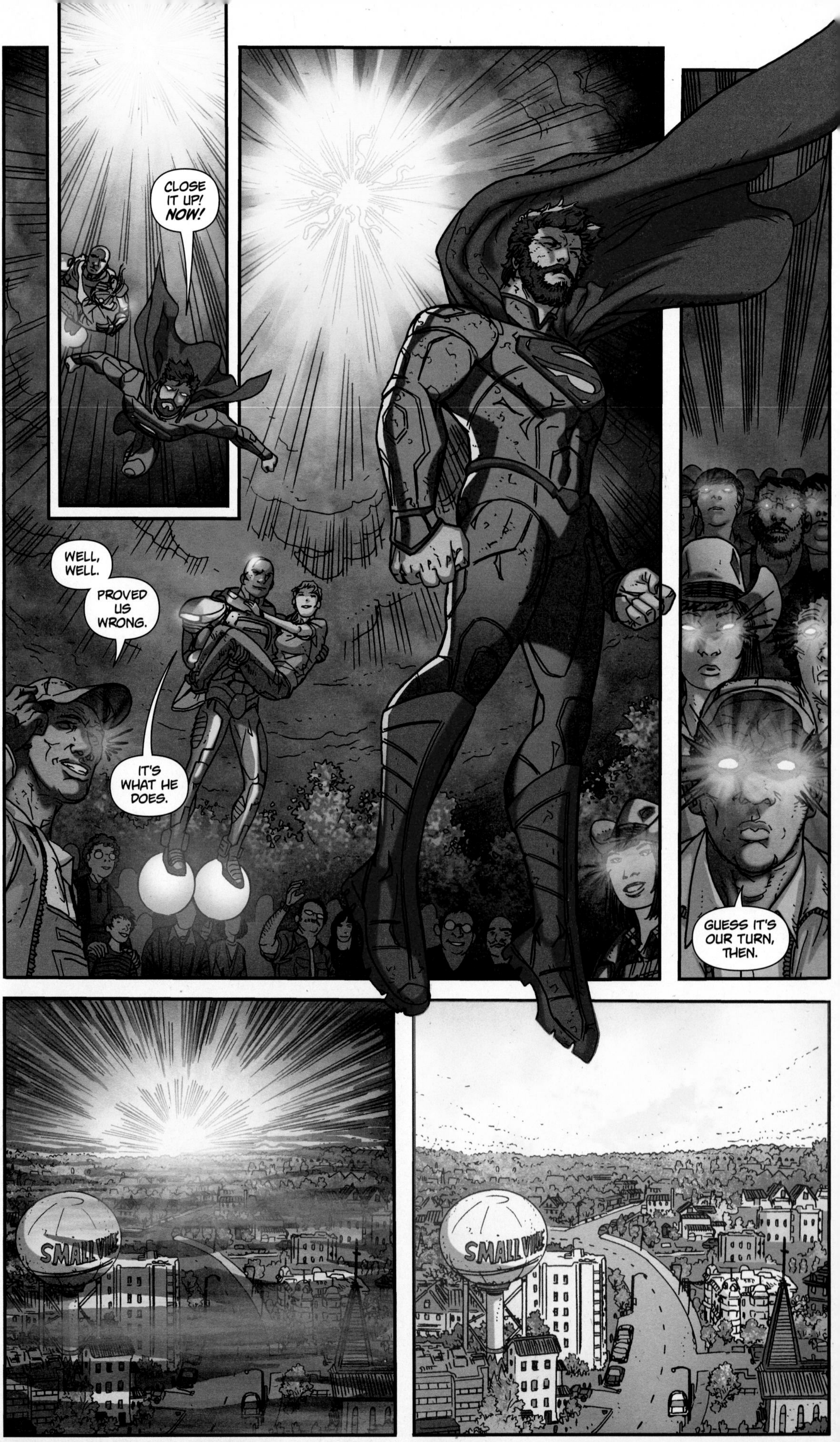
CLOSE IT UP! NOW!
WELL, WELL.
PROVED US WRONG.
IT'S WHAT HE DOES.
GUESS IT'S OUR TURN, THEN.
SMALLVILLE
SMALLVILLE

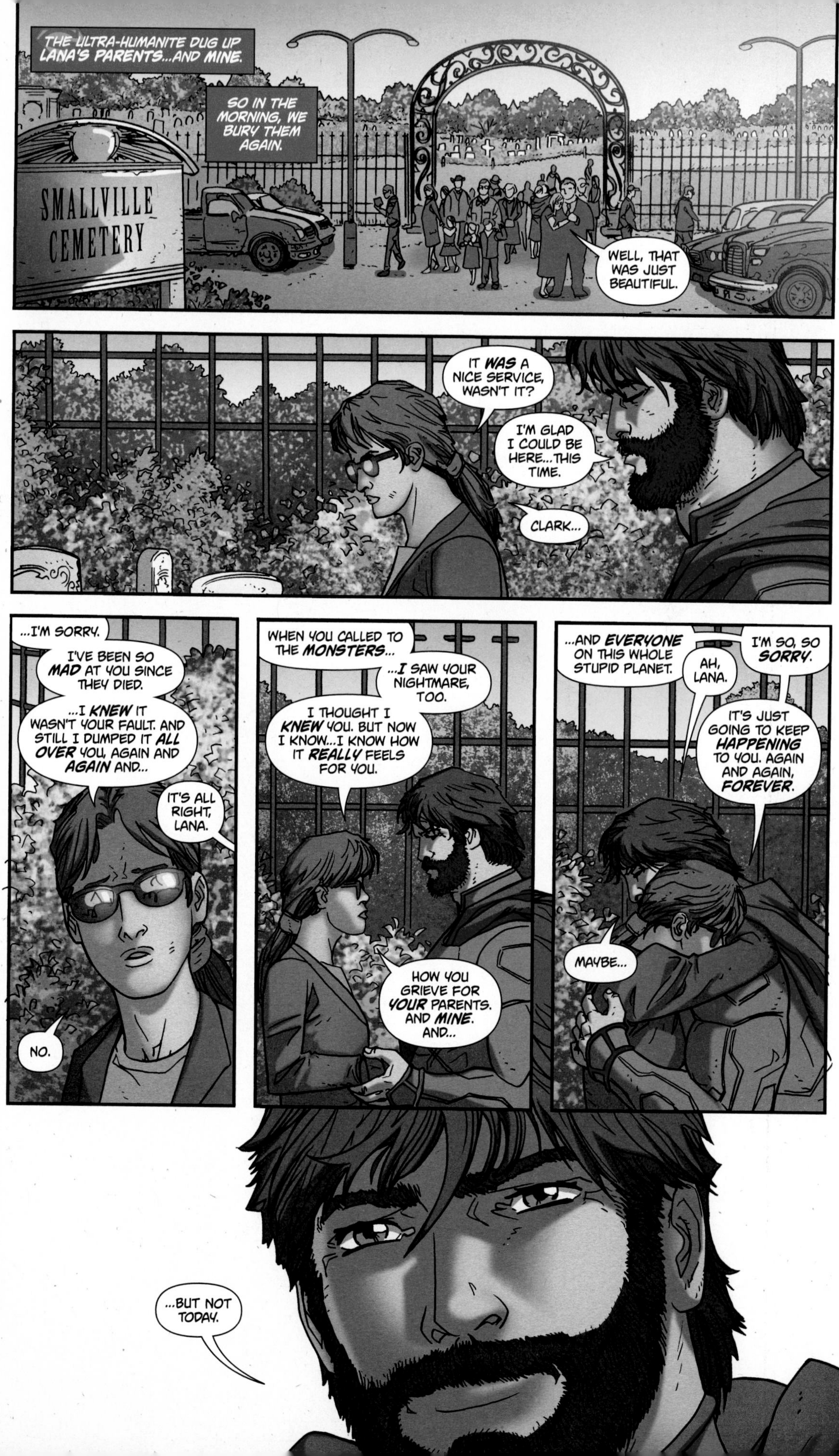
THE ULTRA-HUMANITE DUG UP LANA'S PARENTS...AND MINE.
SO IN THE MORNING, WE BURY THEM AGAIN.
SMALLVILLE CEMETERY
WELL, THAT WAS JUST BEAUTIFUL.
IT WAS A NICE SERVICE, WASN'T IT?
I'M GLAD I COULD BE HERE...THIS TIME.
CLARK...
...I'M SORRY.
I'VE BEEN SO MAD AT YOU SINCE THEY DIED.
...I KNEW IT WASN'T YOUR FAULT. AND STILL I DUMPED IT ALL OVER YOU, AGAIN AND AGAIN AND...
IT'S ALL RIGHT, LANA.
NO.
WHEN YOU CALLED TO THE MONSTERS...
...I SAW YOUR NIGHTMARE, TOO.
I THOUGHT I KNEW YOU. BUT NOW I KNOW...I KNOW HOW IT REALLY FEELS FOR YOU.
HOW YOU GRIEVE FOR YOUR PARENTS. AND MINE. AND...
...AND EVERYONE ON THIS WHOLE STUPID PLANET.
I'M SO, SO SORRY.
AH, LANA.
IT'S JUST GOING TO KEEP HAPPENING TO YOU. AGAIN AND AGAIN, FOREVER.
MAYBE...
...BUT NOT TODAY.

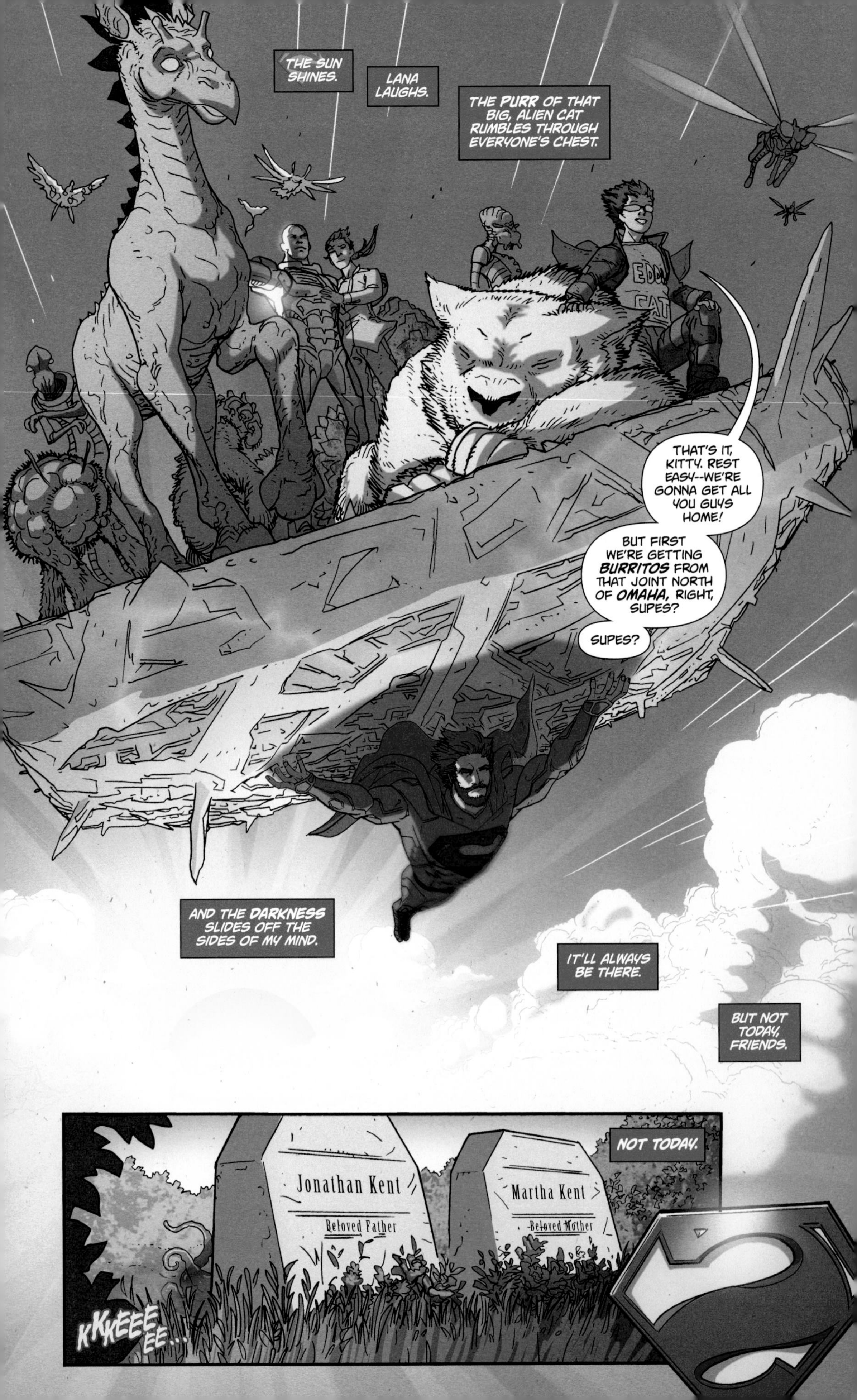
THE SUN SHINES.
LANA LAUGHS.
THE PURR OF THAT BIG, ALIEN CAT RUMBLES THROUGH EVERYONE'S CHEST.
THAT'S IT, KITTY. REST EASY--WE'RE GONNA GET ALL YOU GUYS HOME!
BUT FIRST WE'RE GETTING BURRITOS FROM THAT JOINT NORTH OF OMAHA, RIGHT, SUPES?
SUPES?
AND THE DARKNESS SLIDES OFF THE SIDES OF MY MIND.
IT'LL ALWAYS BE THERE.
BUT NOT TODAY, FRIENDS.
NOT TODAY.
Jonathan Kent
Beloved Father
Martha Kent
Beloved Mother
KKKEEEEE...

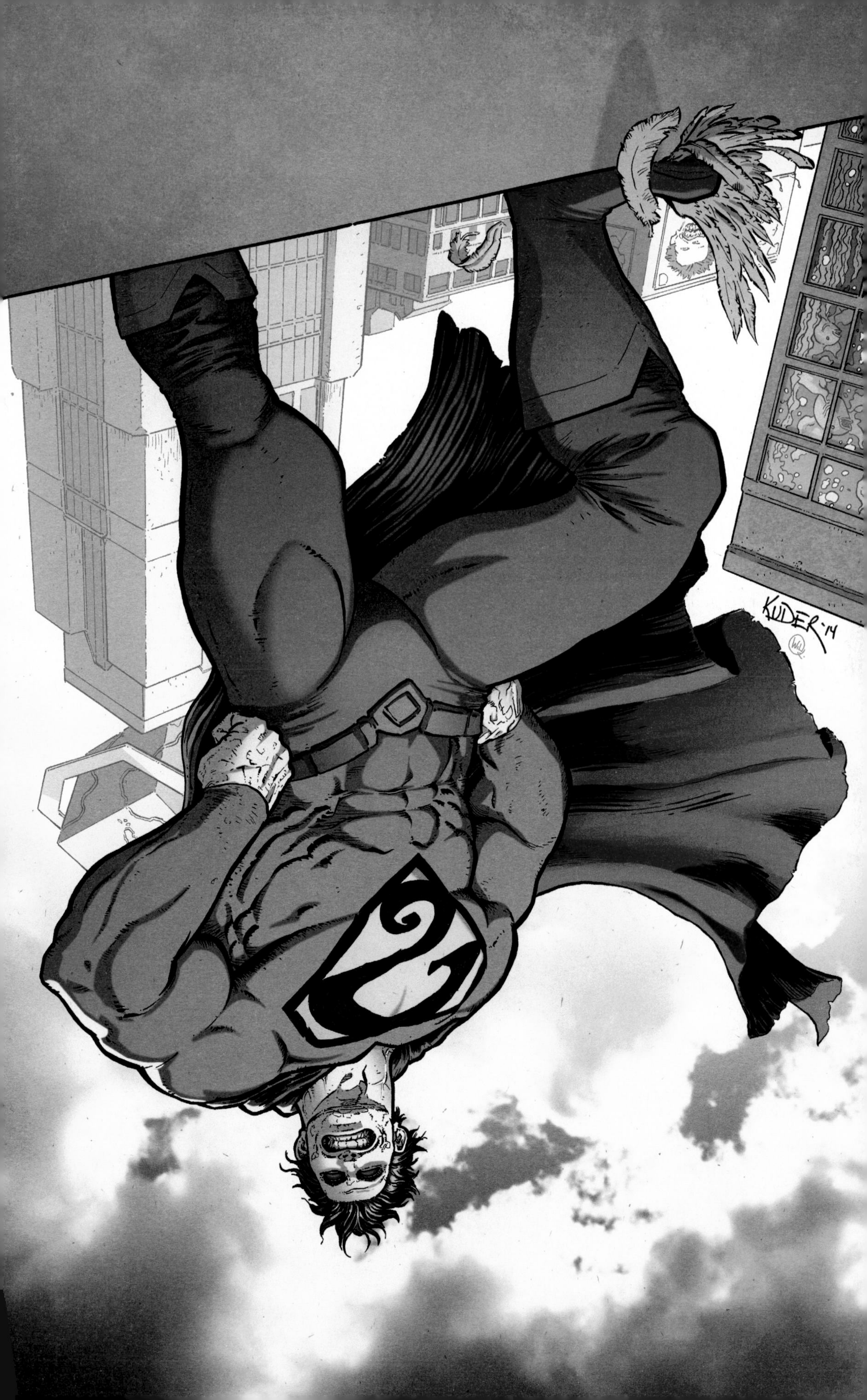
KUDER-'14

MIRЯOR CRACKED

GREG PAK writer **AARON KUDER** artist **WIL QUINTANA** colorist **STEVE WANDS** letterer cover by **AARON KUDER & WIL QUINTANA**

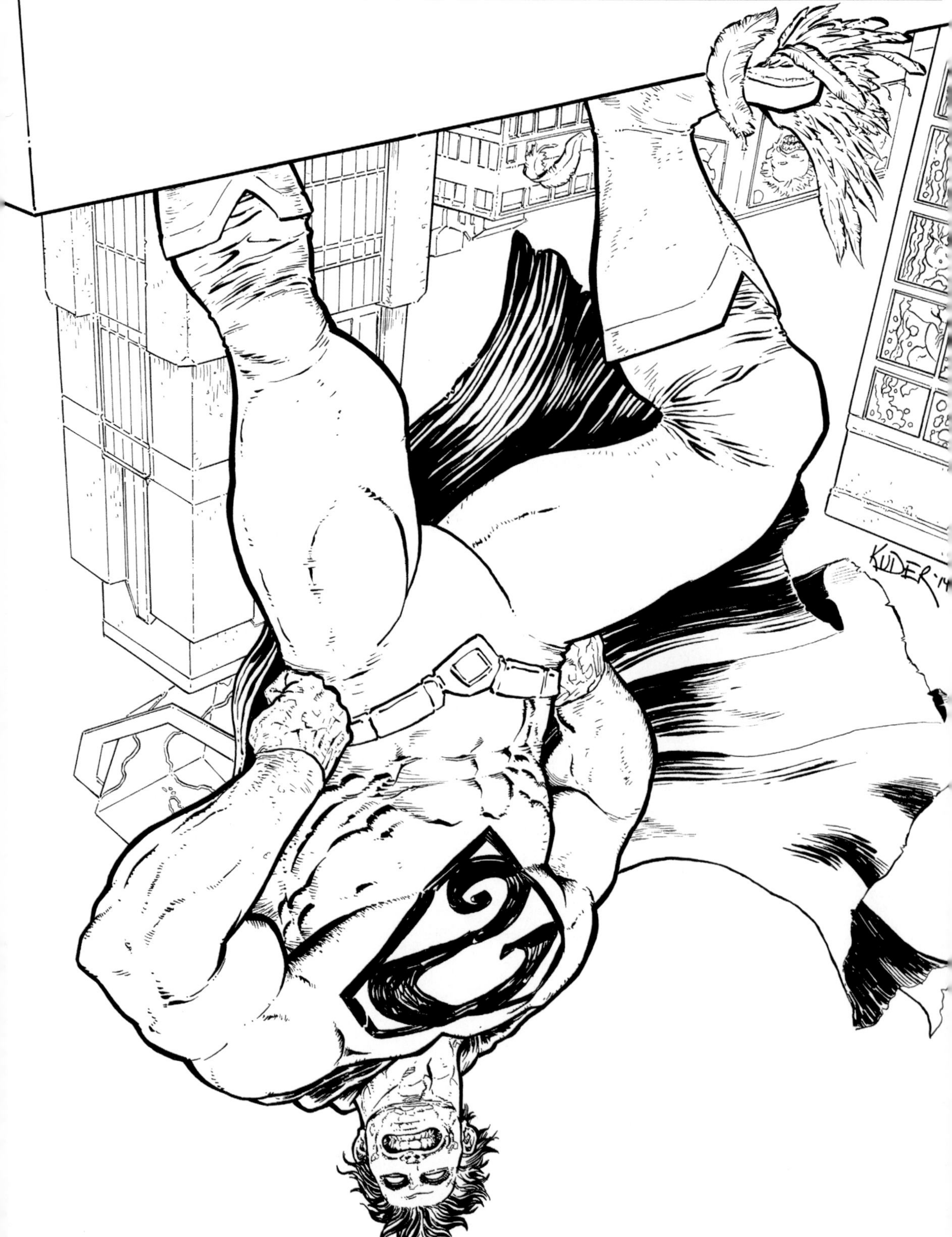
KUDER '14

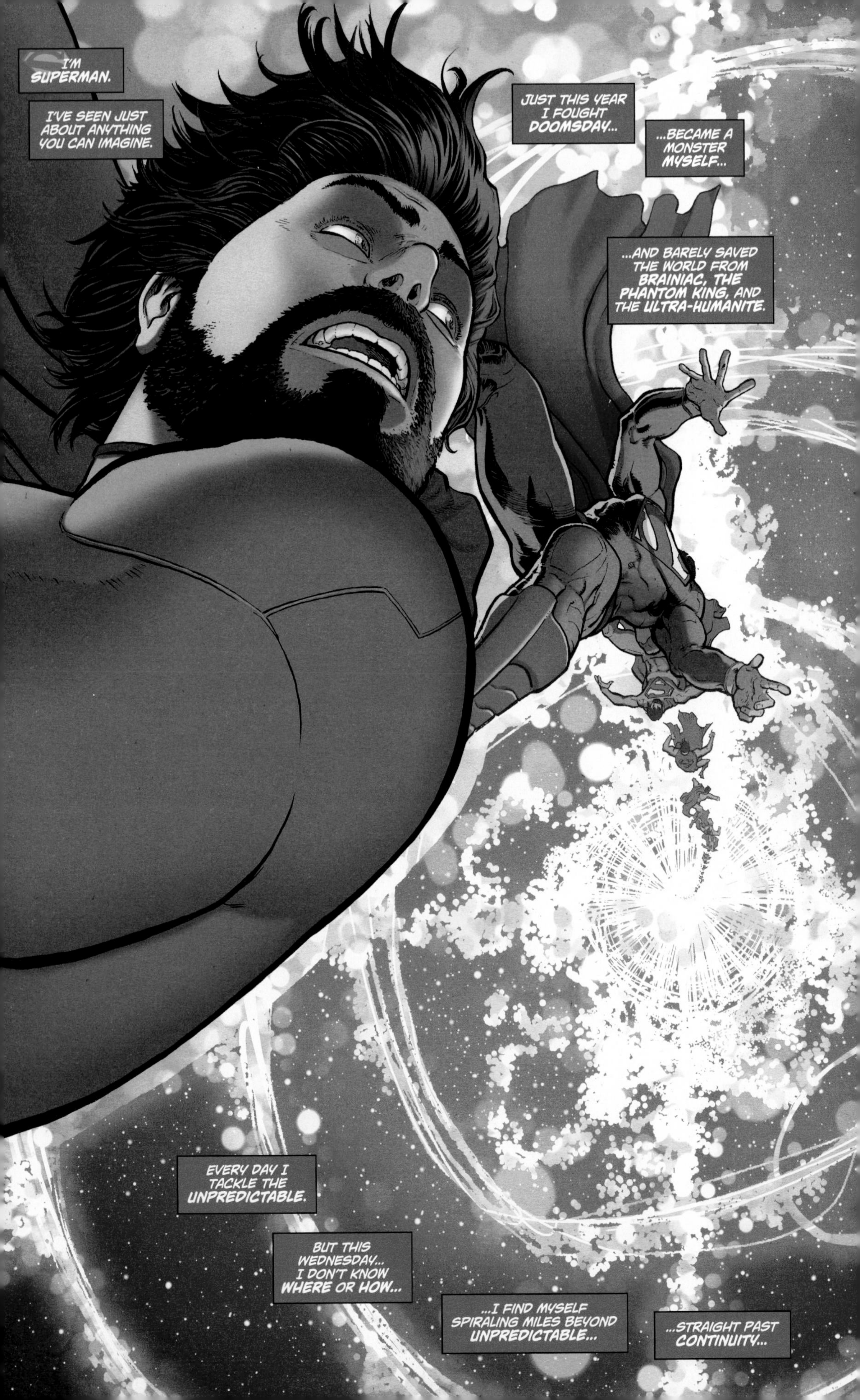
I'M SUPERMAN.
I'VE SEEN JUST ABOUT ANYTHING YOU CAN IMAGINE.
JUST THIS YEAR I FOUGHT DOOMSDAY...
...BECAME A MONSTER MYSELF...
...AND BARELY SAVED THE WORLD FROM BRAINIAC, THE PHANTOM KING, AND THE ULTRA-HUMANITE.
EVERY DAY I TACKLE THE UNPREDICTABLE.
BUT THIS WEDNESDAY... I DON'T KNOW WHERE OR HOW...
...I FIND MYSELF SPIRALING MILES BEYOND UNPREDICTABLE...
...STRAIGHT PAST CONTINUITY...

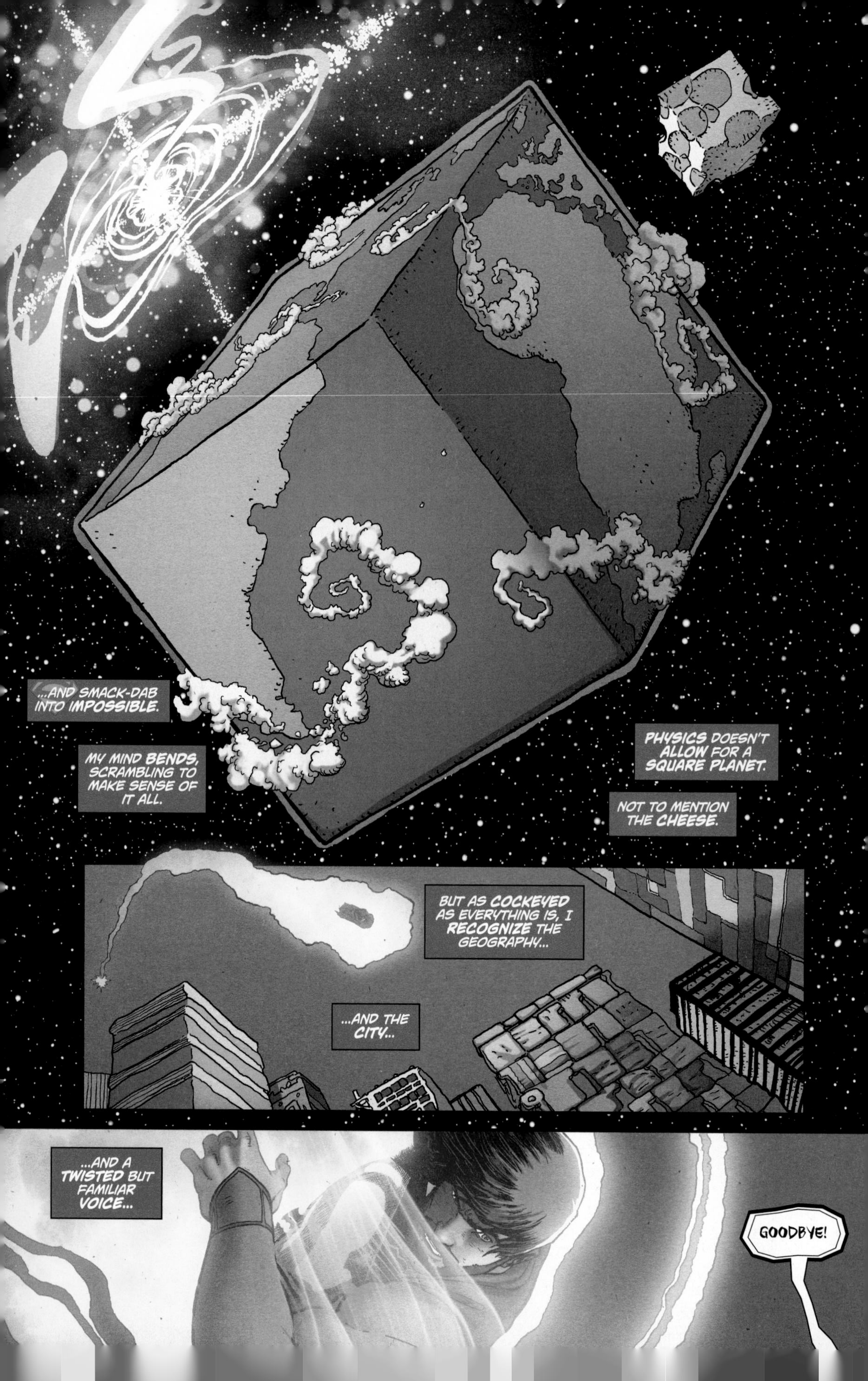
...AND SMACK-DAB INTO IMPOSSIBLE.
MY MIND BENDS, SCRAMBLING TO MAKE SENSE OF IT ALL.
PHYSICS DOESN'T ALLOW FOR A SQUARE PLANET.
NOT TO MENTION THE CHEESE.
BUT AS COCKEYED AS EVERYTHING IS, I RECOGNIZE THE GEOGRAPHY...
...AND THE CITY...
...AND A TWISTED BUT FAMILIAR VOICE...
GOODBYE!

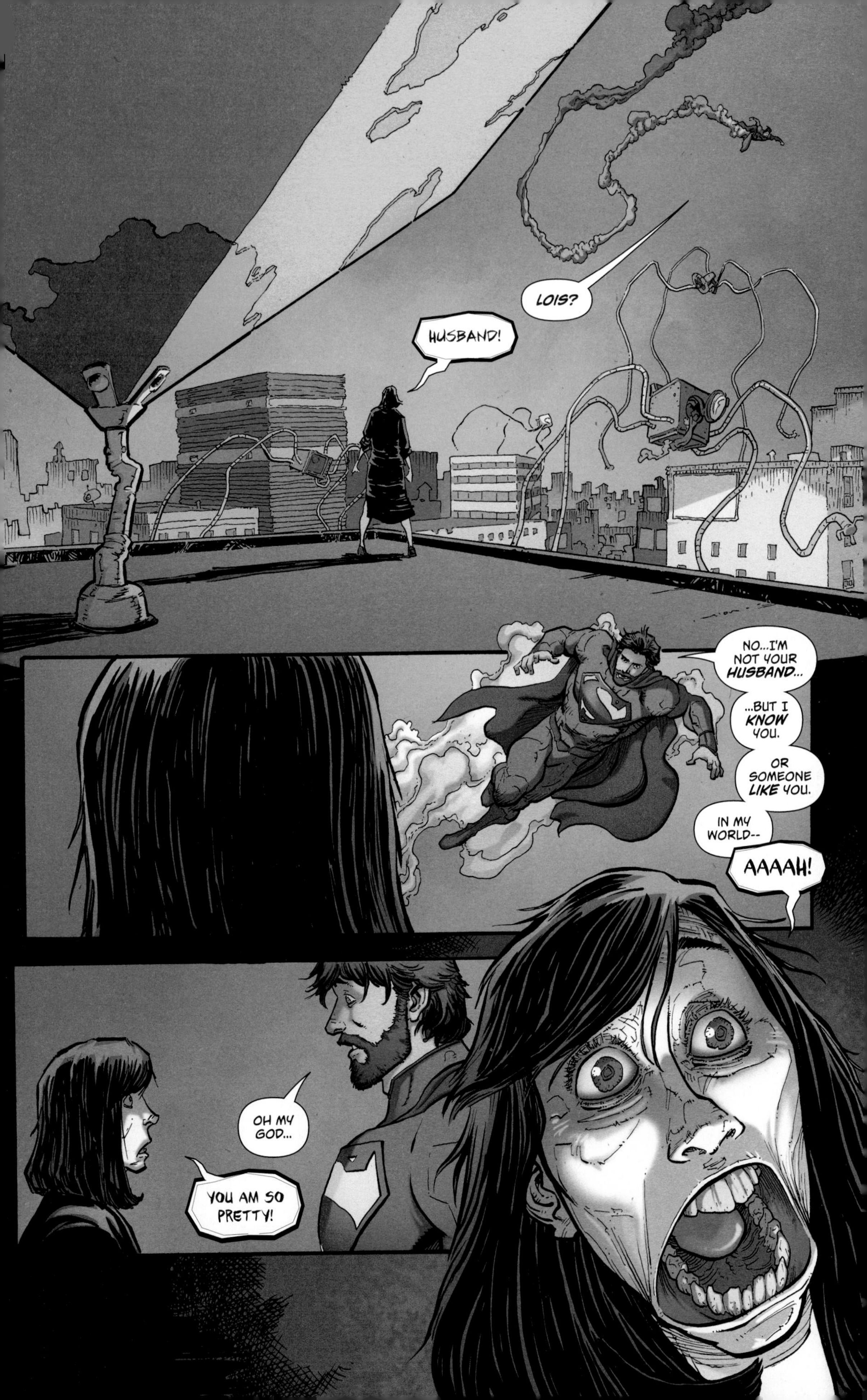
LOIS?
HUSBAND!
NO...I'M NOT YOUR HUSBAND...
...BUT I KNOW YOU.
OR SOMEONE LIKE YOU.
IN MY WORLD--
AAAAH!
OH MY GOD...
YOU AM SO PRETTY!

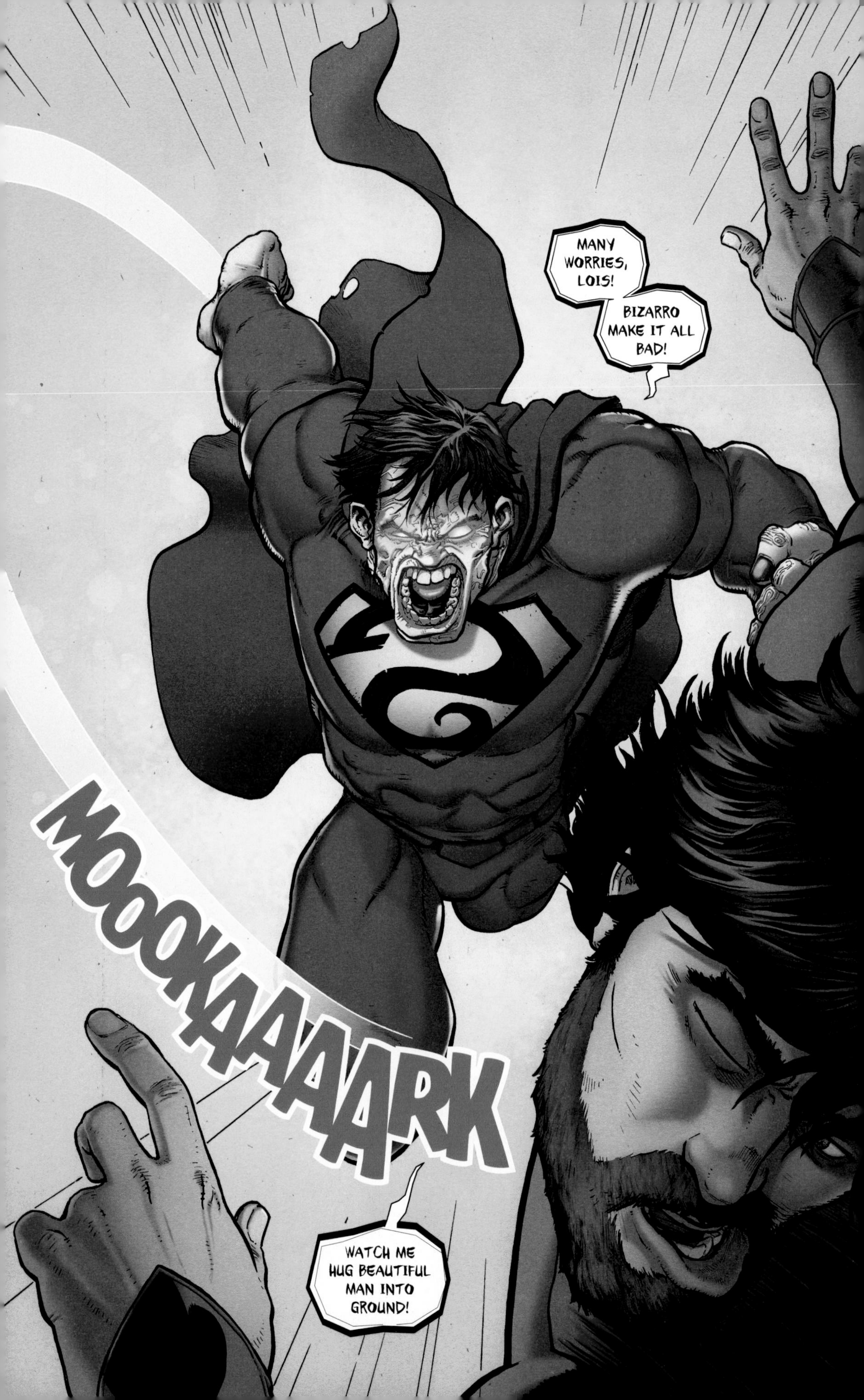
MANY WORRIES, LOIS!
BIZARRO MAKE IT ALL BAD!
MOOOKAAAARK
WATCH ME HUG BEAUTIFUL MAN INTO GROUND!

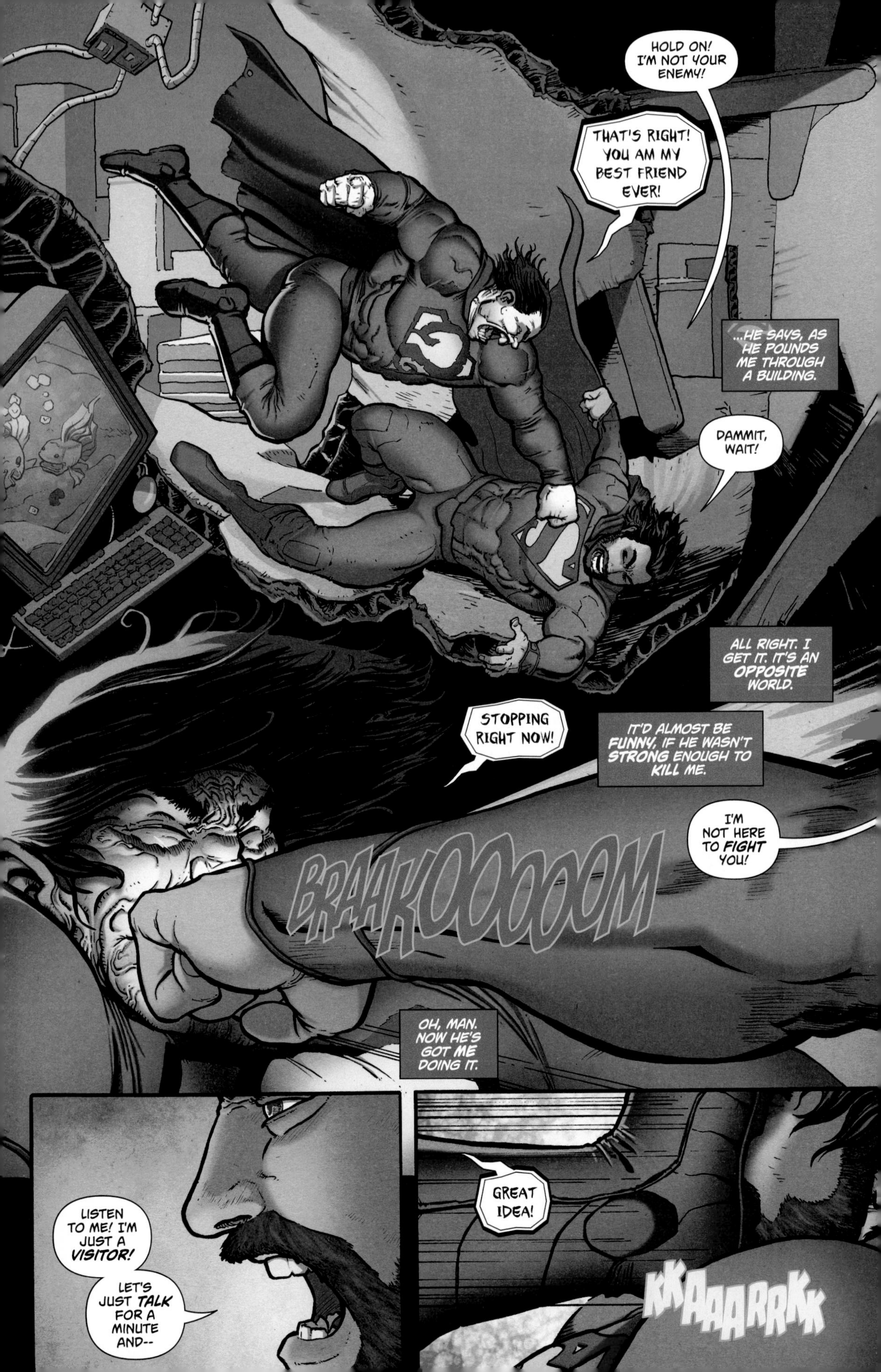
HOLD ON! I'M NOT YOUR ENEMY!
THAT'S RIGHT! YOU AM MY BEST FRIEND EVER!
...HE SAYS, AS HE POUNDS ME THROUGH A BUILDING.
DAMMIT, WAIT!
ALL RIGHT. I GET IT. IT'S AN OPPOSITE WORLD.
STOPPING RIGHT NOW!
IT'D ALMOST BE FUNNY, IF HE WASN'T STRONG ENOUGH TO KILL ME.
I'M NOT HERE TO FIGHT YOU!
BRAAKOOOOOOM
OH, MAN. NOW HE'S GOT ME DOING IT.
LISTEN TO ME! I'M JUST A VISITOR!
LET'S JUST TALK FOR A MINUTE AND--
GREAT IDEA!
KKAAARRKK

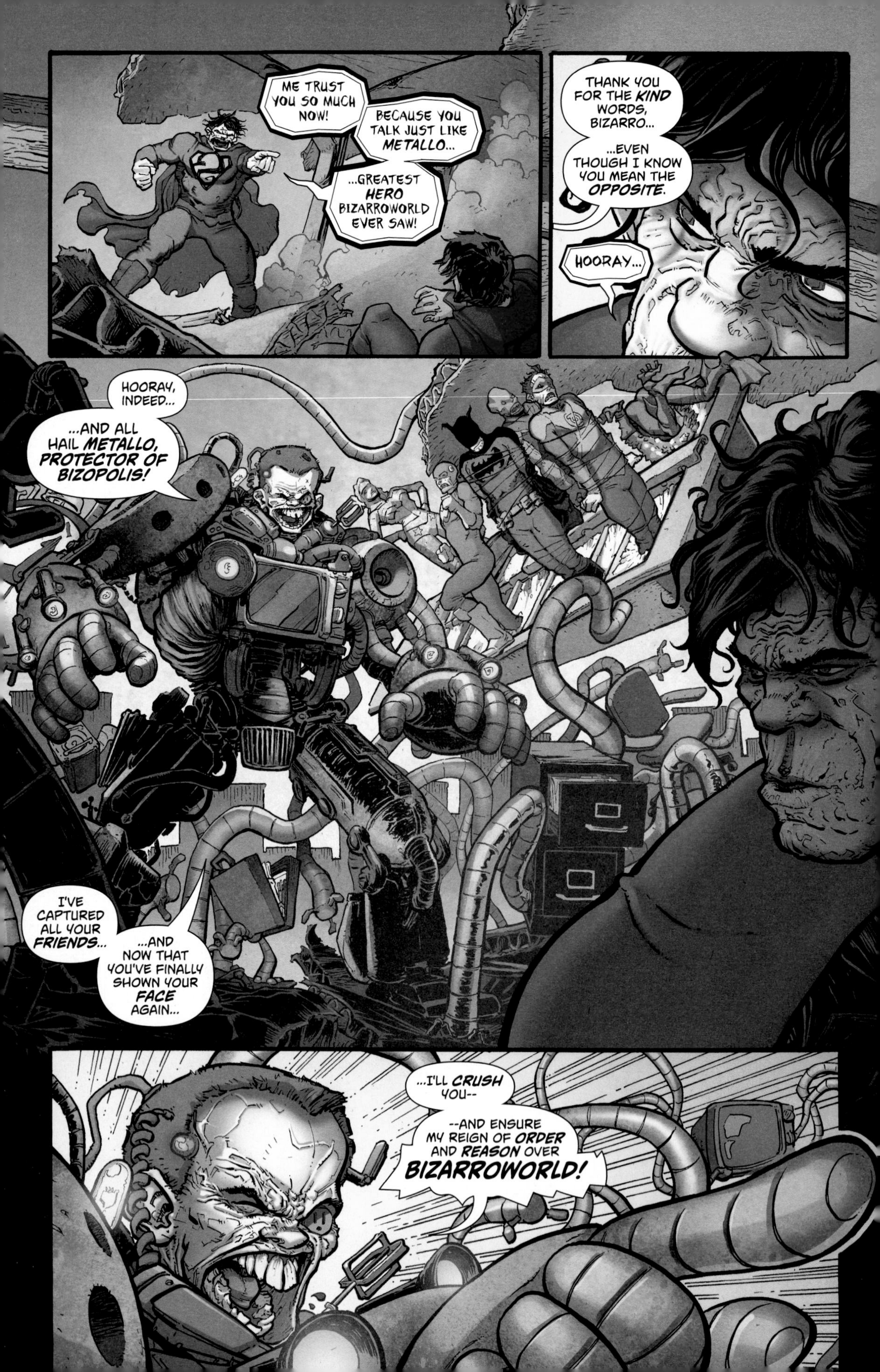

ME TRUST YOU SO MUCH NOW!
BECAUSE YOU TALK JUST LIKE METALLO...
...GREATEST HERO BIZARROWORLD EVER SAW!
THANK YOU FOR THE KIND WORDS, BIZARRO...
...EVEN THOUGH I KNOW YOU MEAN THE OPPOSITE.
HOORAY...
HOORAY, INDEED...
...AND ALL HAIL METALLO, PROTECTOR OF BIZOPOLIS!
I'VE CAPTURED ALL YOUR FRIENDS...
...AND NOW THAT YOU'VE FINALLY SHOWN YOUR FACE AGAIN...
...I'LL CRUSH YOU--
--AND ENSURE MY REIGN OF ORDER AND REASON OVER BIZARROWORLD!

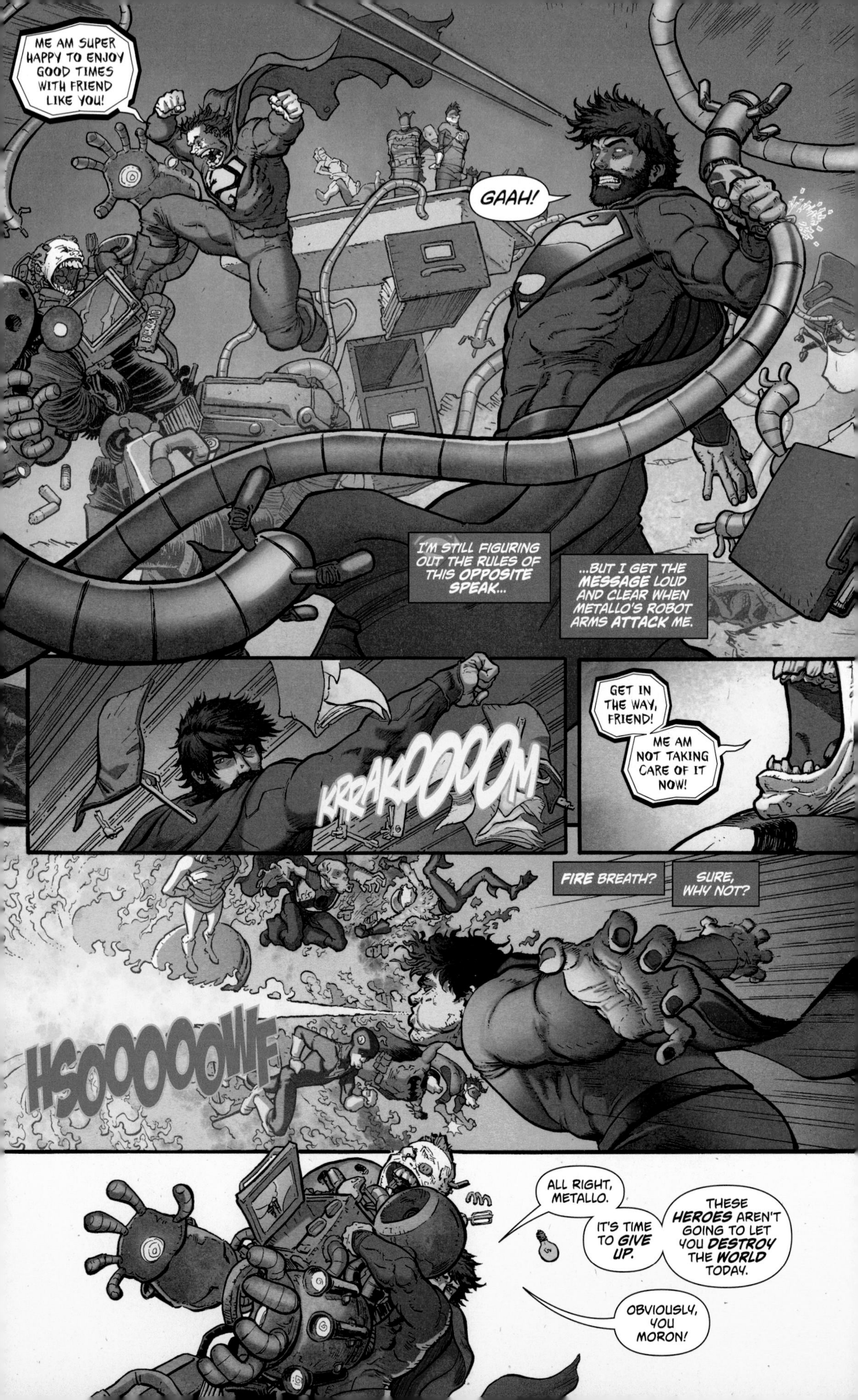
ME AM SUPER HAPPY TO ENJOY GOOD TIMES WITH FRIEND LIKE YOU!
GAAH!
I'M STILL FIGURING OUT THE RULES OF THIS OPPOSITE SPEAK...
...BUT I GET THE MESSAGE LOUD AND CLEAR WHEN METALLO'S ROBOT ARMS ATTACK ME.
KRRAKOOOOM
GET IN THE WAY, FRIEND!
ME AM NOT TAKING CARE OF IT NOW!
FIRE BREATH?
SURE, WHY NOT?
HSOOOOOWF
ALL RIGHT, METALLO.
IT'S TIME TO GIVE UP.
THESE HEROES AREN'T GOING TO LET YOU DESTROY THE WORLD TODAY.
OBVIOUSLY, YOU MORON!

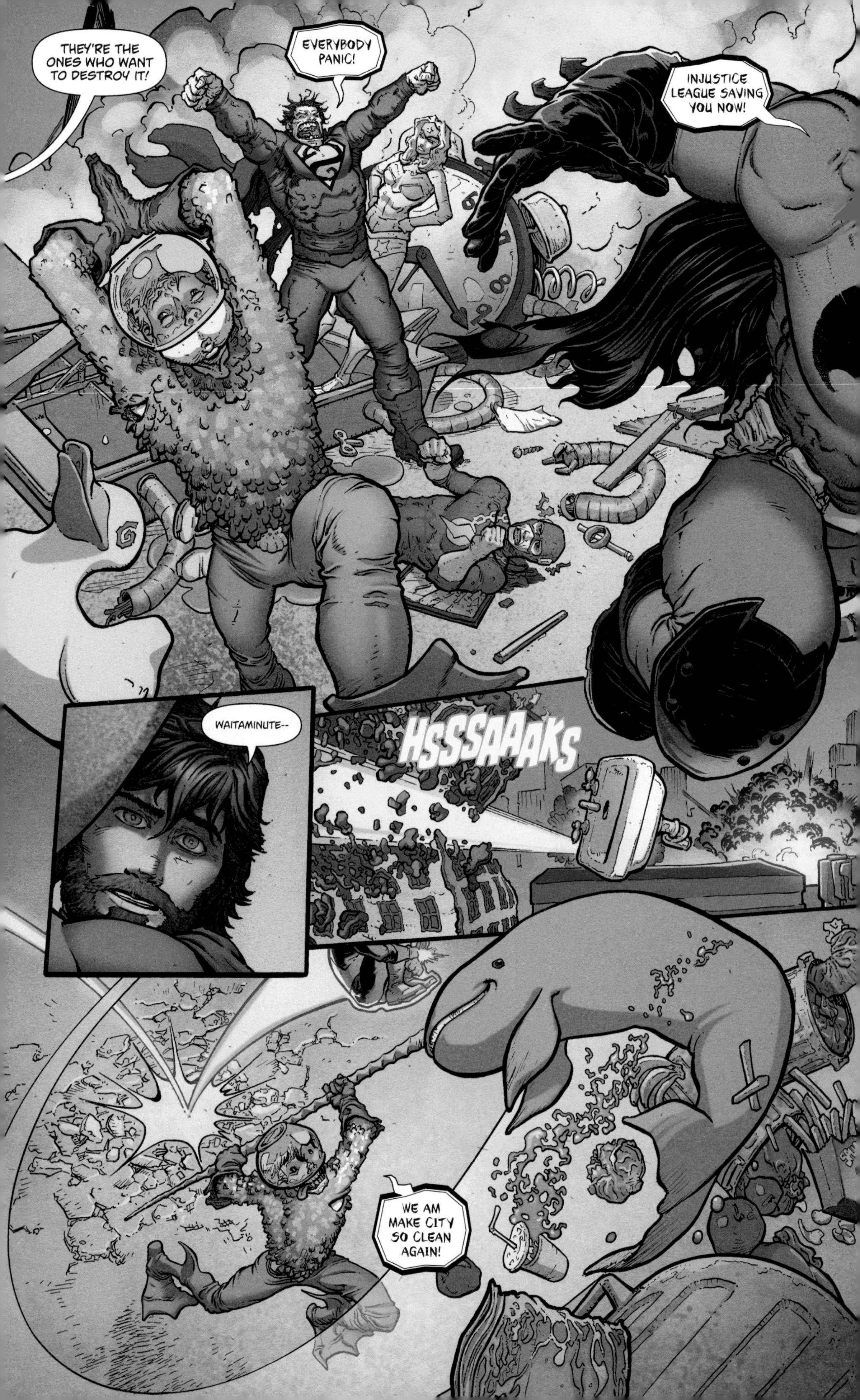
THEY'RE THE ONES WHO WANT TO DESTROY IT!
EVERYBODY PANIC!
INJUSTICE LEAGUE SAVING YOU NOW!
WAITAMINUTE--
HSSSAAAKS
WE AM MAKE CITY SO CLEAN AGAIN!

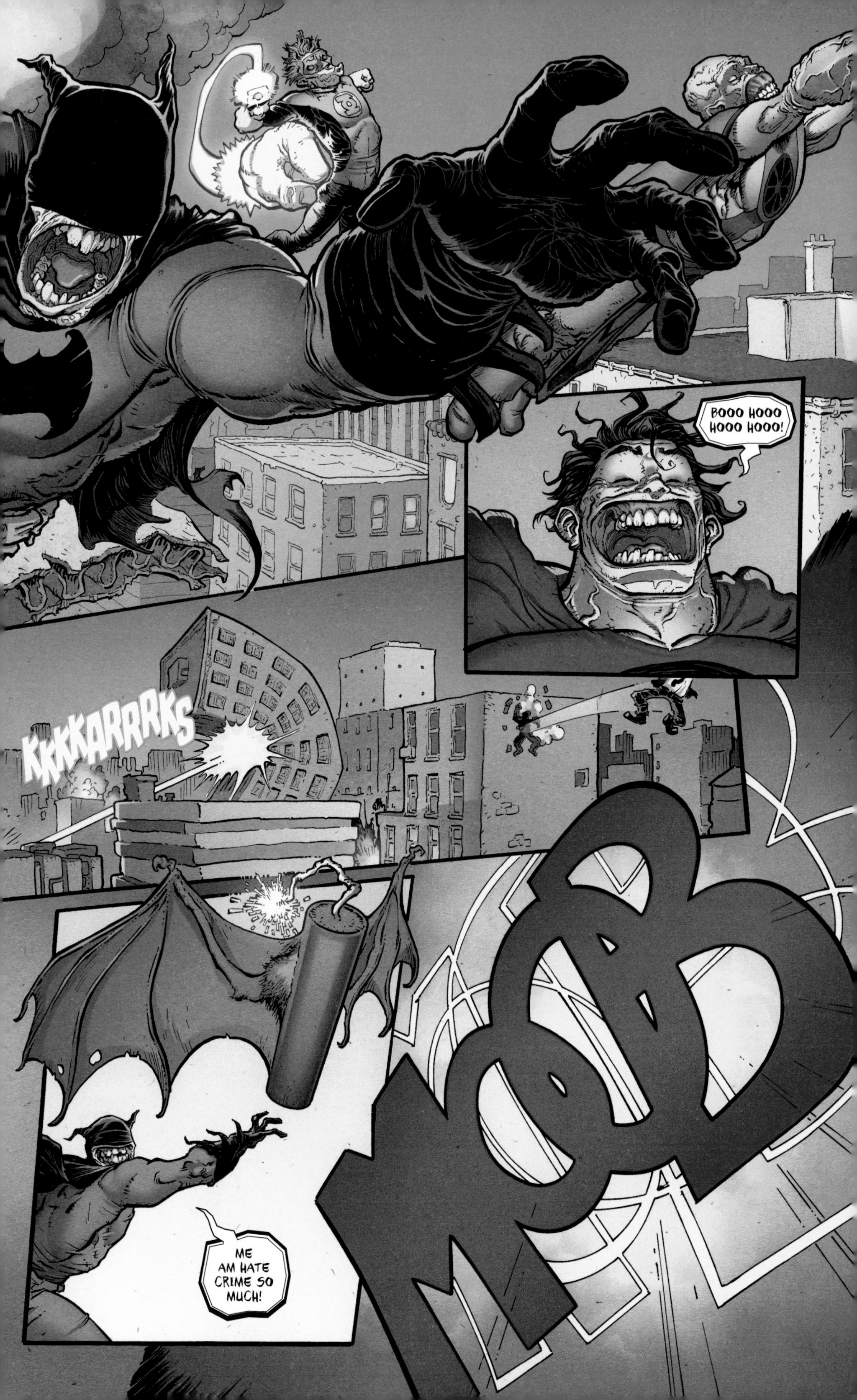
BOOO HOOO HOOO HOOO!
KKKKARRRKS
BOOM
ME AM HATE CRIME SO MUCH!

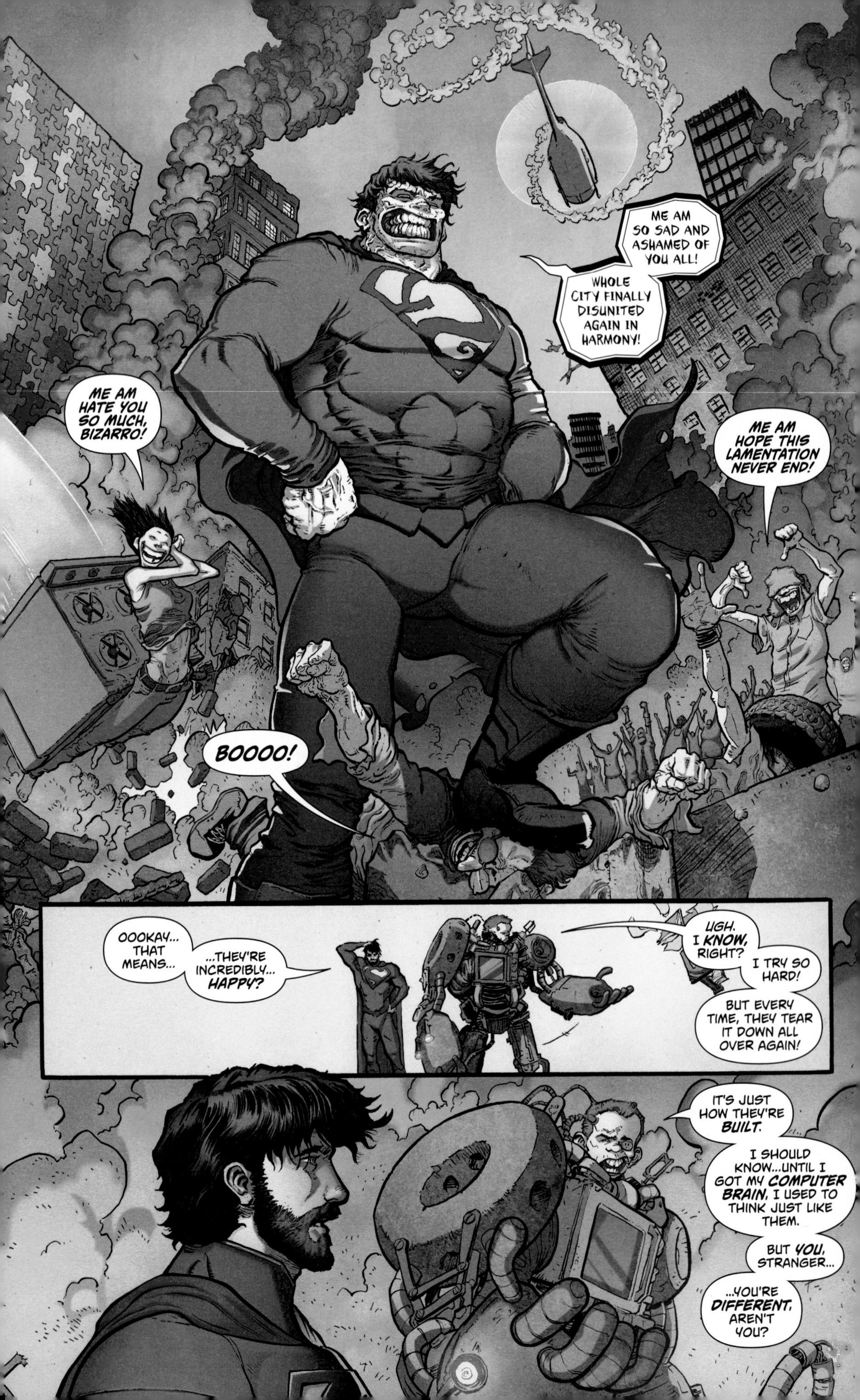
ME AM SO SAD AND ASHAMED OF YOU ALL!
WHOLE CITY FINALLY DISUNITED AGAIN IN HARMONY!
ME AM HATE YOU SO MUCH, BIZARRO!
ME AM HOPE THIS LAMENTATION NEVER END!
BOOOO!
OOOKAY... THAT MEANS...
...THEY'RE INCREDIBLY... HAPPY?
UGH. I KNOW, RIGHT?
I TRY SO HARD!
BUT EVERY TIME, THEY TEAR IT DOWN ALL OVER AGAIN!
IT'S JUST HOW THEY'RE BUILT.
I SHOULD KNOW...UNTIL I GOT MY COMPUTER BRAIN, I USED TO THINK JUST LIKE THEM.
BUT YOU, STRANGER...
...YOU'RE DIFFERENT, AREN'T YOU?

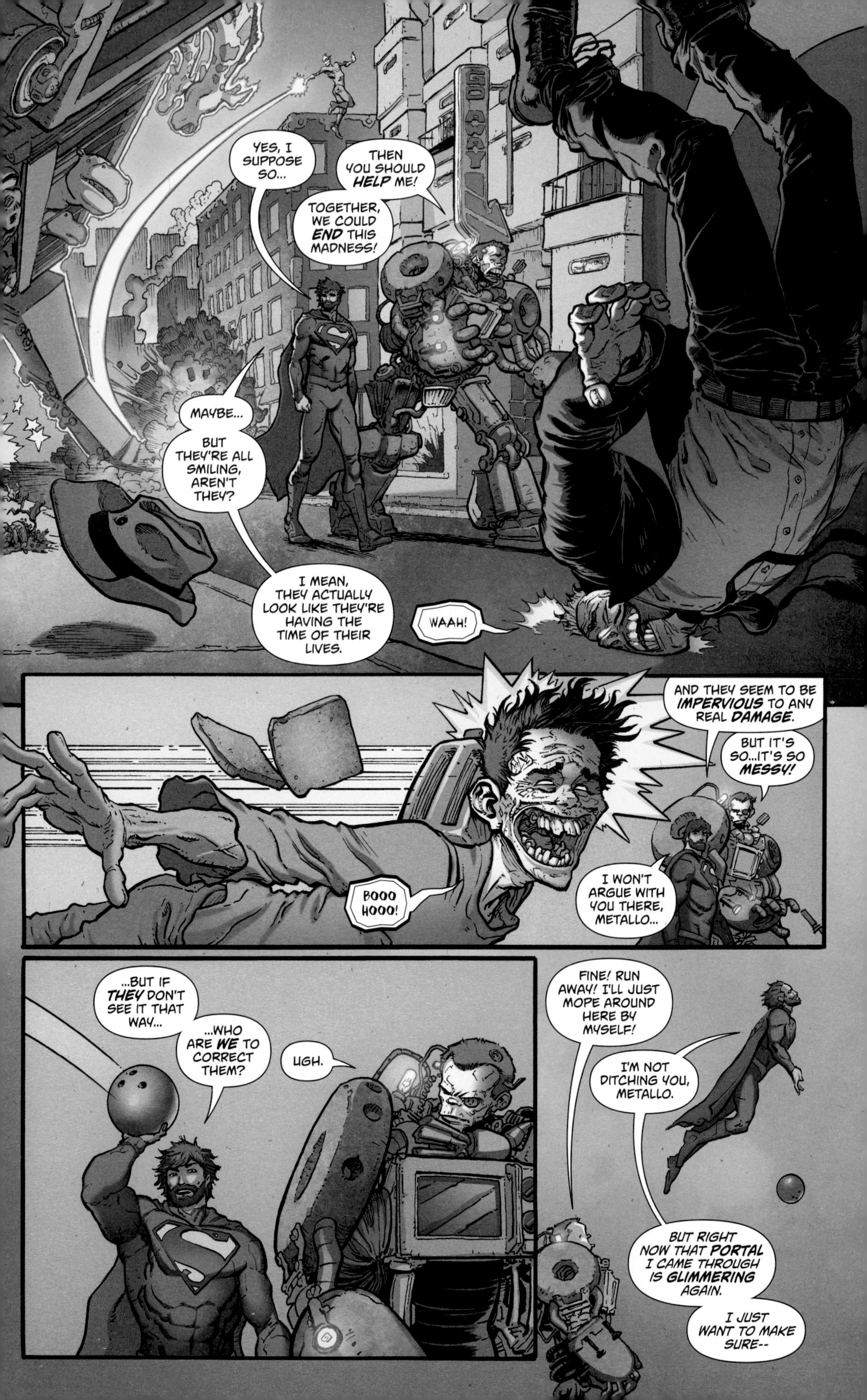
GO AWAY
YES, I SUPPOSE SO...
THEN YOU SHOULD HELP ME!
TOGETHER, WE COULD END THIS MADNESS!
MAYBE...
BUT THEY'RE ALL SMILING, AREN'T THEY?
I MEAN, THEY ACTUALLY LOOK LIKE THEY'RE HAVING THE TIME OF THEIR LIVES.
WAAH!
AND THEY SEEM TO BE IMPERVIOUS TO ANY REAL DAMAGE.
BUT IT'S SO...IT'S SO MESSY!
BOOO HOOO!
I WON'T ARGUE WITH YOU THERE, METALLO...
...BUT IF THEY DON'T SEE IT THAT WAY...
...WHO ARE WE TO CORRECT THEM?
UGH.
FINE! RUN AWAY! I'LL JUST MOPE AROUND HERE BY MYSELF!
I'M NOT DITCHING YOU, METALLO.
BUT RIGHT NOW THAT PORTAL I CAME THROUGH IS GLIMMERING AGAIN.
I JUST WANT TO MAKE SURE--

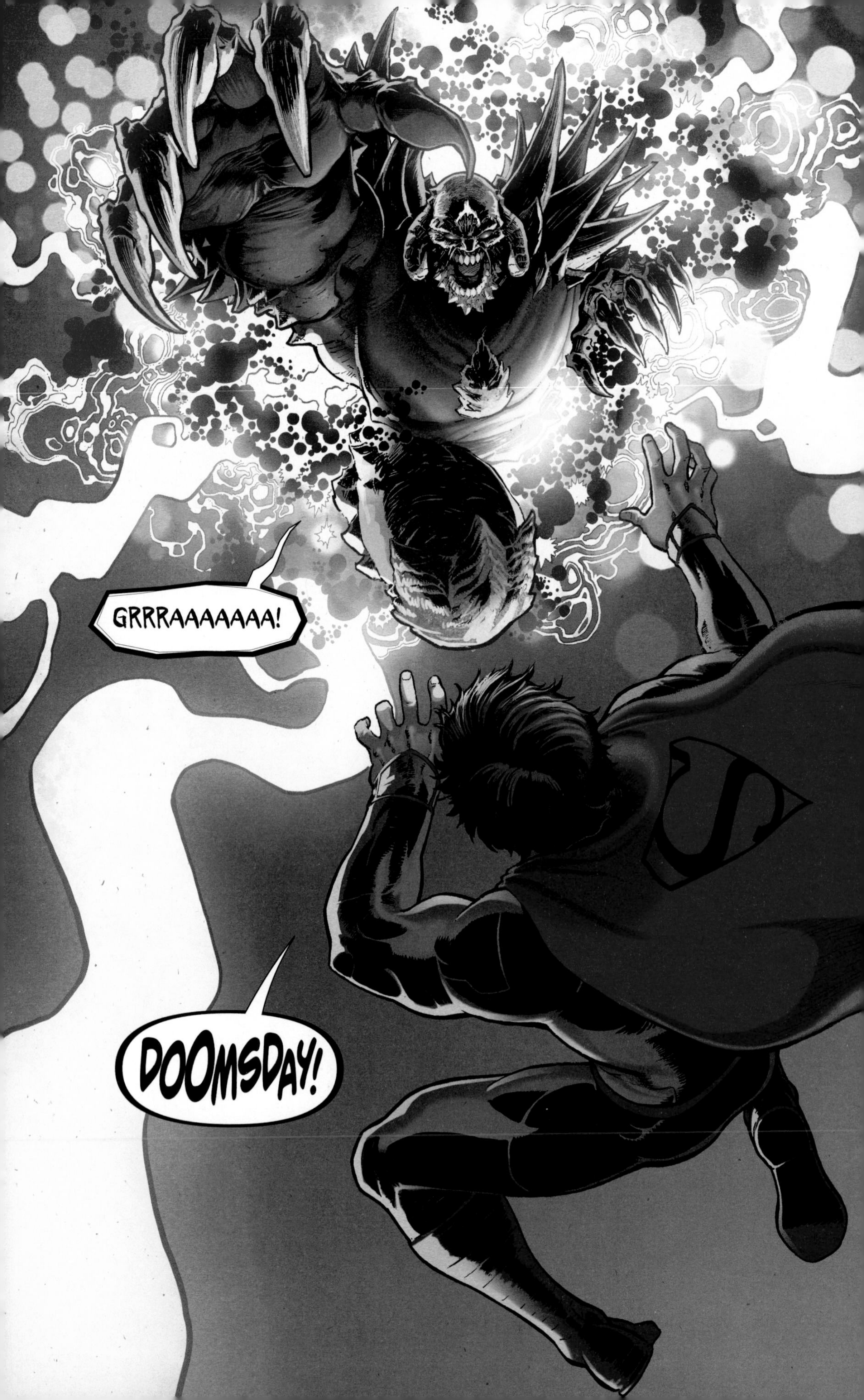
GRRRAAAAAAA!
DOOMSDAY!

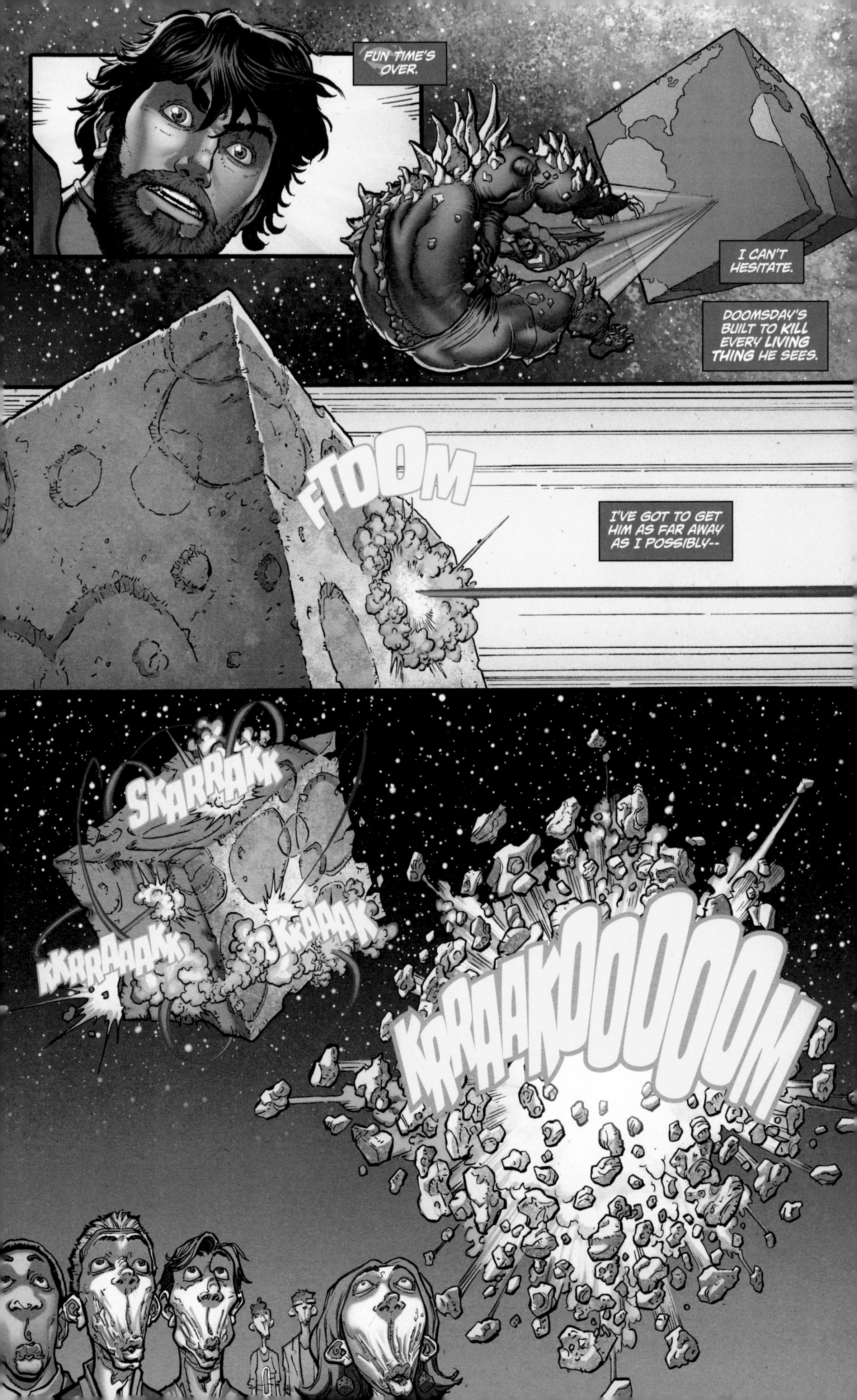
FUN TIME'S OVER.
I CAN'T HESITATE.
DOOMSDAY'S BUILT TO KILL EVERY LIVING THING HE SEES.
FTOOM
I'VE GOT TO GET HIM AS FAR AWAY AS I POSSIBLY--
SKARRAKK
KKRRAAAKK
KRAAAK
KRRAAKOOOOOM

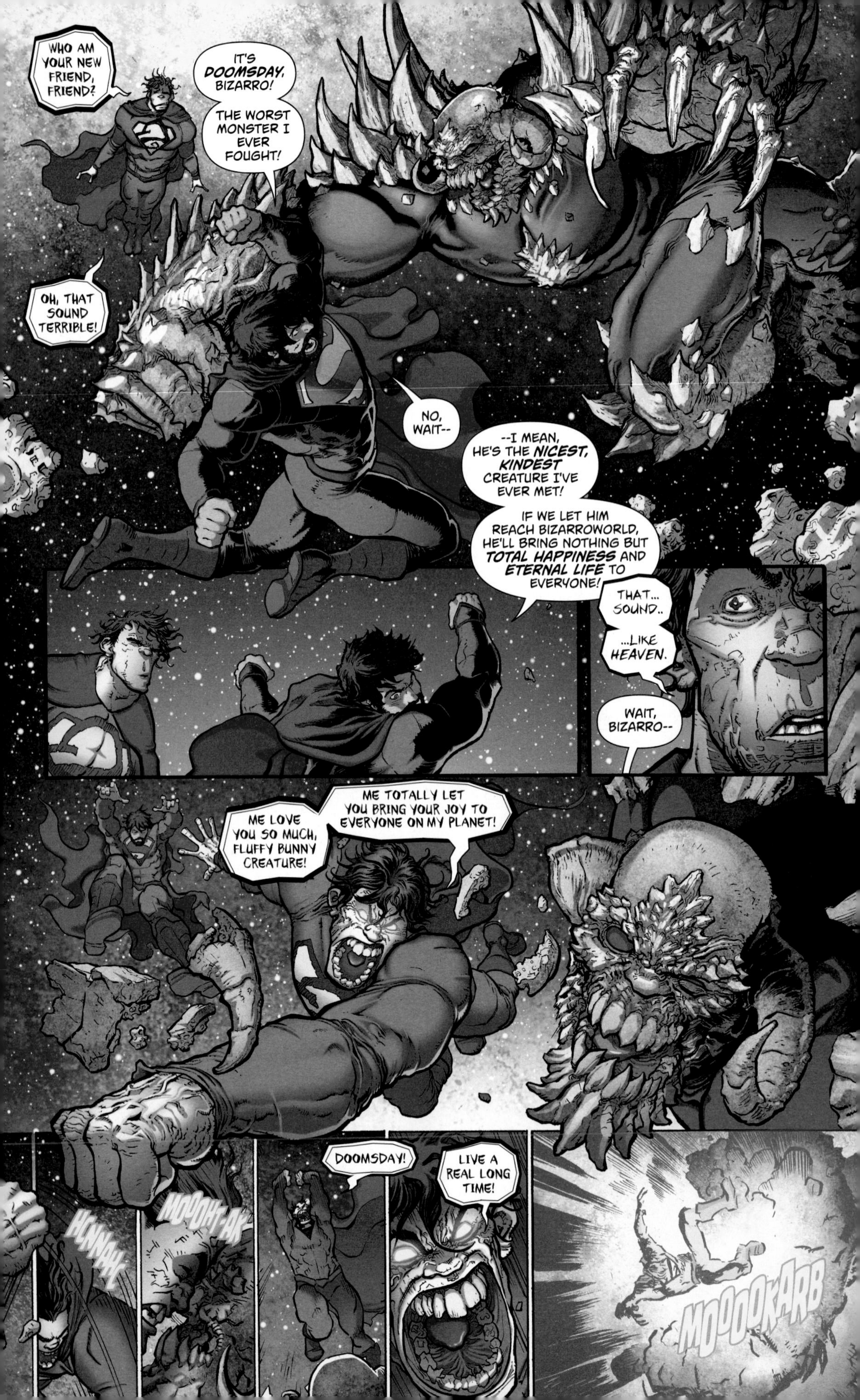

WHO AM YOUR NEW FRIEND, FRIEND?
IT'S DOOMSDAY, BIZARRO!
THE WORST MONSTER I EVER FOUGHT!
OH, THAT SOUND TERRIBLE!
NO, WAIT--
--I MEAN, HE'S THE NICEST, KINDEST CREATURE I'VE EVER MET!
IF WE LET HIM REACH BIZARROWORLD, HE'LL BRING NOTHING BUT TOTAL HAPPINESS AND ETERNAL LIFE TO EVERYONE!
THAT... SOUND..
...LIKE HEAVEN.
WAIT, BIZARRO--
ME LOVE YOU SO MUCH, FLUFFY BUNNY CREATURE!
ME TOTALLY LET YOU BRING YOUR JOY TO EVERYONE ON MY PLANET!
HCNNAHK
MOOOHT-AK
DOOMSDAY!
LIVE A REAL LONG TIME!
MOOOOKARB

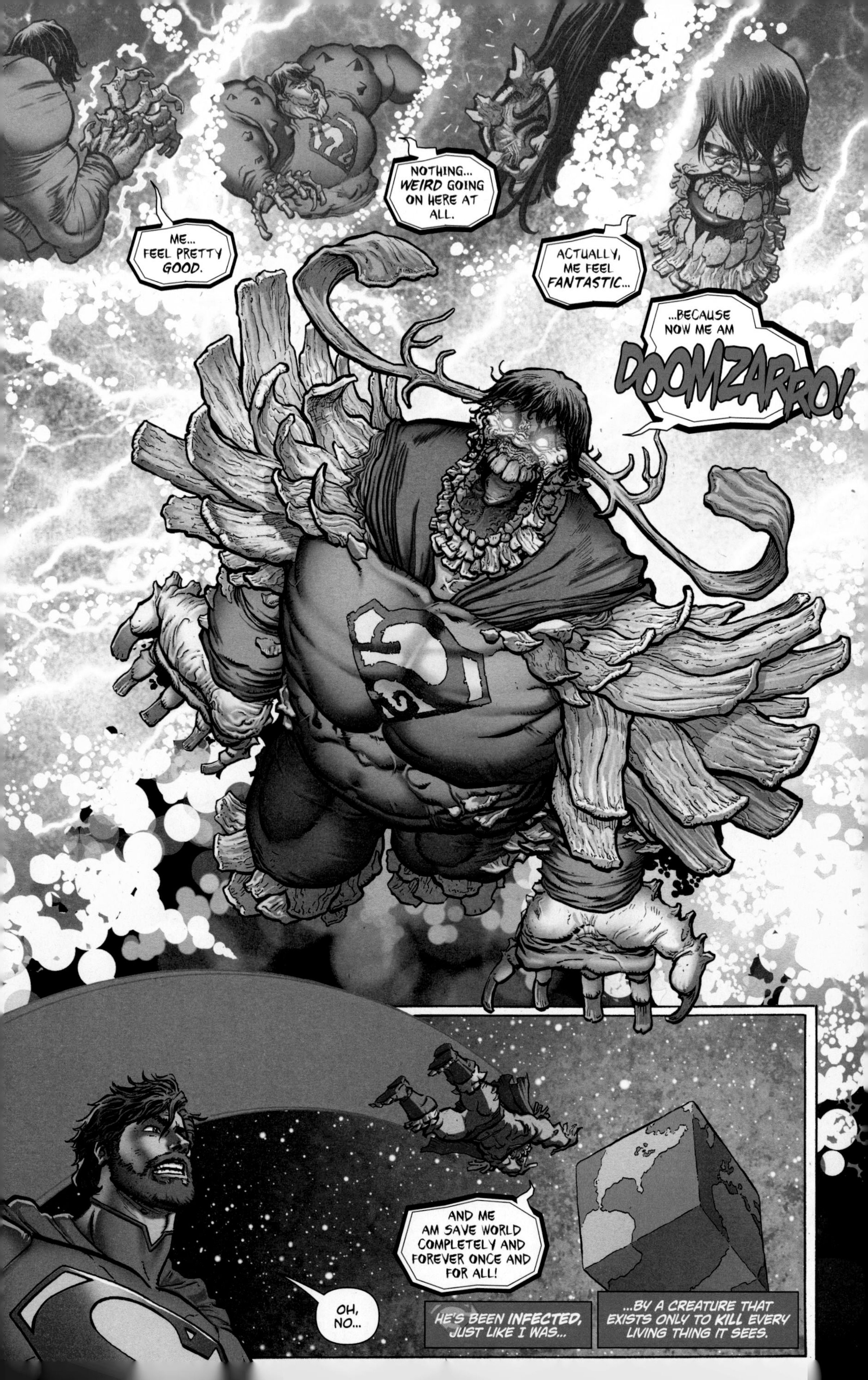
ME... FEEL PRETTY GOOD.
NOTHING... WEIRD GOING ON HERE AT ALL.
ACTUALLY, ME FEEL FANTASTIC...
...BECAUSE NOW ME AM DOOMZARRO!
AND ME AM SAVE WORLD COMPLETELY AND FOREVER ONCE AND FOR ALL!
OH, NO...
HE'S BEEN INFECTED, JUST LIKE I WAS...
...BY A CREATURE THAT EXISTS ONLY TO KILL EVERY LIVING THING IT SEES.

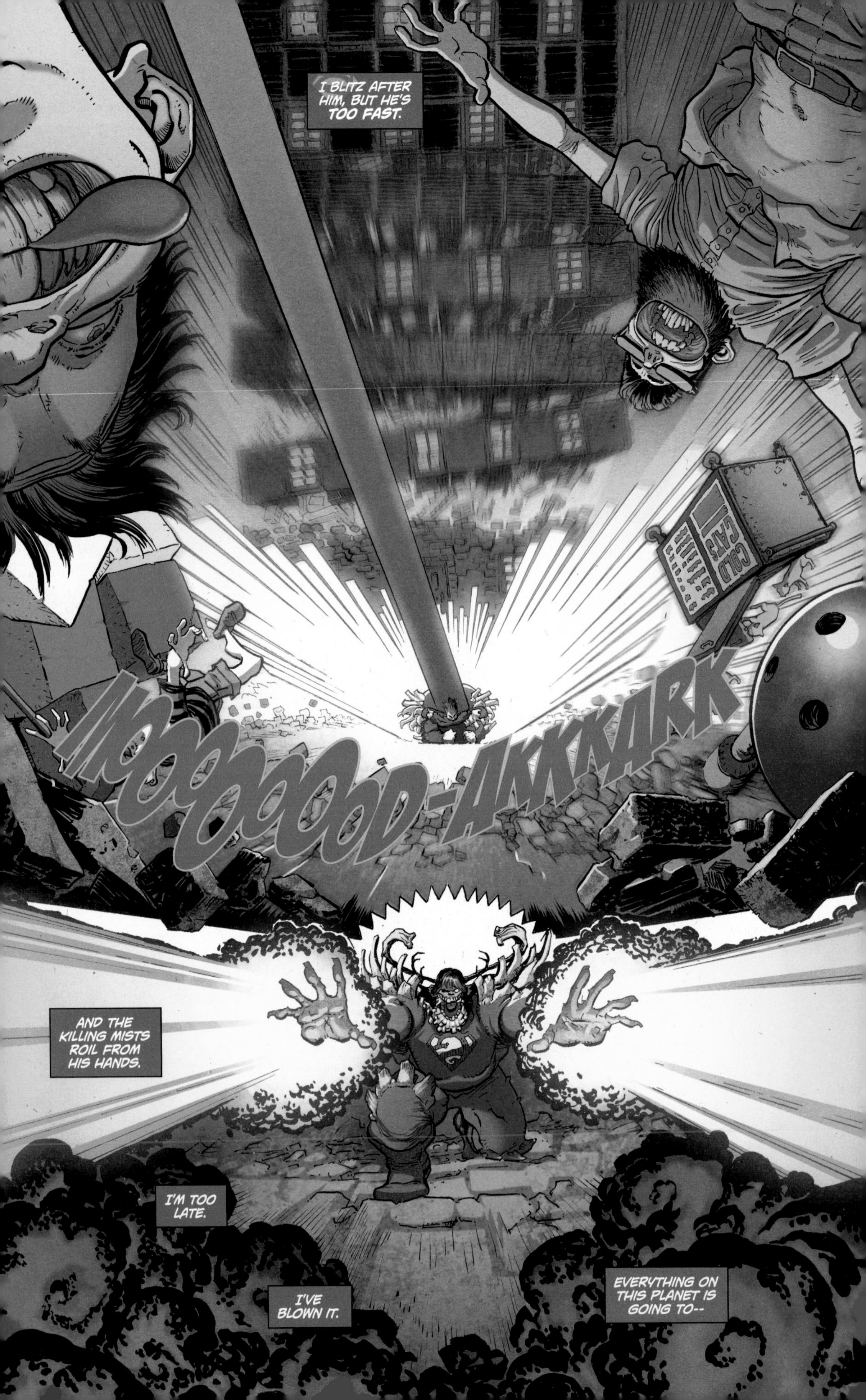
I BLITZ AFTER HIM, BUT HE'S TOO FAST.
WOOOOOOOD-AKKKARK
AND THE KILLING MISTS ROIL FROM HIS HANDS.
I'M TOO LATE.
I'VE BLOWN IT.
EVERYTHING ON THIS PLANET IS GOING TO--

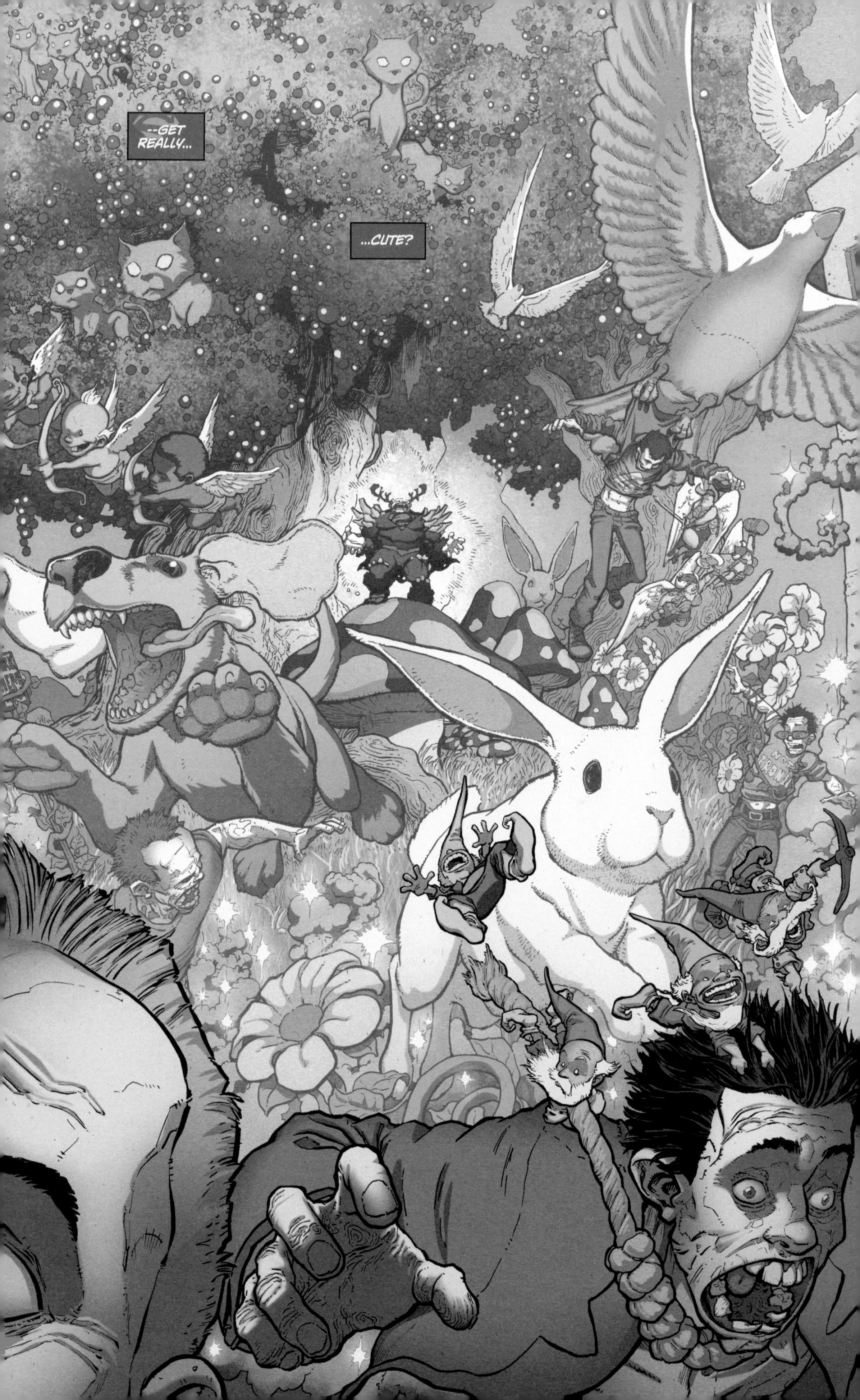
--GET REALLY...
...CUTE?

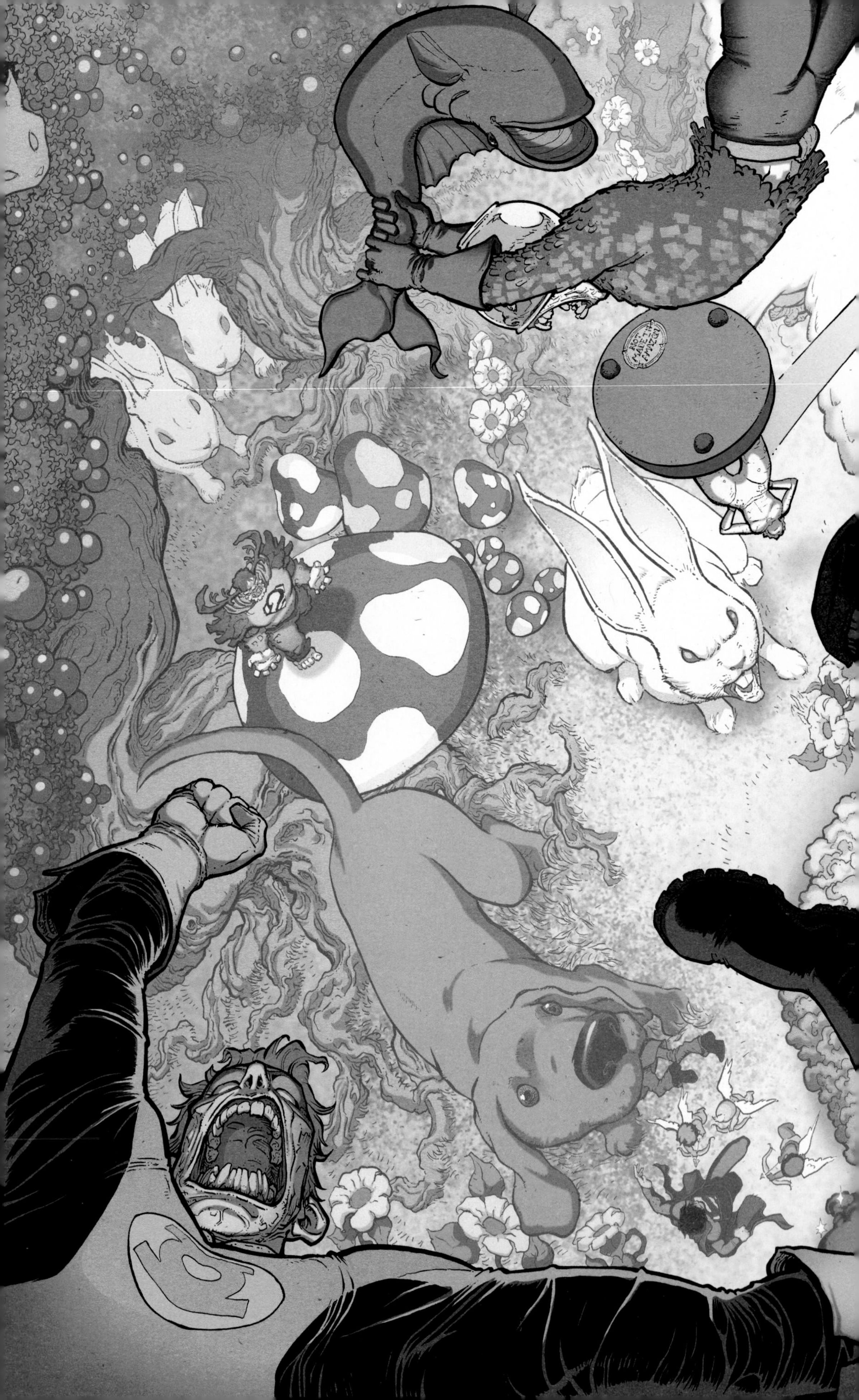

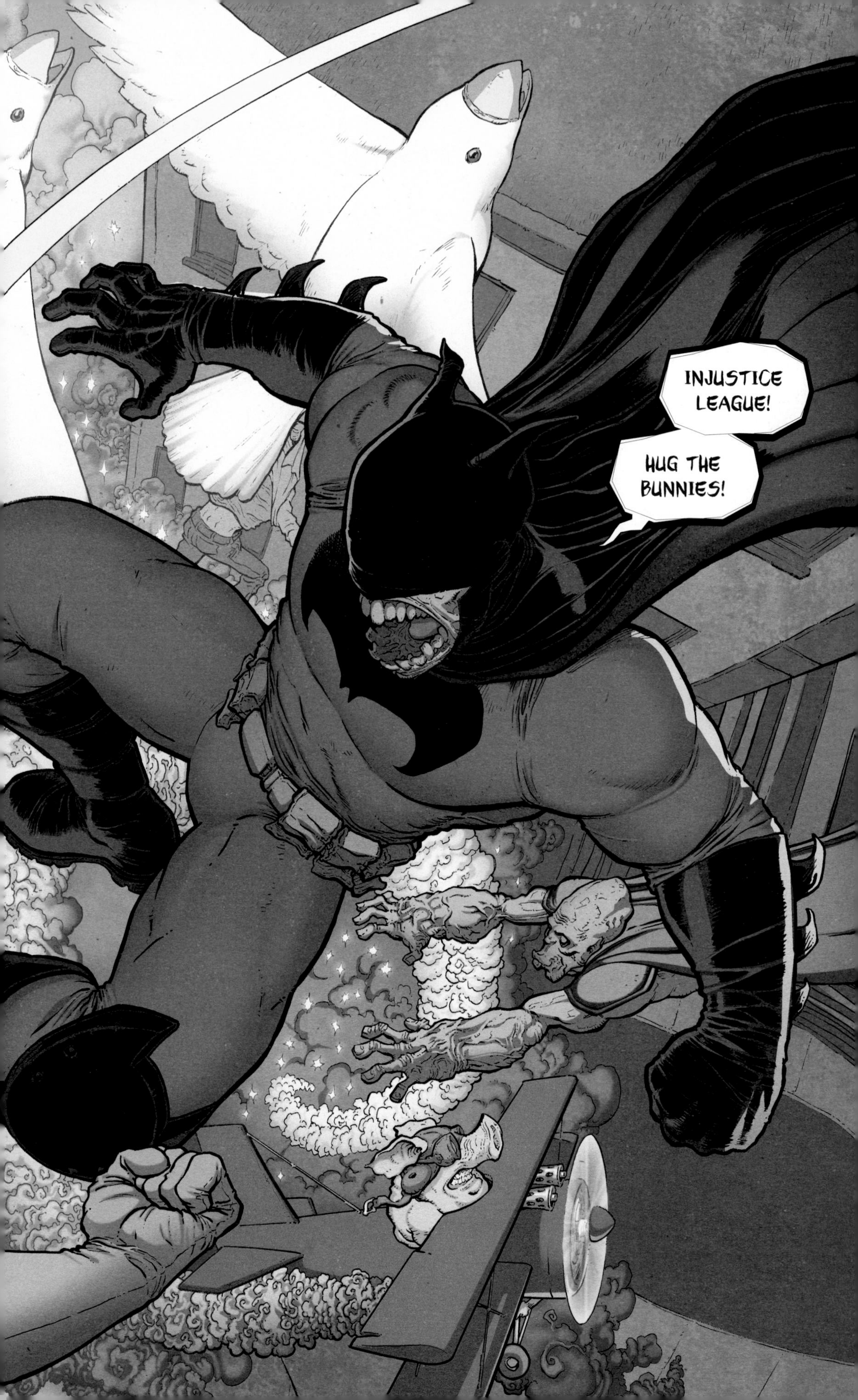
INJUSTICE LEAGUE!
HUG THE BUNNIES!

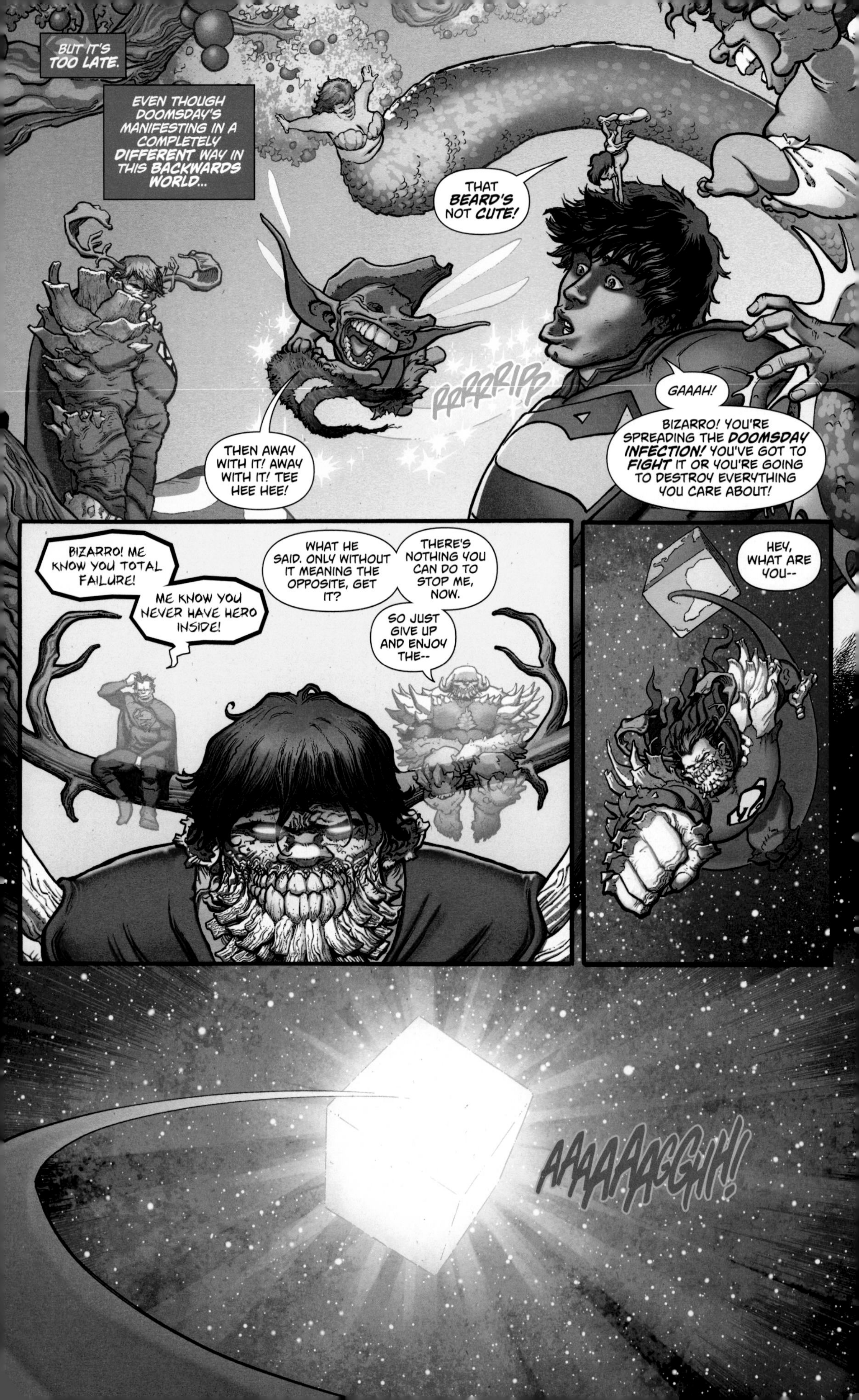
BUT IT'S TOO LATE.
EVEN THOUGH DOOMSDAY'S MANIFESTING IN A COMPLETELY DIFFERENT WAY IN THIS BACKWARDS WORLD...
THAT BEARD'S NOT CUTE!
RRRRRIPP
THEN AWAY WITH IT! AWAY WITH IT! TEE HEE HEE!
GAAAH!
BIZARRO! YOU'RE SPREADING THE DOOMSDAY INFECTION! YOU'VE GOT TO FIGHT IT OR YOU'RE GOING TO DESTROY EVERYTHING YOU CARE ABOUT!
BIZARRO! ME KNOW YOU TOTAL FAILURE!
ME KNOW YOU NEVER HAVE HERO INSIDE!
WHAT HE SAID. ONLY WITHOUT IT MEANING THE OPPOSITE, GET IT?
THERE'S NOTHING YOU CAN DO TO STOP ME, NOW.
SO JUST GIVE UP AND ENJOY THE--
HEY, WHAT ARE YOU--
AAAAAAGGHH!

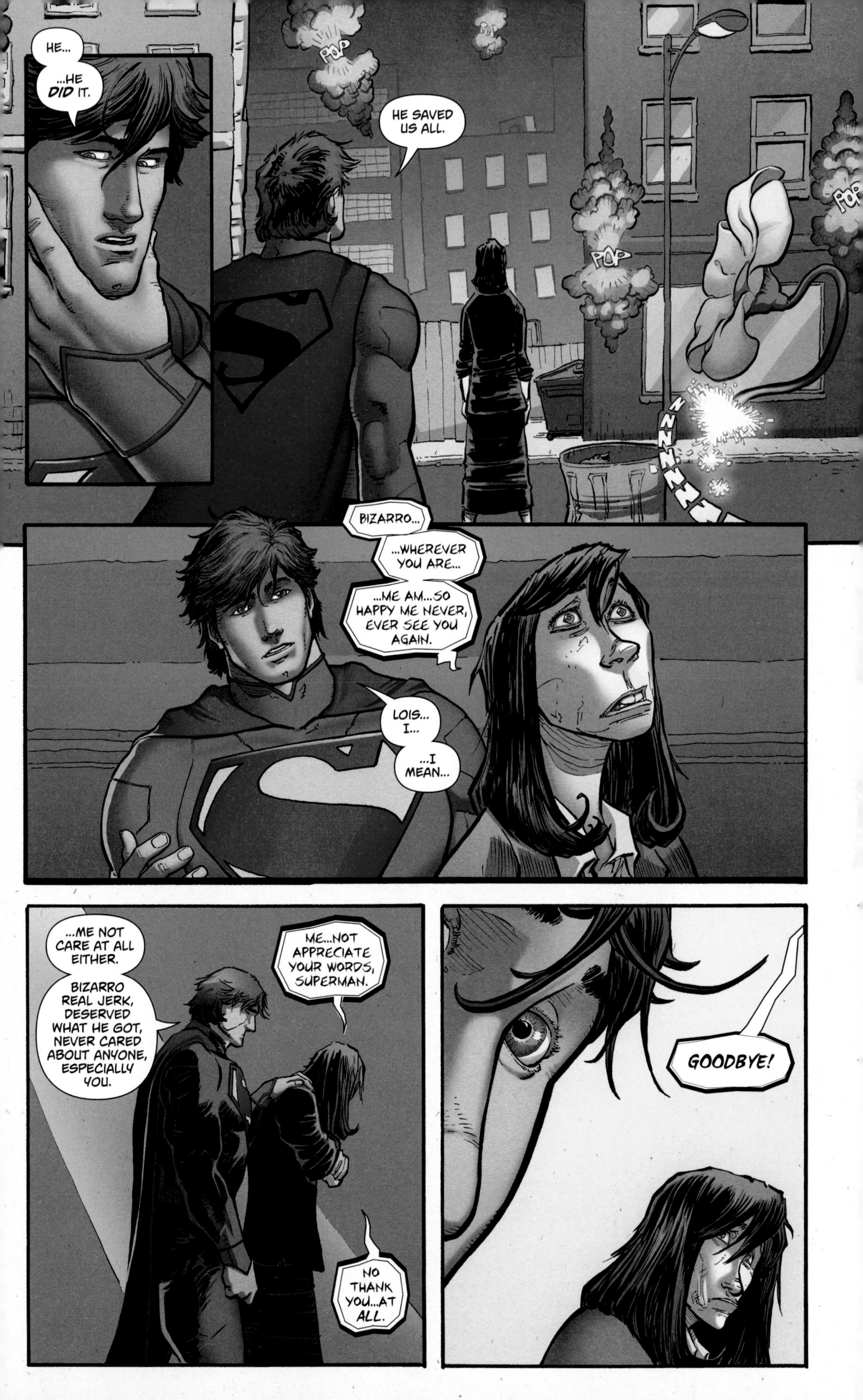
HE...
...HE DID IT.
POP
POP
HE SAVED US ALL.
POP
POP
NNNNNN
BIZARRO...
...WHEREVER YOU ARE...
...ME AM...SO HAPPY ME NEVER, EVER SEE YOU AGAIN.
LOIS... I...
...I MEAN...
...ME NOT CARE AT ALL EITHER.
BIZARRO REAL JERK, DESERVED WHAT HE GOT, NEVER CARED ABOUT ANYONE, ESPECIALLY YOU.
ME...NOT APPRECIATE YOUR WORDS, SUPERMAN.
NO THANK YOU...AT ALL.
GOODBYE!

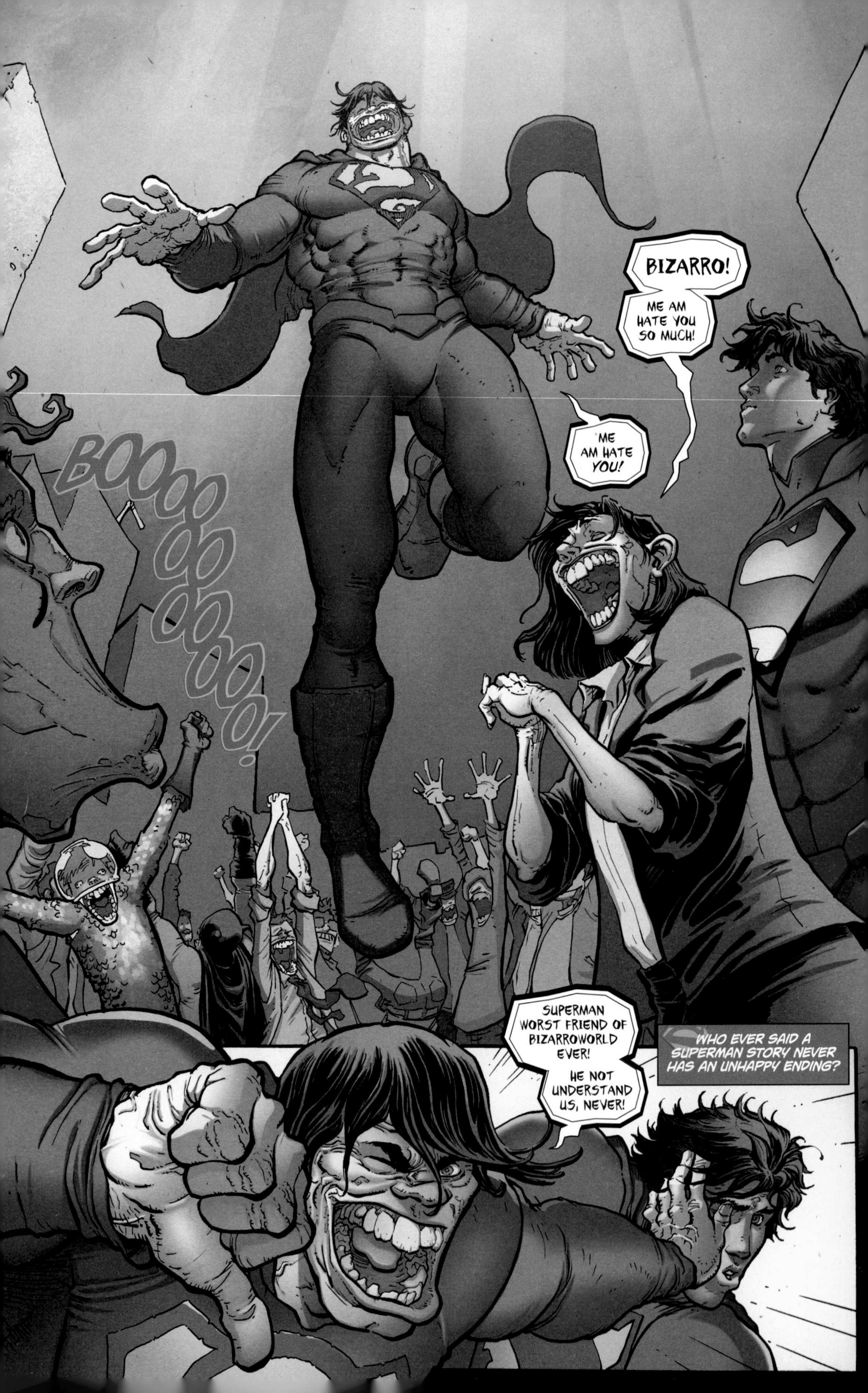
BIZARRO!
ME AM HATE YOU SO MUCH!
ME AM HATE YOU!
BOOOOOOOOOOO!
SUPERMAN WORST FRIEND OF BIZARROWORLD EVER!
HE NOT UNDERSTAND US, NEVER!
WHO EVER SAID A SUPERMAN STORY NEVER HAS AN UNHAPPY ENDING?

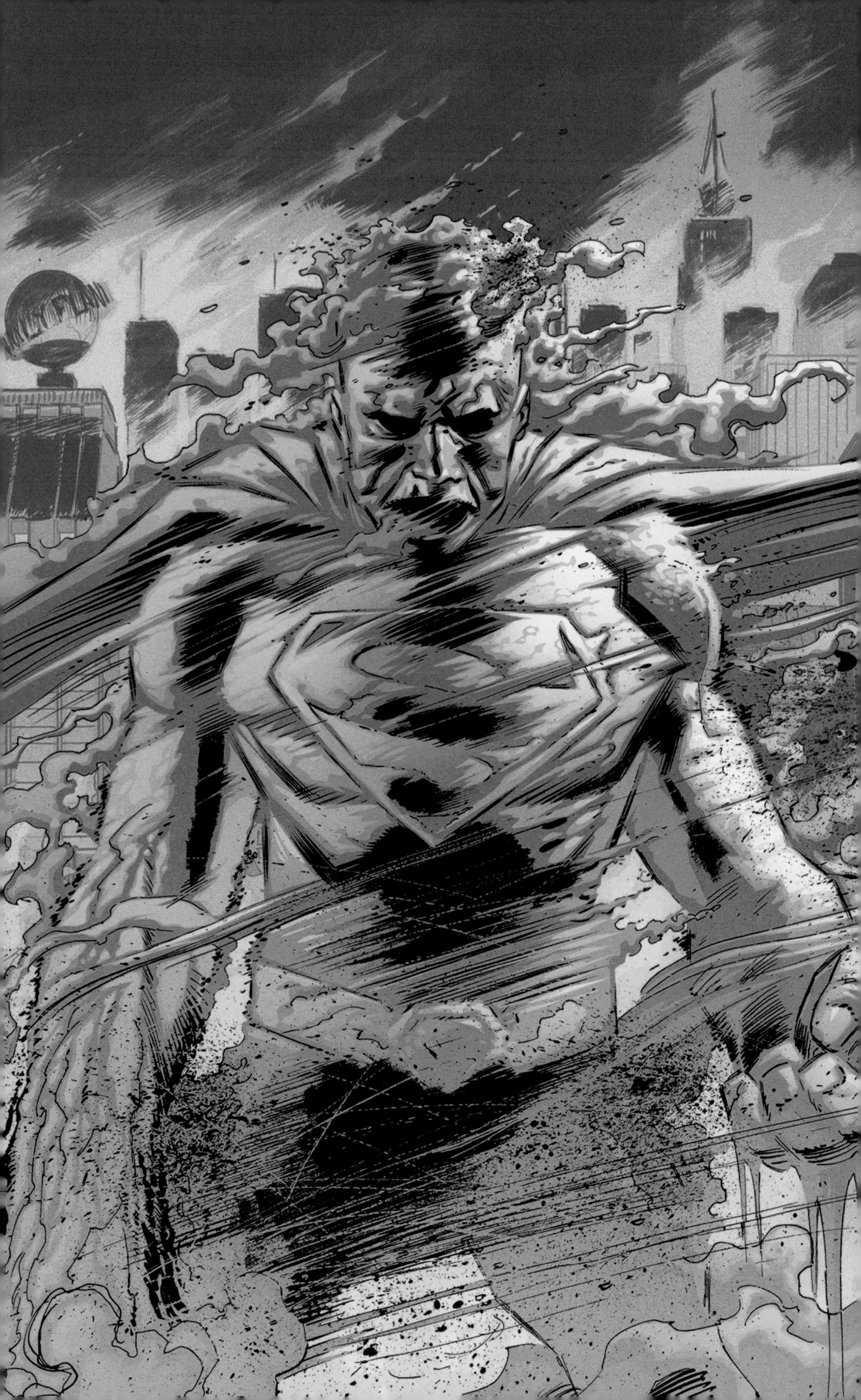

CROSSROADS

SHOLLY FISCH writer **PASCAL ALIXE VICENTE CIFUENTES** artists **PETE PANTAZIS** colorist **CARLOS M. MANGUAL** letterer cover by **LEE WEEKS & DAVE MCCAIG**

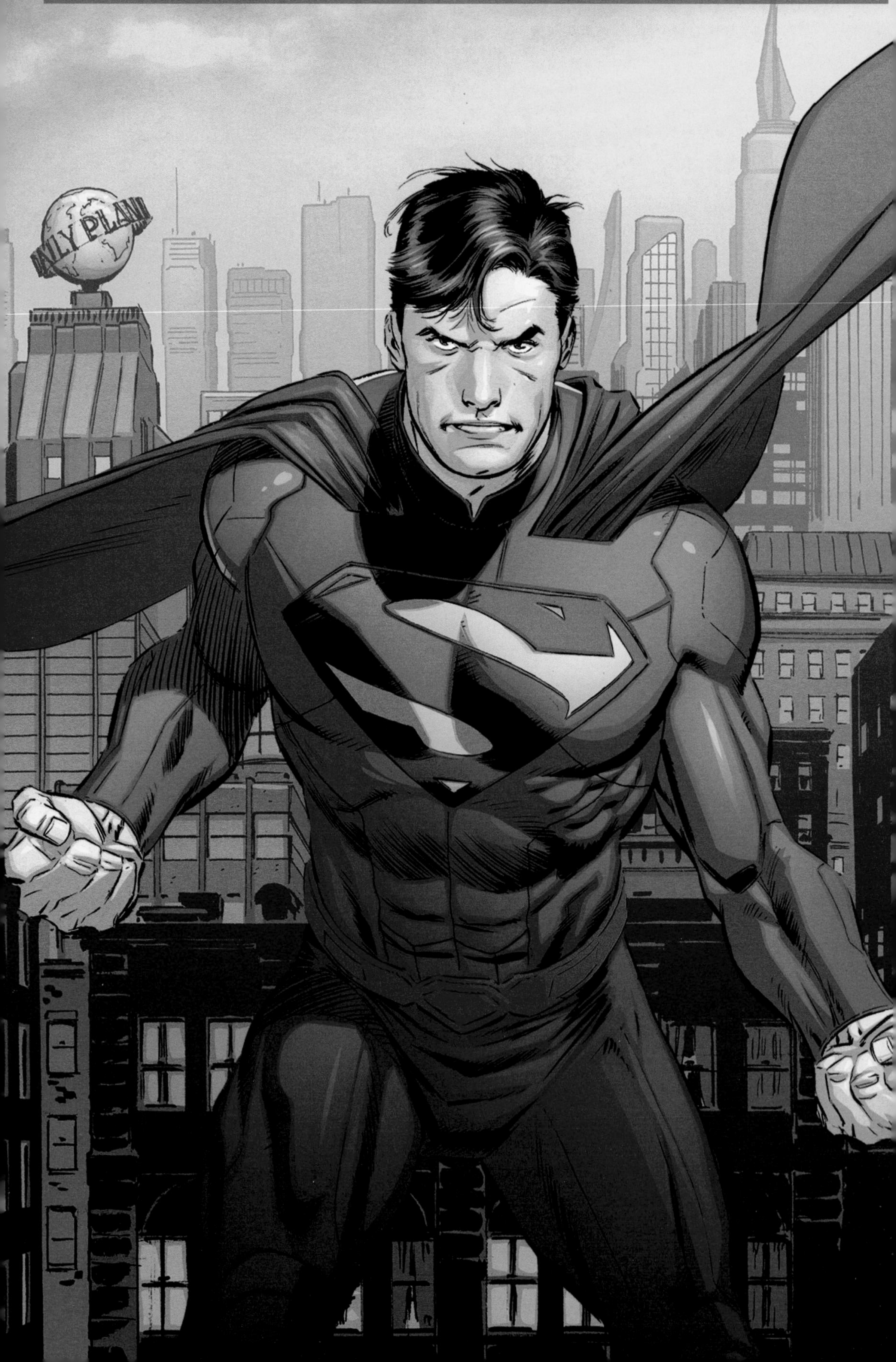

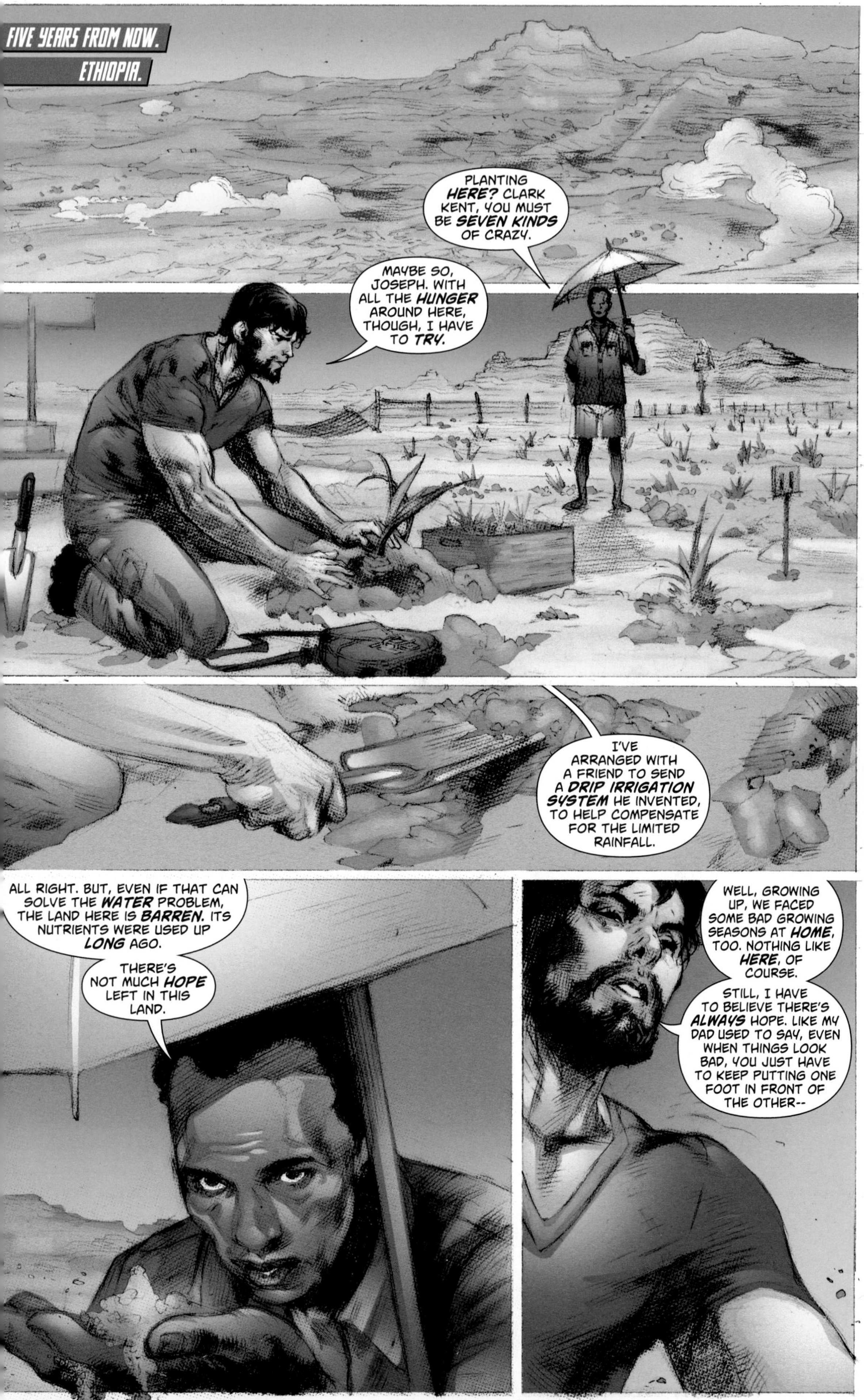
FIVE YEARS FROM NOW.
ETHIOPIA.
PLANTING HERE? CLARK KENT, YOU MUST BE SEVEN KINDS OF CRAZY.
MAYBE SO, JOSEPH. WITH ALL THE HUNGER AROUND HERE, THOUGH, I HAVE TO TRY.
I'VE ARRANGED WITH A FRIEND TO SEND A DRIP IRRIGATION SYSTEM HE INVENTED, TO HELP COMPENSATE FOR THE LIMITED RAINFALL.
ALL RIGHT. BUT, EVEN IF THAT CAN SOLVE THE WATER PROBLEM, THE LAND HERE IS BARREN. ITS NUTRIENTS WERE USED UP LONG AGO.
THERE'S NOT MUCH HOPE LEFT IN THIS LAND.
WELL, GROWING UP, WE FACED SOME BAD GROWING SEASONS AT HOME, TOO. NOTHING LIKE HERE, OF COURSE.
STILL, I HAVE TO BELIEVE THERE'S ALWAYS HOPE. LIKE MY DAD USED TO SAY, EVEN WHEN THINGS LOOK BAD, YOU JUST HAVE TO KEEP PUTTING ONE FOOT IN FRONT OF THE OTHER--

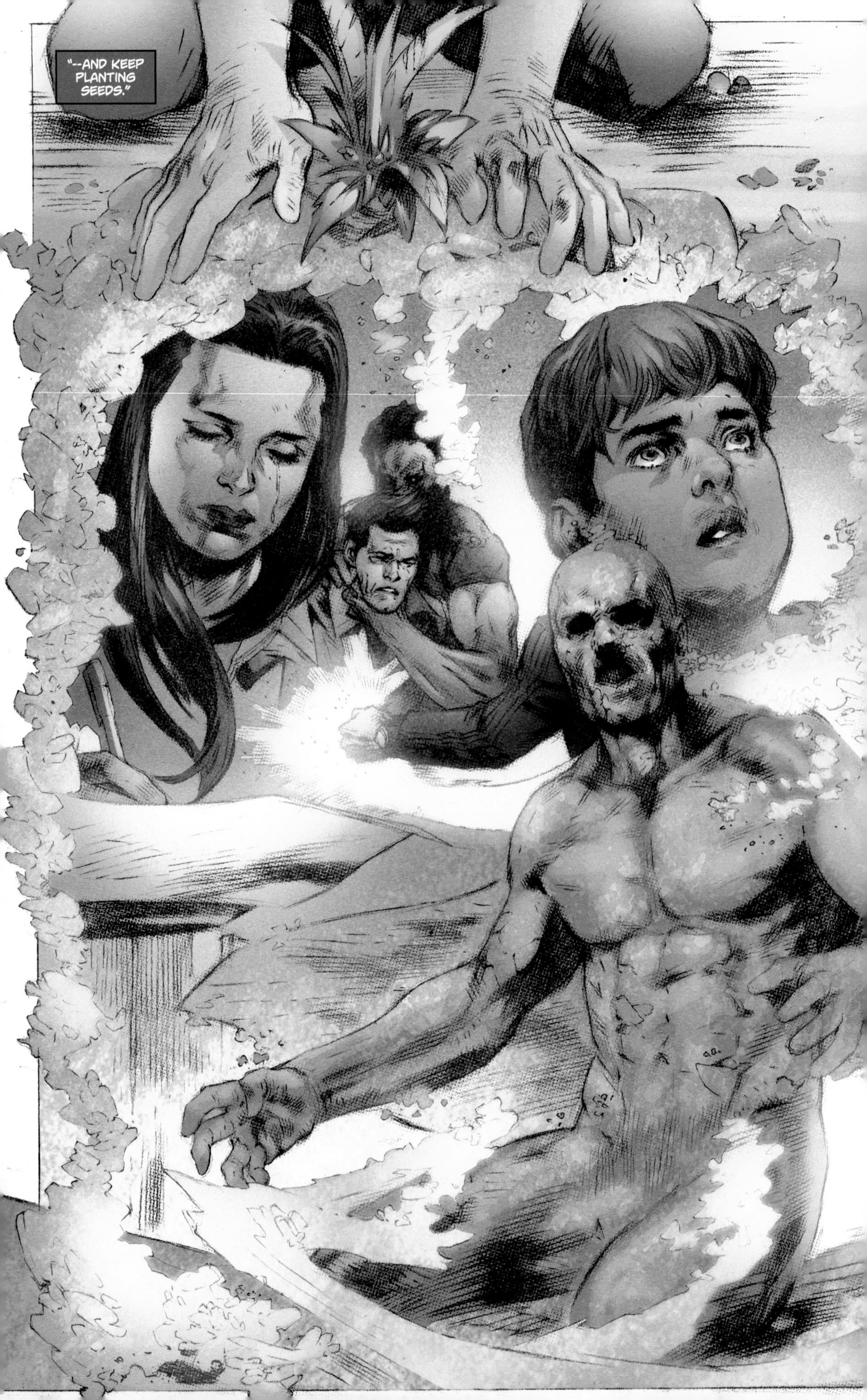
"--AND KEEP PLANTING SEEDS."

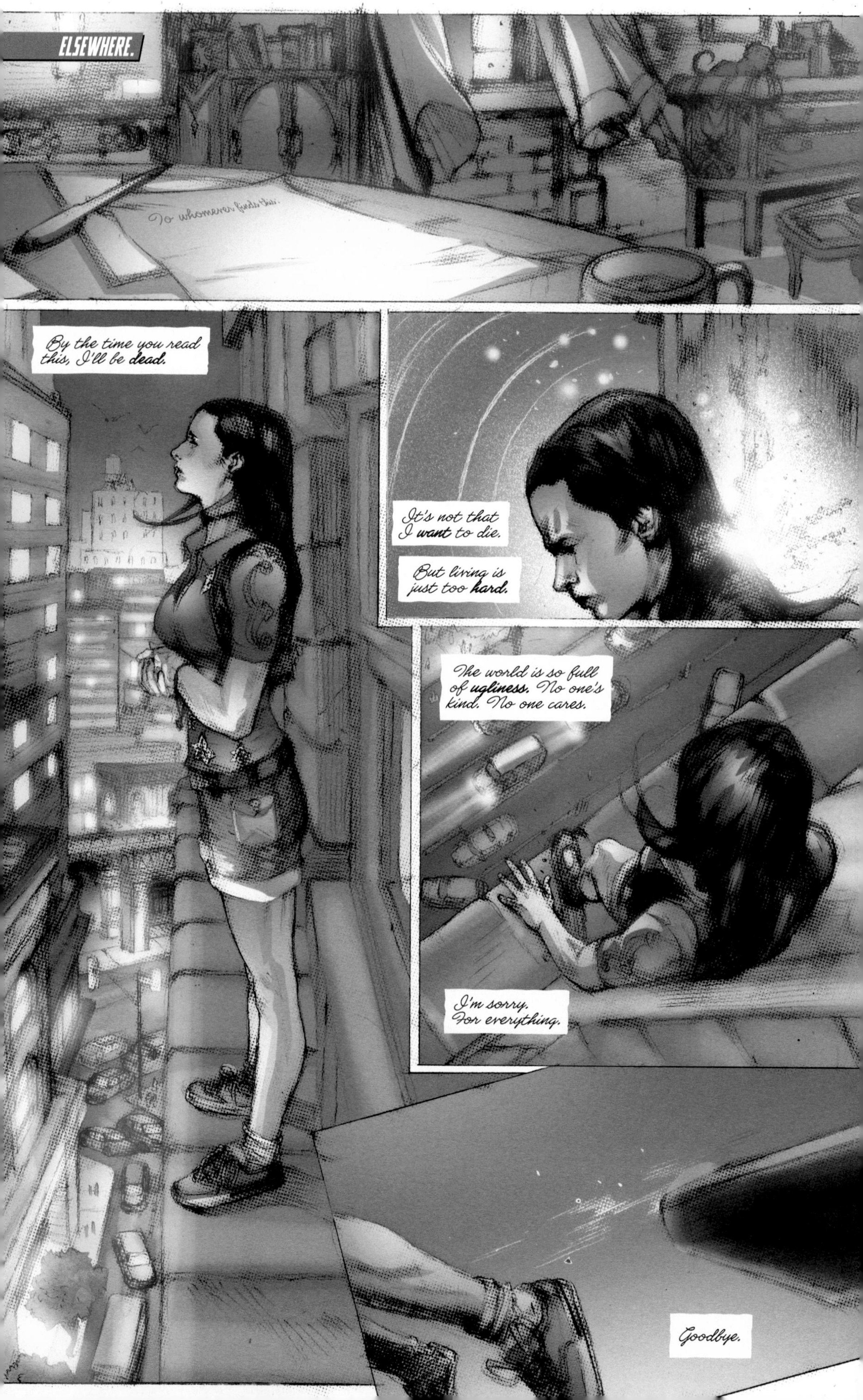

ELSEWHERE.
To whomever finds this.
By the time you read this, I'll be dead.
It's not that I want to die.
But living is just too hard.
The world is so full of ugliness. No one's kind. No one cares.
I'm sorry. For everything.
Goodbye.

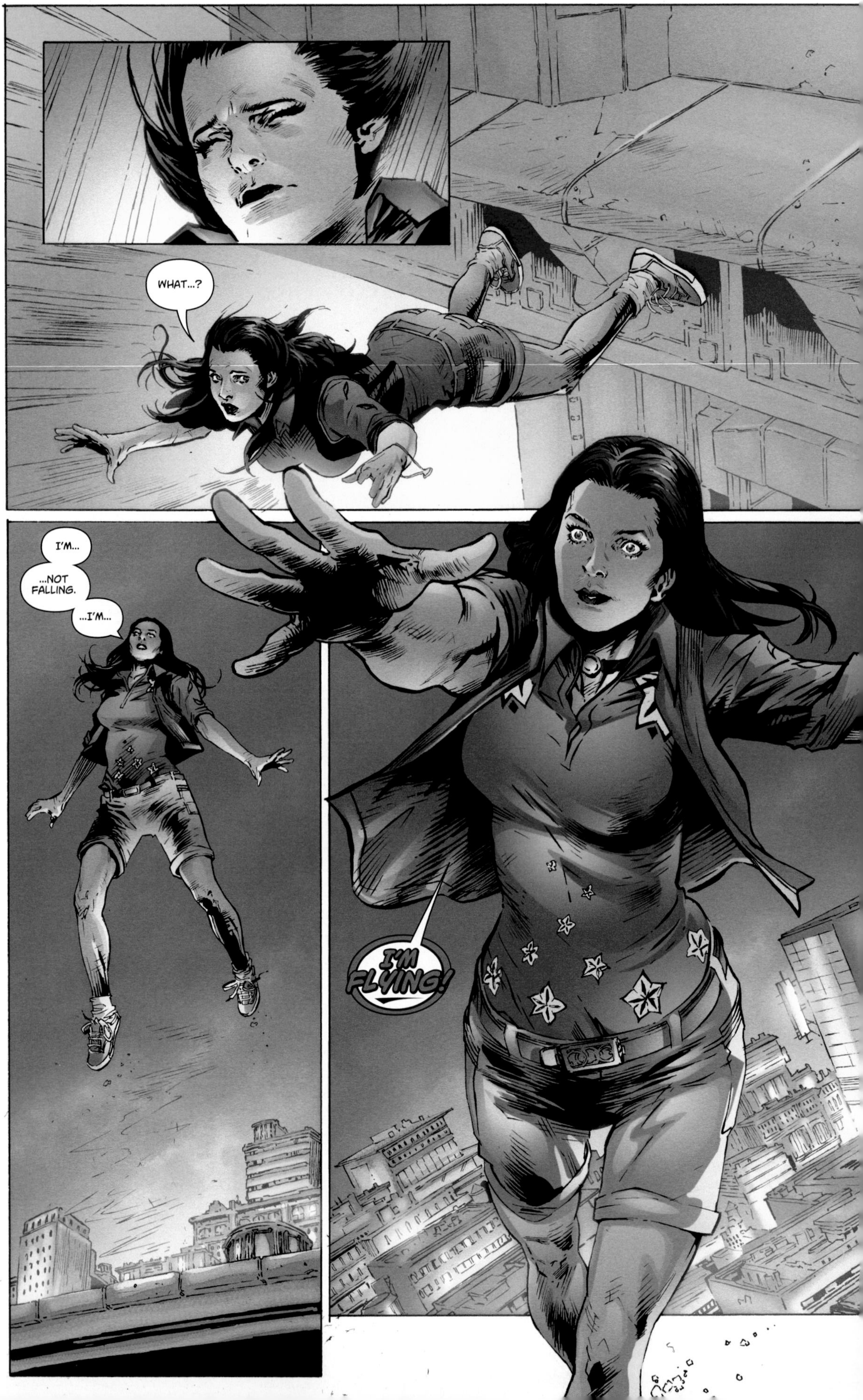
WHAT...?
I'M...
...NOT FALLING.
...I'M...
I'M FLYING!

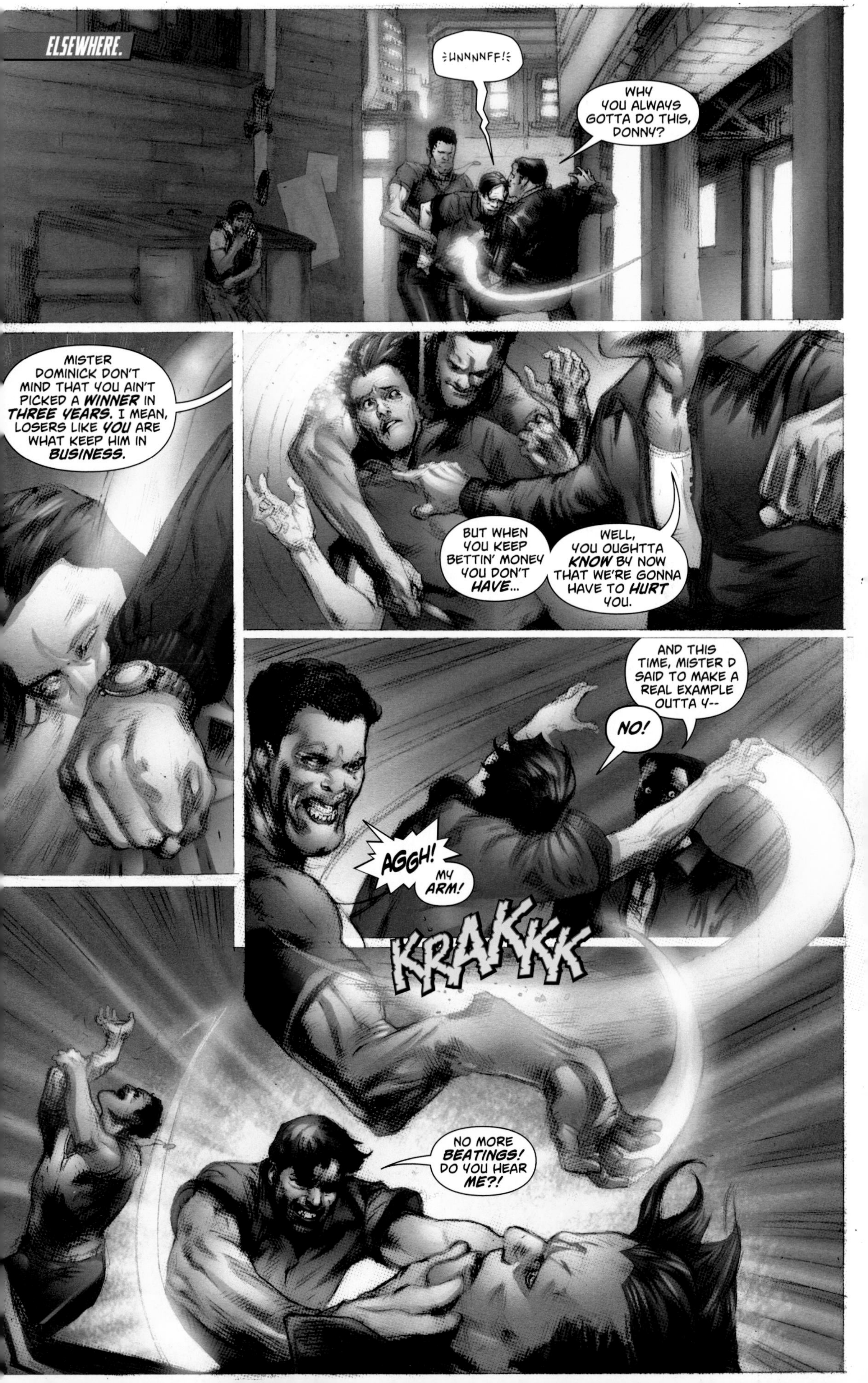
ELSEWHERE.
UNNNNFF!
WHY YOU ALWAYS GOTTA DO THIS, DONNY?
MISTER DOMINICK DON'T MIND THAT YOU AIN'T PICKED A WINNER IN THREE YEARS. I MEAN, LOSERS LIKE YOU ARE WHAT KEEP HIM IN BUSINESS.
BUT WHEN YOU KEEP BETTIN' MONEY YOU DON'T HAVE...
WELL, YOU OUGHTTA KNOW BY NOW THAT WE'RE GONNA HAVE TO HURT YOU.
AND THIS TIME, MISTER D SAID TO MAKE A REAL EXAMPLE OUTTA Y--
NO!
AGGH! MY ARM!
KRAKKK
NO MORE BEATINGS! DO YOU HEAR ME?!

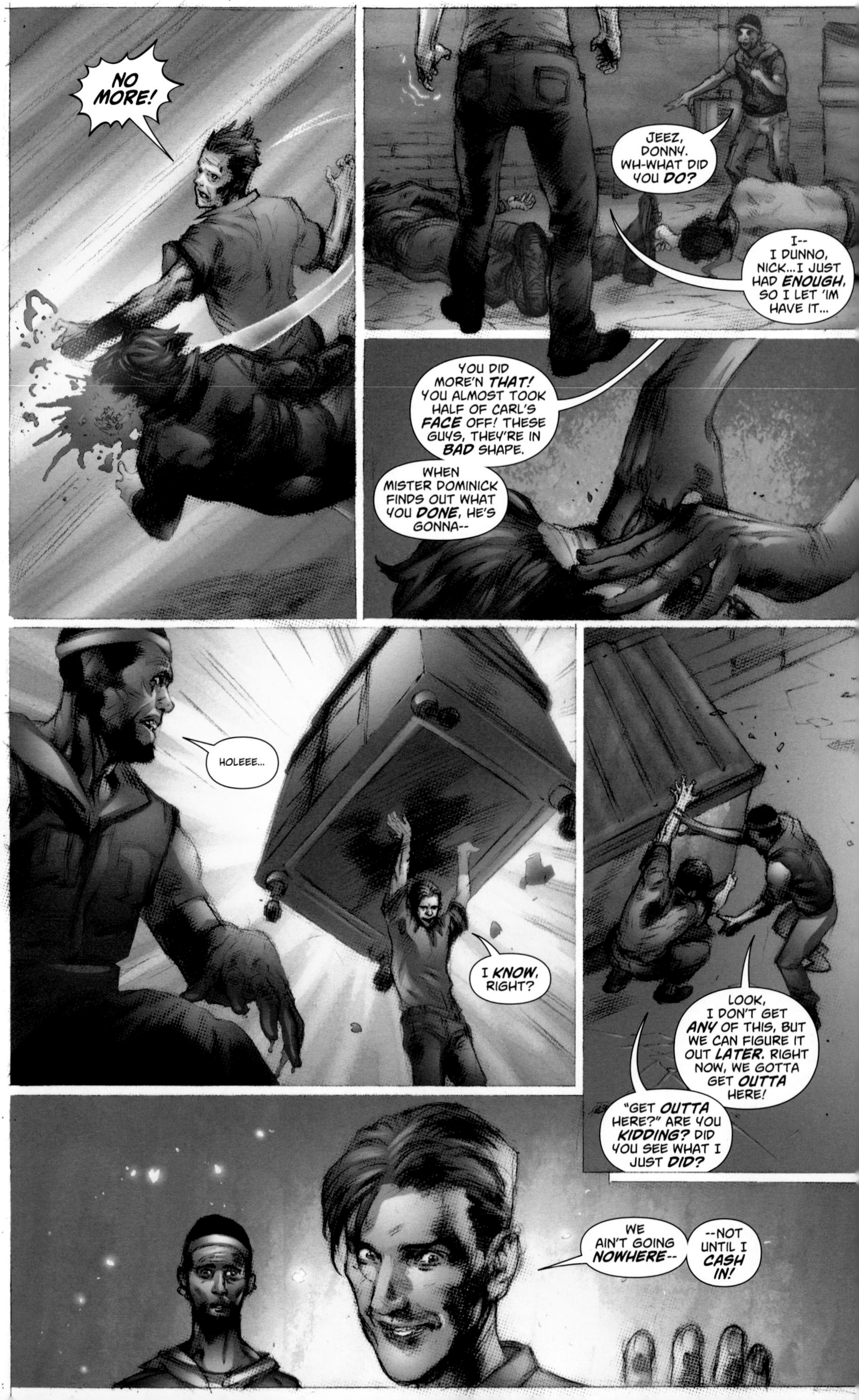
NO MORE!
JEEZ, DONNY. WH-WHAT DID YOU DO?
I-- I DUNNO, NICK...I JUST HAD ENOUGH, SO I LET 'IM HAVE IT...
YOU DID MORE'N THAT! YOU ALMOST TOOK HALF OF CARL'S FACE OFF! THESE GUYS, THEY'RE IN BAD SHAPE.
WHEN MISTER DOMINICK FINDS OUT WHAT YOU DONE, HE'S GONNA--
HOLEEE...
I KNOW, RIGHT?
LOOK, I DON'T GET ANY OF THIS, BUT WE CAN FIGURE IT OUT LATER. RIGHT NOW, WE GOTTA GET OUTTA HERE!
"GET OUTTA HERE?" ARE YOU KIDDING? DID YOU SEE WHAT I JUST DID?
WE AIN'T GOING NOWHERE--
--NOT UNTIL I CASH IN!

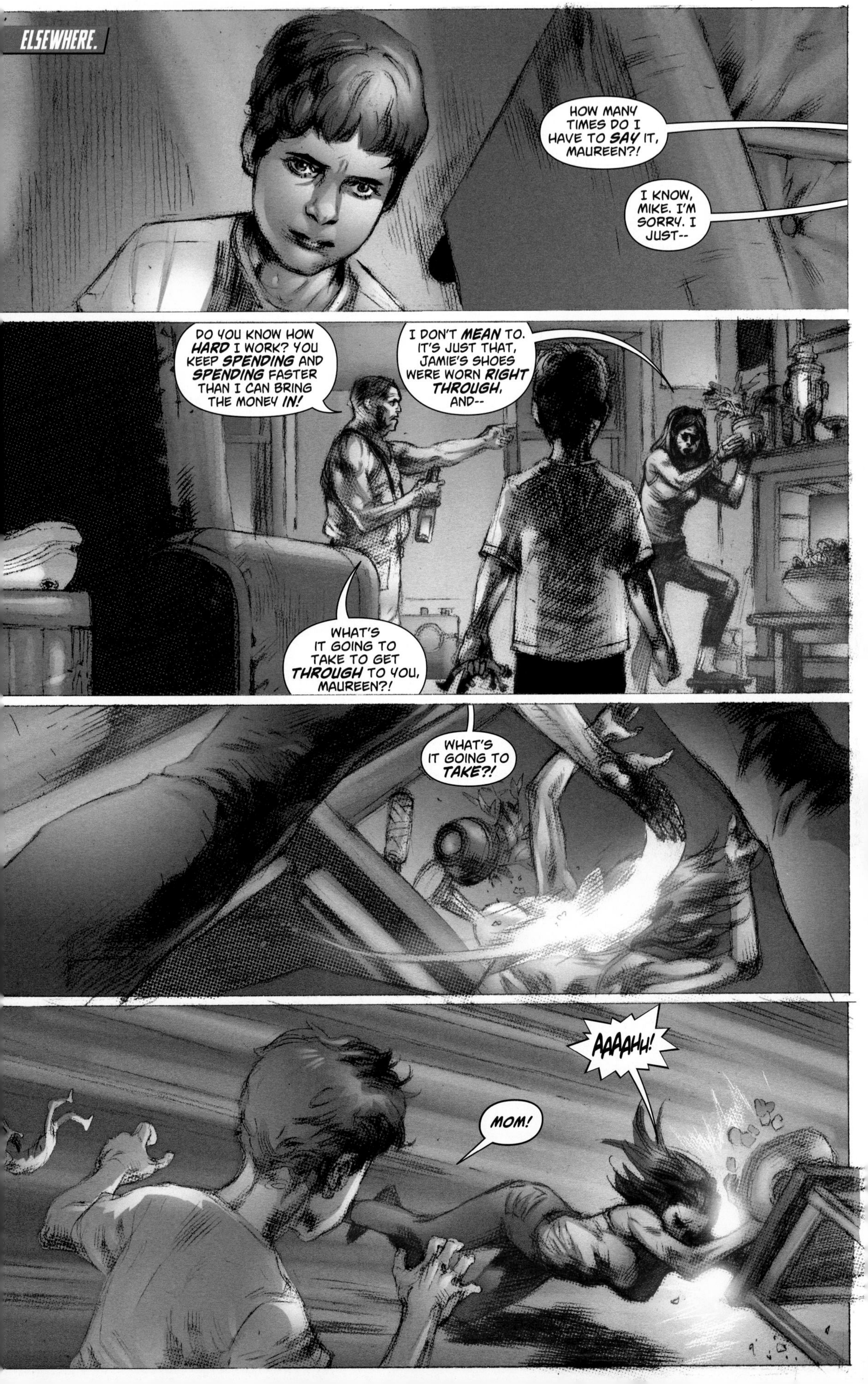
ELSEWHERE.
HOW MANY TIMES DO I HAVE TO SAY IT, MAUREEN?!
I KNOW, MIKE. I'M SORRY. I JUST--
DO YOU KNOW HOW HARD I WORK? YOU KEEP SPENDING AND SPENDING FASTER THAN I CAN BRING THE MONEY IN!
I DON'T MEAN TO. IT'S JUST THAT, JAMIE'S SHOES WERE WORN RIGHT THROUGH, AND--
WHAT'S IT GOING TO TAKE TO GET THROUGH TO YOU, MAUREEN?!
WHAT'S IT GOING TO TAKE?!
AAAAHH!
MOM!

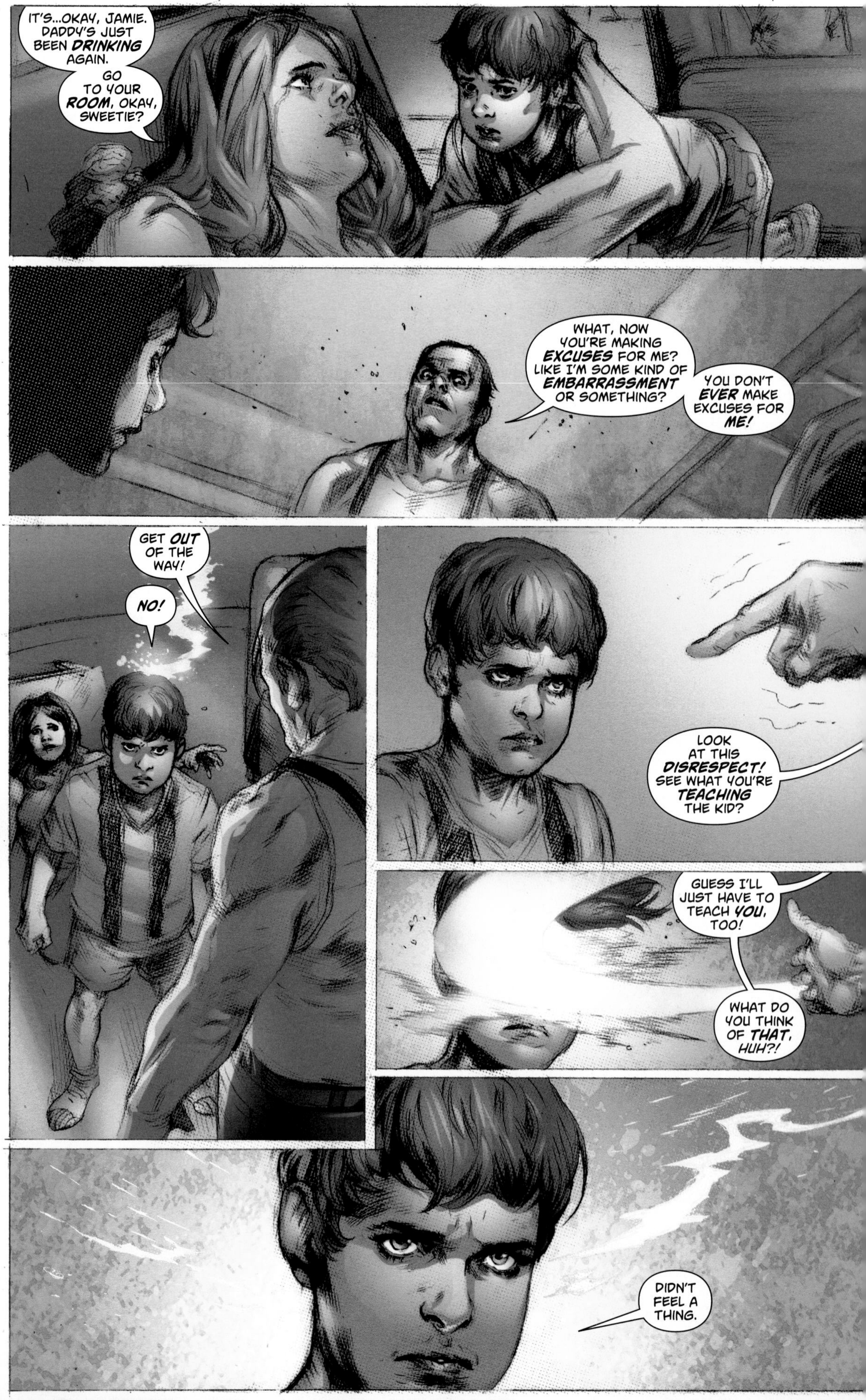

IT'S...OKAY, JAMIE. DADDY'S JUST BEEN DRINKING AGAIN.
GO TO YOUR ROOM, OKAY, SWEETIE?
WHAT, NOW YOU'RE MAKING EXCUSES FOR ME? LIKE I'M SOME KIND OF EMBARRASSMENT OR SOMETHING?
YOU DON'T EVER MAKE EXCUSES FOR ME!
GET OUT OF THE WAY!
NO!
LOOK AT THIS DISRESPECT! SEE WHAT YOU'RE TEACHING THE KID?
GUESS I'LL JUST HAVE TO TEACH YOU, TOO!
WHAT DO YOU THINK OF THAT, HUH?!
DIDN'T FEEL A THING.

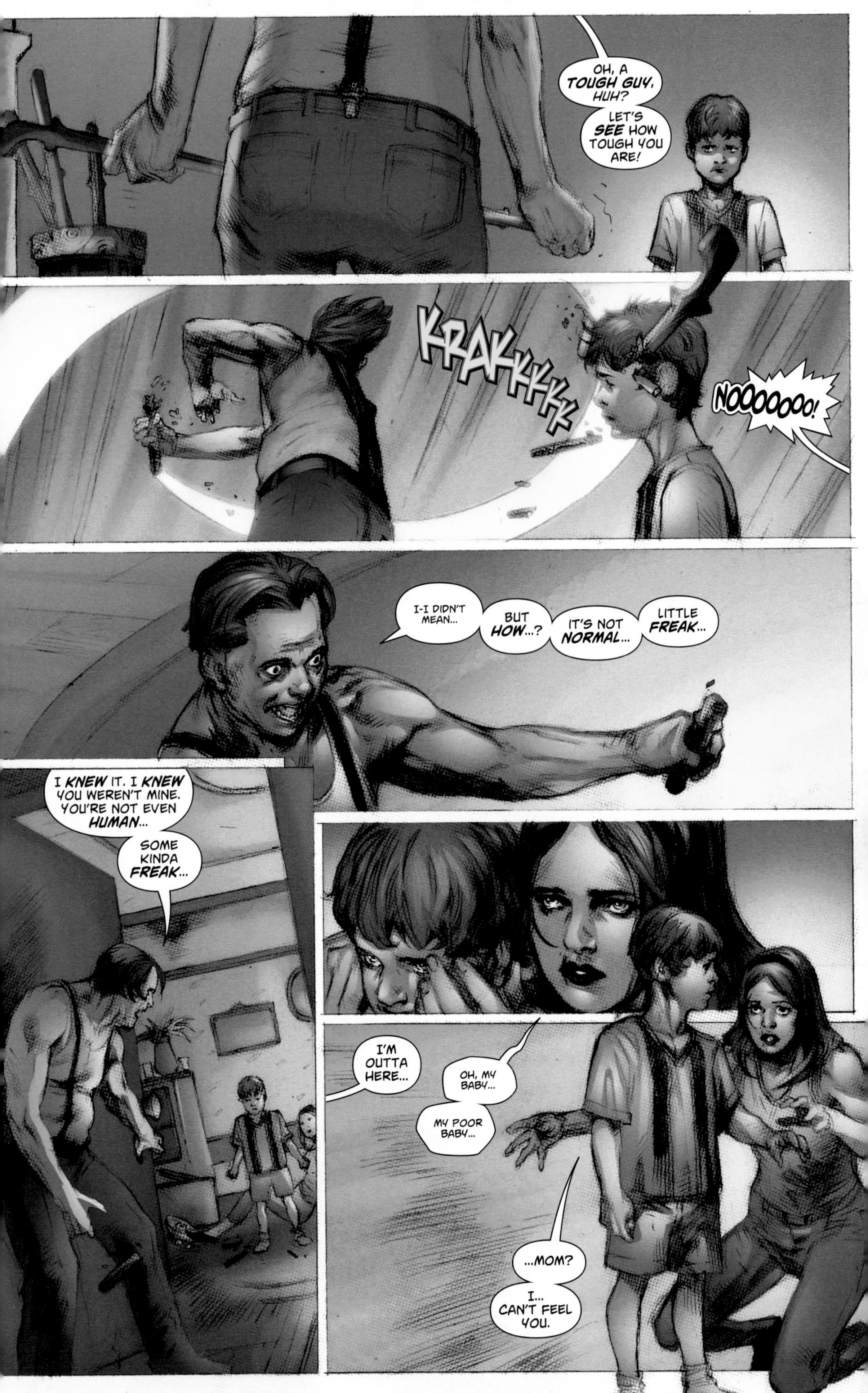
OH, A TOUGH GUY, HUH?
LET'S SEE HOW TOUGH YOU ARE!
KRAKKKKK
NOOOOOOO!
I-I DIDN'T MEAN...
BUT HOW...?
IT'S NOT NORMAL...
LITTLE FREAK...
I KNEW IT. I KNEW YOU WEREN'T MINE. YOU'RE NOT EVEN HUMAN...
SOME KINDA FREAK...
I'M OUTTA HERE...
OH, MY BABY...
MY POOR BABY...
...MOM?
I... CAN'T FEEL YOU.

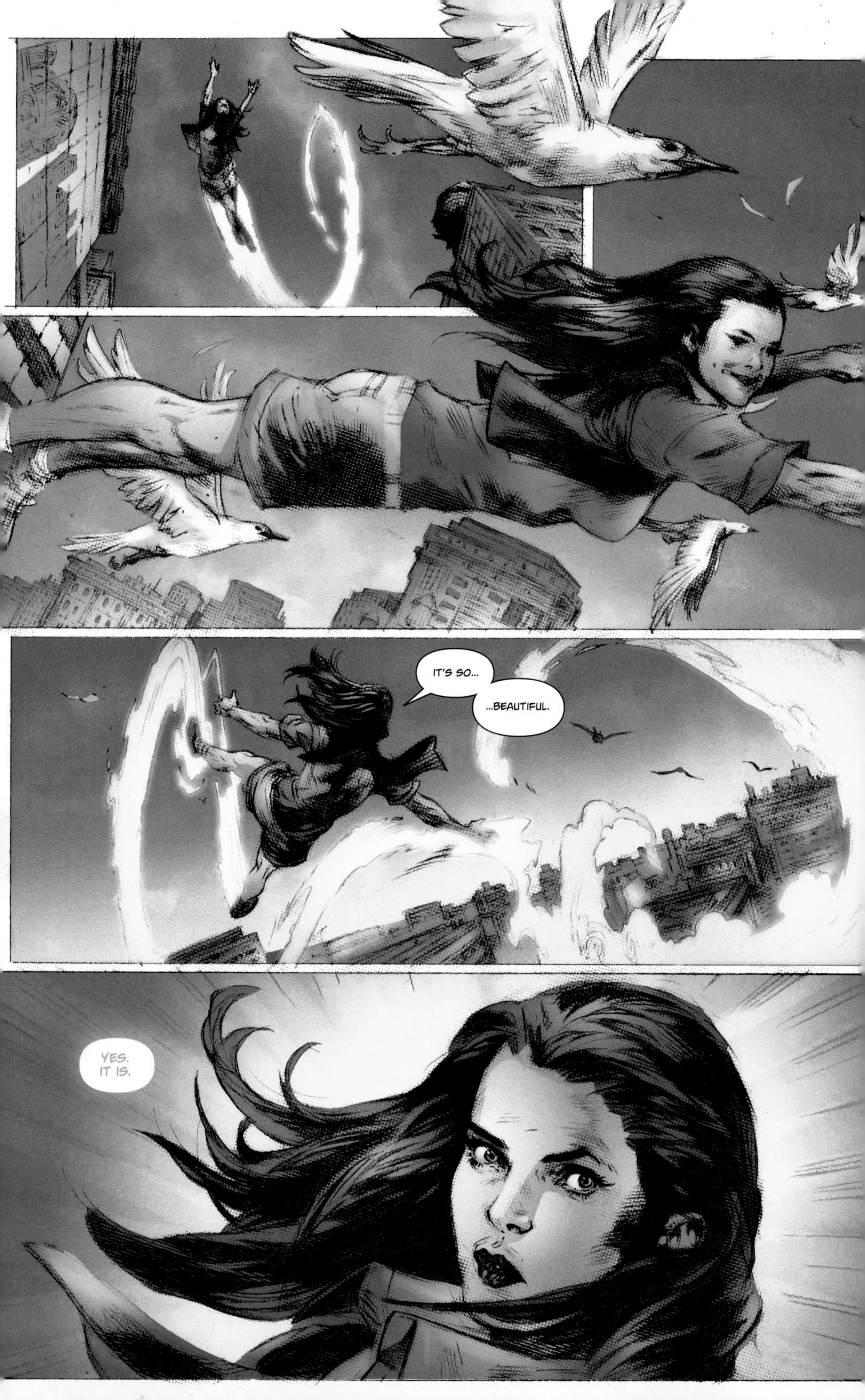
IT'S SO...
...BEAUTIFUL.
YES. IT IS.

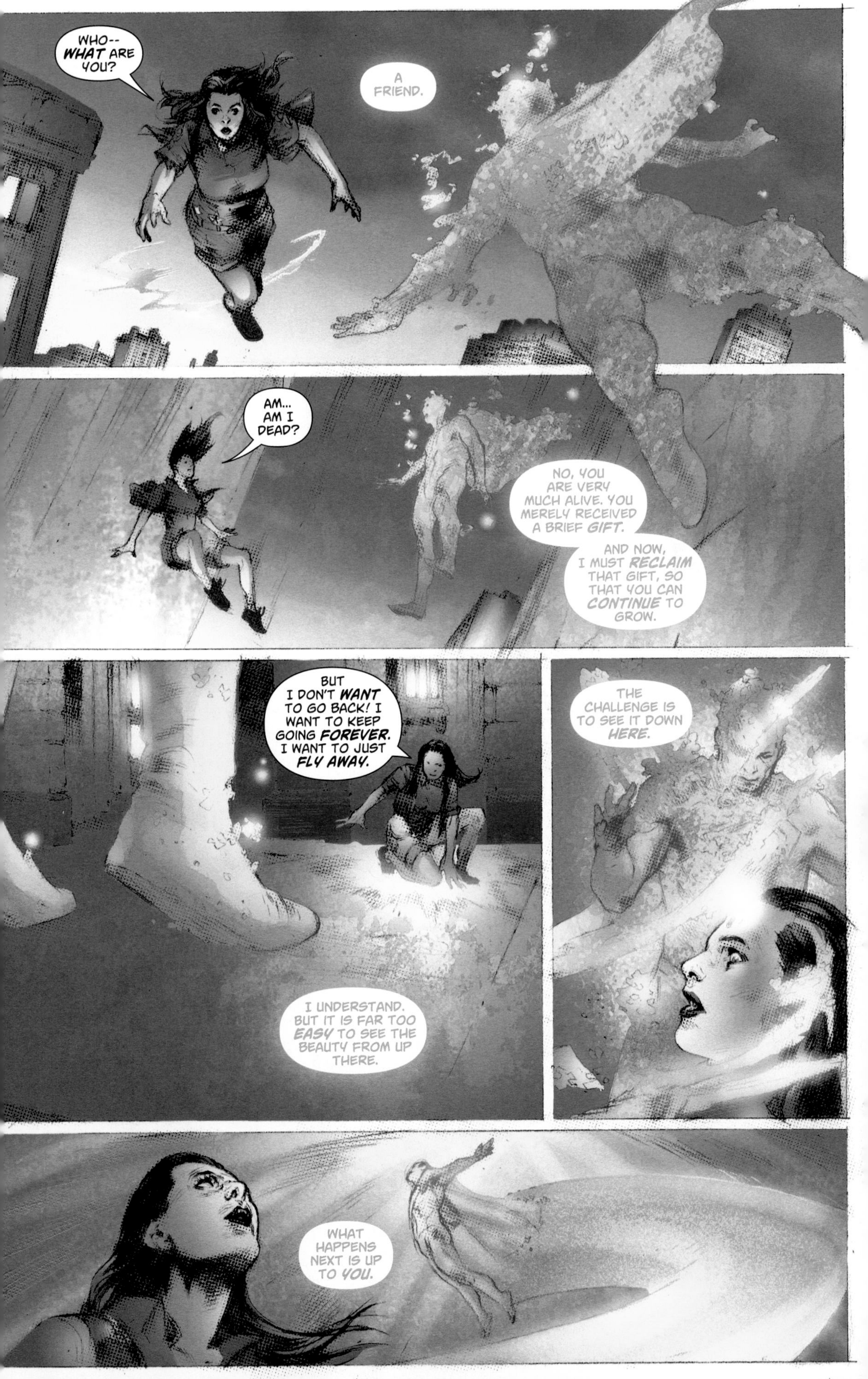
WHO-- WHAT ARE YOU?
A FRIEND.
AM... AM I DEAD?
NO, YOU ARE VERY MUCH ALIVE. YOU MERELY RECEIVED A BRIEF GIFT.
AND NOW, I MUST RECLAIM THAT GIFT, SO THAT YOU CAN CONTINUE TO GROW.
BUT I DON'T WANT TO GO BACK! I WANT TO KEEP GOING FOREVER. I WANT TO JUST FLY AWAY.
I UNDERSTAND. BUT IT IS FAR TOO EASY TO SEE THE BEAUTY FROM UP THERE.
THE CHALLENGE IS TO SEE IT DOWN HERE.
WHAT HAPPENS NEXT IS UP TO YOU.

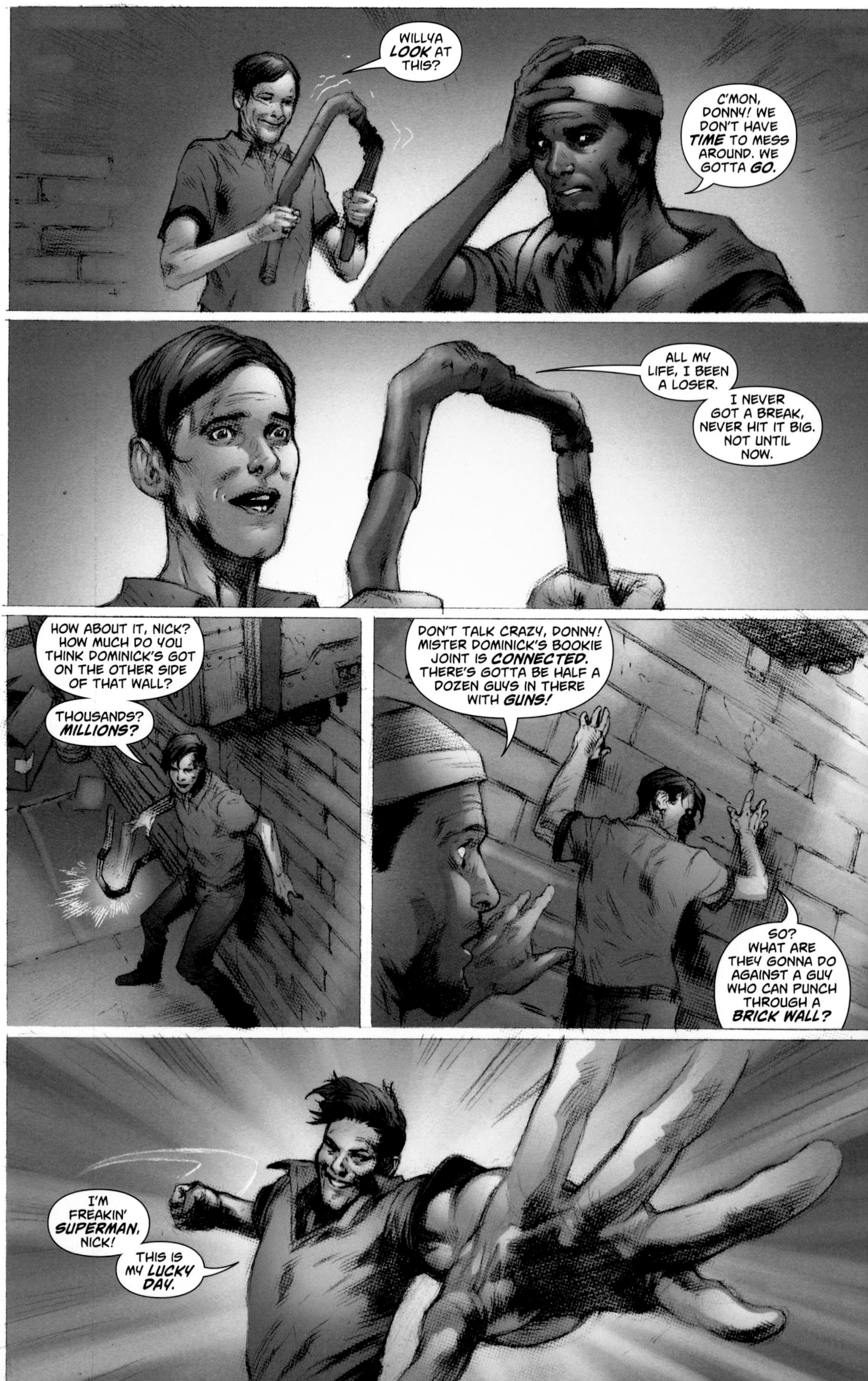
WILLYA LOOK AT THIS?
C'MON, DONNY! WE DON'T HAVE TIME TO MESS AROUND. WE GOTTA GO.
ALL MY LIFE, I BEEN A LOSER.
I NEVER GOT A BREAK, NEVER HIT IT BIG. NOT UNTIL NOW.
HOW ABOUT IT, NICK? HOW MUCH DO YOU THINK DOMINICK'S GOT ON THE OTHER SIDE OF THAT WALL?
THOUSANDS? MILLIONS?
DON'T TALK CRAZY, DONNY! MISTER DOMINICK'S BOOKIE JOINT IS CONNECTED. THERE'S GOTTA BE HALF A DOZEN GUYS IN THERE WITH GUNS!
SO? WHAT ARE THEY GONNA DO AGAINST A GUY WHO CAN PUNCH THROUGH A BRICK WALL?
I'M FREAKIN' SUPERMAN, NICK!
THIS IS MY LUCKY DAY.

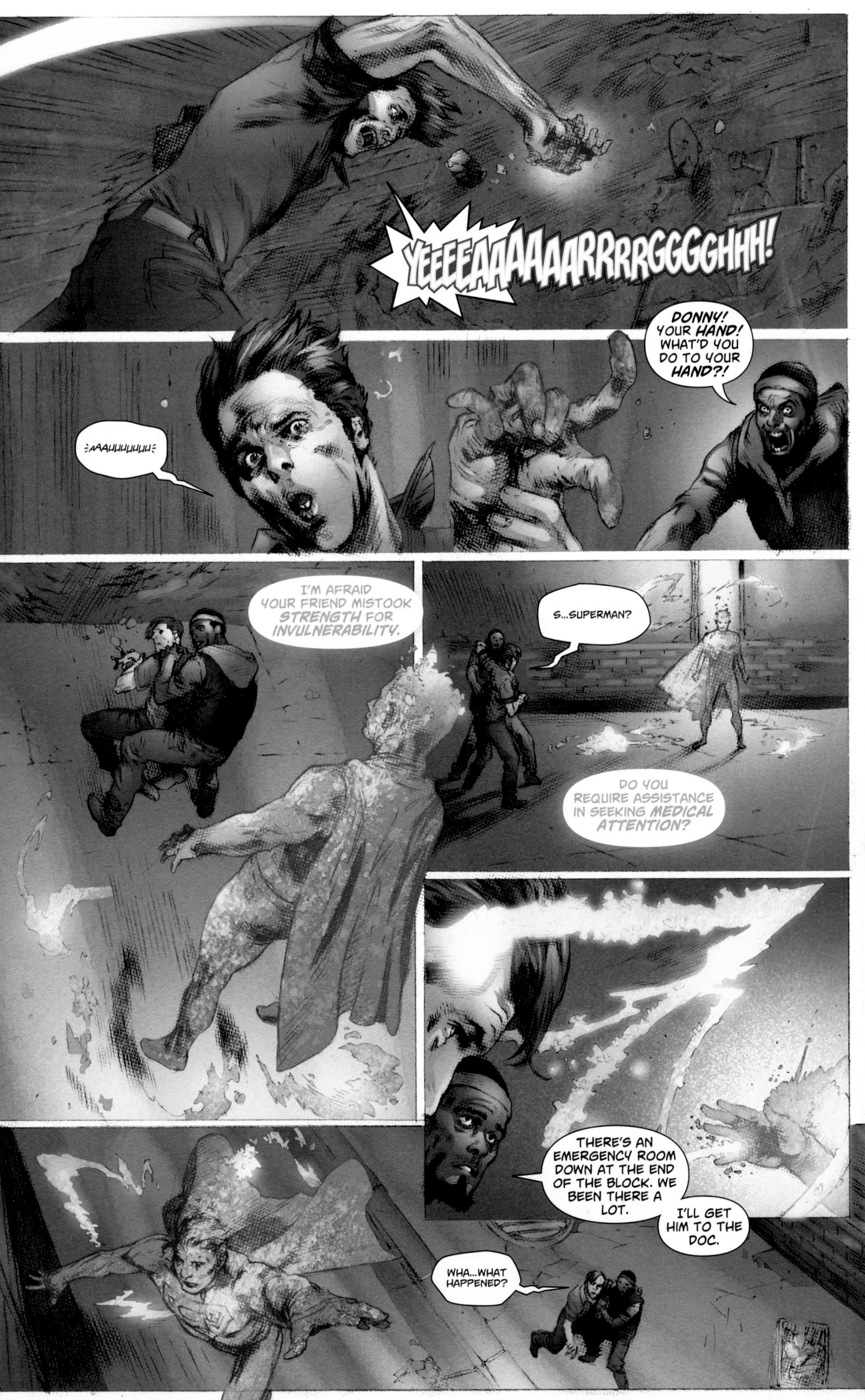
YEEEEAAAAAARRRRGGGGHHH!
DONNY! YOUR HAND! WHAT'D YOU DO TO YOUR HAND?!
AAAUUUUUUU
I'M AFRAID YOUR FRIEND MISTOOK STRENGTH FOR INVULNERABILITY.
S...SUPERMAN?
DO YOU REQUIRE ASSISTANCE IN SEEKING MEDICAL ATTENTION?
THERE'S AN EMERGENCY ROOM DOWN AT THE END OF THE BLOCK. WE BEEN THERE A LOT.
I'LL GET HIM TO THE DOC.
WHA...WHAT HAPPENED?

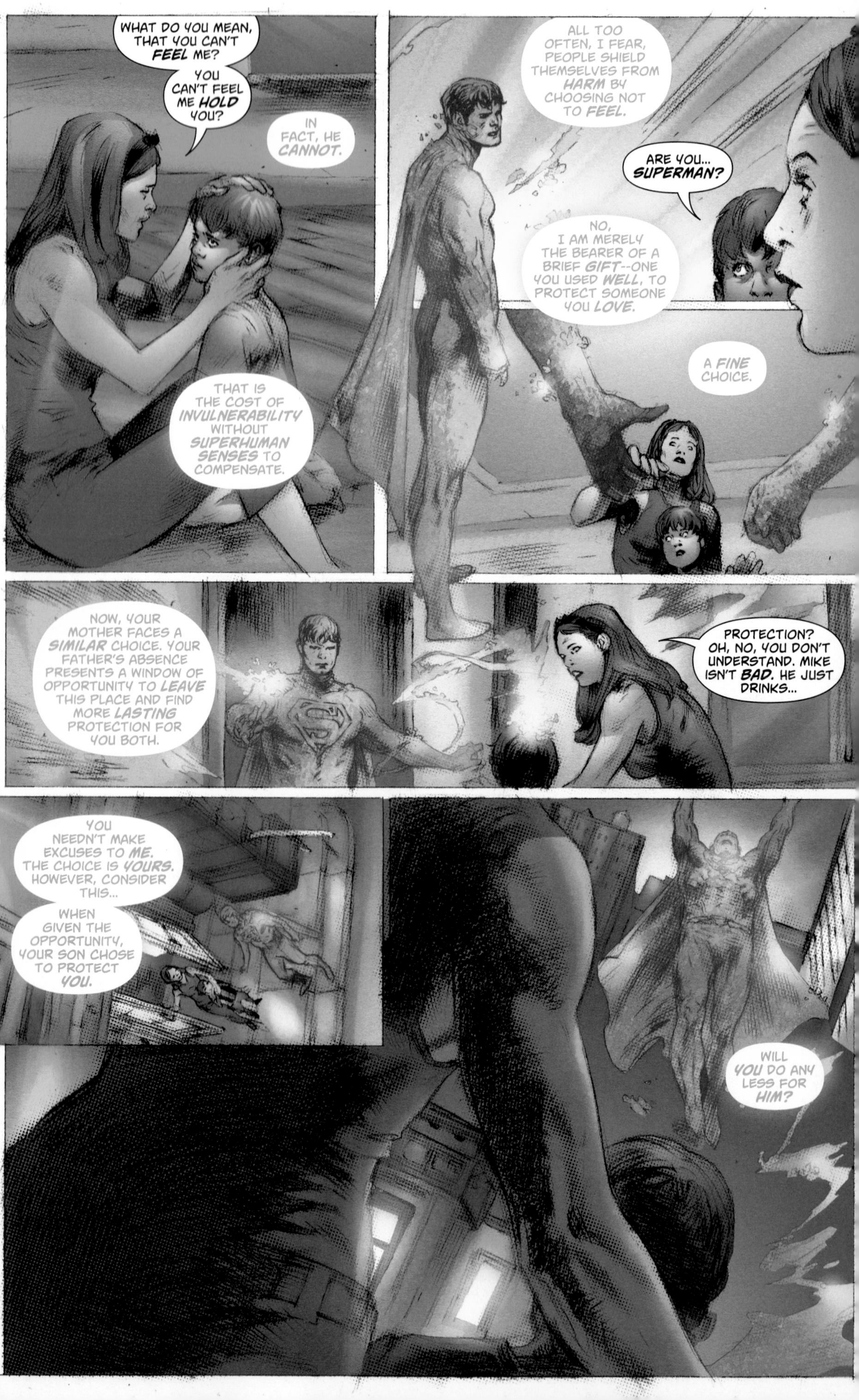
WHAT DO YOU MEAN, THAT YOU CAN'T FEEL ME?
YOU CAN'T FEEL ME HOLD YOU?
IN FACT, HE CANNOT.
THAT IS THE COST OF INVULNERABILITY WITHOUT SUPERHUMAN SENSES TO COMPENSATE.
ALL TOO OFTEN, I FEAR, PEOPLE SHIELD THEMSELVES FROM HARM BY CHOOSING NOT TO FEEL.
ARE YOU... SUPERMAN?
NO, I AM MERELY THE BEARER OF A BRIEF GIFT--ONE YOU USED WELL, TO PROTECT SOMEONE YOU LOVE.
A FINE CHOICE.
NOW, YOUR MOTHER FACES A SIMILAR CHOICE. YOUR FATHER'S ABSENCE PRESENTS A WINDOW OF OPPORTUNITY TO LEAVE THIS PLACE AND FIND MORE LASTING PROTECTION FOR YOU BOTH.
PROTECTION? OH, NO, YOU DON'T UNDERSTAND. MIKE ISN'T BAD. HE JUST DRINKS...
YOU NEEDN'T MAKE EXCUSES TO ME. THE CHOICE IS YOURS. HOWEVER, CONSIDER THIS...
WHEN GIVEN THE OPPORTUNITY, YOUR SON CHOSE TO PROTECT YOU.
WILL YOU DO ANY LESS FOR HIM?

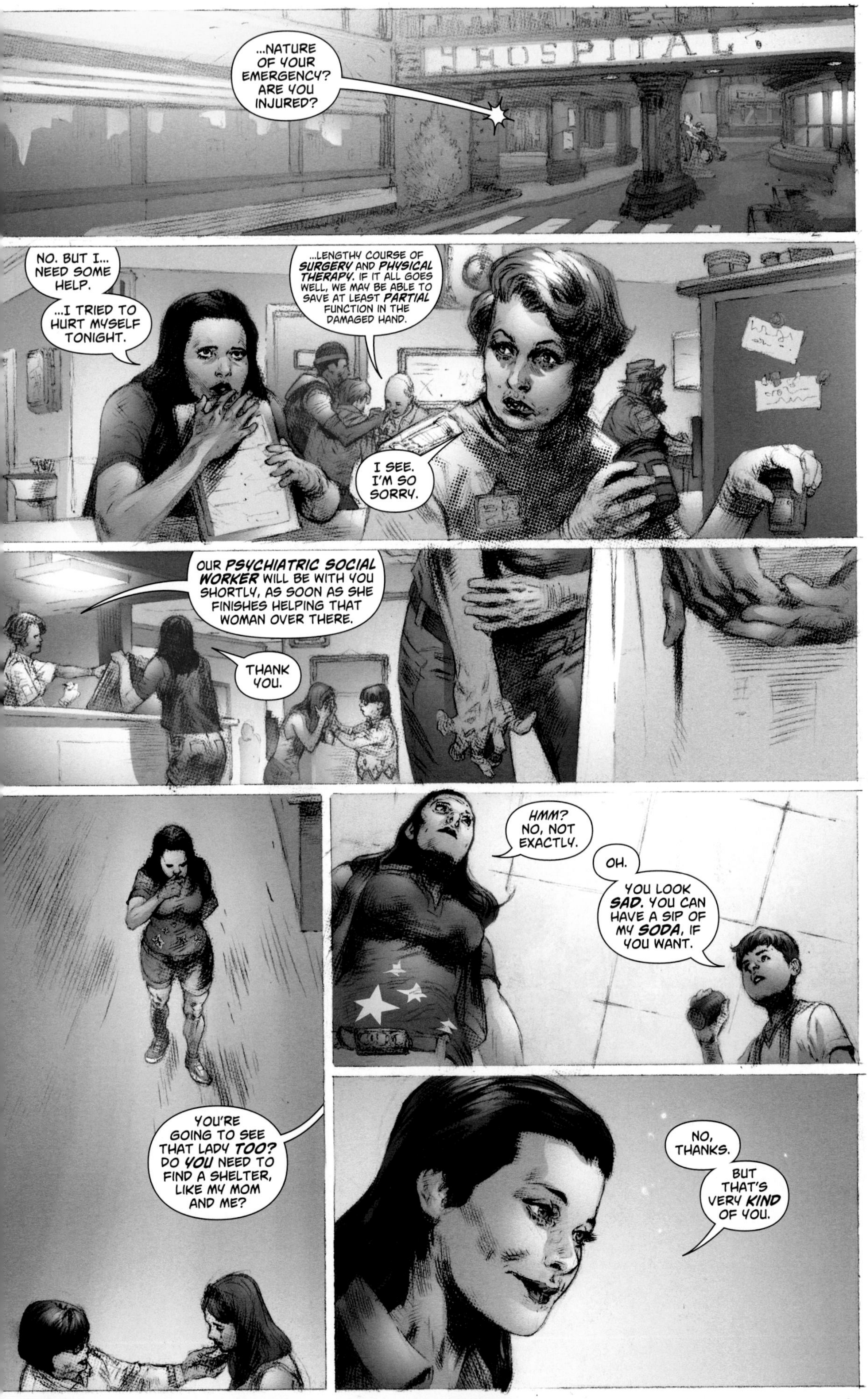
HOSPITAL
...NATURE OF YOUR EMERGENCY? ARE YOU INJURED?
NO. BUT I... NEED SOME HELP.
...I TRIED TO HURT MYSELF TONIGHT.
...LENGTHY COURSE OF SURGERY AND PHYSICAL THERAPY. IF IT ALL GOES WELL, WE MAY BE ABLE TO SAVE AT LEAST PARTIAL FUNCTION IN THE DAMAGED HAND.
I SEE. I'M SO SORRY.
OUR PSYCHIATRIC SOCIAL WORKER WILL BE WITH YOU SHORTLY, AS SOON AS SHE FINISHES HELPING THAT WOMAN OVER THERE.
THANK YOU.
YOU'RE GOING TO SEE THAT LADY TOO? DO YOU NEED TO FIND A SHELTER, LIKE MY MOM AND ME?
HMM? NO, NOT EXACTLY.
OH.
YOU LOOK SAD. YOU CAN HAVE A SIP OF MY SODA, IF YOU WANT.
NO, THANKS.
BUT THAT'S VERY KIND OF YOU.

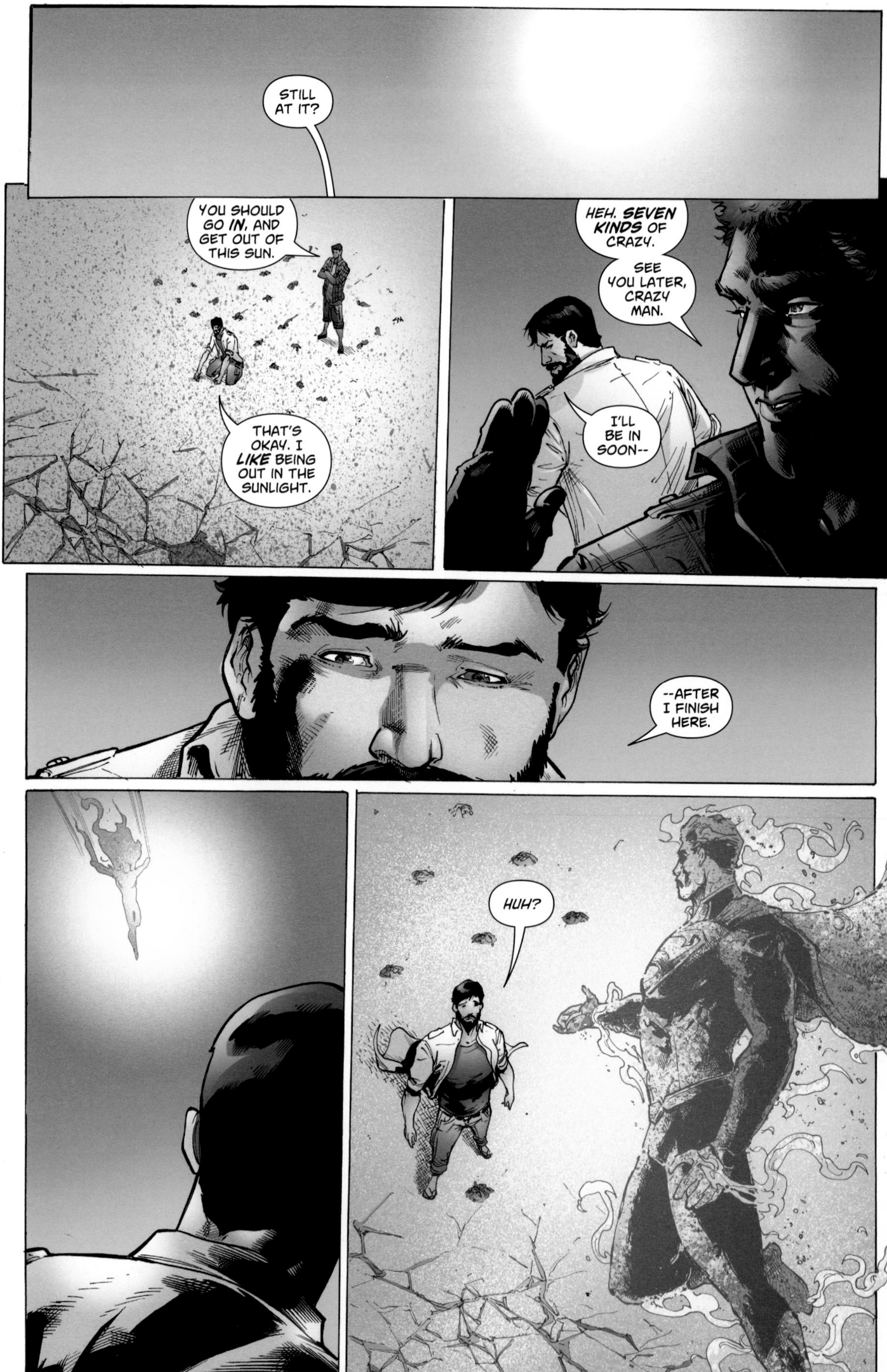
STILL AT IT?
YOU SHOULD GO IN, AND GET OUT OF THIS SUN.
THAT'S OKAY. I LIKE BEING OUT IN THE SUNLIGHT.
HEH. SEVEN KINDS OF CRAZY.
SEE YOU LATER, CRAZY MAN.
I'LL BE IN SOON--
--AFTER I FINISH HERE.
HUH?

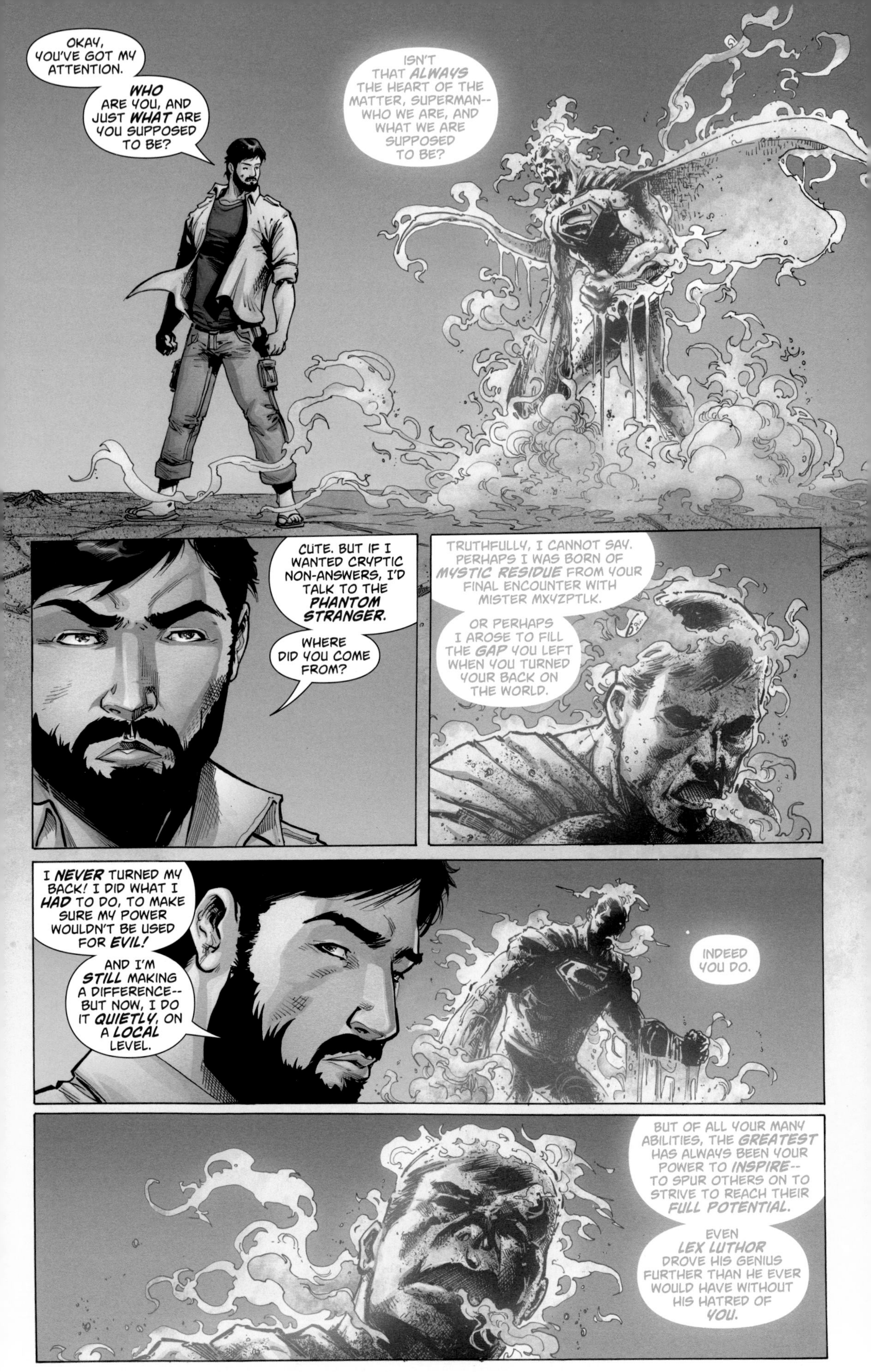
OKAY, YOU'VE GOT MY ATTENTION.
WHO ARE YOU, AND JUST WHAT ARE YOU SUPPOSED TO BE?
ISN'T THAT ALWAYS THE HEART OF THE MATTER, SUPERMAN-- WHO WE ARE, AND WHAT WE ARE SUPPOSED TO BE?
CUTE. BUT IF I WANTED CRYPTIC NON-ANSWERS, I'D TALK TO THE PHANTOM STRANGER.
WHERE DID YOU COME FROM?
TRUTHFULLY, I CANNOT SAY. PERHAPS I WAS BORN OF MYSTIC RESIDUE FROM YOUR FINAL ENCOUNTER WITH MISTER MXYZPTLK.
OR PERHAPS I AROSE TO FILL THE GAP YOU LEFT WHEN YOU TURNED YOUR BACK ON THE WORLD.
I NEVER TURNED MY BACK! I DID WHAT I HAD TO DO, TO MAKE SURE MY POWER WOULDN'T BE USED FOR EVIL!
AND I'M STILL MAKING A DIFFERENCE-- BUT NOW, I DO IT QUIETLY, ON A LOCAL LEVEL.
INDEED YOU DO.
BUT OF ALL YOUR MANY ABILITIES, THE GREATEST HAS ALWAYS BEEN YOUR POWER TO INSPIRE-- TO SPUR OTHERS ON TO STRIVE TO REACH THEIR FULL POTENTIAL.
EVEN LEX LUTHOR DROVE HIS GENIUS FURTHER THAN HE EVER WOULD HAVE WITHOUT HIS HATRED OF YOU.

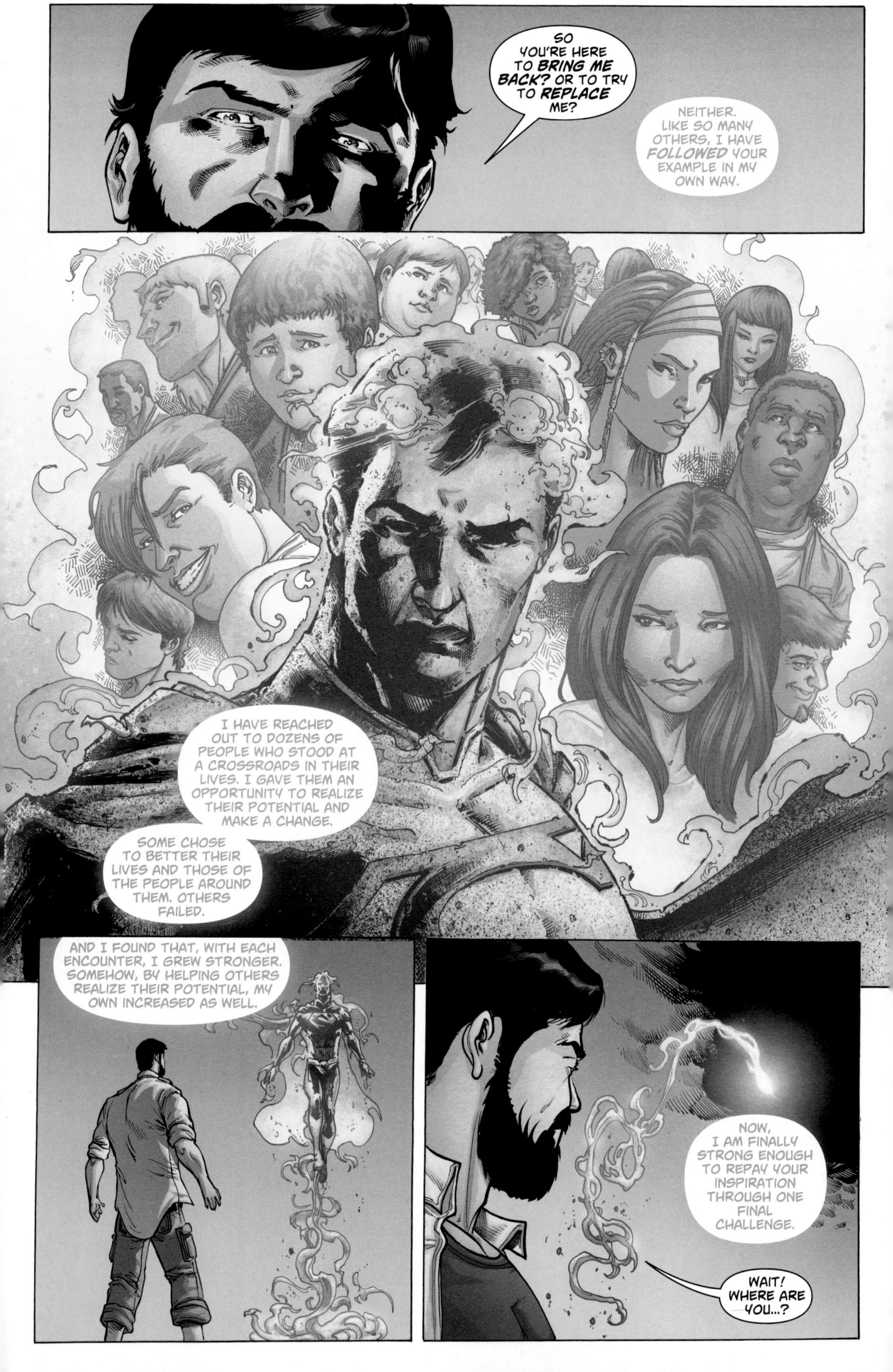
SO YOU'RE HERE TO BRING ME BACK? OR TO TRY TO REPLACE ME?
NEITHER. LIKE SO MANY OTHERS, I HAVE FOLLOWED YOUR EXAMPLE IN MY OWN WAY.
I HAVE REACHED OUT TO DOZENS OF PEOPLE WHO STOOD AT A CROSSROADS IN THEIR LIVES. I GAVE THEM AN OPPORTUNITY TO REALIZE THEIR POTENTIAL AND MAKE A CHANGE.
SOME CHOSE TO BETTER THEIR LIVES AND THOSE OF THE PEOPLE AROUND THEM. OTHERS FAILED.
AND I FOUND THAT, WITH EACH ENCOUNTER, I GREW STRONGER. SOMEHOW, BY HELPING OTHERS REALIZE THEIR POTENTIAL, MY OWN INCREASED AS WELL.
NOW, I AM FINALLY STRONG ENOUGH TO REPAY YOUR INSPIRATION THROUGH ONE FINAL CHALLENGE.
WAIT! WHERE ARE YOU...?

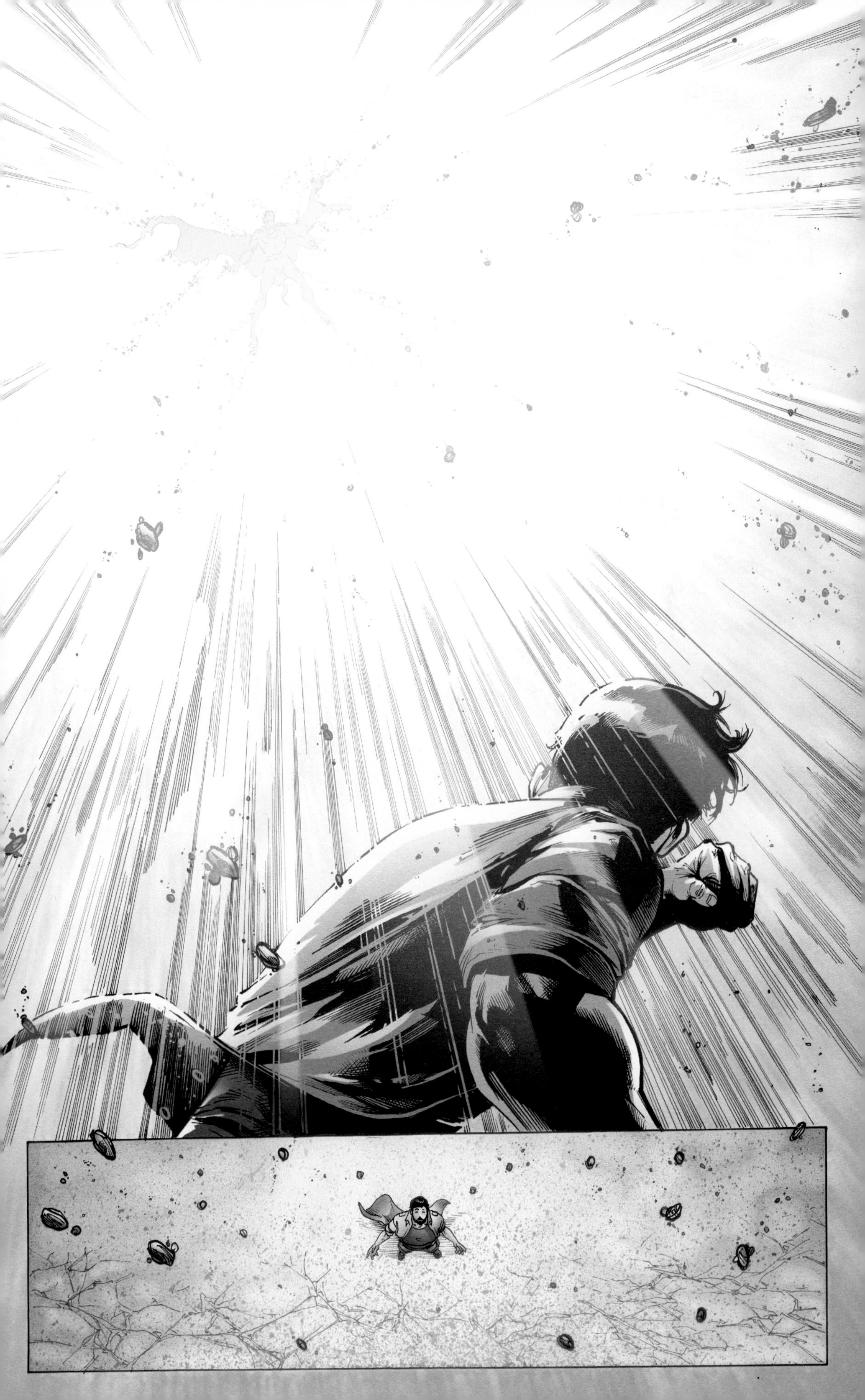

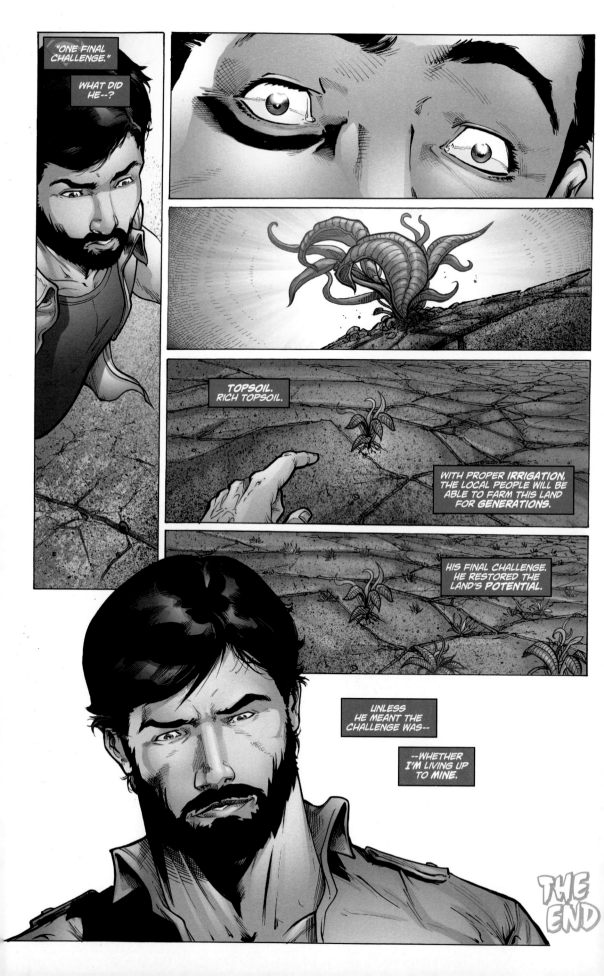

"ONE FINAL CHALLENGE."

WHAT DID HE--?

TOPSOIL. RICH TOPSOIL.

WITH PROPER IRRIGATION, THE LOCAL PEOPLE WILL BE ABLE TO FARM THIS LAND FOR GENERATIONS.

HIS FINAL CHALLENGE. HE RESTORED THE LAND'S POTENTIAL.

UNLESS HE MEANT THE CHALLENGE WAS--

--WHETHER I'M LIVING UP TO MINE.

THE END

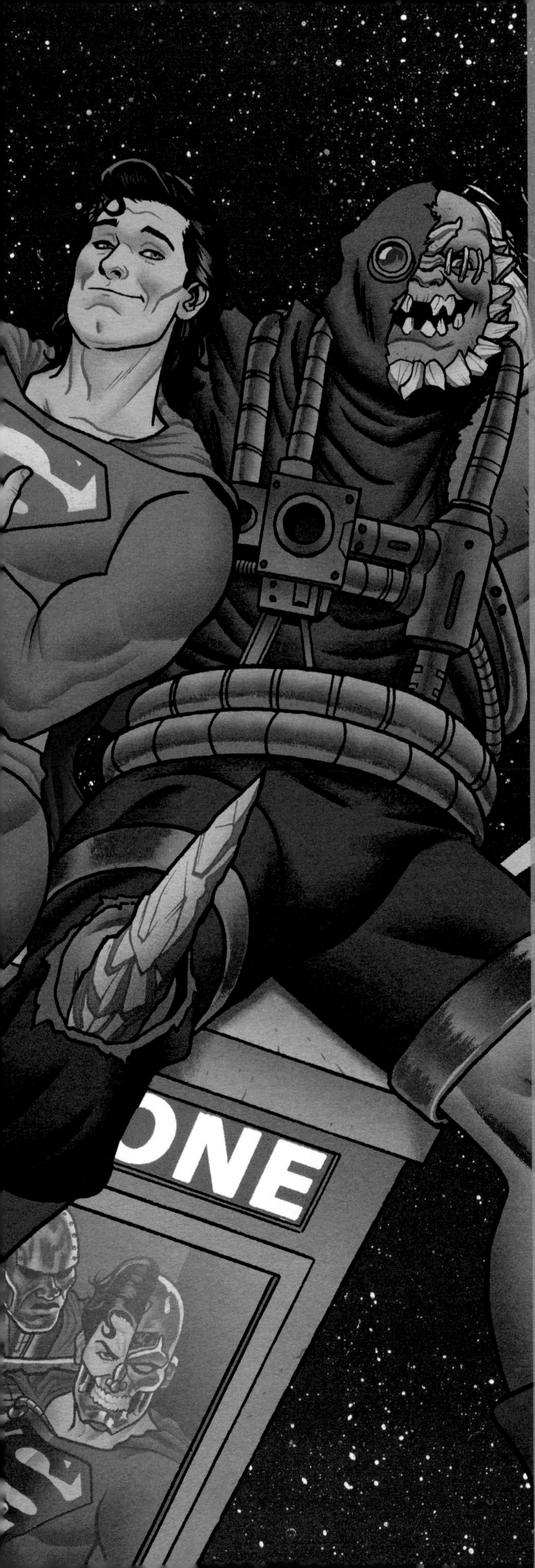
ONE

VARIANT COVER GALLERY

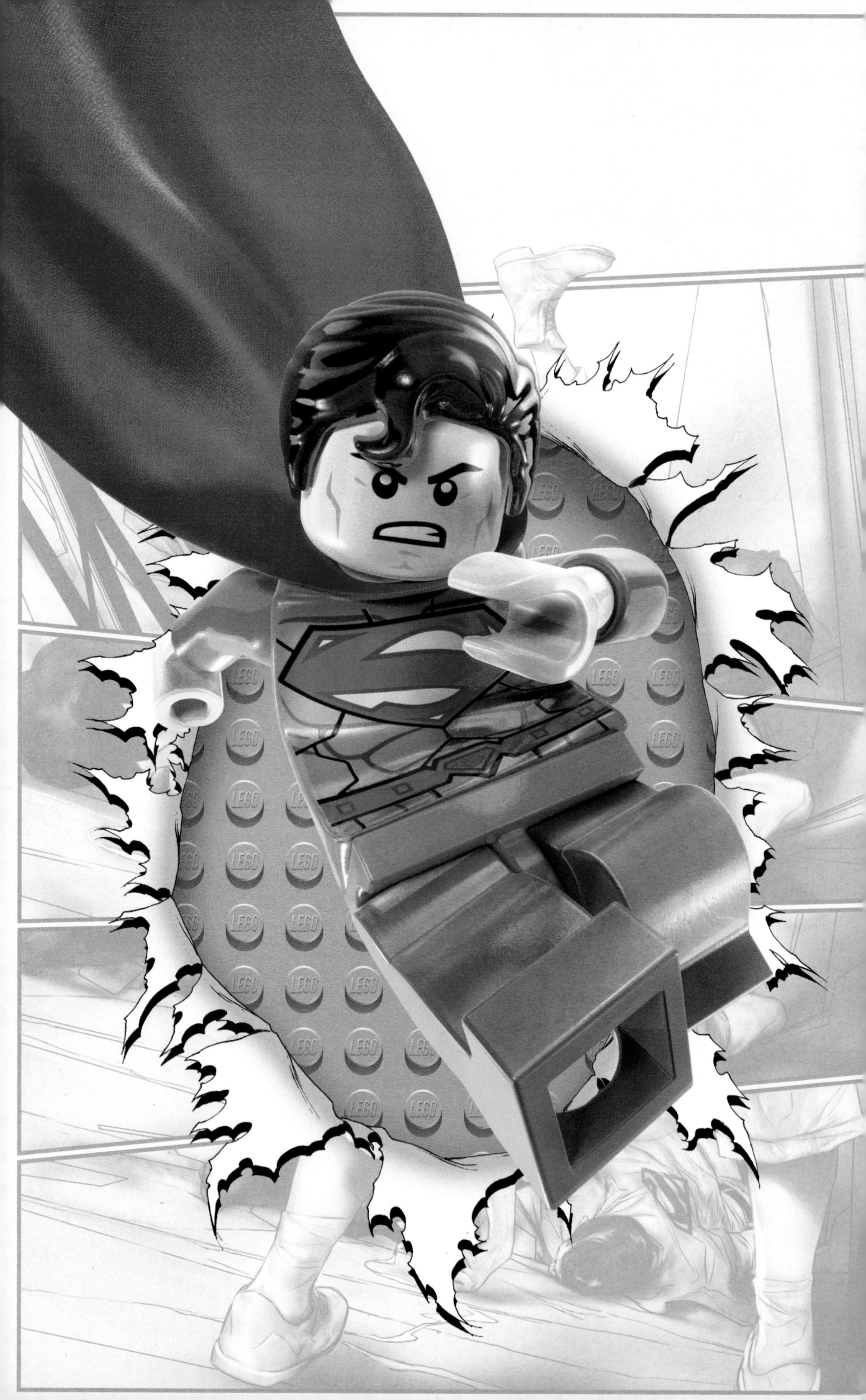

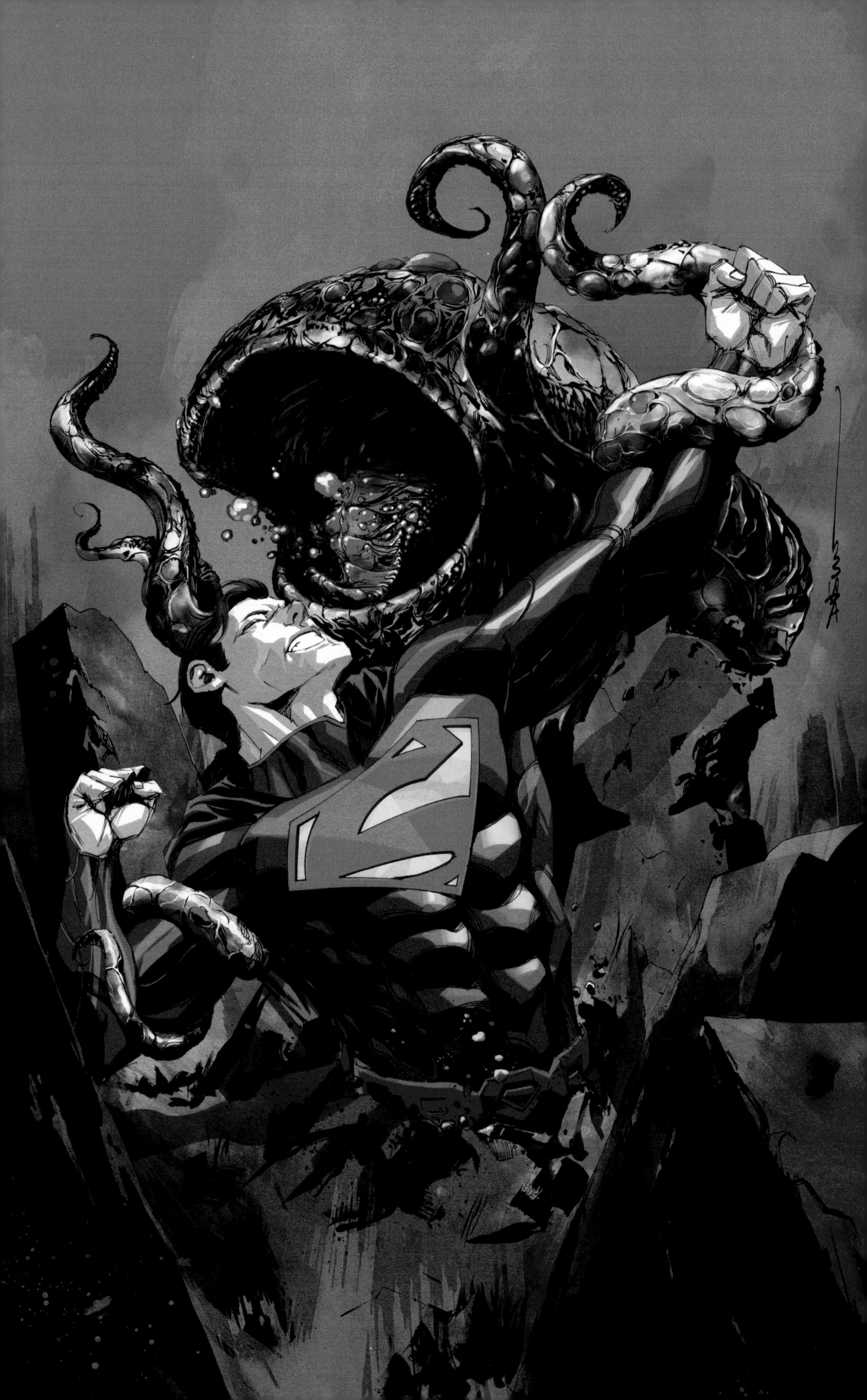

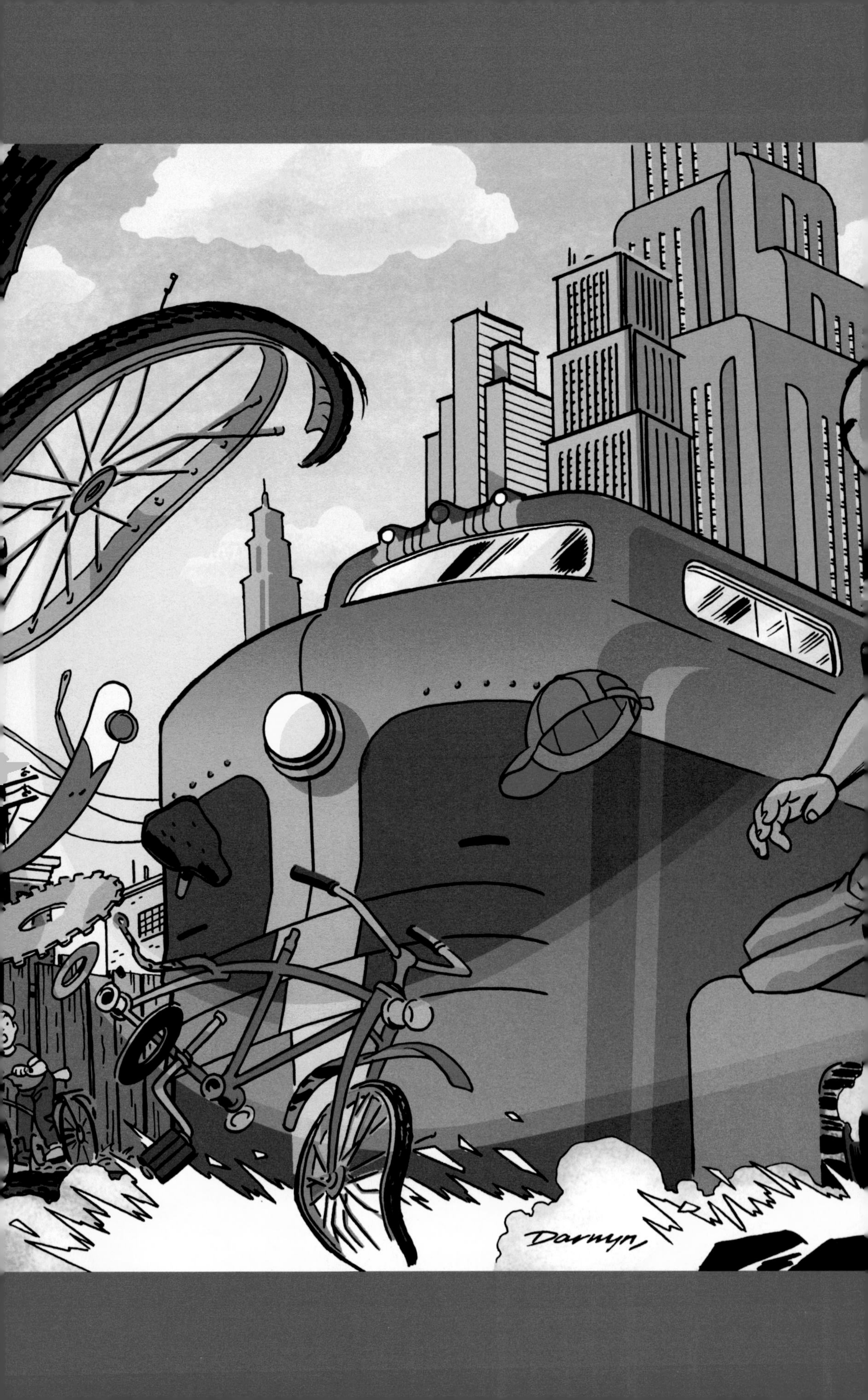
Darwyn

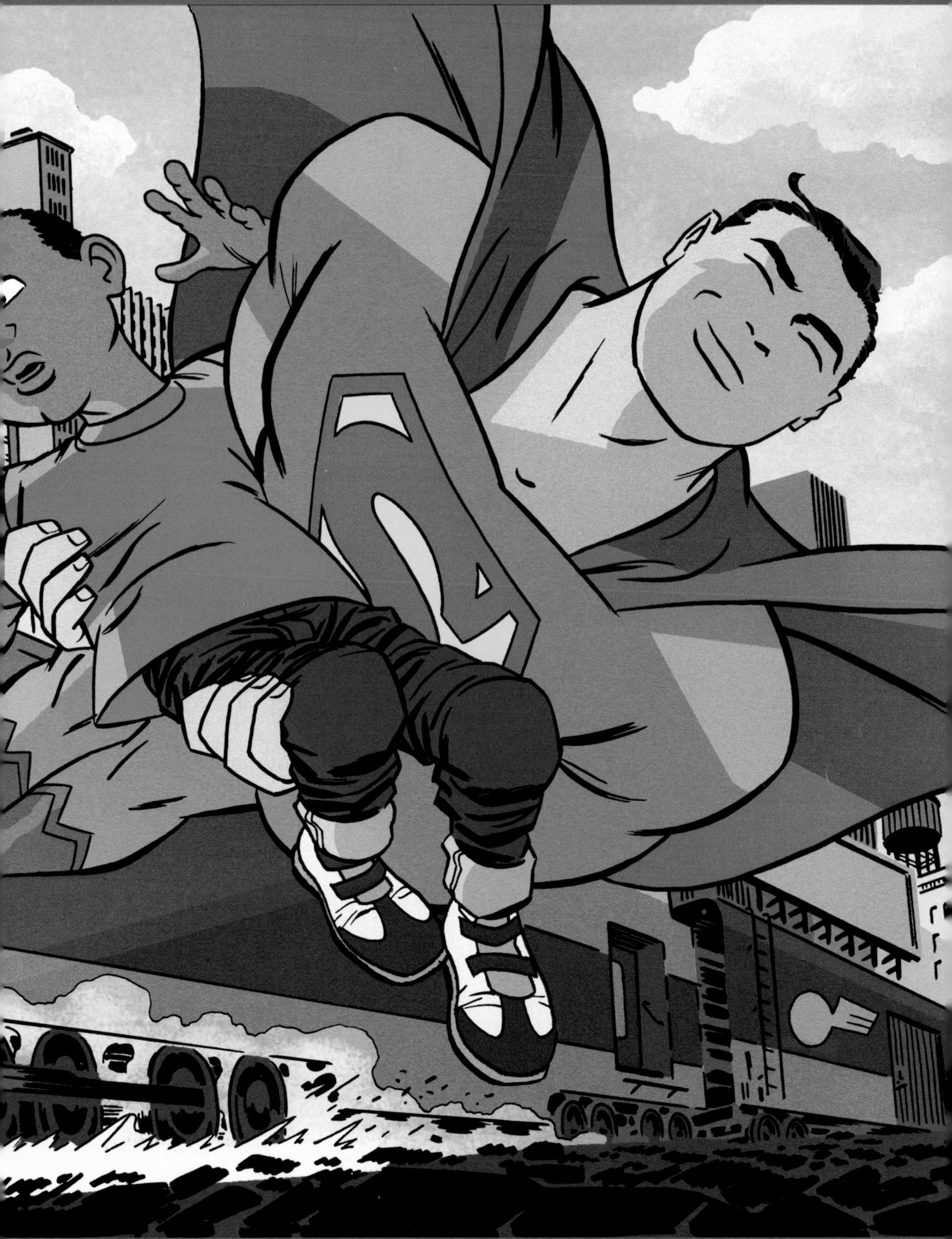

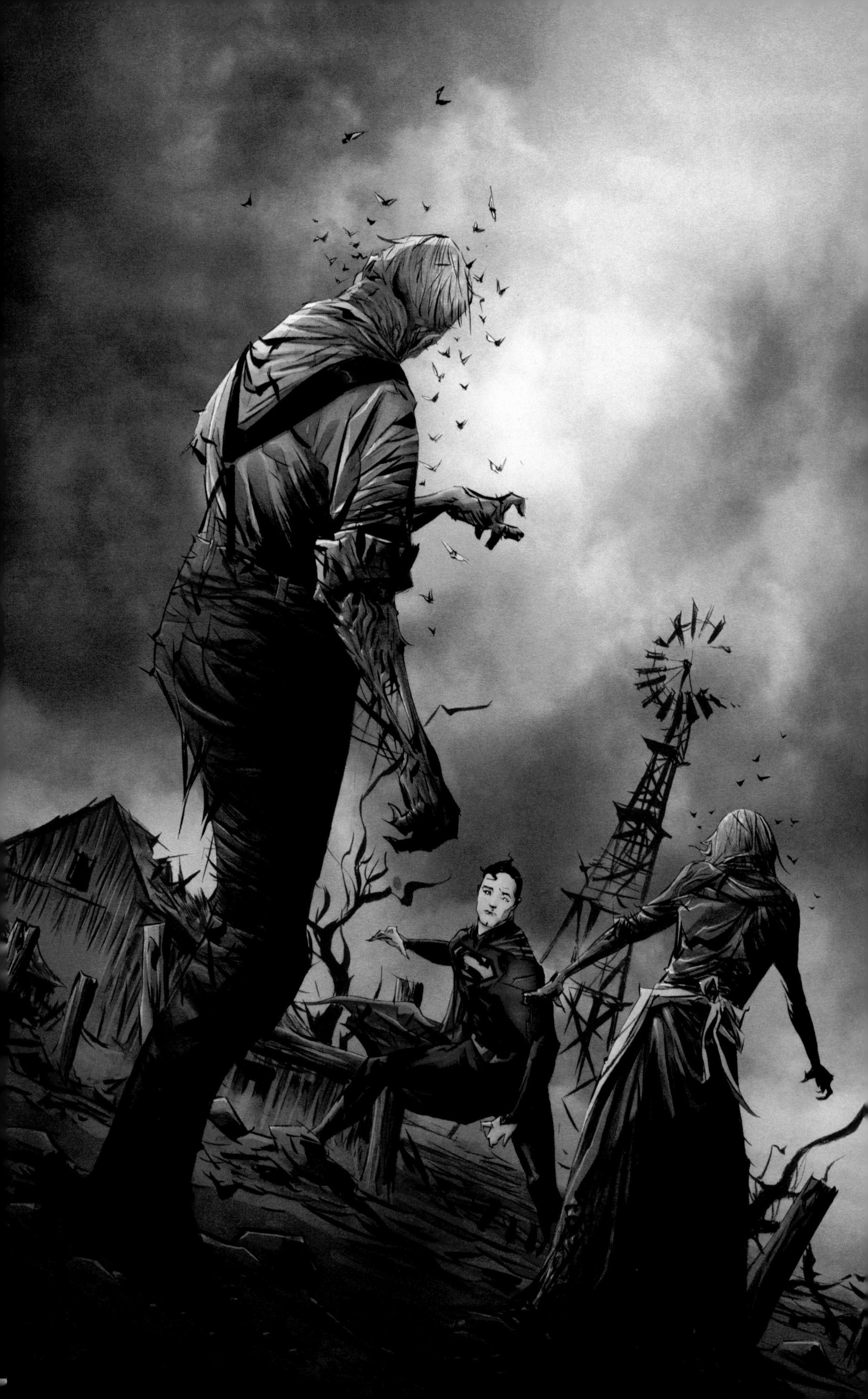

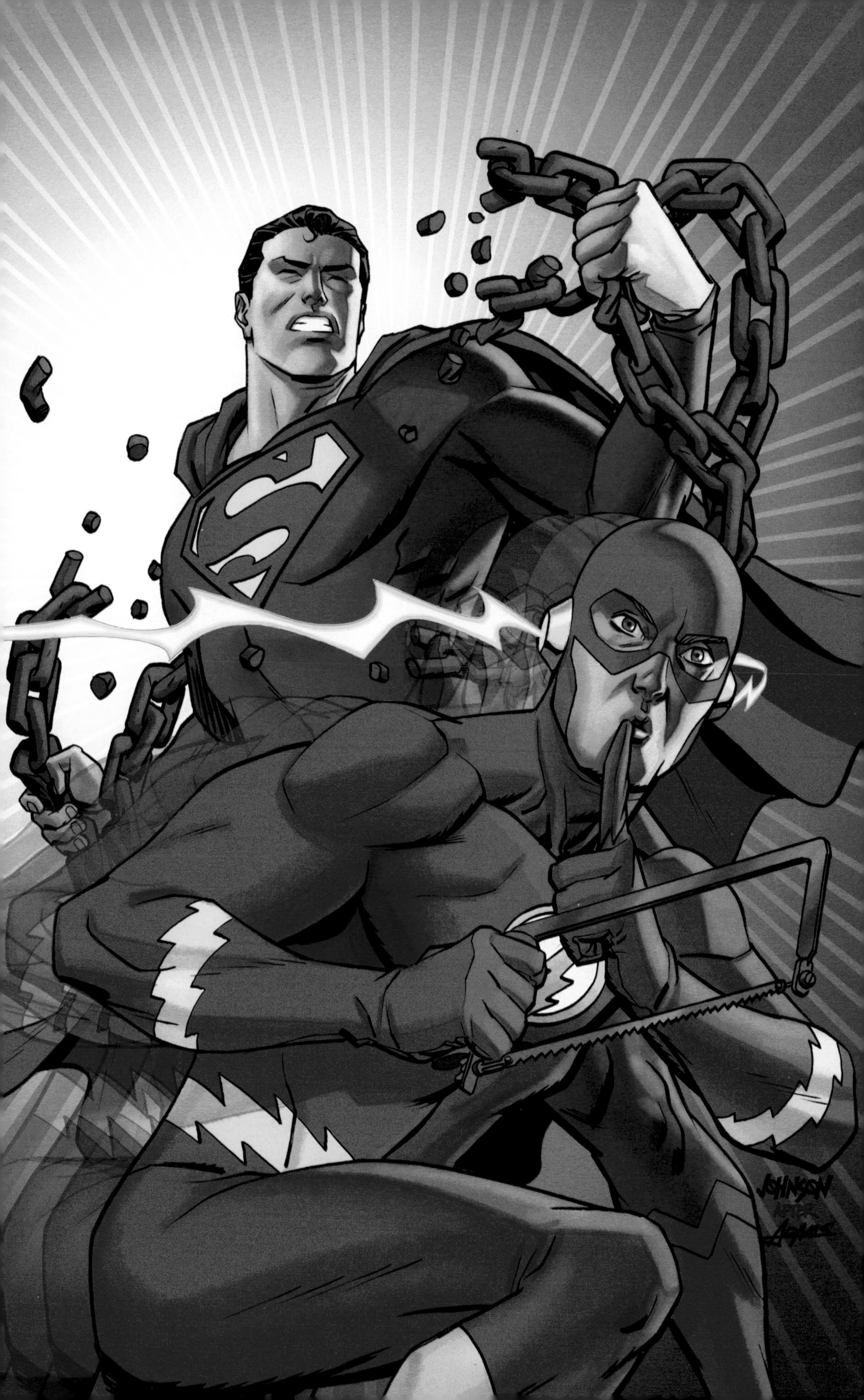
JOHNSON

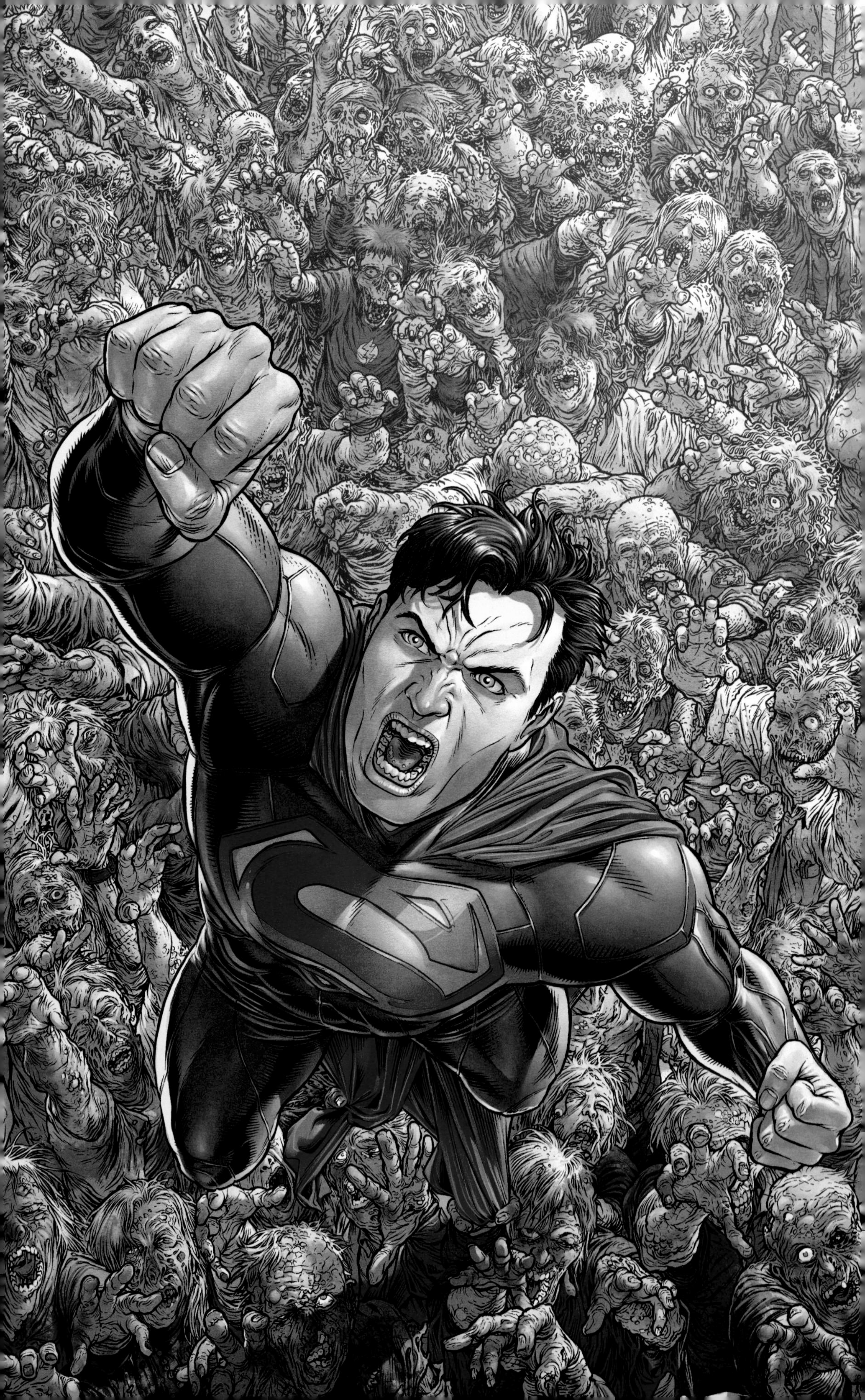

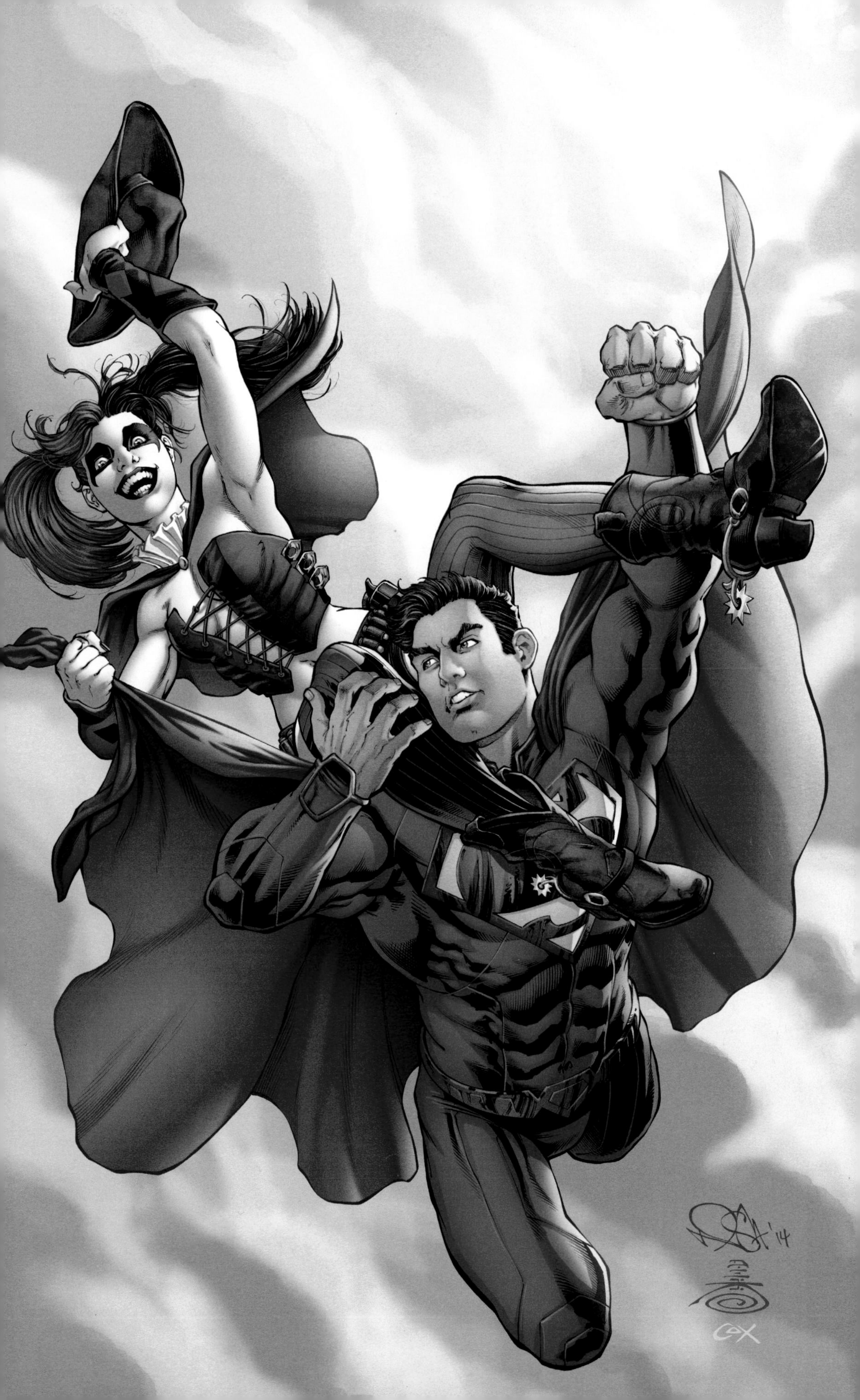

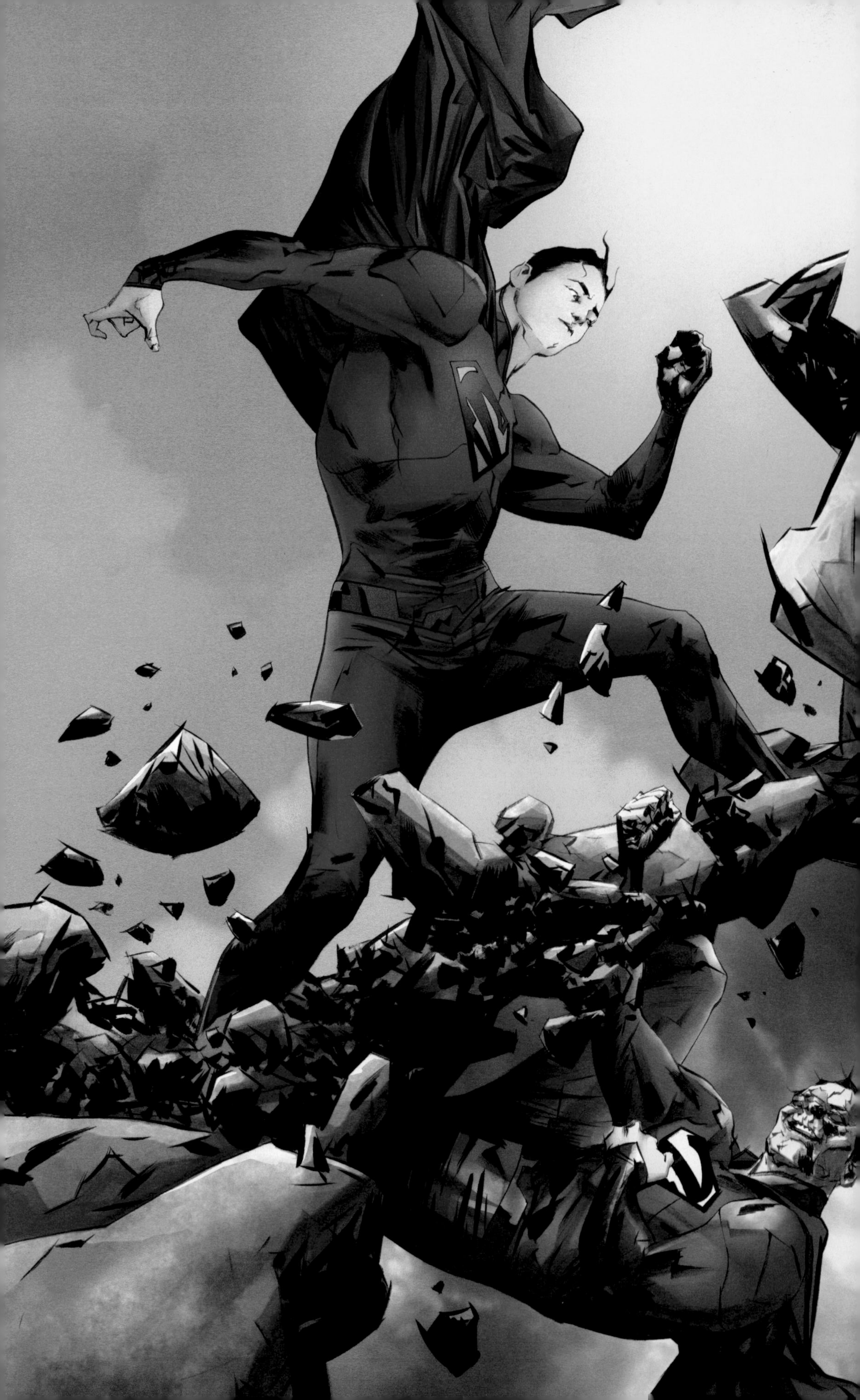

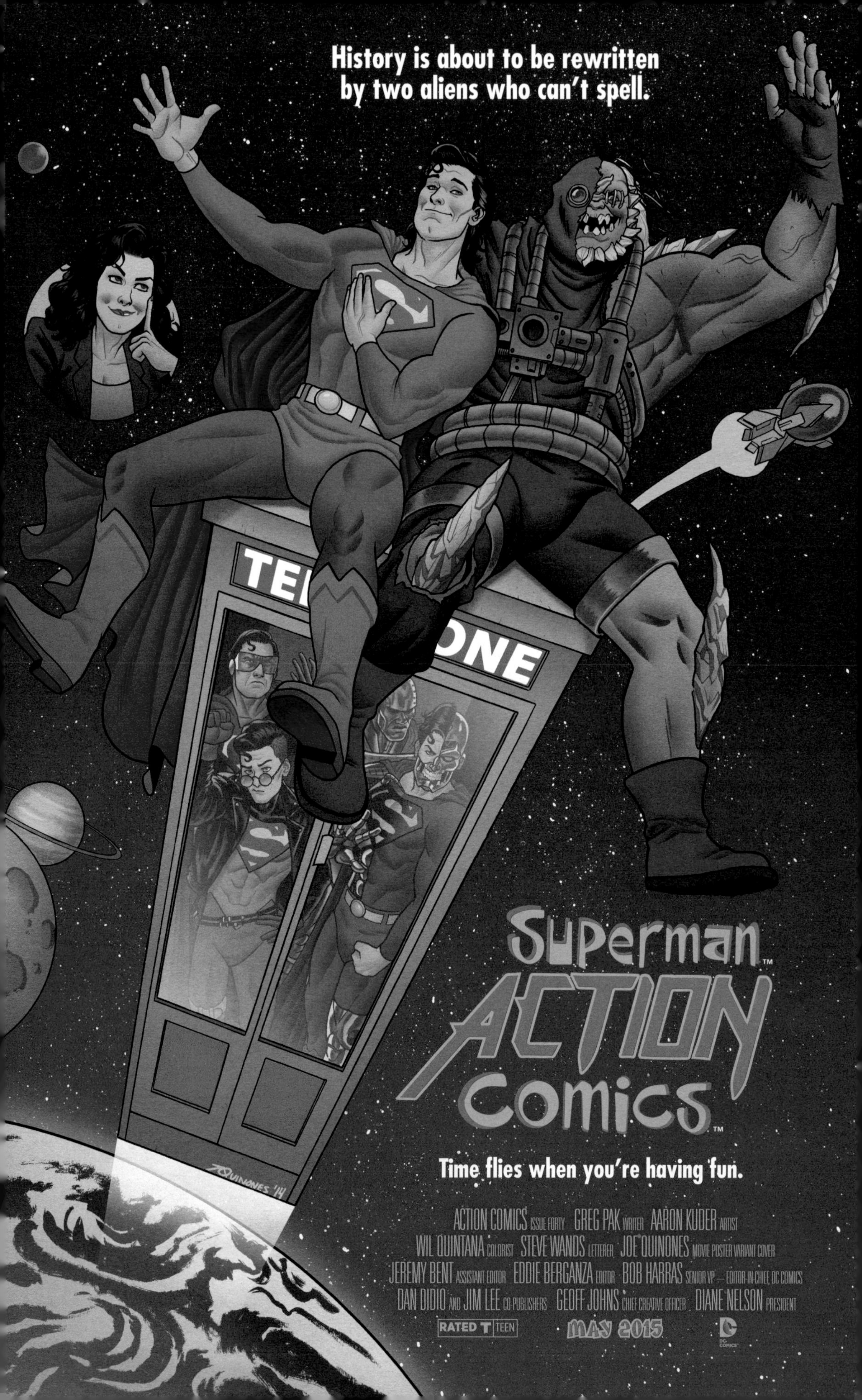
History is about to be rewritten
by two aliens who can't spell.
Superman
ACTION
Comics
Time flies when you're having fun.
ACTION COMICS ISSUE FORTY GREG PAK WRITER AARON KUDER ARTIST
WIL QUINTANA COLORIST STEVE WANDS LETTERER JOE QUINONES MOVIE POSTER VARIANT COVER
JEREMY BENT ASSISTANT EDITOR EDDIE BERGANZA EDITOR BOB HARRAS SENIOR VP — EDITOR-IN-CHIEF, DC COMICS
DAN DIDIO AND JIM LEE CO-PUBLISHERS GEOFF JOHNS CHIEF CREATIVE OFFICER DIANE NELSON PRESIDENT
RATED T TEEN
MAY 2015

"ACTION COMICS has successfully carved its own territory and continued exploring Morrison's familiar themes about heroism and ideas."—IGN

"Casts the character in a new light, opens up fresh storytelling possibilities, and pushes it all forward with dynamic Rags Morales art. I loved it."—THE ONION/AV CLUB

START AT THE BEGINNING!

SUPERMAN: ACTION COMICS VOLUME 1:
SUPERMAN AND THE MEN OF STEEL

SUPERMAN: ACTION COMICS VOL. 2: BULLETPROOF

with GRANT MORRISON and RAGS MORALES

SUPERMAN: ACTION COMICS VOL. 3: AT THE END OF DAYS

with GRANT MORRISON and RAGS MORALES

SUPERBOY VOL. 1: INCUBATION

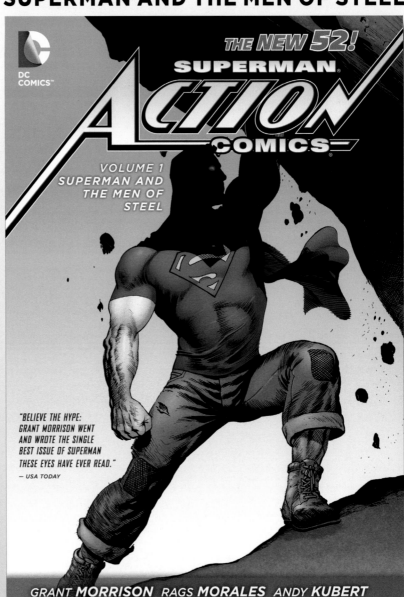

"BELIEVE THE HYPE: GRANT MORRISON WENT AND WROTE THE SINGLE BEST ISSUE OF SUPERMAN THESE EYES HAVE EVER READ." — USA TODAY

GRANT MORRISON RAGS **MORALES** ANDY **KUBERT**